Susan A. Howard
550 Collingwood Dr.
East Lansing, MI 48823

Alastair Sawday's

Special Places to Stay

FRENCH BED & BREAKFAST

4th EDITION

Typesetting, Conversion & Repro:	Avonset, Bath
Maps:	HarperCollins
Printing:	Jarrold Book Printing, Norwich
Design:	Springboard Design, Bristol
UK Distribution:	Portfolio, London
US Distribution:	St Martin's Press, New York

First published in 1998 by Alastair Sawday Publishing Co. Ltd
44 Ambra Vale East, Bristol BS8 4RE, UK

Alastair Sawday's
Special Places to Stay

FRENCH BED
& BREAKFAST

4th EDITION

"Une lourde porte de bois, arrondie dans le haut et cloutée comme une
porte de presbytère, était à demi ouverte.... Il s'y engouffra... et se trouva...
entouré de rires, de chants, d'appels..."
Alain Fournier – *Le Grand Meaulnes*

(A heavy, nail-studded, wooden door like a presbytery door, was half-
open. He plunged in and found himself surrounded by laughter,
singing and joyous cries.)

Alastair Sawday Publishing

ACKNOWLEDGEMENTS

Once the golden fruit of the frenzied musings and travellings of an eclectic band of enthusiasts, this book has become Ann Cooke-Yarborough's. She is the impresario, the dreamer, the catalyst and galvanizer... the dynamo behind this new edition. She makes it happen, infuses the book with her own remarkable personality and stimulates us all into further support.

My own role is little more than that of *Chef Animateur*, as the French would call it. I love just being in these places. I drool over their descriptions while editing them. May the bureaucracy of France and the E.U. long keep their hands off those expressions of individuality that you see in these pages. Will the bureaucrats force stainless steel kitchens on the owners of ancient wooden ones? Will every door have to carry a luminous EXIT sign? Will the chickens in the yard be asked to go inside, and certainly NOT mix with the pigs? Will the owners of chain hotels force small hotels and B&Bs to toe their own anodyne and culture-crushing line? This is all a genuine threat... so my second acknowledgement is of the stout rearguard that faces it: the many owners in this guide in whose originality we revel. I salute them. Vive la France!

Alastair Sawday

Series Editor:	Alastair Sawday
Managing Editor:	Ann Cooke-Yarborough
Production Manager:	Julia Richardson
Administration:	Amy Clifton, Julia Richardson
Inspections:	Clive & Patricia Brooks, Alyson & Colin Browne, Ann Cooke-Yarborough, Meredith Dickinson, Valerie Foix, Diana Harris, Guy Hunter-Watts, Susanna Isaac, Ian Kelly & Claire Davies, Carol Lenthal, Mike Millbourn, Lucie Nérot, Jess Newton, Paddy Nicholls, Caroline Portway, Heidi Steffes, Louise Vaughan-Arbuckle, Elizabeth Yates.
Additional writing:	James Elsey, Sally Walters
Accounts:	Sheila Clifton, Maureen Humphries, Julie Edosa
Cover Design:	Caroline King
Photographs:	Sara Hay, Amy Wynn, Brendan Flanagan, Ann Cooke-Yarborough

And our unseen but essential support teams. In Paris, they were Brendan Flanagan, Marie Guimezanes and Rose Bacquet. In Bristol they were the staff of Alastair Sawday's Tours: Annie Shillito, Eliza Meredith, Dave Kelly, Anne Woodford, Emma Scragg and Amy Wynn.

INTRODUCTION

As I was proof-reading these entries I was struck again and again by their vitality. No dull lists of available facilities, but a throbbing appreciation of what each individual host and house has to give you. This book really DOES contain a remarkable collection of people and places. Read this extract from a reader's letter, for example:

"Madame offers a uniquely memorable experience, welcoming guests not just with warmth but with an extraordinarily sympathetic interest in them as living flesh and blood, rather than as mere suppliers of French francs. In projecting this warmth she managed to be at once formidable and lovable, dignified and mischievous. Soon after we arrived we were gorging on figs freshly picked for jam-making..."

Not only do many of 'our' owners combine lovability with dignity, but they put themselves out for you too:

"What a lovely woman, and such a fabulous cook. The family room was nothing to write home about but the evening meal she prepared and served so beautifully and with such concern for the vagaries of my children's taste was exquisite..."

By now, however, we have learned that half the fun of using the book is the two-way experience, in which readers add so much to it all with their own sense of adventure and fun:

"I was quickly asleep only to be woken by my son saying: "Daddy, Tom has had an accident in the loo." Fearing the result of adolescent enthusiasm for the wine, I was quickly on the scene to be confronted by a waterfall pouring from the base of the cracked cistern and along the passage. Your section on 'When things go wrong' did not provide a translation of "Madame, where is your stopcock?". Fortunately she arrived and the tide was stemmed, eyes averted from skimpy summer nightwear."

So, with a mixture of colourful, attractive hosts and open-minded travellers, there is every reason why this book should have quickly become the most popular of its kind. But the final ingredient must be the sheer, and most welcome, Frenchness of travelling with it:

"We spent our first night in an idyllic Norman manoir, complete with turrets, stone steps - worn away by the plod of mediæval back-packers - and sheep, chickens and rabbits, all of which we counted assiduously as we left each morning... to ascertain whether the sumptuous casserole we had enjoyed the previous evening had in fact contributed to the decline in the extended family."

If you don't get a huge kick out of these places then there is something the matter. Let us know.

One thing which I MUST tell you: you will save a small fortune using this book. The average price per person for B&B in a double room is £15. France is wonderful value, and not just because the franc is now weak.

Alastair Sawday

INTRODUCTION

Places in the guide

Your comments

We owe quantities of gratitude to our readers for their reports on B&Bs in the guide and for their recommendations of others. Their contributions are hugely appreciated.

- First, we are delighted by the very large proportion of positive comments - they all go on file.
- Secondly, all poor reports are followed up and the owners' side of the question examined as well (no mention of the writer's name, of course) - there is often a simple, human explanation. Really bad reports lead us to make an incognito visit, after which we may exclude a house. It happens. If you are unhappy with a B&B, <u>please</u> tell the owners there and then - they are, after all, the only ones who can change things. Then do write to us - we need to know too. But being clear with your hosts is the first step.
- All recommended addresses are inspected if appropriate. We trust our readers' suggestions.

Non-French owners

The non-French names in this book often belong to 'mixed couples' (one Anglo-Saxon, one French) or even to thoroughly French families with Irish, Scottish or English ancestors.

We receive bagfuls of requests from British and American B&B owners wanting to be in the guide and we have had to disappoint many. Our aim is essentially to guide you to fruitful encounters with French families in their homes, so non-French owners have a smaller chance of being chosen.

However, many of you have written to say how restful it can be, after several evenings of valiant French conversation, to have a 'day off' and relax in your native tongue. Our Native Speaker homes are dotted around the country so we hope you find the linguistic break you need!

How to use this book

French words and expressions used in the entries are explained at the end of the book.

Activities

Another new 'service' for you : a page at the back of the book listing the courses, workshops, activities and facilities owners organise or offer, though many are occasional or seasonal. We have not included farm visits as most farmers love showing you around anyway.

By the way, should you need to get a fishing permit, it can be bought at any fishing tackle shop.

Finding the houses

NB. The individual **ENTRY REFERENCE** is **at the bottom of the page**. This is the number to use when writing to us, please (!), as well as when looking places up in the book. Each entry (except the Parisians) also has the 1/200000 **Michelin Regional Map** reference as **MM** followed by the relevant map and fold numbers, e.g. MM 245-31 is Regional Map No 245, fold No 31 - we hope this is useful to you for detailed pinpointing of houses.

OUR MAPS

Our maps are thoroughly up to date but **are designed for B&B flagging only** - you will be frustrated if you try and use them as road maps! Take a good detailed road map such as Michelin or Collins.

If you know where you are going, turn to the general map to find the number of the relevant area map then turn to that map to find the B&Bs listed in 'your' area. Finally, turn to those entry reference numbers and read all about those lovely places.

DIRECTIONS

Apart from motorway exits, which are usually valid on both sides, our directions take you to each house **from one side only**. If you approach another way, make adjustments. We name the French roads with the letters they carry on French maps and road signs :

A = *Autoroute*. Toll motorways with junctions that usually have the same name/number on both sides.

N = *Route Nationale*. The old trunk roads that are still pretty fast, don't charge tolls, but often go through towns.

D = *Route Départementale*. Smaller country roads with relatively little traffic.

If our directions are not perfect, PLEASE tell us how to improve them; you could save other people a major row over map-reading!

Reading the entries

OUR LANGUAGE

We intend to be as honest and informative as possible in our descriptions of places and people but insist that, whatever the caveats, all the places in this book are here because WE LIKE THEM and believe they should be here. We hope you will quickly learn to read between our lines and pick up the subtleties of what one reader has called "Sawday-speak". If we love the people but find the decor odd, we often just describe it in factual terms.

Quotation marks are for passages from readers' letters.

TELEPHONING

Our telephone numbers give the ten-digit number every French subscriber now has, e.g. *(0)5 15 25 35 45*. You should know that:
- the *initial zero* (bracketed here) is for use when telephoning *inside* France only, i.e. dial *05 15 25 35 45* from any private or public telephone;
- when dialling from *outside* France use the international access code then the country code for France - *33* - followed by the *last 9 digits* of the number you want, e.g. *00 33 5 15 25 35 45*;
- numbers beginning *(0)6* are mobile phone numbers and will cost you accordingly;
- to telephone <u>from France</u> –
  – to <u>Great Britain</u>, dial 00 44 and your correspondent's number *without the initial zero*,
  – to <u>the USA</u>, dial 00 1 and your correspondent's number *without the initial zero*.

(See also *Times for Telephoning* under <u>BOOKING</u> below.)

ROOMS & BATHROOMS

French bathrooms and washing arrangements vary enormously and, if you have a sense of humour and are a good traveller, are part of the fun of being in France. A few are American-style luxurious, many are family-style. We have tried to tell you this year whether to expect shower or bath and whether the shower and/or wc are just curtained or screened off. Most baths will have a shower attachment but not necessarily a protective screen or curtain to go with it. It is impossible for us to tell you every case of 'shower en-suite, wc across landing' or 'separate but private bathroom' or even 'shower down corridor, wc on floor above'.

OPEN SEASON

When given in months, this means the WHOLE of both months named; thus *April to November* means 1 April to 30 November.

INTRODUCTION

PRICES

The prices we give are indicative and **not binding** on the owners, but are presumed to be their 1998 prices. If you travel with this edition after 1998 you must expect an increase on both rooms and meals, though you won't necessarily find it - some owners are very proud of not having put their prices up for years!

Where we give a price range, it generally means one of two things :
- different rooms have different prices
- prices vary according to season

As always, enquire when booking.

Reductions

Most French B&Bs offer reductions for stays of 2 or more nights; some have very attractive half-board terms, or special prices for children. Enquire when you book, for they are too numerous and complex for us to print them all.

Dinner prices

(VERY few places do lunch but the occasional picnic is available.) We have tried to show what the price quoted for dinner includes, but 'including wine' means many things. It may mean just a standard quarter-litre carafe per person; it may mean a bottomless barrel of table wine; it may mean a very decent bottle of local produce or, in some rare cases, of excellent estate wine. Whatever it is, it is usually wonderful value. When wine is not included, we have sometimes shown what it might cost you.

(See also **How to use Chambres d'Hôtes** below.)

MEALS - _Table d'Hôte_

You should seize the opportunity to eat honest - and sometimes sophisticated or even gourmet - food in an authentic family atmosphere. However, dinner at a B&B is NEVER automatic - it must be booked beforehand, at least in the morning, sometimes the day before. And cooks in their own houses are allowed their days off so don't expect dinner every day!

Where there is no _Table d'Hôte_, we have mentioned places to eat in the area but, here again, country restaurants and _auberges_ are seldom open every day. And most of them stop taking orders at about 9pm.

ICONS

Two symbols here - one for the animal you bring, one for the animal already there (did you know that 36% of French families are dog-owners as compared to 28% of English?).

 The 🐕 means YOUR animal, i.e. you may take your pet(s) but only if you check with the owners first - they may have a grandchild staying who has nightmares about fat cats. We print the symbol on the tacit understanding that your pet will behave itself, not dirty or damage the house nor disturb other people. (If we had room, we would write 'well-behaved' in front of every 🐕!)

 The 🐈 means THEIR animal, i.e. the owners themselves have animals of **some** sort (other than farm animals) - usually a dog or two, often a cat, sometimes parrots, horses, llamas. Don't be shy about asking which...

 In theory, our no-smoking icon is only printed for houses that are 100% non-smoking. Therefore, those without it do not refuse smokers but it is only common politeness not to smoke in a <u>bedroom</u> that might be occupied by a non-smoker tomorrow. It is hard to get curtains and bedclothes free of the smell of stale smoke.

 This new icon identifies places where walkers (with muddy boots and wet clothes) are welcome and can expect to find good hikes from the house or village, either in loops or on to another B&B, with luggage transported by your hosts. In a few cases, owners have said they will drive you to a starting point. Enquire when booking.

Gîtes for ... people
The intention is to tell you how many other people may be staying on the property in *gîtes* (holiday cottages). Then you will have an idea of what the total population is liable to be - the Happy-Families-Round-the-Pool Factor.

Tips for our American readers

One of America's favourite series on where to stay in Europe is Karen Brown's. She knows her readers well and leads them to places where she knows they will feel safe and comfortable.

Our book is VERY different! It too has a lot of lovely and utterly safe places for you to visit. But we also offer you the chance to venture forth and experience France in a perhaps more eclectic (and exciting?) way.

One reader wrote to question our inclusion of such widely differing places. Setting forth to find "romantic, luxurious and exotic" places, she had experienced a quintessentially French house with chaotic plumbing and mismatching decor and then a magnificently luxurious château. What she had missed was the significance of the very different prices and the subtleties of the descriptions - which are designed to spell out the truth in a sort of coded way.

Experience tells us that many of you are coming over to Europe with a different 'vocabulary', so the following hints may be of help:

B&B
In the US, the standard of B&Bs is extremely high with superb plumbing and heating, lots of vast fluffy towels and good furniture. In France, it ranges from the very basic farm, with a bath down the corridor or even in the room itself (!), to the most luxurious private château. In between, there will be gorgeous private châteaux with very basic plumbing and lovely old houses with perfectly adequate plumbing. Do remember that we choose these places with mostly European readers in mind, so the more in tune you are with European thinking the more you will enjoy our selection. This book is for the more sophisticated travellers.

Sophisticated
In the US, the word tends to relate to wealth and material needs. In Europe, it speaks rather of intellectual and cultural qualities. Thus, a 'sophisticated' US traveller may look for a luxurious B&B whereas a 'sophisticated' British traveller may not mind fairly basic facilities if the conversation and food are good.

Plumbing
We deal with bathrooms elsewhere in this Introduction, but it is worth emphasising that US plumbing is magnificent compared to much of ours and that we have learned to accept, even to love, rattling pipes, hip-baths behind curtains in bedrooms, exposed pipes and other oddities. If you are wary of such things then only go for the places which are obviously modernised... and probably more expensive.

Having said all this... if you come with a sense of adventure and are keen to meet interesting French people (often in beautiful homes), you will have a ball; thousands of US readers already have, and now swear by this book. You may also wallow in a surprising amount of luxury... and have more FUN than you thought possible in France.

How to use Chambres d'Hôtes

MUTUAL WELCOME

They are not hotels - that surely is why you choose them? Every time we write to the B&B owners in our guides we remind them what you, our readers and users of B&Bs, hope to find in the way of family welcome and atmosphere. Here is an anecdote to illustrate one French owner's attitude :

We had a handicapped visitor who wanted to dine with us but couldn't fit his legs under the table. So we put four 5-inch blocks of wood under the legs of the table and there he was, happily ensconced. It was a joyful and unforgettable meal, even though the other guests had their chins practically in their plates.

And there is another side to the relationship. Owners tell us over and over again how much they appreciate guests who come bearing Alastair Sawday's guide - "they are educated and civilised, interesting and interested; really good people to have in one's house".

BUT - there has to be a but - I quote here what some of our B&B owners would like to say to their less delicate guests. One wrote :

We are private people in our own homes NOT "professionnels du tourisme". Imagine inviting friends to stay - would you :

Make their beds for them every morning? Clean their bathroom, change their towels every day? Lay their breakfast at separate little tables? No? We treat our B&B guests like friends too... and make them pay when they go!

Another had this to say :

We always offer our guests a free drink, ranging from tea to gin and tonic, but we do have the occasional person who only just stops short of clicking his fingers and saying "Two beers, a gin and tonic and a coke for my daughter and we'll be out on the terrace". In such cases, I simply cannot produce my usual welcoming attitude.

We want you to feel you are our guest. We know that most people only have one or two holidays a year and we try to make it special for them. This includes excellent food and unlimited wine at dinner. Why do some people abuse this and expect to drink non-stop until 2am for the price of a meal? The record was a woman who consumed 2 litres of wine AFTER dinner with us - and was heard in a restaurant next day declaring that she was going to stick to her quarter-litre ration because any more would be too expensive...

Lastly, a detail but an important one :

One thing that does bug us is people not putting things back where they took them from. It seems to us a common courtesy.

Common courtesy is, I believe, the least we can each expect and give. It opens the door, as so many readers tell us, to relationships that can lift a holiday into another dimension.

NO-SHOWS

The majority of owners hope you will treat them like friends too, with sensitivity, tidiness and punctuality. The most upsetting thing for them, apart from the perfunctory behaviour described above, is preparing rooms and waiting up late for 'guests' who never come, never ring, never give any further sign of life. They gently tell us of *"des personnes indélicates"* who stand them up thus.

So if you find you are not going to take up a booking, PLEASE telephone right away.

By the way, there is a tacit agreement among a number of B&B owners that no-show + no-call by 8pm can be taken as a refusal of the booking and they will re-let the room if another asker turns up. This can be a touch embarrassing...

BOOKING

It is _**essential to book ahead in summer**_ (July and August) and recommended in other months - these places often have very few rooms. You can, of course, travel spontaneously and try your luck... Otherwise, the fax is the ideal way of booking and avoiding misunderstandings over the telephone - more and more French B&Bs have fax machines.

You will occasionally receive a _Contrat de Location_ ("Tenancy Contract") as confirmation (bureaucracy creeping into the most private corners, I fear). It must be filled in and sent back, probably with a deposit (see _All about Money_ below) and commits both sides to the stated dates and terms.

**Times for telephoning**. Two points need making :

- The French never ring people they don't know intimately after 9.30pm, and some even put the deadline at 9pm;
- Do remember that Ireland and the UK are one hour behind the Continent so your latest time for ringing France from the UK is 8.30pm. Some country folk have been quite upset by enquiries coming through at midnight when they were fast asleep.

ARRIVING

Most owners expect you to arrive between 5pm and 7pm. If you come earlier, you may find the rooms not finished or your hosts still out at work. Yet again, these are private houses and people have their private lives to get on with as well. We do ask them to leave a note if they are going to be late or have an emergency errand to run, but some are chary of announcing 'House Empty' to the world at large. Similarly, if you are going to be late (or early, unavoidably), PLEASE telephone and say so.

CHILDREN

Don't expect charming Madame automatically to LOVE looking after your children while you sleep late or go out to dinner (I invent nothing - these are real cases quoted to us). She is not insured for unattended children falling in her pond or tumbling downstairs in search of comfort at ten o'clock at night. Anyway, she may have other things to do, like go to bed herself.

Some owners **will** occasionally look after children but please don't take it for granted.

Dare we quote the horror story of the two nine-year-olds whose parents went for a walk, leaving the children "to play in the garden"? These children cut off the cat's whiskers and "rode" the dog, thereby crippling it. Your perfect children <u>may</u> just be hellish when your back is turned!

How to use Tables d'Hôtes

ALWAYS BOOK AHEAD. And please telephone to cancel if you are not going to be able to make it. Dinner will be at a fixed time but very seldom earlier than 7.30pm. In some houses, particularly in the south, it is normal to sit down at any time between 8.30 and 10 in the evening.

En famille or not _en famille_? Ideally, it should be; very often, it is. Practically, there are reasons why it won't be. Two of these reasons will make sense to a lot of you :

- the owners' young family need their parents' presence at dinner and for homework time and/or are not considered 'civilised' enough to dine with guests;
- your hostess is minding her figure and simply cannot afford to eat as much as she serves her guests every day!

VEGETARIANS, _please_ let your hosts know beforehand, otherwise they can hardly be expected to rustle up anything more original than the eternal '*omelette-salade*' or just offer you another helping of spinach. A handful of houses in this book actually specialise in vegetarian cooking but the 🌱 is given to all those who say they have a veggie dish or two up their sleeves if forewarned.

Practical Expectations

110 VOLTS

Our American cousins should be aware that the whole of Europe runs on 220-240 volts so leave your 110-volt appliances at home... or bring an adaptor.

TOWELS, etc.

Towels may not always be up to scratch. There may not always be soap. Do ask for things you lack. It is usually just an oversight when only two hand towels are provided for three people, though the French DO use smaller towels than we do. It's a good idea to take your favourite soap and towels with you.

All about Money

CASH, CHEQUE OR CREDIT CARD?

Most French B&B owners are still not equipped to take plastic payment. We feel it is reasonable for them to ask you to take your card to the nearest cash machine.

However, more and more of the plusher places are going over to plastic and the Internet - are they still true B&Bs? Let us know.

Travellers cheques and Eurocheques may also be a problem - French banks often charge a large lump-sum commission to honour them so the (smallish) amounts charged by B&Bs are half-annihilated by the charges. However, you CAN pay with either if the amount is stated in French francs (and your cheque guarantee card number is on the back of the cheque).

DEPOSITS

Some owners ask for a deposit - many readers have found it virtually impossible or horribly expensive to do this by direct transfer. One reader and one owner suggested the following solutions :
1. Have a number of French banknotes at home (you will need some for your travels anyway) and send the appropriate amount with your confirmation by 'International Recorded' mail.
2. Send a Eurocheque <u>which the owner will destroy when you arrive</u> (so no-one pays the charges); when you leave, they will ask you for cash for your whole stay.

TAXE DE SÉJOUR

This is a small sum per person that local councils are allowed to levy on all visitors paying for accommodation. Some councils do, some don't. So you may find you bill increased by a petty 4, 5, or 9 Francs. Owners do not like this at all, are even embarrassed about it, and don't know how to present it. They would like to disguise it inside their quoted rate; some do, but it is against the rules. So do be understanding about their subjection, once again, to heedless bureaucracy.

DISCLAIMER

We make no claims to pure objectivity in judging B&Bs. We have included these ones because we have some powerful reason for considering them special. Our inspectors are as human as you are - and we cherish that. Please read the description carefully for hints that Madame may be a bit barmy or that the decor inside is somewhat kitsch, in spite of a splendid exterior. These are our choices. Our opinions and tastes are ours alone and this book is a statement of them; we hope you will share them. If you don't, it's not because we've been sloppy, but probably because things have changed or you are very different from the inspector! Do let us know.

SYMBOLS

Explanation of Symbols Treat each one as a guide rather than a concrete indicator.

 Working farm or vineyard.

 Fairly good English is spoke here.

 One of your hosts speaks enough English for simple communication.

 Children are positively welcomed but cots, high chairs, etc., are not necessarily available. The text gives restrictions where relevant.

 You can either borrow or hire bikes here.

 Good hiking walks from house or village.

 Some, but not necessarily all, ingredients are organically grown.

 Vegetarians catered for with advance warning.

 Full disabled facilities provided.

 Accessible for people of limited mobility.

 Pets are welcome but may be housed in an outbuilding rather than in your room. Check when booking if restrictions/small supplements apply.

 This house has pets of its own: dog, cat, horse, duck, parrot,...

 Applies to totally non-smoking houses.

 Swimming may be in a swimming pool on the property, a pond, a lake, a river or the sea.

MM Michelin Map reference: number of Michelin 1/200 000 regional map followed by number of fold in that map.

 Entry number of each inspected property.

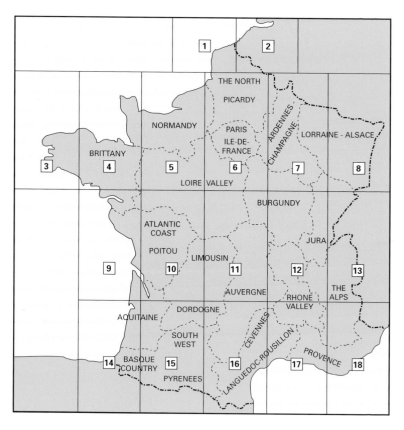

France : General Map

CONTENTS

ENTRIES   MAP

The North – Picardy
- Pas-de-Calais (62) ——————— 1-23   ❶ ❷
- Nord (59) ——————— 24-27   ❶ ❷ ❻
- Somme (80) ——————— 28-41   ❶ ❻
- Oise (60) ——————— 42-47   ❻
- Aisne (2) ——————— 48-54   ❻ ❼

The Ardennes – Champagne
- Ardennes (8) ——————— 55   ❼
- Marne (51) ——————— 56-61   ❼
- Aube (10) ——————— 62   ❼
- Haute-Marne (52) ——————— 63-65   ❼

Lorraine – Alsace – Franche-Comté
- Meuse (55) ——————— 66-68   ❼
- Moselle (57) ——————— 69-73   ❽
- Meurthe-et-Moselle (54) ——————— 74   ❼/❽
- Bas-Rhin (67) ——————— 75-78   ❽
- Haut-Rhin (68) ——————— 79   ❽
- Territoire de Belfort (90) ——————— 80   ❽
- Haute-Saône (70) ——————— 81-82   ❽ ⓬

Burgundy
- Jura (39) ——————— 83-85   ⓬
- Saône-et-Loire (71) ——————— 86-98   ⓬
- Côte d'Or (21) ——————— 99-105   ❼
- Nièvre (58) ——————— 106-114   ❻ ⓫ ⓬
- Yonne (89) ——————— 115-125   ❻ ❼ ⓬

Paris – Ile-de-France
- Seine-et-Marne (77) ——————— 126-128   ❻
- Essonne (91) ——————— 129-130   ❻
- Yvelines (78) ——————— 131-133   ❻
- Val d'Oise (95) ——————— 134-135   ❻
- Paris (75) ——————— 136-142   ❻

CONTENTS

ENTRIES   MAP

Normandy
- Seine-Maritime (76) ————— 143-149   ❺ ❻
- Eure (27)————————— 150-160   ❺ ❻
- Orne (61) ————————— 161-168   ❺
- Calvados (14) ———————— 169-197   ❺
- Manche (50) ———————— 198-224   ❹ ❺

Brittany
- Ille-et-Vilaine (35) ————— 225-233   ❹
- Côtes-d'Armor (22) ————— 234-247   ❸ ❹
- Finistère (29) ——————— 248-262   ❸
- Morbihan (56) ——————— 263-268   ❸ ❹
- Loire-Atlantique (44)————— 269-274   ❹ ❾

The Loire Valley
- Maine-et-Loire (49) ————— 275-299   ❺ ❾
- Vienne (North) (86) ————— 300-301   ❿
- Mayenne (53) ——————— 302-308   ❺
- Sarthe (72) ———————— 309-316   ❺
- Loir-et-Cher (41) ————— 317-324   ❺ ❻ ❿
- Eure-et-Loir (28) ————— 325-332   ❻
- Loiret (45) ———————— 333-336   ❻
- Cher (18)————————— 333-344   ⓫
- Indre (36) ————————— 345-350   ❿ ⓫
- Indre-et-Loire (37)————— 351-376   ❺ ❿

Poitou – The Atlantic Coast
- Vienne (Centre/South) (86)——— 377-395   ❿
- Deux-Sèvres (79) ————— 396-399   ❿
- Vendée (85)————————— 400-403   ❾ ❿
- Charente-Maritime (17) ———— 404-419   ❾ ❿
- Charente (16) ——————— 420-425   ❿

Limousin – Dordogne
- Haute-Vienne (87)————— 426-434   ❿ ⓫
- Creuse (23) ———————— 435-437   ⓫
- Corrèze (19) ———————— 438-443   ⓫
- Dordogne (24) ——————— 444-458   ❿ ⓯
- Lot (46) —————————— 459-464   ⓯ ⓰
- Lot-et-Garonne (47) ————— 465-470   ⓯

CONTENTS

	ENTRIES	MAP

Aquitaine
- Gironde (33) ——————— 471-480   ❾ ❿ ⓯
- Landes (40) ——————— 481-483   ⓮ ⓯

Basque Country – The South-West – Pyrenees
- Pyrénées-Atlantiques (64) ——— 484-492   ⓮ ⓯
- Hautes-Pyrénées (65) ——————— 493-499   ⓯
- Haute-Garonne (31) ——————— 500-506   ⓯ ⓰
- Ariège (9) ——————————— 507-515   ⓯ ⓰
- Gers (32) ————————————— 516-519   ⓯
- Tarn-et-Garonne (82) ————— 520-526   ⓯ ⓰

Roussillon – Languedoc – Cévennes
- Pyrénées-Orientales (66) ——— 527-529   ⓰
- Aude (11) —————————— 530-533   ⓰
- Tarn (81) ——————————— 534-544   ⓰
- Hérault (34) ————————— 545-551   ⓰ ⓱
- Gard (30) ——————————— 552-563   ⓱

The Auvergne
- Aveyron (12) ————————— 564-567   ⓰
- Cantal (15) —————————— 568-570   ⓫
- Puy-de-Dôme (63) ——————— 571-572   ⓫
- Allier (3) ———————————— 573   ⓫
- Loire (42) ——————————— 574-575   ⓬
- Haute-Loire (43) ——————— 576-581   ⓫ ⓬

The Rhône Valley
- Ardèche (7) ——————————— 582-587   ⓬ ⓱
- Drôme (26) —————————— 588-600   ⓬ ⓱
- Isère (38) —————————— 601   ⓬
- Rhône (69) ——————————— 602   ⓬
- Ain (1) ———————————— 603   ⓬

The Alps
- Haute-Savoie (74) ——————— 604-610   ⓬
- Savoie (73) —————————— 611-615   ⓭
- Hautes-Alpes (5) ——————— 616   ⓭

Provence – The Riviera
- Vaucluse (84) ————————— 617-632   ⓱
- Bouches-du-Rhône (13) ———— 633-643   ⓱ ⓲
- Var (83) ——————————— 644-655   ⓲
- Alpes-Maritimes (6) ————— 656-667   ⓲

Amiens	Bâle	Bayonne	Besançon	Bordeaux	Brest	Caen	Calais	Clermont-Ferrand	Dijon	Geneva	Grenoble	Le Havre	Lille	Limoges	Lyon	Le Mans	Marseille
568																	
918	1028																
560	151	888															
726	836	184	696														
614	1097	814	956	622													
239	783	770	643	578	373												
155	683	1062	595	870	718	343											
546	478	555	337	372	751	544	690										
459	244	833	104	641	856	542	603	282									
684	259	932	177	695	1081	767	828	323	199								
711	403	815	287	658	1108	794	855	286	296	144							
179	746	842	606	650	482	107	283	571	505	730	757						
115	610	989	522	797	814	344	112	617	530	755	782	284					
542	612	412	472	220	599	437	686	178	417	486	464	548	613				
607	389	813	249	550	1004	690	751	178	192	156	104	653	678	356			
349	703	619	563	427	402	151	415	382	462	687	714	223	420	286	610		
923	694	683	564	649	1319	1005	1067	459	507	435	282	969	994	637	316	926	
345	253	1095	257	903	920	568	471	546	264	424	559	531	387	680	455	526	771
906	677	519	547	484	1092	989	1050	364	490	418	300	952	977	432	299	718	169
527	35	1016	139	824	1085	771	653	466	232	294	438	734	569	600	377	691	693
362	209	1031	199	839	884	541	488	495	213	366	508	504	404	629	404	491	720
530	847	518	707	326	296	284	674	452	606	725	738	380	601	303	628	183	961
1078	737	838	804	1474	1161	1222	614	662	478	334	1124	1149	792	471	1081	188	
277	538	649	398	457	545	255	421	295	297	522	549	283	348	272	445	138	761
148	554	771	413	579	596	240	292	400	313	538	565	203	219	396	461	203	776
1054	825	483	695	448	1056	972	1198	465	638	566	448	1100	1125	514	447	821	317
157	412	906	324	714	731	379	271	502	284	470	580	342	198	531	476	338	791
417	849	629	708	437	245	177	522	536	608	833	860	286	566	374	756	154	1071
115	682	814	542	622	499	124	219	507	441	666	693	87	220	484	589	196	905
659	441	701	301	519	909	742	803	147	244	214	139	705	730	325	59	507	309
503	145	1122	244	930	1077	725	617	571	338	404	548	688	544	706	483	684	798
984	755	744	625	710	1380	1067	1128	520	568	496	335	1030	1055	698	377	987	64
852	913	299	783	244	852	768	996	397	726	654	536	858	923	310	535	617	405
381	656	537	516	345	484	233	525	300	415	527	534	305	452	204	430	82	745

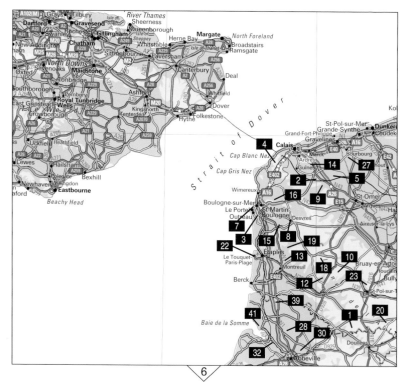

Scale for colour maps 1:1 600 000

(1cm:16km or 1 inch:25.25 miles)

Distances between major towns

Example: Montpellier – Toulon 240km

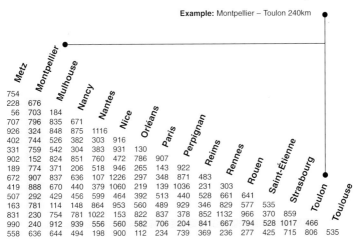

Metz	Montpellier	Mulhouse	Nancy	Nantes	Nice	Orléans	Paris	Perpignan	Reims	Rennes	Rouen	Saint-Étienne	Strasbourg	Toulon	Toulouse
754															
228	676														
56	703	184													
707	796	835	671												
926	324	848	875	1116											
402	744	526	382	303	916										
331	759	542	304	383	931	130									
902	152	824	851	760	472	786	907								
189	774	371	206	518	946	265	143	922							
672	907	837	636	107	1226	297	348	871	483						
419	888	670	440	379	1060	139	219	1036	231	303					
507	292	429	456	599	464	392	513	440	528	661	641				
163	781	114	148	864	953	560	489	929	346	829	577	535			
831	230	754	781	1022	153	822	837	378	852	1132	966	370	859		
990	240	912	939	556	560	582	706	204	841	667	794	528	1017	466	
558	636	644	494	198	900	112	234	739	369	236	277	425	715	806	535

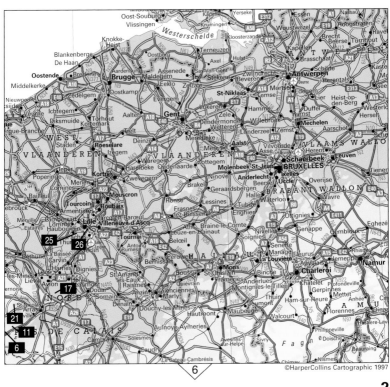

©HarperCollins Cartographic 1997

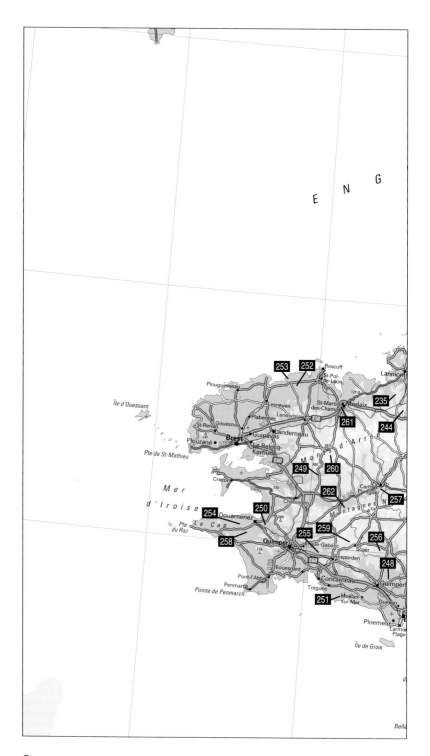

3

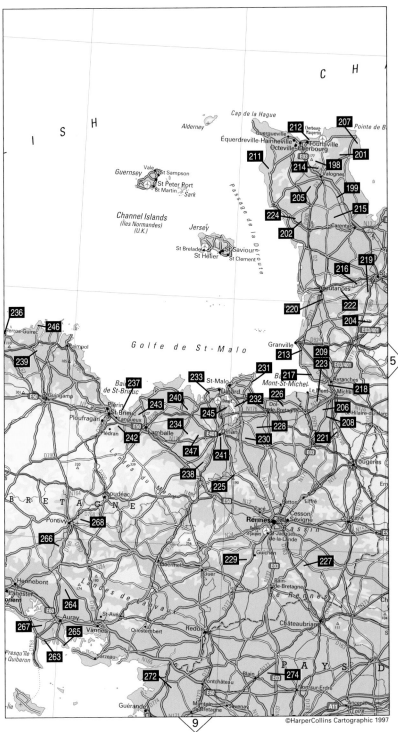

CH

C H

I S H

Cap de la Hague

Alderney

Querqueville
Équerdreville-Hainneville
Octeville-Cherbourg

Cherbourg-Maupertus
212
207 Pointe de B

Fourlaville
201

Guernsey
Vale St Sampson
St Peter Port
St Martin Sark

211

214
198
Valognes

199

Channel Islands
(Îles Normandes)
(U.K.)

Jersey

St Brelade St Saviour
St Hélier St Clement

205

224

202

215

Carentan N13

219

216

Coutances

222

204

220

Granville
213

209
223
217

Bai
Mont-St-Michel

218

Avranches

Le Mont-St-Michel

236
246
Perros-Guirec

Golfe de St-Malo

233 St-Malo

231

240
Dinard

232
226
Dol-
de-Bretagne

206
St-Hilaire-du-Harc

208

239

Baie
de St-Brieuc

237

Guingamp

Plérin
St-Brieuc
Langueux

243

245

228

221

230

234

Camballe

242

P1édran

247

Dinan

241

238

225

Fougères

BRETAGNE

Loudéac

Gifflé

Betton

Cesson-
Sévigné

Pontivy

268

Rennes

266

St-Jacques
de-la-Lande

229 Guichen

227

Ploërmel

Guer

Bain-
de-Bretagne

Hennebont
Lanester
orient

Landes de Lanvaux

264
Auray

St-Avé

267

265 Vannes

Questembert

Redon

Châteaubriant

263

Sarzeau

N165

Presqu'île
Quiberon

PAYS D

Blain

272
Pontchâteau

274
Nort-sur-Erdre

Guérande

Montoir-de
Bretagne Savenay

Ancenis
Loire

A11

©HarperCollins Cartographic 1997

4

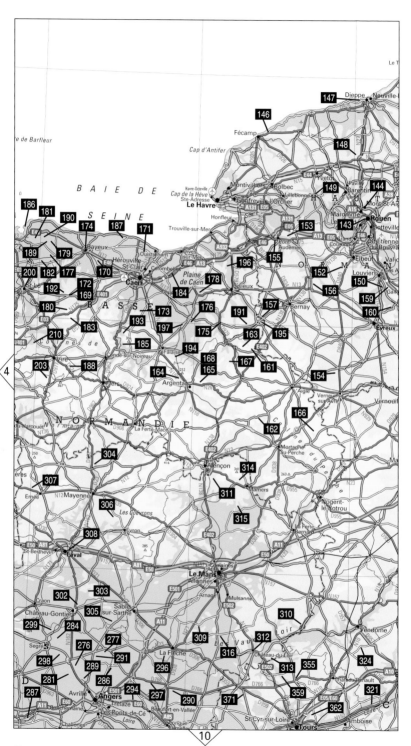

5

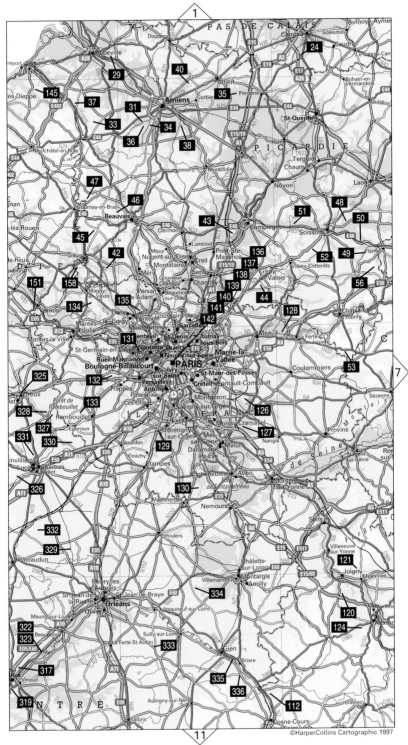

PAS DE CALAIS

PICARDIE

ÎLE DE FRANCE

PARIS

©HarperCollins Cartographic 1997

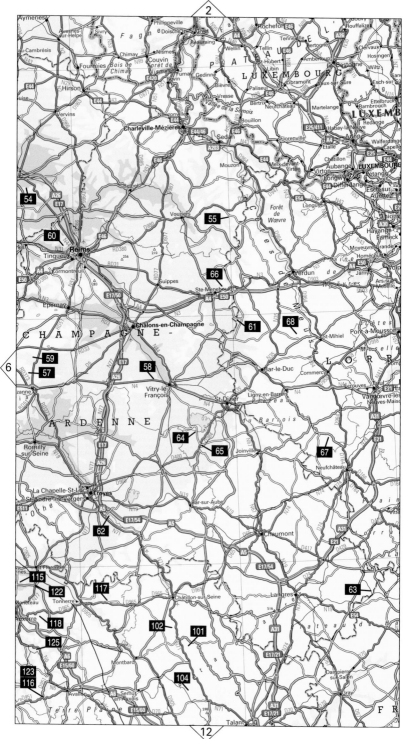

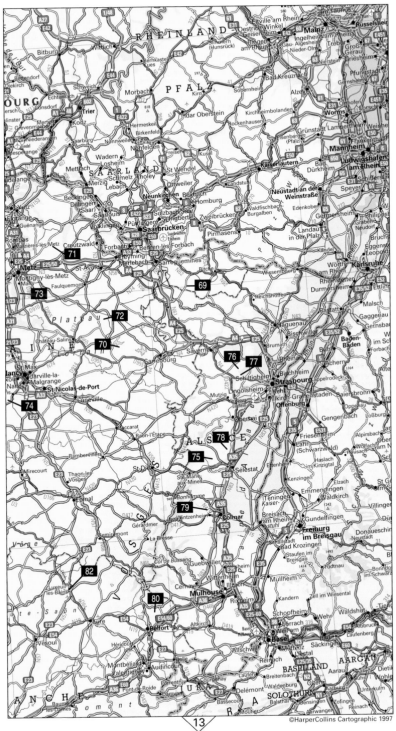

©HarperCollins Cartographic 1997

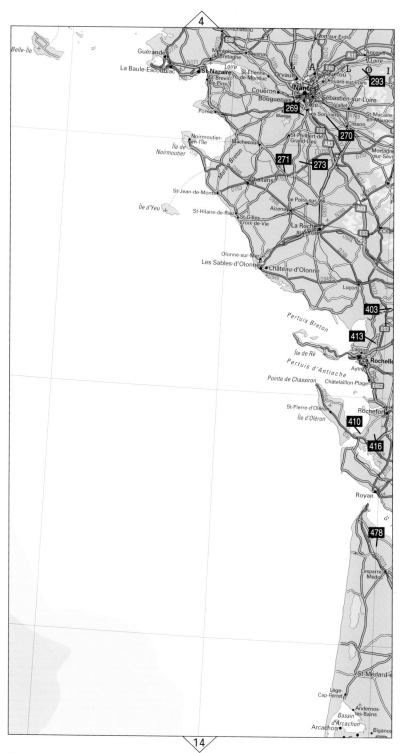

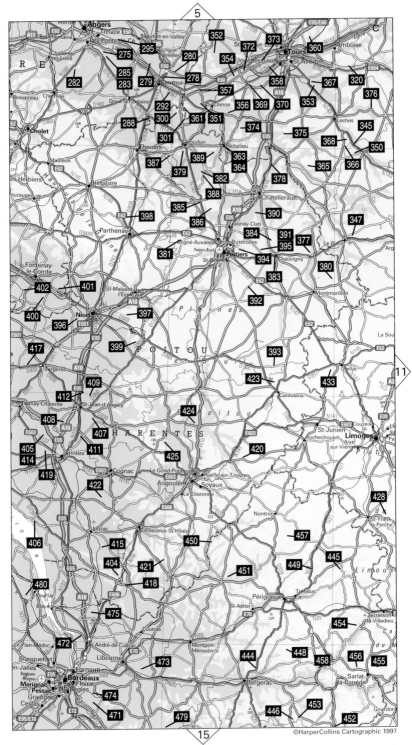

©HarperCollins Cartographic 1997

10

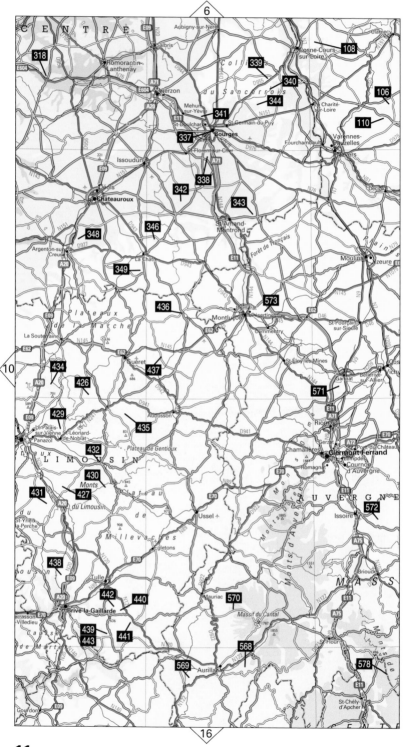

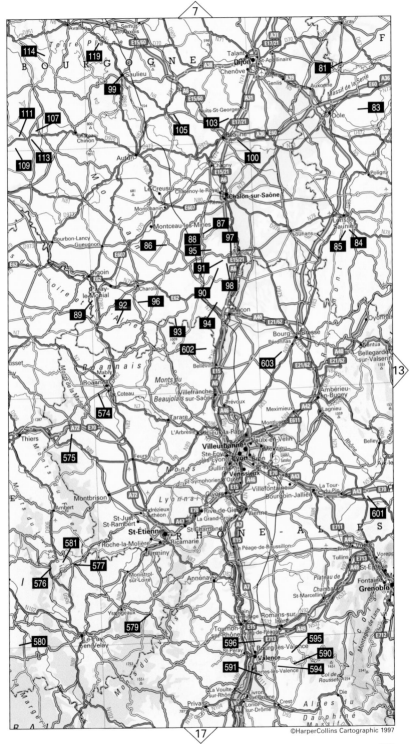

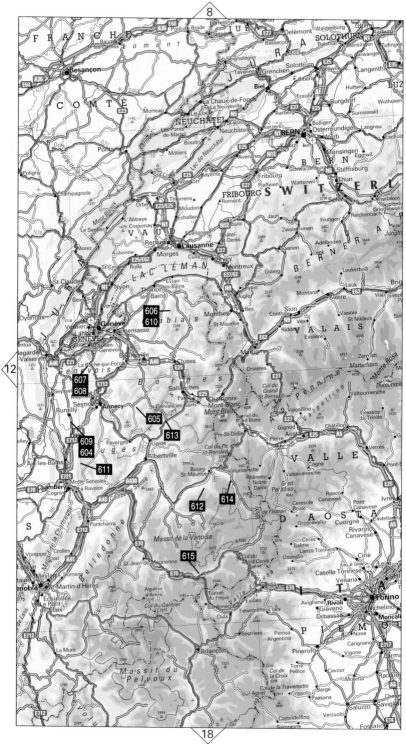

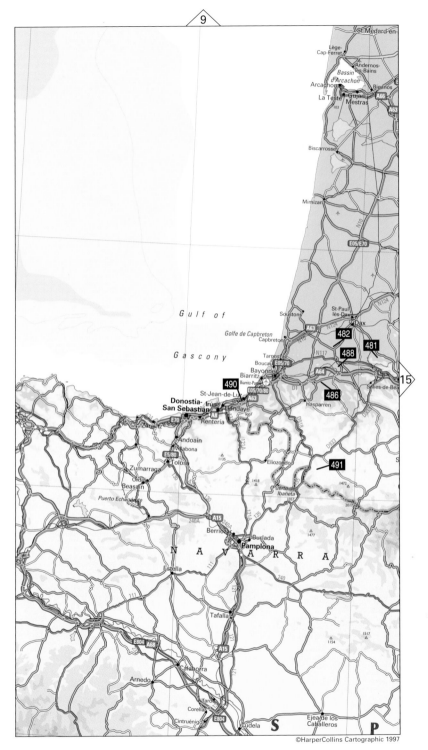

St-Médard-en-

Lège-
Cap-Ferret

Andernos-
lès-Bains

Bassin
d'Arcachon

Arcachon
La Teste
103

Biganos

A66

A63

Gujan
Mestras

Biscarrosse

Mimizan

E05 E70

N10

N124

Gulf of

Soustons

St-Paul-
lès-Dax

Dax

Golfe de Capbreton

Capbreton

A63

482

N117

488

481

Gascony

Tarnos
Boucau
Bayonne

E05/70

490

Biarritz

Biarritz-Parme

E05/70/80

A64

Salies-de-Béa

15

St-Jean-de-Luz

A63

486

Donostia-
San Sebastián

Irun
Hendaye
A8

Hasparren

Zarautz

E70

Rentería

906?

Andoain

Villabona

E5/80

491

Tolosa

Zumarraga

Eliozondo

1135

Ordizia
Beasain

1418

1472

Puerto Echegárate

Puerto de
Ibañeta
1057

2017

A15

Berriozar

240A

Burlada

1477

N A V A R R A

Pamplona

Estella

240

Tafalla

A15

1517

1154

E804 A68

Calahorra

Arnedo

Alfaro

Ejea de los
Caballeros

Corella

E804

S

P

Cintruénigo

Tudela

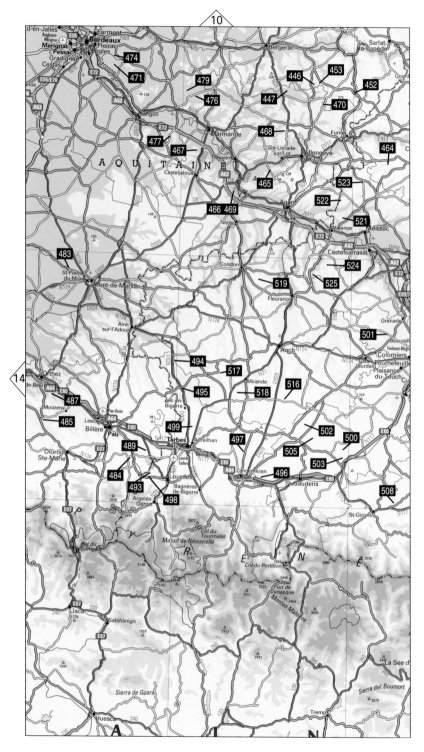

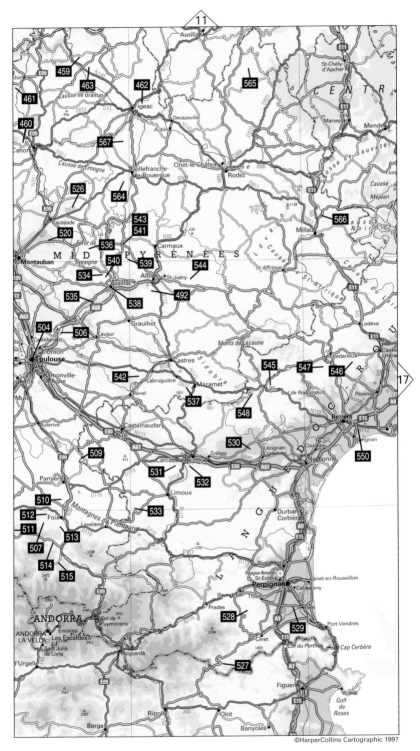

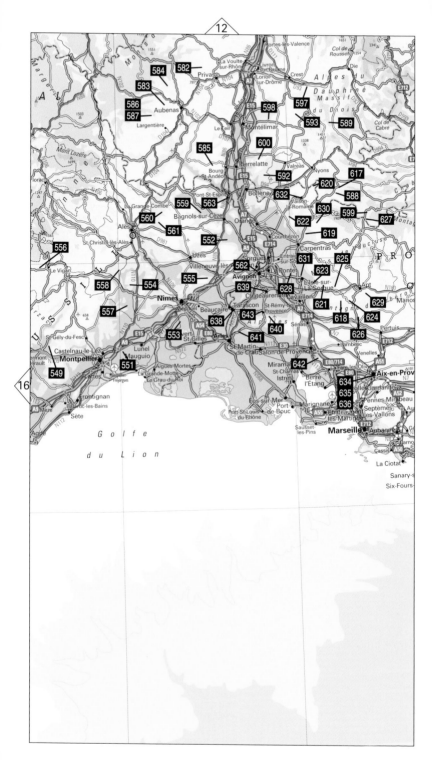

Perhaps the exterior might lead you to expect something grander within, but this is much more a working farmer's house than a château, with family furniture and plastic flowers, a gorgeous white-and-black tiled floor and a tired sitting-room. Guests sleep in an outbuilding which has some big solid period pieces in one or two of the large bedrooms and a huge fireplace downstairs. It is, quite properly, inexpensive; but it is good value and your hosts are an affable, down-to-earth couple.

Rooms: 1 large double, 2 smaller double above, all in one dwelling with one bathroom.

Price: 220-250 Frs for two, including breakfast.

Meals: Doullens 13km.

Open: All year.

In Abbeville N1 towards Paris then D925 towards Arras; after St Riquier, left on D941; through Auxi-le-Château; right on D938 to Beauvoir Wavens: château is first building on right as you enter village.

Map No: 1   MM 236-23

René AUGUSTIN
Château de Drucas
Beauvoir Wavens
62390 Auxi-le-Château
Pas-de-Calais
Tel: (0)3 21 04 01 11

The North – Picardy

The people are delightful — an open, smiling, intelligent family who will also sell you wine. The big park is soft and appealing; the nearness to ferry ports is seductive although the nearby main road and TGV line may disturb some people. Straightforward and simple are the key words here — no luxury (showers are behind curtains). Breakfast is in the separate guest quarters (or the family kitchen for very early starts), where basic pine furniture and slatting grace the smallish rooms and windows look onto lawn and trees.

Rooms: 2 triple, each with shower, sharing wc; 1 quadruple with shower & wc.

Price: 210 Frs for two, including breakfast.

Meals: 1km or Ardres 5km. Self-catering.

Open: All year.

Gîtes for 11 people

There are only a few horses in the stables now: the main stud farm is further away. This means that your hosts have a very busy life and may be a little preoccupied, though Madame is lively and fun when relaxed. The bedrooms, in a self-contained unit which looks out onto the courtyard and surrounding wooded hills, have simple, modern decor and the breakfast/living-room is also very straightforward. The garden and orchard go down to the river and this is a good family stopover.

Rooms: 2 double, 2 twin, all with shower & wc.

Price: 250 Frs for two, including breakfast.

Meals: In village.

Open: All year except Christmas & New Year

From A26 (exit 2 on N43) towards Calais. Wolphus is on left 1km after the junction, with woods beside road. Be careful turning in!

Map No: 1   MM 236-3

Jean-Jacques & Mimi BEHAGHEL
La Ferme de Wolphus
No 39, RN43, Wolphus
62890 Zouafques
Pas-de-Calais
Tel: (0)3 21 35 61 61
Fax: (0)3 21 35 61 61

From Boulogne-sur-Mer, D940 towards St Léonard. There, at 2nd lights, left onto small road (to Echingen, not signed); in village centre, left into tiny street immediately after sharp bend then left into first gateway.

Map No: 1   MM 236-2

Jacqueline & Jean-Pierre
BOUSSEMAERE
Rue de l'Eglise
62360 Echinghen
Pas-de-Calais
Tel: (0)3 21 91 14 34

A good place to stay and visit this dramatic, cliff-lined coast. The enclosed farmyard envelopes and protects; the old dovecote, its landing ledges intact, still welcomes pigeons; the roses bloom; Madame serves breakfast and warming dinners in the newish conservatory where wooden birds fly. The rooms, in converted outbuildings with rafters and character, are a good size, nicely decorated, tempting. We would choose the studio over the stables... And there is a games room where children can play table-tennis or paint on rainy afternoons.

Rooms: 3 triple, 2 double, 1 quadruple, all with bath or shower & wc.

Price: 220 Frs or 280 Frs, including breakfast.

Meals: 90 Frs, including wine (not Saturdays).

Open: All year.

Gîtes for 27 people

She's a lovely old lady! She talks lots, in French, and otherwise relies on radio and telly for company. Hers is a piecemeal family house with comfortable old furniture and masses of photographs (37 grandchildren). Rooms are rustically attractive with good beds and windows onto the peace outside. Madame loves cooking her delicious country dishes for visitors and readers have praised her natural hospitality. Ask to see the exquisite vaulted stables — built for cows and carthorses, fit for thoroughbreds!

Rooms: 2 double, one with cot + child's bed, each with shower & wc.

Price: 190 Frs for two, including breakfast.

Meals: 80 Frs, including wine & coffee.

Open: April to October.

From A16 exit 11 into Peuplingues. 2km beyond, left at first houses in Haute Escalles. Park in farmyard.

Map No: 1 — MM 236-2

Jacqueline & Marc BOUTROY
La Grand' Maison
Haute Escalles
62179 Escalles
Pas-de-Calais
Tel: (0)3 21 85 27 75
Fax: (0)3 21 85 27 75

From Calais, N43 towards St-Omer. At Nordausques, D218, then D217 towards Ruminghem. Signposted in Muncq-Nieurlet — house 500m beyond hamlet.

Map No: 1 — MM 236-3

Mme Françoise BRETON
La Motte Obin, 191 rue du Bourg
62890 Muncq-Nieurlet
Pas-de-Calais
Tel: (0)3 21 82 79 63

This stately home is actually a warm, embracing country house. The hall/breakfast-room has all the features of the stolid, studied early 19th century: black and white floor, moulded ceiling, arches framing (later) stained glass windows. Madame is as bustling and chatty as any busy young grandmother with guests to care for (and delicious 'real' apples to sell). Two rooms are in traditional French style, four have fresh modern pine furniture and pretty colours, all have space and quiet. Only 4 rooms available at any one time.

Rooms: 5 triple, 1 double, all with bath or shower & wc (extra beds available).

Price: 260 Frs for two, including breakfast. Extra bed 70 Frs.

Meals: Choice 5-8km.

Open: All year except February.

Gites for 4 people

Distinctive it certainly is. Huge heavy family furniture, a great high-arched fully floral hall, dining space and French upholstered upright chairs for twelve. Madame is an effervescent animal-lover whose guests have "opened the world anew to her". The 'Big Room' is fabulous, its bathroom almost more so; the top-floor suite is more rustic. It's all fascinating and captures the flavour of one very particular (and lovable) kind of France. Just 100 yards from the lovely old walled town of Boulogne.

Rooms: 1 double with bath & wc; 1 triple with shower & wc on different floor; 1 suite for 4 with shower, sharing wc.

Price: 250-350 Frs for two, including breakfast.

Meals: Wide choice within the ramparts (walking distance).

Open: All year except February.

From Doullens, N25 towards Arras. In L'Arbret, first left to Saulty and follow signposts.

Map No: 2   MM 236-24

Pierre & Françoise DALLE
82 rue de la Gare
62158 Saulty
Pas-de-Calais
Tel: (0)3 21 48 24 76
Fax: (0)3 21 48 18 32

Rue Flahaut is off Boulevard Mariette which runs below the ramparts on the northern side of the city past the Porte des Dunes.

Map No: 1   MM 236-1

Simone & Édouard DELABIE
26 rue Flahaut
62200 Boulogne-sur-Mer
Pas-de-Calais
Tel: (0)3 21 31 88 74

The Desalases are friendly and helpful, eager to please and make friends. The house is simple and undemanding, a long low farm wih plain rooms, beams, showers and loos curtained off among the rafters... all comfortable, scruffy in places and pleasant. The bedrooms have forest views, their own entrance and a dayroom with refrigerator and collection of books. Breakfast is a feast (try the smoked turkey) and you can work it off with a good walk. They welcome walkers and cyclists, and you can even bring your horse.

Rooms: 2 double, each with shower & wc.

Price: 250 Frs for two, including breakfast.

Meals: Barbecue available.

Open: All year.

A stunning house, not big but an architectural historian's delight. It is 'French traditional' with masses of original, highly perishable details intact such as stained glass, trompe-l'œil wall-paintings (admire the 1850s fake marble), superb green and white tiling in the kitchen. The quiet rooms are trad-furnished too, with rich dark wardrobes and good beds. Madame works on weekdays so you see more of her at weekends. Otherwise, arrive 6pm onwards (though a friend is always available earlier).

Rooms: 1 double with shower & wc; 1 twin, 2 double with washbasins, sharing bath & wc; 2 double with showers, sharing wc (+ 3rd shower).

Price: 200-220 Frs for two, including breakfast.

Meals: Restaurant 3km. Ardres 10km.

Open: All year.

From Boulogne-sur-Mer, D341 to Desvres, then D215 towards Menneville; just outside Desvres, left at sign 'Le Mont Eventé'.

Map No: 1   MM 236-12

M & Mme DESALASE
Le Mont Eventé
Menneville
62240 Desvres
Pas-de-Calais
Tel: (0)3 21 91 77 65

A26 exit 2 towards Tournehem then immediately right to Zouafques then Tournehem. There D217 to Bonningues. House on right just after entering village.

Map No: 1   MM 236-3

Mme Christiane DUPONT
Le Manoir
40 rue de Licques
62890 Tournehem-sur-Hem
Pas-de-Calais
Tel: (0)3 21 82 69 05

Close your eyes and you can almost hear the clanking swords of the 1415 Battle of Agincourt (this 1750s house stands on the site). Open them and you may see mediæval knights — that's just your hosts on their way to a re-enactment battle. Tales abound here of ghosts and archers, soldiers and horses. The guestrooms (one with shower behind curtain) are in an adjoining wattle-and-daub house with its own dayroom and log fire. Breakfast is served in a room crammed with bric-à-brac on the ground floor of the house's tower.

Rooms: 3 double, 1 triple, all with own shower & wc.

Price: 250 Frs for two, including breakfast.

Meals: Good choice in Fruges 6km.

Open: All year.

Well-placed for Arras, Calais and the military cemeteries of the Vimy Ridge, this 1847 timber-frame and stone house hides in a peaceful spot behind the church. The rural simplicity of the outside contrasts with the handsome interior, furnished with fine antiques. Madame provides the little touches that make the difference, such as bathrobes and bottled water in the rooms. She also serves a generous and imaginative breakfast and is the sort of person who will spontaneously post back to you anything you leave behind.

Rooms: 2 double, 1 twin, all with bath or shower & wc.

Price: 200 Frs for two, including breakfast.

Meals: Good inexpensive restaurant nearby.

Open: All year.

From St Omer D928 towards Abbeville. At Ruisseauville right on D104. At Agincourt Battle Centre crossroads left towards Tramecourt — house 100m on right.

Map No: 1   MM 236-13

Patrick & Marie-Josée FENET
La Gacogne
62310 Azincourt
Pas-de-Calais
Tel: (0)3 21 04 45 61
Fax: (0)3 21 04 45 61

From Arras N25 towards Doullens. At Bac-du-Sud right on D66 to Gouy-en-Artois and Fosseux. House is near village church.

Map No: 2   MM 236-15

Geneviève GUILLUY-DELACOURT
3 rue de l'Église
62810 Fosseux
Pas-de-Calais
Tel: (0)3 21 48 40 13

This house has been allowed to keep its solid, genuine, elegant personality. Those bricks are original 18th-century, as are the bowed doorframes and drawing-room panelling inside. Mrs James's exquisite taste matches the house: unpretentious but stylish, harmonious yet comfortable, chandeliers to light books, swags to hold fine textiles, excellent bedrooms, luxurious bathrooms. The small art gallery might inspire you to stay a while and paint the gentle views over the valley or the ghosts at Agincourt, 3km away.

Rooms: 2 twin, 1 family room, each with own bathroom.

Price: 360-400 Frs for two, family room 400-500 Frs, including breakfast.

Meals: In village or 5 minutes drive.

Open: All year.

From Hesdin, D928 towards St Omer, then D155 left to Fressin. On entering village cross bridge, turn left & take 1st right; house is 200m on right.

Map No: 1   MM 236-13

Mrs Lesley JAMES
La Maison des Violettes
Rue de l'Avocat
62140 Fressin
Pas-de-Calais
Tel: (0)3 21 81 80 94

The house feels almost monastic (it never was), even Gothic on a dark night, in its white-stoned simplicity and eerie hush; it is a pure, pleasing renovation. The vaulted dining-room is a triumph; bedrooms and bathrooms are remarkable with lit candles, old mirrors, large beds and views over the immaculate courtyard and its historic pigeon-tower. Madame is flexible and helpful, her mornings are all light, space and home-made jams, her passions include rescuing animals (a menagerie to delight any child) and 1900s dress-dummies.

Rooms: 2 double, 1 suite for 4, each with bath & wc.

Price: 280 Frs for two, including breakfast.

Meals: Wide choice 5km.

Open: All year.

From Montreuil, D901 to Neuville. In Neuville, on sharp bend, D113 towards Marles-sur-Canche. Shortly after la Chartreuse follow signposts for 3km.

Map No: 1   MM 236-12

Mme Dominique LEROY
Manoir Francis
1 rue de l'Eglise
62170 Marles-sur-Canche
Pas-de-Calais
Tel: (0)3 21 81 38 80
Fax: (0)3 21 81 38 56

Bernard, who has had six children, is an exceptional host — several readers have said so. Sheltering behind thick trees, this recent conversion of the old château stables has a glorious family atmosphere, games in the big walled garden, a vastly welcoming living-room with a fireplace and the most amazing carved, ochre-tiled, water-themed table made for them in Provence (where they lived by a lake). The bedrooms have windows onto the garden, country-style beds, razors and chocolates; the breakfast room has a billiards table.

Rooms: 2 double, 1 triple, all with bath & wc; 1 triple with shower & wc (behind curtain). Connecting children's room available.

Price: 220 Frs for two, including breakfast. Reductions for children.

Meals: Choice 3km.

Open: All year (except 23-26 December).

This charming, genuine *Notaire*'s house (the shield on the front is his symbol of office) has a gloriously eccentric attic *salon* for guests with all the furniture gathered in the centre. The big bedrooms are decorated in traditional French style with antiques, shutters and modern bathrooms. Breakfast — including *clafoutis* if you're lucky — is served on the terrace in good weather. The pretty, authentic village makes no concessions to tourism, and the owners have a similar olde-worlde air to them.

Rooms: 2 double, 1 twin, each with bath or shower & wc. Extra beds available.

Price: 250 Frs for two, including breakfast.

Meals: 80 Frs, including wine.

Open: All year.

From Calais, N43 towards St Omer. At Bois-en-Ardres, house (just after the roundabout) is second B&B on right; signposted. (12 mins from tunnel & ferries.)

Map No: 1   MM 236-3

Bernard & Geneviève LÉTURGIE
La Chesnaie
N43 Bois-en-Ardres
62610 Ardres
Pas-de-Calais
Tel: (0)3 21 35 43 98
Fax: (0)3 21 36 48 70

From Boulogne N1 S towards St Léonard & Montreuil for approx. 15km. In Samer, take road that goes down to right of church — house on left.

Map No: 1   MM 236-12

Joëlle MAUCOTEL
127 rue du Breuil
62830 Samer
Pas-de-Calais
Tel: (0)3 21 33 50 87/
      (0)3 21 87 64 19
Fax: (0)3 21 83 00 43

Readers have told of remarkable hospitality, food and beds in antique-furnished rooms where sweeties and bathrobes are laid out — so it's immaterial that the loos are down a long corridor. It's nicer than it looks in the photos, slightly scuffed and run in a comfortingly amateur way. Our inspector loved it for just being itself: "...so interesting and so real. My ideal place to stay; a big family home with special people". The main bedroom has walls panelled with painted cupboards, antiques and courtyard views.

Rooms: 2 twin, 2 double, all with shower, sharing 2 wcs.

Price: 170-195 Frs for two (+25 Frs for 2nd 'twin' bed), including breakfast. Extra person 60 Frs.

Meals: 70 Frs, including wine & coffee.

Open: All year.

A fine example of northern French brick-building, as is the splendid 19th-century brewery across the road with its curious double swastika emblem. The Peugniez are lovely, gentle people whose children have grown and flown; they still farm (cereals only now, having given up beef) and enjoy good company. Their house is simple and most welcoming, not at all pretentious, just with a warm family feel. The attic-floor guestrooms have screened-off showers, old timbers and floorboards and make a good-value stopover.

Rooms: 3 double, 1 twin, 1 quadruple, all with own shower, all sharing 2 wc's.

Price: 180 Frs for two, including breakfast.

Meals: In village or Arras 7km.

Open: All year except Christmas — New Year.

Gîtes for 12 people

From Calais, A16 for Boulogne. At Marquise, D238 to Wierre Effroy. Follow D234 southwards; left onto D233 and left to Le Breucq.

Map No: 1   MM 236-2

Jacques & Isabelle de MONTIGNY
Le Breucq
62142 Belle-et-Houllefort
Pas-de-Calais
Tel: (0)3 21 83 31 99
Fax: (0)3 21 83 31 99

From A1 exit 16 on N50 for 2km then left to Fampoux. In village follow Chambre d'Hôte signs. House on right in Rue Paul Verlaine.

Map No: 2   MM 236-16

Dominique & Marie-Thérèse PEUGNIEZ
17 rue Paul Verlaine
62118 Fampoux
Pas-de-Calais
Tel: (0)3 21 55 00 90
Fax: (0)3 21 55 00 90

Both suites are generous in comforts and floral cosiness, both give onto the wide terrace and the green and flowery garden. One has a huge carved Henri III bed, a totally French heavy-framed mirror and loads of lace. The breakfast is as generous as the decor and your hosts, who are very young grandparents, will keep you informed and entertained. Madame makes superb jams, Monsieur's passion is Arab horses but as he can no longer ride he keeps two animals from an equine refuge in his pasture.

Rooms: 1 suite for 3/4, 1 suite for 6, both with bath or shower & wc.

Price: 250 Frs for two, 400 Frs for 4, including breakfast.

Meals: 110 Frs, including wine & coffee.

Open: All year.

Gîtes for 3 people

From Montreuil N39 towards Hesdin. Left on D928 towards St Omer. After Hesdin Forest 2nd left on D155 to Sains-lès-Fressin. House is at PR5 milestone.

Map No: 1   MM 236-16

Jo & Jacques RIEBEN
Chantelouve
35 rue Principale
62310 Sains-lès-Fressin
Pas-de-Calais
Tel: (0)3 21 90 60 13
Fax: (0)3 21 90 60 13

Perfectly placed for touring, this 18th-century house sits on the quiet main street of a small village. The cosiest room (for three) is in the beamed attic. Madame is fairly elderly, anxious that you should enjoy your stay and she is so attentive a hostess we know her lack of English will not be a problem. There are bathrobes for 'detached' bathroom users and toothbrushes and toothpaste for the forgetful! Breakfast is stupendous with four varieties of homemade jam, delicious bread, yoghurt, cheese and *pain au chocolat*.

Rooms: 2 double, 1 triple, each with shower & wc; 1 twin, 1 double, with basins, sharing shower & wc.

Price: 180 or 210 Frs for two, including breakfast. Extra bed 70 Frs. Children 2-10 yrs: 50 Frs.

Meals: Wide choice in Montreuil (10km); self-catering possible.

Open: All year.

From Hesdin N39 towards Montreuil. At Brimeux right on D129 to Aix-en-Issart. House on right in village centre.

Map No: 1   MM 236-12

Mme Gilberte SANTUNE
42 rue Principale
62170 Aix-en-Issart
Pas-de-Calais
Tel: (0)3 21 81 39 46

It feels miles from anywhere, like a lost domain, but the hospitality is stupendous, especially at weekends when great parties are held for village, family and guests — the lawns are dotted with pretty frocks and chandeliers ring with friendly laughter. The housekeeper is delightful and Madame will come back from Paris for guests on weekdays. Built in 1745, the château has much grandeur but is still in need of great works of restoration by its down-to-earth owners: the relaxed and friendly atmosphere easily makes up for a little damp.

Rooms: 5 double, each with bath or shower & wc.

Price: 350 Frs for two, including breakfast.

Meals: 100 Frs, excluding wine.

Open: All year.

The sheltered garden is lovely (swings for the children too) and the lime trees are a fitting backdrop to this imposing manor built in soft grey stone between the 17th and 19th centuries. It originally belonged to the château next door and the drive is still flanked by a fine laurel hedge. Rooms are high-ceilinged, bright and comfortable, with some antique furniture (particularly the Grandparents' Room). Madame is warmly relaxed and attentive, very much the pivot of her family and has photographs of them everywhere.

Rooms: 1 family suite, 1 double, both with bath or shower & wc.

Price: 240 Frs for two, including breakfast.

Meals: Choice 4-7km.

Open: All year.

From Arras, N25 towards Doullens. At L'Arbret, right on D8 to Avesnes-le-Comte. D75 to Grand-Rullecourt (4km); château in village centre, on the square.

Map No: 1   MM 236-14

Patrice & Chantal de SAULIEU
Château de Grand-Rullecourt
Avesnes-le-Comte
62810 Grand-Rullecourt
Pas-de-Calais
Tel: (0)3 21 58 06 37
Fax: (0)1 41 27 97 30
e-mail: Routiers@Club-Internet.fr

From Arras, N39 towards Le Touquet. After 7km, left along D56 towards Duisans. House on left.

Map No: 2   MM 236-15

Annie & Patrick SENLIS
Le Clos Grincourt
18 rue du Château
62161 Duisans
Pas-de-Calais
Tel: (0)3 21 48 68 33
Fax: (0)3 21 48 68 33

Georges is an Orson-Wellsian figure, larger than life and well able to talk at the same time as his wife... a sort of double act that is irresistible and lovable. The house is an architectural flourish, the contents are modern but in good taste, the rooms simple, with pretty bedding and one or two antiques. The only possible drawback is the Holiday Inn and all its vulgarity opposite, but the sea is only ten minutes away through the trees and there is stacks to do locally. It is all perfect for children, raucous and great fun.

Rooms: 1 double, 1 twin, each with bath & wc.

Price: 300-350 Frs for two, including breakfast.

Meals: Wide choice within walking distance.

Open: Easter to mid-November.

This house is loaded with character and history — you will breakfast in both dining-rooms if you stay two nights. One has a unique '1830s-mediaeval' fireplace, the other is classically French with curly furniture. Madame, who teaches accounting, is shy and helpful; they both work constantly on the house and cope with teenage children. In an independent building, guestrooms are simpler, each with some old furniture and a neat shower room. A quiet garden (but weekend race-track in the valley).

Rooms: 2 double, 2 twin, each with shower & wc.

Price: 240 Frs for two, including breakfast.

Meals: Choice in village, 10 mins. walk.

Open: All year.

In Le Touquet follow signs to Holiday Inn — house is directly opposite.

Map No: 1   MM 236-11

Georges & Marie VERSMÉE
Birdy Land
Avenue du Maréchal Foch
62520 Le Touquet
Pas-de-Calais
Tel: (0)3 21 05 31 46 or
    (0)3 27 46 39 41

From Montreuil N39 to St Pol-sur-Ternoise. Left on D343 towards Fruges. Just before entering Gauchin Verloingt right into Rue des Troisvaux then right into Rue des Montifaux. House along on right.

Map No: 1   MM 236-14

Marie-Christine & Philippe VION
Le Loubarré
550 rue des Montifaux
62130 Gauchin Verloingt
Pas-de-Calais
Tel: (0)3 21 03 05 05

Originally a staging post on the windswept plain, this impressive house carries local history in its bones: destroyed in 1916, it was rebuilt in 1920 then the staircase had to be replaced in 1945. The balcony room is splendid but all rooms have high ceilings, marble fireplaces and good old furniture. They are sober and peaceful. The breakfast room is more eclectically furnished with individual tables and toasters. Your wonderfully attentive hosts make it a perfect ferry stopover. Fully-equipped 'disabled' room in converted outbuilding.

Rooms: 1 double, 1 twin, 1 triple, 1 suite for 6, all with shower & wc.

Price: 230-315 Frs for two, including breakfast.

Meals: Restaurant 100 metres.

Open: All year.

Gîtes for 8 people

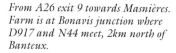

From A26 exit 9 towards Masnières. Farm is at Bonavis junction where D917 and N44 meet, 2km north of Banteux.

Map No: 6   MM 236-27

Michel & Thérèse DELCAMBRE
Ferme de Bonavis
Route Nationale
59266 Banteux
Nord
Tel: (0)3 27 78 55 08
Fax: (0)3 27 78 55 08

Jeannine Hulin's beautiful townhouse reflects her personality: artistic, warm and friendly, and she takes obvious pleasure in both her house and her guests. You breakfast at a tiled table in the clean, bright kitchen, and the delightful bathroom, shared with the family, has a claw-footed bath. Original floor tiles, stripped pine doors and masses of plants add to the atmosphere. The bedroom is lovely with matching *lit bateau*, wardrobe and desk, antique white linen and mirrors. Conservatory for guests with sofas.

Rooms: 1 double with bath & wc on floor below.

Price: 190 Frs for two, incl. breakfast.

Meals: Full choice in town.

Open: All year.

In Lille find Hôtel de Ville; drive away from it on small street into wider Bd Jean-Baptiste Lebas; at end, bear left Rue de Douai; under metro; Rue Armand Carel/Rue du Faubourg de Douai; under railway bridge; right then 2nd left, left and left again = Rue des Hannetons (one-way).

Map No: 2   MM 236-16

Jeannine HULIN
28 rue des Hannetons
59000 Lille
Nord
Tel: (0)3 20 53 46 12

A modern house on a fairly busy street with a lovely surprise: the picture window in the uncluttered living room gives onto an intimate garden full of flowers where guests can sit after exploring the treasures of Lille. The bedrooms are small but pleasing, carpeted and cosy. Chantal is bright and energetic and typically French. She used to teach English then adapted her house specially to receive guests; this is what she loves, particularly when she can communicate with them in her excellent English.

Rooms: 1 double with shower & wc; 1 double with shower, 1 double with bath, sharing wc.

Price: 210-260 Frs, including breakfast.

Meals: 100 Frs, including wine & coffee.

Open: All year.

The outside may be unprepossessing — don't be put off; you will get a marvellous welcome and be treated with immense care. Your hosts are eager to please, competent and pleasant. The entrance to the house is striking with its real marble floor. Lots of stuffed animals, a very sober breakfast room, another nice room with painted panelling. All is impeccably clean and orderly and there is a lovely little garden at the back. A very good, and genteel, stop for those going to and from the ferry.

Rooms: 2 doubles, each with shower & wc.

Price: 250 Frs for two, including breakfast.

Meals: Restaurant 100m.

Open: All year

From A1 exit 19 on D549 to Wattignies (7km). At 'Pharmacie' bear left to village centre. House is on left hand side just before the church on the right.

Map No: 2   MM 236-16

Yves & Chantal LE BOT
59 rue Faidherbe
59139 Wattignies
Nord
Tel: (0)3 20 60 24 51

From Calais A16 E to exit 23b and into Bourbourg. From Place de l'Hôtel de Ville the road is left of the town hall as you face it.

Map No: 1   MM 236-3

Marilou & Jacques VANDEWALLE-MILLEVILLE
25 rue des Martyrs de la Résistance
59630 Bourbourg
Nord
Tel: (0)3 28 22 21 41

An excellent stopover, clean and simple and very much what you would expect from an old French farmhouse: traditional floral decoration in the bedroom, kind hosts, shared breakfast s*alon* for a quiet read or chat with your hosts. The studio has its own entrance and garden, its own terrace and its own sitting area. The garden, full of flowers, is the owners' pride and joy; indeeed, the whole village is a *village fleuri*. In the large forest nearby there are good walks.

Rooms: 1 double with shower & wc; 1 studio with double room, *salon*, kitchen, shower & wc.

Price: Double 300 Frs, studio 350 Frs, both for two including breakfast.

Meals: Abbeville 10km.

Open: All year.

The ancient garden, with its straight lines of dwarf box hedging and flower beds, is very attractive. (There is a roofed barbecue area which you are encouraged to use.) Joanna, a gentle and grandmotherly woman with seven children, makes small ceramic figures — her kiln is in the barn. At breakfast you eat jam made from her own organic fruit, sitting in the glass-fronted porch among her plants and *objets*, using very pretty crockery. One bedroom is off the kitchen, so not so private. In a pretty village and opposite the church.

Rooms: 3 double, each with shower or bath & wc.

Price: 280-300 Frs for two, including breakfast.

Meals: Barbecue available. Choice in Abbeville.

Open: All year.

From Abbeville, N1 towards Nouvion. At Hautvillers, D105 to Forest-l'Abbaye; signposted.

Map No: 1   MM 236-22

M & Mme Michel BECQUET-CHATEL
161 place des Templiers
80150 Forest-l'Abbaye
Somme
Tel: (0)3 22 23 24 03

From Boulogne A16, Abbeville/St Riquier exit. At first roundabout, to Vauchelles-lès-Quesnoy. House on main square opposite church.

Map No: 6   MM 236-22

Mme Joanna CRÉPELLE
121 place de l'Eglise
80132 Vauchelles-les-Quesnoy
Somme
Tel: (0)3 22 24 18 17

These farmers specialise in the noble material that is flax (beets, peas and cattle too). Hélène is a treat, bubbling with enthusiasm for her rooms, for England (she used to teach English), for the heron she saw this morning or her shop (in the main house) where she sells linen goods produced with their own flax. She loves telling you all about it and in June its incomparable soft mauve breathes across the land. A separate, converted timber-frame stable block houses the guestrooms. It is clean, very comfortable and totally French.

Rooms: 4 double, one studio, each with own shower or bath & wc. Extra beds available.

Price: 300 Frs for two, including breakfast.

Meals: Two restaurants in village.

Open: All year.

Gîtes for 15 people

The 'best' room is worth it: white all over with pools of colour in the bed hangings, soft kilim rugs, dark polished antiques, old oil paintings, gilt-framed prints. White doors lead to a gorgeous bathroom (antique basin and taps) and a private sitting alcove. The smaller rooms also have lovely furniture. Madame is a painter and the charm and peace of her garden, with bantams and rabbits all about, deepen the warm, friendly atmosphere she creates. Breakfast, served in a delightful room next to Madame's studio, is a most happy affair.

Rooms: 3 double and 1 twin, all with bath or shower & wc.

Price: 250 or 350 Frs for two, including breakfast.

Meals: Self-catering possible.

Open: All year.

From Abbeville, D82 to Caours. House on far side of village; signposted.

Map No: 1   MM 236-22

Marc & Hélène de LAMARLIÈRE
La Rivièrette
2 rue de la Ferme
80132 Caours
Somme
Tel: (0)3 22 24 77 49
Fax: (0)3 22 24 76 97

From Amiens, N29 towards Poix, then left on D162 to Creuse; signposted.

Map No: 6   MM 236-23

Mme Monique LEMAÎTRE
26 rue Principale
80480 Creuse
Somme
Tel: (0)3 22 38 91 50

A superb group of mainly brick buildings round a square garden and pool. Madame is a fanatical gardener and the results are stunning. The attic rooms are full of character, the first-floor room is cosy with old furniture, the garden rooms are fresh and independent. Madame is intelligent and informed and likes to chat over breakfast, which is served in the elegant dining-room on china that matches the pale green of the curtains. Small pets welcome.

Rooms: 1 suite for 4, 1 twin, 1 double/twin, all with bath & wc; 2 twin sharing shower & wc.

Price: 380 Frs for two, suite 600 Frs, including breakfast. Reservation only.

Meals: Choice in Abbeville.

Open: Mid-Feb to mid-Nov.

Gîtes for 5 people

From Abbeville, D40 towards St Valéry-le-Crotoy. Right in Port-le-Grand & follow small road for 2km; path for Bois Bonance is on right, 300m after a railing. (1 hour from Calais by A16.)

Map No: 1   MM 236-22

Jacques & Myriam MAILLARD
Le Bois Bonance
Port-le-Grand
80132 Abbeville
Somme
Tel: (0)3 22 24 11 97
Fax: (0)3 22 31 63 77

Enfolded in rolling, wooded country, this very attractive house was the first to offer B&B hospitality in the Somme (though Rommel was not really invited, he just came) and the tradition holds. Madame is the local mayor and Monsieur, who is Dutch, makes cider, calvados and honey, keeps that supremely French animal, a *trotteur* horse and will happily tell you stories. They are calm, hospitable people, the rooms are comfortable, the views restful, the panelled dining-room a proper setting for a fine breakfast. A good place to stay.

Rooms: 3 triple, each with shower & handbasin, sharing wc.

Price: 230-250 Frs for two, including breakfast.

Meals: Barbecue and guests' kitchen available.

Open: All year.

Gîtes for 13 people

From Abbeville, N28 towards Rouen. After 28km, left at Bouttencourt on D1015 to Sénarpont then D211 towards Amiens. After 4.5km, left into Le Mazis; follow Chambres d'Hôtes signs.

Map No: 6   MM 236-22

Dorette & Aart ONDER DE LINDEN
80430 Le Mazis
Somme
Tel: (0)3 22 25 90 88
Fax: (0)3 22 25 76 04

A typical, blessedly unmodernised, Picardy farm with low buildings, white walls and greenery. And a typically warm northern welcome from Madame who used to be a social worker — she is at ease with all sorts and has the most infectious laugh. Guestrooms, each with separate entrance, are decorated and furnished with panache and simple basics. Ask for the big room in the *grenier* (loft). The lush green garden at the back has wrought-iron furniture, a lily pond and hens scratching in a large pen.

Rooms: 3 triple, all with shower, wc & kitchenette.

Price: 220-240 Frs for two, including breakfast.

Meals: 60 Frs, excluding wine (by arrangement). Self-catering.

Open: Easter to October

Come down into the valley as you approach the village and take in this spectacular view of the beautiful Somme river and a network of lakes. 15 hectares of it belong to this working farm, an obvious attraction for those who enjoy fishing or boating. There are views of a bridge and the lock from the bedrooms. The friendly Madame Randjia offers adequate guestrooms and cooks excellent regional specialities, served in the flower-filled dining-room. Families can have their noisy breakfasts in a separate room!

Rooms: 2 double, 1 twin, all with shower & wc.

Price: 260 Frs for two, including breakfast.

Meals: By arrangement, 85 Frs, excluding wine.

Open: All year.

Gîtes for 5 people

From Amiens N1 south to Hébécourt. Opposite church follow Chambre d'Hôte signs to Plachy-Buyon.

Map No: 6   MM 236-23

Mme Jacqueline PILLON
L'Herbe de Grâce
Hameau de Buyon
80160 Plachy-Buyon
Somme
Tel: (0)3 22 42 12 22

From A1, Péronne exit onto N29 westwards and immediately right on D146 towards Feuillères. Before village, D146E to Frise. First farm after bridge.

Map No: 6   MM 236-25

Michel & Annick RANDJIA
La Ferme de l'Ecluse
1 rue Mony
80340 Frise
Somme
Tel: (0)3 22 84 59 70
Fax: (0)3 22 83 17 56

The ground floor of the converted chapel, also used by the *gîte d'étape* (B&B bookings are not taken when groups are expected), has a kitchen area, a free-standing fireplace in the shape of an oil lamp (the local masonry students' masterpiece), a massive table which converts into... a snooker table. Guests may light a fire, play snooker, use garden and kitchen. The smallish bedrooms are upstairs under the rafters. Nearby are water sports, fishing and Amiens' great Gothic cathedral. A pleasant and unusual stopover.

Rooms: 1 double, 1 triple, each with bath & wc in bedroom.

Price: 200 Frs for two, including breakfast.

Meals: In village. Self-catering.

Open: All year.

Gîtes for 12 people

This is above all a family house where Madame, mother of four and lover of things outdoor — dogs, horses, gardening, shoring up the outbuildings — reigns with energy and a refreshingly natural attitude: what matter if a little mud is walked into the hall? In pleasing contrast is the formal dining-room with its fabulous patterned parquet floor, vast table, family silver and chandeliers, plus very fine food. Rooms may seem slightly worn — renovation is laborious and there have been disastrous leaks — so come for lively hospitality not plush decor.

Rooms: 1 double, 1 suite for four, each with bath or shower & wc; 2 double sharing bathroom.

Price: 350-450 Frs for two, including breakfast.

Meals: 110 Frs, excluding wine (65 Frs).

Open: All year.

Gîtes for 16 people

From Amiens, N1 towards Beauvais. Between St Sauflieu and Essertaux, right on D153 to Loeuilly; signposted.

Map No: 6   MM 236-33

Claudine & Bernard RICHOUX
36 route de Conty
80160 Loeuilly
Somme
Tel: (0)3 22 38 15 19

From Abbeville, N28 towards Rouen. At St Maxent, D29 to Oisemont, then D25 towards Sénarpont. Signposted on outskirts of Foucaucourt.

Map No: 6   MM 236-22

Mme Elisabeth de ROCQUIGNY
Château de Foucaucourt
80140 Foucaucourt
Somme
Tel: (0)3 22 25 12 58
Fax: (0)3 22 25 25 58

This house has such a lovely face! The guest bedrooms and sitting-room, however, are in a well-converted barn that gives onto the courtyard. They are furnished with a mix of old and new, adorned with fresh flowers in summer and double-glazed against any road noise. If you arrive at a sensible time you will be offered a glass of homemade cider. Breakfast in the pretty room with its fireplace (in the main house) is a feast. Pony-and-trap rides in summer. The spire of Amiens cathedral reaches up into the sky nearby.

Rooms: 3 double, 1 twin, each bath or shower & wc

Price: 310 Frs for two, including breakfast.

Meals: Within walking distance.

Open: All year.

Gites for 11 people

It glows with colour, comfort and good taste; everything is just so, almost like a dolls' house, Madame's perfect plaything. The impression is of character and antiques, with some modern bits. The living-room is huge, with pink walls, beams, a black slate floor and a big fireplace. The breakfast room is almost overwhelmingly pretty, full of *objets trouvés*, plants and a big crackling fire. The single room is small and pretty; the double/triple is comfortable, has lovely bedding, a good bathroom, beams and a view over church and garden.

Rooms: 1 triple, 1 single, each with shower & wc.

Price: 350 Frs for two, including breakfast.

Meals: Choice 5km.

Open: All year.

From Abbeville N1 N dir. Montreuil/Boulogne for 25km. In Vron left to Villers-sur-Authie. There take Rue de l'Eglise (opposite café). At end of road, left up tree-lined lane; house on left.

Map No: 1   MM 236-12

Pierre et Sabine SINGER de WAZIÈRES
La Bergerie
80120 Villers-sur-Authie
Somme
Tel: (0)3 22 29 21 74

From A16 Dury exit onto N1 S towards Breteuil and Paris. Just before Dury, left towards St Fuscien; signposted.

Map No: 6   MM 236-24

Alain & Maryse SAGUEZ
2 rue Grimaux
80480 Dury
Somme
Tel: (0)3 22 95 29 52

THE NORTH – PICARDY

A rambling garden with stone love-seats, swings and a play-house give this old manor house the feel of a child's adventure story — grandchildren roam in the yard and there's a shimmering duck pond across the road. Behind the wrought-iron front door the emphasis is on family hospitality. Madame, smiling and uncomplicated, often clad in a white linen apron, gives guests a big welcome. Bedrooms have marble fireplaces, square French pillows on the beds, floral 1950s country-style décor and complicated bathroom arrangements.

Rooms: 1 double on ground floor with bath & wc; 2 double on 1st floor with showers sharing wc; 1 twin, 1 double on 2nd floor sharing bath & wc. 2 small extra rooms for children.

Price: 230-250 Frs for two, including breakfast.

Meals: Restaurants 5-10km.

Open: March to November.

From Amiens D929 towards Albert. At Pont-Noyelles, left onto D115 towards Contay; signposted in Bavelincourt.

Map No: 6   MM 236-24

M & Mme Noël VALENGIN
Bavelincourt
80260 Villers Bocage
Somme
Tel: (0)3 22 40 51 51

Catherine is a wildly enthusiastic, possibly mercurial but caring hostess. Claude is quiet and attentive. Their house displays his talent for dramatic design — dark or black walls, much use of mirrors, draperies and large patterns — and their combined collectionitis. It is welcoming, interesting and vastly comfortable with good, utterly personal rooms and bathrooms. Also, the food (dinner is usually compulsory) is an example of really good French cuisine. The top-floor dining-room has a terrace onto the ineffably beautiful Baie de Somme. What a lovely spot!

Rooms: 2 suites for 3/4, 2 double, 2 twin/double, all with bath or shower & wc.

Price: 380-420 Frs for two, including breakfast.

Meals: (Compulsory unless agreed otherwise) 160-180 Frs, including aperitif, wine, coffee, calvados.

Open: All year.

From Abbeville D40 to Le Crotoy. In town bear right towards 'La Plage' along Rues Desjardins, Victor Peletier, Gourlain, Victor Petit. House on sea front.

Map No: 1   MM 236-22

Claude & Catherine WEYL
Villa La Mouclade
32 rue Victor Petit
80550 Le Crotoy
Somme
Tel: (0)3 22 27 09 44
Fax: (0)3 22 27 88 29
e-mail: cweyl@nordnet.fr

The old house is pretty, the 'new' wing by Auguste Perret, king of concrete, a piece of design history. His immense living room is squares set in squares: the panelling, bookshelves, floor tiles, even the table. Madame loves her house and enjoys sharing its delights with you. The guestrooms are pleasing: ethnic fabrics, good colours and light with sophisticated bathrooms. Monsieur is mad about horses; their pasture is foreground to the sweeping view from the quiet garden. And the train can carry you straight from the village to Paris.

Rooms: 2 double, 1 triple, each with bath or shower & wc.

Price: 300 Frs for two, including breakfast.

Meals: 120 Frs, incl. aperitif, wine & coffee (reservations only) or 4km.

Open: All year.

Behind the austere brick walls and imposing archway you will discover a homely museum of exotica. Your hostess, a retired chemist, loves travelling; she also loves her dogs — and contact with visitors. Your beamed, fireplaced, mellow rooms furnished with old pieces are in the original house; she lives in the brilliantly converted barn, and all is harmony and warm, natural living. Drink in her talk of France, the French and the rest of the world. Rest in peace, rouse to the dawn chorus, then enjoy breakfast in the sunshine. (Cats won't like it here.)

Rooms: 1 double with shower & basin, 1 double with bath & basin, sharing wc.

Price: 300 Frs for two, including breakfast.

Meals: Restaurants 4-6km.

Open: All year: booking essential.

Gîtes for 4 people

From Gisors, D133 to Chaumont-en-Vexin. Right on D567 to Liancourt-St-Pierre. Left into village, left to post office & follow road left into rue du Donjon (cul de sac); high gate on left.

Map No: 6   MM 237-4

Monique & Luc GALLOT
La Pointe
10 rue du Donjon
60240 Liancourt-St-Pierre
Oise
Tel: (0)3 44 49 32 08
Fax: (0)3 44 49 32 08

From A1 exit 10 towards Compiègne/Arsy for 4km. By caravan yard right at small turning towards Jaux. 1st right to Varanval, up hill then down. House on right opposite château gates (1.2km from N31 turning).

Map No: 6   MM 236-35

Françoise GAXOTTE
La Gaxottière
363 rue du Champ du Mont
60880 Jaux-Varanval
Oise
Tel: (0)3 44 83 22 41
    (0)3 44 83 22 41

This cereal farm, surrounded by woods and fields, has an elegant, old, cobbled farmyard at its heart. Cleverly renovated farm cottages provide delightful, clean, modern rooms with pretty fabrics and good bedding. In a converted barn, under a brick-vault ceiling, are a games room with original mangers to catch the ping-pong balls and a stone-walled, log-fired sitting/dining-room with an old dresser and painted jugs. The Hamelins, smiling, light-hearted and keen to please, have thoughtfully installed swings and slides and a tennis court.

Rooms: 2 twin, 1 family suite (twin & bunks), all with bath or shower & wc.

Price: 300 Frs for two, including breakfast.

Meals: Choice in Crépy 9km.

Open: All year except January.

A delightfully eccentric elderly couple with an ever-youthful attitude to life — among our very favourites. The house is dated early 1900s; downstairs there are flowers and plants, Monsieur's sculpture, Madame's paintings, objects collected when they were teaching and nursing in Africa. Rooms are slightly cramped but the owners' company over breakfast is fascinating. There are no rules and the house exudes peace and tenderness. There is even a banister lift for the disabled and the huge garden boasts ancient forest trees.

Rooms: 1 suite with salon, 1 double, 1 twin, each with bath or shower & wc.

Price: 300 Frs for two, suite 450 Frs, including breakfast.

Meals: Supper for tired, late arrivals. Good-value restaurant 6km.

Open: All year.

From A1 Senlis exit onto N324 to Crépy-en-Valois, then D332 towards Lévignen and Betz. 3km after Lévignen right to Macquelines. Right at T-junction; farm immediately on right.

Map No: 6   MM 237-20

Philippe & Marthe HAMELIN
Ferme de Macquelines
60620 Betz
Oise
Tel: (0)3 44 87 20 21

From Beauvais, N31 towards Gournay-en-Bray. At Orsimont, left onto D129, through St Germer-de-Fly, to Le Coudray; in village opposite water tower.

Map No: 6   MM 236-32

Marc & Eugénie LE MARCHAND de SAINT PRIEST
58 rue Paul Dubois
60850 Le Coudray-Saint-Germer
Oise
Tel: (0)3 44 81 56 74
Fax: (0)3 44 81 56 74

Your rooms are NOT in that pigeon-tower but in the former bakery where bread was made for humans and potatoes cooked for pigs. Oven, beams and character have been preserved. The bedrooms are good-sized, simply furnished with an Indian cotton throw at each bedhead, original timbers and sober carpets. This is a working farm whose active, quiet owners have turned their small farmhouse rooms into a lovely open-plan space with timber framing. Dine here with them in all simplicity once the children are in bed.

Rooms: 1 quadruple, 3 double, all with shower & wc.

Price: 220 Frs for two, including breakfast. Extra bed 50 Frs.

Meals: 70 Frs, including wine & coffee.

Open: All year.

An idyllic village of handsome old houses surrounded by rolling farmland and green forests. There are cows in the field and a small orchard beside the house. Guests sleep in a modern extension (though on beds that are a bit less modern?) to a fine old building of uncertain age. This is every bit the lived-in farmhouse and Madame is every inch the chatty, friendly, elderly farmer's wife. She is also a charming hostess who loves tending her orchard and kitchen garden... and her guests.

Rooms: 2 double, each with shower, bath & wc.

Price: 230-250 Frs for two, including breakfast.

Meals: 3 restaurants within 2km.

Open: All year.

From Beauvais D31 towards Rouen. Just on leaving Beauvais pick up signs to Savignies. Farm in village, 50m from church.

Map No: 6   MM 236-33

Annick & Jean-Claude LETURQUE
La Ferme du Colombier
14 rue du Four Jean Legros
60650 Savignies
Oise
Tel: (0)3 44 82 18 49
Fax: (0)3 44 82 53 70

From Beauvais, D901 towards St Omer-en-Chaussée. At Troissereux, D133 towards Songeons. There, D143 towards Gournay-en-Bray. On leaving forest, right to Buicourt; house near church.

Map No: 6   MM 236-32

Eddy & Jacqueline VERHOEVEN
3 rue de la Mare
60380 Buicourt
Oise
Tel: (0)3 44 82 31 15

A working farm set amid parkland and lakes. Fancy a spot of fishing? That's one 'water sport' which is encouraged here. Guestrooms are in a renovated barn with all mod cons, heating that works and windows that don't let in draughts. Madame takes pride in keeping everything spotlessly clean. Monsieur is retired and retiring. They live in a separate building, rather like a baby château from the outside, plain and traditional inside. Meals are taken *en famille* in the hosts' dining-room; nothing fancy, just good, simple farm food.

Rooms: 1 double room and 1 twin room, each with bath & wc.

Price: 260 Frs for two, including breakfast.

Meals: 100 Frs, including wine & coffee (book ahead).

Open: All year.

This is a big, active farm (producing 'happy' veal), with an unspoilt house among rolling hills and champagne vineyards. Your hosts are hard-working, active and good company; they also hunt. Madame, an architect, works from home, brings up two small children AND nurtures her guests. The superb deeply-carved Henri III furniture is an admirable family heirloom; rooms are colour-coordinated, beds are beautiful, views are stunning; bring rod and permit and you can fish in the pond. There are open arms for you here.

Rooms: 2 double with own bath shower & wc; 2 double & 1 twin, each with bath, sharing wc.

Price: 250-300 Frs for two, including breakfast.

Meals: 90 Frs, excluding wine.

Open: All year except Christmas.

Gîtes for 6 people

From Soissons, N2 towards Laon. At Bucy-le-Long, D925 towards Vailly. House on right just before entering Missy.

Map No: 6   MM 236-37

Georges & Jacqueline DUFFIÉ
La Biza
02880 Missy-sur-Aisne
Aisne
Tel: (0)3 23 72 83 54
Fax: (0)3 23 72 91 43

From Fismes D967 towards Fère-en-Tardenois & Château Thierry for 4km. DON'T go to Mont St Martin. Continue 800m beyond turning; white house on left.

Map No: 6   MM 237-10

Valérie & Jean-Paul FERRY
Ferme de Ressons
02220 Mont-Saint-Martin
Aisne
Tel: (0)3 23 74 71 00
Fax: (0)3 23 74 28 88

Your cup will overflow with the kindness heaped upon you by Madame's partner. He is all heart. Together they run this charmingly faded grand house with great energy. There have been some strange sightings — a kingfisher in the garden and some lesser-spotted leopard-print sheets on the Empire bed. Madame will help you with your French, talk fascinatingly about local history (including the First World War) and guide you to magnificent forest walks. A charming place and breakfast is every bit as generous as your hosts.

Rooms: 2 twin with shower & wc, 2 triple sharing a bathroom.

Price: 250 Frs for two, including breakfast.

Meals: 5 minutes walk to restaurants.

Open: All year.

Beneath the looming mediæval keep, in an attractive old village, the house was built in 1611 and was once the property of Napoleon's Finance Minister. The grounds run down to the river Aisne, creating an almost rural impression just 3 minutes' walk from the centre. Fish in the river, swim in the pool in summer (at the higher price), play tennis or, less energetically, draughts on the giant 10ft x 10ft board. A tranquil, clean-aired place where your hosts run a *brocante*. Baby-sitting possible.

Rooms: 2 double, 3 triple, all with shower & wc.

Price: 330 or 390 Frs for two, including breakfast.

Meals: 100 Frs, excluding wine.

Open: All year.

Gîtes for 14 people

From Soissons, N31 towards Reims. In Braine, house is set back on this road next to Peugeot garage.

Map No: 6   MM 237-9

Mme Jacqueline MARTIN
14 rue Saint-Rémy
02220 Braine
Aisne
Tel: (0)3 23 74 12 74

From Compiègne, N31 towards Soissons; after 22km, left to Vic-sur-Aisne; opposite Mairie, right and first right again.

Map No: 6   MM 236-36

Jean & Anne MARTNER
Domaine des Jeanne
Rue Dubarle
02290 Vic-sur-Aisne
Aisne
Tel: (0)3 23 55 57 33
Fax: (0)3 23 55 57 33

This farm is utterly 'country French' and friendly to all (extra special attention to children). Flagstones and stone benches, 12th-century cellars, coppers and big mirrors, plus a piano, old photographs and vases of flowers to add to the atmosphere. Madame deals with ease and energy with family and friends (that's you). Cottage-style bedrooms (one is particularly fine) with pretty linen and marble-topped washstands. Ample breakfasts; robust farmhouse dinners *en famille* if you wish. Pool for children.

Rooms: 1 double, 1 twin, with bath or shower & wc; 1 double, 1 twin, 1 single sharing shower & wc.

Price: 250 Frs for two, including breakfast.

Meals: 100 Frs, excluding wine.

Open: All year.

Is this sprawling 13th-16th century homestead a country house or an art gallery? Your efficient and knowledgeable hosts delight in appreciative guests. Dinner is elegant and intimate, even when shared with 15 others. All rooms are big and furnished with taste; the family suite is 5-star quality. A large spring-fed pond will delight fishermen while the beautiful gallery houses a unique collection of contemporary illustrations of La Fontaine's fables. A place of culture and great style and only one hour from Paris.

Rooms: 2 double (1 kingsize), 1 twin, 1 triple, 2 suites for 4, all with bath or shower & wc.

Price: 330-480 Frs for two, including breakfast. Extra bed 120 Frs.

Meals: 140-160 Frs, including wine.

Open: All year.

From Soissons, N2 towards Paris. At 4th main crossroads, D172 left towards Chaudun. About 4km on, D177 left to Léchelle. (1 hour from Paris.)

Map No: 6   MM 237-9

Jacques & Nicole MAURICE
Ferme Léchelle
02200 Berzy-le-Sec
Aisne
Tel: (0)3 23 74 83 29
Fax: (0)3 23 74 82 47

From A4 junction Château Thierry onto D1 towards Montmirail then right on D933 to La Haute Épine; or from A4 junction La Ferté s/Jouarre on N3, D407, D933 to La Haute Épine. Signposted.

Map No: 6   MM 237-21

Mary-Ann & Marc ROYOL
Domine des Patrus
02540 L'Epine-aux-Bois
Aisne
Tel: (0)3 23 69 85 85
Fax: (0)3 23 69 98 49

A big old house, welcoming and warmly tatty with mix 'n not-match wallpapers and posters on long corridor walls and funny old prints in the bedrooms. The owners are great fun, energetic, loving their dinner parties in the dining-room with its old family furniture, where guests of all nations communicate as the wine flows. "So much more alive than any hotel, this is real contact with French people." The rooms are simple and good; one has a ship's shower room, another a Louis XVI bed, all look onto green pastures.

Rooms: 1 suite for 4, 2 double, 1 twin, each with bath or shower & wc; 1 double, 1 twin with basins, sharing bathroom.

Price: 200-250 Frs for two, including breakfast. Extra bed 100 Frs.

Meals: 95 Frs, including wine.

Open: 15 March to 15 October.

Gîtes for 12 people

From A26-E17, Laon/Chambry exit south on N2 then 2nd left to Athies s/Laon. There D516 to Bruyères-Monbérault. There left on D967 towards Fisme. Chérêt signposted on leaving Bruyères.

Map No: 7   MM 238-38

Mme Monique SIMONNOT
Le Clos
02860 Chérêt
Aisne
Tel: (0)3 23 24 80 64

Well, neither Holiday Inn nor Novotel can put you to sleep in a mediæval tower. One of the three tower rooms has a Louis XV stone fireplace and a pale blue bathroom. Another huge old room has the usual fireplace, bedstead with family crest, wooden floor with rug. The *salon* has a 1567 painted ceiling, a huge Renaissance fireplace with family crest, formal chairs and sofas, desk and table. It is all very grand but your hosts are down-to-earth and charming people. The house is 800 years old — utterly splendid. Pets by arrangement.

Rooms: 4 double, all with own bath or shower & wc.

Price: 480-530 Frs for two, including breakfast.

Meals: Choice 10-20km.

Open: March to December.

Ardennes – Champagne

From Reims, N46 then N47 towards Luxembourg; go through Vouziers to Buzancy, turn right onto D12 and follow signs.

Map No: 7   MM 241-18

Jacques & Véronique de
MEIXMORON
Château de Landreville
08240 Bayonville
Ardennes
Tel: (0)3 24 30 04 39
Fax: (0)3 24 30 04 39

These independent champagne-growers delight in showing guests round vineyards and cellars (tastings included). Up its own staircase, the bright, airy attic bedroom has beams, dormers, handmade matching curtains and covers, and wicker furniture. Breakfast is served in the lovely old family house with Madame's fine jams and the black dog Champagne (*naturellement*) lying under the table waiting for crumbs. She is a wonderful woman who started B&B for champagne buyers who did not want to leave the same day!

Rooms: 1 double with shower & wc.

Price: 205 Frs for two, including breakfast.

Meals: Choice in Fismes (11km).

Open: All year except 2 weeks in August.

The great Forêt du Gault borders this C17 farmhouse and provides beautiful walks. Two rooms are in a converted stable with a living-room (with original mangers), kitchenette and steep stairs up. The decor is modest and modern with carpeted floor. The third, in the main house, has old furniture and a view of the pond. You breakfast in another former stable on the courtyard but you dine with your serious/amusing hosts by their fireplace where home-produced fruit, vegetables, eggs and poultry are served.

Rooms: 1 twin, 1 double, 1 triple, all with shower or bath & wc.

Price: 210 Frs for two, including breakfast.

Meals: 70-90 Frs, including wine & coffee. Self-catering.

Open: All year.

From Epernay N51 N towards Reims for 4km then left onto D386 towards Fismes for 30km. At Crugny left onto D23 to Brouillet. House WITH 'Ariston Fils' sign on right (Gîtes de France sign).

Map No: 7   MM 237-10

Rémi & Marie ARISTON
Ariston Fils
4 & 8 Grande Rue
51170 Brouillet
Marne
Tel: (0)3 26 97 43 46
Fax: (0)3 26 97 49 34

From Calais (map 61 fold 5) to St Quentin, Soissons, Château-Thierry, Montmirail. There, D373 towards Sézanne for 7 km. On leaving Le Gault left at silo; signposted.

Map No: 7   MM 237-22

Nicole & Guy BOUTOUR
Ferme de Désiré
51210 Le Gault-Soigny
Marne
Tel: (0)3 26 81 60 09
Fax: (0)3 26 81 67 95

The Collots are hard-working, naturally welcoming farmers whose family has owned this house for several generations. The modernised 18th-century farmhouse has two newly-decorated sizeable guestrooms furnished with nice old beds and wardrobes and views over either the active farmyard, with its fine collection of agricultural machinery, or over the little village street. The family dining-room where you have breakfast is pleasingly homely and cluttered and Madame takes the time to chat. Really excellent value.

Rooms: 2 double, each with shower & wc.

Price: 200 Frs for two, including breakfast.

Meals: Choice in Vitry-le-François 6km. Barbecue available.

Open: All year.

Cows, chickens, ducks, guinea-fowl, turkeys, donkey, sheep, goats... children love it here, and love the higgledy-piggledy buildings too; school groups come for visits. The house is full of beams, the rooms are full of swags, flowers and antique bits, and one bathroom is behind a curtain. Our readers have loved the house, the family and the food. Little English is spoken but the welcome is so exceptional, the generosity so genuine, that communication is easy. Superb outings in the area for all.

Rooms: 1 suite, 2 double, each with bath & wc. Extra beds available.

Price: 260-320 Frs for two, including breakfast.

Meals: 105 Frs, excluding wine. Self-catering in suite.

Open: All year.

Gîtes for 7 people

From Vitry-le-François, N4 towards Fère-Champenoise. 3km after N4/D2 roundabout turn right. In village, left 100m after Mairie; signposted.

Map No: 7   MM 241-30

Brigitte & Michel COLLOT
19 rue de Coole
51300 Maisons-en-Champagne
Marne
Tel: (0)3 26 72 73 91

From Epernay, D51 towards Sézanne. At Baye, just before church, right onto D343. At Bannay turn right. Farm is before small bridge.

Map No: 7   MM 237-22

Muguette & Jean-Pierre CURFS
Ferme de Bannay
51270 Bannay
Marne
Tel: (0)3 26 52 80 49
Fax: (0)3 26 59 47 78

The Harlauts produce their own marque of champagne and, although bottles are for sale, it is for the first-class food and the atmosphere that guests return. Dinner is eaten with the family, either in the dining-room, or on the terrace overlooking the garden. Your hosts love entertaining and are keen to provide good value. The guestrooms share a loo but this is a minor concern as everything is as spotless as it should be. The views are great over the plains of Reims. Try the champagne cakes.

Rooms: 1 double with shower & wc; 1 double & 1 twin, each with shower & washbasin, sharing wc.

Price: 220-250 Frs for two, including breakfast.

Meals: 100 Frs, including champagne aperitif, wine & coffee.

Open: All year.

Near the beautiful forest of Argonne, the farm is now run by M Patizel Junior while your hosts have converted the stables into a modern house. It has an attractive mixture of beautifully-restored antiques and good-quality new furniture, lovely linen and good mattresses, bright colours and clean-cut bathrooms. Madame is an excellent cook, Monsieur is a notable crafter of local wood and stone; both are proud of their country heritage, wonderful with children and deeply committed to 'real B&B'. Nothing is too much trouble for them.

Rooms: 2 double, 1 quadruple, all with shower & wc.

Price: 220 Frs for two, including breakfast.

Meals: 75 Frs, including wine & coffee.

Open: All year.

From A26 exit 15 'Reims La Neuvillette' onto N44 towards Laon for 2km. Left to St Thierry. House in village.

Map No: 7   MM 237-11

Evelyne & Remi HARLAUT
5 rue du Paradis
51220 Saint-Thierry
Marne
Tel: (0)3 26 03 13 75
Fax: (0)3 26 03 03 65

From A4 exit Ste Menehould on D982 (382 on some maps) to Givry-en-Argonne. There left on D54 to Les Charmontois (9km).

Map No: 7   MM 241-26

M & Mme Bernard PATIZEL
51330 Les Charmontois
Marne
Tel: (0)3 26 60 39 53
Fax: (0)3 26 60 39 53

The key to the local church is with Madame; do look round it. Her own house is a mediæval priory with two 11th-century towers... superb. She is an extremely friendly, busy, chatty young mother with teenage children, a farming husband and parents-in-law 'through the wall'. Splendid rooms; the ground floor one, for example, is enormous, with a huge stone fireplace, two queen beds, wattle walls between great beams, wooden roof with more beams, and a basic bathroom.

Rooms: 1 double, 1 twin, each with bath or shower & wc.

Price: 200-250 Frs for two, including breakfast.

Meals: Restaurant 5 mins walk.

Open: All year.

Gîtes for 15 people

If your family are straining at the leash, bring them here to let off steam: there is riding (and space for 15 passing horses), pony-trapping, walking, mountain-biking, archery, orienteering and a bit of gentle ping-pong. This is a most friendly place, simple and easy, with breakfasts (homemade jams, fresh *brioche*, lots of coffee) available until midday. The rooms are right for the price; note the corridor upstairs with 'artexed' walls and 'lino' floor. You dine well in the nearby village: the Mayoress is the chef.

Rooms: 3 double, 1 twin sharing shower & wc.

Price: 170 Frs for two, including breakfast.

Meals: Good auberge 3km.

Open: All year.

Gîtes for 19 people

From Troyes N71 SE for 13 km. In Fouchères left onto D81 towards Poligny — house just behind Fouchères church.

Map No: 7   MM 237-48

M & Mme BERTHELIN
Le Prieuré
Place de l'Église
10260 Fouchères
Aube
Tel: (0)3 25 40 98 09
Fax: (0)3 25 40 98 09

From Langres, N19 towards Vesoul. Left on D460 towards Bourbonne; right on D34; 3rd left to Velles. Through village to grass triangle; house on left.

Map No: 7   MM 241-48

Alain & Christine ROUSSELOT
Les Randonnées du Précheny
52500 Velles
Haute-Marne
Tel: (0)3 25 88 85 93

In the mould of contemporary Jane Austen characters, Madame and her daughters renovated this delightful, two-centuries-old timber-framed house with only occasional help from local craftsmen. They pride themselves on being independent and discussion with these remarkable women at breakfast (with eggs from their hens) is fascinating. The village is high up — take warm clothes. Many activiites (Europe's largest artificial lake is here, plus superb bird-watching) make the evening in front of the open fire a special treat.

Rooms: 1 quadruple, 1 triple, each with shower & wc.

Price: 250 Frs for two, including breakfast.

Meals: In village, 100m away.

Open: All year.

This is an irresistible spot for no-kill fishermen (including *carpistes*), water-sportsmen, bird-watchers and architecture buffs; the local tour of half-timbered churches is considered one of the 100 most beautiful attractions in France. Afternoon tea is served in the *salon*; later, an elegant chandeliered dinner awaits you, possibly with home-raised boar or home-fished scaly things but not with your hosts, delightful as they are. Bedrooms are comfortable and attractive. Children over 7 welcome.

Rooms: 2 double, 2 twin, 1 suite, all with bath or shower & wc.

Price: 270-330 Frs for two, including breakfast.

Meals: 130 Frs, including aperitif, wine & coffee.

Open: All year.

From Vitry-le-François D13 towards Montier-en-Der. 2km before Giffaumont-Champ Aubert right towards Châtillon s/Broué & Droyes. In village, main road to Y-junction. Left towards Lycée Agricole then left again. House straight ahead.

Map No: 7   MM 241-34

Pascale STEIN
6 rue de la Motte
52220 Droyes
Haute-Marne
Tel: (0)3 25 94 32 44

From Troyes, D960 to Brienne, D400 towards St Dizier. At Louze, D182 to Longeville then D174 towards Boulancourt; house on left at 1st crossroads.

Map No: 7   MM 241-34

Philippe & Christine VIEL-CAZAL
Domaine de Boulancourt
Boulancourt
52220 Montier-en-Der
Haute-Marne
Tel: (0)3 25 04 60 18

This is an ever-lasting project, so chat to Monsieur as he assiduously restores the house to its former glory — some rooms and bathrooms have been redecorated but many bits are still in need — and enjoy Madame's charming affability. There are elegant terraces, a super garden, stylish furniture to impress, lots of religion on view, a genuine welcome to win you over. The house is beside a fairly busy road, so if traffic noise bothers you ask for one of the quieter bedrooms.

Rooms: 2 double, 1 twin, 1 triple, 1 suite with kitchenette & garden, each with shower & wc.

Price: 250-300 Frs for two, including breakfast.

Meals: Self-catering in suite.

Open: All year.

From A4, St Menehould exit onto N3 towards Verdun-Chalons. House is signposted in La Vignette, the hamlet before Les Islettes.

Map No: 7 MM 241-22

Lorraine –
Alsace –
Franche-Comté

M & Mme Léopold CHRISTIAENS
Villa des Roses
La Vignette, Les Islettes
55120 Clermont-en-Argonne
Meuse
Tel: (0)3 26 60 81 91
Fax: (0)3 26 60 23 09

Readers of previous editions will be sad to hear that *Grandmère*, the redoubtable single-handed war-time farmer, has died. But the 200-hectare farm is still welcoming guests and producing veal and cereals. You may eat your breakfast (eggs included) here in the farmhouse, where your hosts live, or in the *chambre d'hôte...* where their children sometimes stay too. The house is comfortable and functional, filled with knick-knacks in the inimitable rural style and very real. There is a fine garden but the road is nearby.

Rooms: 2 triple, sharing shower & separate wc.

Price: 170 Frs for two, including breakfast.

Meals: In Domrémy-la-Pucelle, 8km.

Open: All year.

Gîtes for 8 people

There is now an 'artists' path' to explore in the nearby forest and a golf practice area laid out by Monsieur in the garden. They are very proud of their house and, though renovation may have hidden two centuries of history, it has produced very big, plush, slightly hotel-like guestrooms. Dinner is a chance to sample some of the region's best dishes (*terrines, magret*, homemade pastries); Madame will join you for dessert and a chat. An excellent stopover between the ferries and Germany.

Rooms: 2 double, each with shower & wc, 1 suite with bath, shower & wc.

Price: 300-400 Frs for two, including breakfast.

Meals: 130 Frs, including wine. By arrangement.

Open: All year.

50 Frs

From Nancy, A31/N4 east. At Void, D964 dir. Vaucouleurs for 1km then right onto D10 to Rosières-en-Blois then D168 through Badonvilliers to Vouthon; house at end of village.

Map No: 7   MM 241-35

Simone & Roger ROBERT
Le Bourg
55130 Vouthon-Bas
Meuse
Tel: (0)3 29 89 74 00
Fax: (0)3 29 89 74 42

From Reims take A4, Voie Sacrée exit; take N35 dir. Bar-le-Duc. At Chaumont-sur-Aire, D902 left to Longchamps-sur-Aire then D121 left to Thillombois. House is next to château.

Map No: 7   MM 241-27

Lise TANCHON
Le Clos du Pausa
Rue du Château
55260 Thillombois
Meuse
Tel: (0)3 29 75 07 85
Fax: (0)3 29 75 00 72

This house, built in 1750 and once a watermill, was destroyed in the war. Louis's father restored the (now purely decorative) wheel. Inside, the house — modernised, with lots of new wood — is a bit out of kilter with the charming exterior but it has very clean, comfortable rooms (showers curtained off from bedrooms). Breakfast, served in the living/dining room, is hosted by various members of the family who look down from two large studio-style family portraits. Madame has three children and is welcoming, hospitable and talkative.

Rooms: 1 double, 2 triple, all with shower & wc.

Price: 220 Frs for two, including breakfast.

Meals: Self-catering.

Open: All year.

Stay a night at this grand and very stylish château, now in the hands of an engaging, lively and able couple: it's really worth it and not at all daunting. Two utterly French *salons* with the right number of antiques, huge oils of the Napoleonic wars (French version), a library with a billiards table, dinner with candles and flowers and the unadulterated pleasure of dining like a 17th-century French aristo (there may be wild boar in season). Guestrooms and bathrooms are suitably luxurious.

Rooms: 3 double and 3 twin, all with bath & wc.

Price: 590 Frs for two, including breakfast.

Meals: 200-250 Frs, excluding wine(book ahead).

Open: 1 April to 31 October.

Gites for 4 people

From A4 exit 42 on N61 towards Sarreguemines then onto N62 to Rohrbach. There right on D35 towards Bining/Rahling. In village 1st right (after small bridge) then right again; signposted.

Map No: 8   MM 242-15

Louis & Annie BACH
2 rue du Vieux Moulin
57410 Rahling
Moselle
Tel: (0)3 87 09 86 85

From Nancy, N74 towards Château Salins. At Burthecourt crossroads D38 to Dieuzé, then D999 south; after 5km, left on D199F and D199G to the château.

Map No: 8   MM 242-18

Livier & Marie BARTHÉLÉMY
Château d'Alteville
Tarquimpol
57260 Dieuzé
Moselle
Tel: (0)3 87 86 92 40
Fax: (0)3 87 86 02 05

A most interesting couple: he's a retired French architect (who's done wonders in the kitchen), she's a Polish painter (work in progress on the easel), patchworker (her bedcovers adorn your room) and dancer. They are both passionate about the environment and keen to chat over dinner. And good news for vegetarians who like a change: Gérard is a 'veggie' and Alina will happily rustle up a warm red *borsch* or a dish of *pierogi* (vegetable *ravioli*) though her talent stretches to delicious meaty things too. An excellent and friendly house.

Rooms: 1 twin room with shower & wc.

Price: 250 Frs for two, including breakfast.

Meals: 95 Frs standard, 70 Frs vegetarian, including wine.

Open: All year.

From Metz D3 NE towards Bouzonville for about 21km then right on D53a to Burtoncourt. House on left on main street.

Map No: 8   MM 242-10

Alina & Gérard CAHEN
51 rue Lorraine
57220 Burtoncourt
Moselle
Tel: (0)3 87 35 72 65
Fax: (0)3 87 35 72 65

Want to keep in touch with the office? All the gear is here, plus most of the modern extras that hotels provide, plus the wilder side. Set in the Lorraine Nature Park, the house is older than it looks, an ancient Lorraine farm, now a *Gîte Panda*, with two of the friendliest possible owners. They have done the restoration themselves; it is cluttered but comfortable... no shortage of chairs to sag into. Come for the walks — Bride Forest, lakes, a big bird sanctuary (they'll lend rucksacks and binoculars) — the vast breakfasts and the company.

Rooms: 2 double, 1 twin, each with shower or bath & wc.

Price: 310 Frs for two, including breakfast.

Meals: 110 Frs, excluding wine.

Open: April to October.

From A31, exit 28 for St Avold (D910) for 30km. At Han-sur-Nied, D999 towards Morhange and Dieuze. 10km after Morhange, left to Lidrezing.

Map No: 8   MM 242-14

René & Cécile MATHIS
La Musardière
2 rue le Faubourg
Lidrezing
57340 Morhange
Moselle
Tel: (0)3 87 86 14 05
Fax: (0)3 87 86 40 16

Clearly not the place to stay if you want to be modern: partly 13th-century (part of the defensive ring around Metz), it is now a farmhouse with 110 acres of cereals. Brigitte relishes her role as your hostess, does it with great talent and makes friends easily. She also cooks superb, largely organic, meals and keeps goats, rabbits, donkey and dog. All the bedrooms are in another building, filled with her own paintings. There is a handsome dining-room with great beams; try the local Moselle wine. A wonderful family and a friendly village.

Rooms: 1 triple, 1 double, each with bath & wc; 1 twin, 1 triple, each with shower, sharing wc.

Price: 250 Frs for two, including breakfast.

Meals: 100 Frs, including wine & coffee (by arrangement).

Open: March to November.

South of Metz on A31 Féy exit; right at junction; do not go into Féy but straight on for Cuvry. Farm on edge of village past 'Mairie'; signposted.

Map No: 8   MM 242-13

Brigitte & Jean-François MORHAIN
Ferme de Haute-Rive
57420 Cuvry
Moselle
Tel: (0)3 87 52 50 08
Fax: (0)3 87 52 60 20

Just 16km from historic Nancy, a walled garden enfolds you as your eye wanders out to the warm fields and woods beyond. The house too has history in its bones: once the summer residence of the Bishops of Toul, it has C12 tiles still visible by one superb C16 stone fireplace, cornices, panelling, family antiques. Cotels have owned it for 300 years, losing their titles but keeping their beloved house. Bedrooms are all different with pale-papered walls, larger or smaller washing places, old furniture, atmosphere. Great value.

Rooms: 1 quadruple, 2 double, each with bath or shower & wc.

Price: 200 Frs for two, including breakfast.

Meals: 70 Frs, excluding wine (60 Frs).

Open: All year.

From Toul D904 S for 15km. At junction left onto D974 towards Neuves-Maisons for 8km. In Maizières, house is 50m into village near church.

Map No: 7/8   MM 241-36

M Laurent COTEL
69 rue Carnot
54550 Maizières
Meurthe-et-Moselle
Tel: (0)3 83 52 75 57
Fax: (0)3 83 52 75 57

Young Madame Engel greets you with the warmest welcome and the finest Alsace cooking. The peaceful Swiss-style chalet, commanding breathtaking views of the mountains and forests, is just the place to enjoy both. All you need to do is take a deep breath, forget everything — and relax. The rooms are simply comfortable, geraniums cascade from every window and there's a guest entrance. Breakfast tables are laden with goodies — try the homemade organic fruit jams and *kougelopf* (Alsace cake to the uninitiated).

Rooms: 2 double, 1 twin, each with shower & wc.

Price: 240-260 Frs for two, including breakfast.

Meals: Choice 4km.

Open: February to December.

The owners live a few blocks away but this pretty townhouse still displays character in an area that is difficult for tourists to get to. It has a quiet courtyard with garden and stables. The sparkling rooms — two are actually duplex apartments — named after trees and furnished with the appropriate wood (elm, larch, maple, etc), were completed by Monsieur, a woodworker by profession who is every bit as friendly as his wife. Breakfast is served with fresh orange juice, homemade jam and cakes.

Rooms: 2 duplexes, 2 twin, 1 double, all with shower (one behind curtain) & wc.

Price: 240-300 Frs for two, including breakfast.

Meals: Strasbourg 12km. Self-catering in duplexes.

Open: All year.

Gîtes for 11 people

From Colmar, A35 and N83 towards Sélestat (exit 11) then N59 and D424 to Villé. There, D697 to Dieffenbach-du-Val. Careful: ask for exact address as 2 other Engels do B&B!

Map No: 8   MM 242-27

Doris ENGEL-GEIGER
Maison Fleurie
19 route de Neuve Eglise
Dieffenbach-au-Val
67220 Villé
Bas-Rhin
Tel: (0)3 88 85 60 48

From A4 exit 48 onto N63 towards Vendenheim/Strasbourg. Right on D64 towards Lampertheim. At Pfulgrieshiem right on D31 to Pfettisheim. In village follow main road; signposted.

Map No: 8   MM 242-20

Marie-Célestine GASS
La Maison du Charron
15 rue Principale
67370 Pfettisheim
Bas-Rhin
Tel: (0)3 88 69 60 35
Fax: (0)3 88 69 77 96

LORRAINE – ALSACE – FRANCHE COMTÉ

So close to expensive but gorgeous Strasbourg, yet such good value. You are also right at the start of the *Route des Vins*, in the heart of a pretty Alsatian village. The house is, extraordinarily, a working farm, producing rosé as well as milk. Although on a fairly busy main road its bedrooms are at the back and quiet; they are simple, small, yet comfortable. Marie teaches German; Paul, the farmer, serves the breakfast in the garden or in the dining-room with its brown tiles and blue walls.

Rooms: 3 double, each with shower & wc.

Price: 200 or 220 Frs for two, including breakfast.

Meals: Restaurant in village.

Open: All year.

Gîtes for 8 people

The first Ruhlmann wine-grower built this lovely Alsatian house in 1688. Wine buffs will enjoy visiting the wine cellar and non-drinkers can taste the spring water straight from the Vosges hills. The charming rooms under the sloping roof have new carpets and old family furniture; breakfast is served in a huge room full of relics: barrels, a wine press, a grape basket, a china stove. You will meet the whole fun-loving family — children love this place and *Le Petit Train* that tours the striking old village and the vineyards.

Rooms: 2 double, each with shower, sharing wc.

Price: 230 Frs for two, including breakfast and wine-tasting.

Meals: 6 choices within walking distance.

Open: April to November.

From A4 exit 45 onto N404/N4 towards Strasbourg for 16km. Farm is in middle of the village of Marlenheim on left, before post office.

Map No: 8   MM 242-19

Paul & Marie-Claire GOETZ
86 rue du Général de Gaulle
67520 Marlenheim
Bas-Rhin
Tel: (0)3 88 87 52 94

Dambach is about 8km north of Sélestat on D35. House in village centre, about equidistant between two gateways.

Map No: 8   MM 242-27

Jean-Charles & Laurence RUHLMANN
34 rue Maréchal Foch
67650 Dambach-la-Ville
Bas-Rhin
Tel: (0)3 88 92 41 86
Fax: (0)3 88 92 61 81

Two villages, two houses — one blue, one yellow — a mixture of B&B and self-catering, this is a special Alsatian find. The enthusiastic owners, wine-growers and activity-providers — walks with donkeys, wine-tastings, nature trails for children — offer one cosy, environmentally-conscious room at home and two others in exquisite Riquewihr where the 16th-century Blue House is run by friendly Nicole Sirot. Smallish rooms, organic breakfasts in baskets, roof terrace, holiday atmosphere.

Rooms: 1 suite for 4, 2 double, each with shower, wc & kitchenette.

Price: 360-480 Frs for two, 510 Frs for four, including breakfast; 3 nights min.

Meals: Good choice in both villages.

Open: All year.

From Colmar N83 dir. St Dié 'par le col' then N415 towards Kaysersberg for 1km then left on D10 to Katzenthal. Enter village to fountain, fork left, house along on left. For Riquewihr, request directions by fax.

Map No: 8   MM 242-31

Francine & Clément
KLUR-GRAFF
105 rue des Trois Épis
68230 Katzenthal
Haut-Rhin
Tel: (0)3 89 27 53 59
Fax: (0)3 89 27 30 17
e-mail: katz@nucleus.fr

Madame, an artist, has adorned her home and furniture with hand-painted stencils. One of her daughters is studying Fine Art and they often paint quietly together on the landing. Nearby are golf and skiing (in equally breathtaking locations) and the *Ballons des Vosges* Regional Park. Dinner is shared with your hosts and possibly their three daughters plus a few friends. Madame should charge extra for her conversation! "Lucky is the traveller who stops here," said the Canadian reader who led us to Le Montanjus.

Rooms: 1 double, 1 suite for 3, each with own shower & wc.

Price: 295 Frs for two, including breakfast.

Meals: 95 Frs (weekdays) & 115 Frs (w/e), incl. wine & coffee.

Open: All year.

Gites for 3 people

From A36 exit 4 onto D466 towards Masevaux. At Lauw left on B14bis (later D2) to Rougement & Ettuefont. In village pass 1st Chambres d'Hôtes sign, right at T-junction; house, marked 'Le Placard d'Astride', is 100m up.

Map No: 8   MM 243-10

Astride & Daniel ELBERT
Le Montanjus
8 rue de la Chapelle
90170 Ettuefont
Territoire de Belfort
Tel: (0)3 84 54 68 63

Once part of the C15 fortress of Pesmes, one of France's prettiest villages, it is vast. Guy bought only walls, and built a house within them. The staircase is grey-painted concrete with wooden bannister; some of the rooms are magnificent, the sort you pay to visit on a wet Sunday afternoon. As the bedrooms are so huge the furniture can appear sparse, but they are colourful and stylish. There is a library plus a small *salon*, a 200m² reception room, a boat on the river and... too much to describe in this space. Children over 5 welcome.

Rooms: 4 double, 1 twin, 1 triple, 1 family room, each with bath or shower & wc.

Price: 400-450 Frs for two, including breakfast.

Meals: Choice within short walking distance.

Open: Mid-March to mid-October.

From A36 exit 2 onto D475 to Pesmes (20km). House is at top of village on left.

Map No: 12   MM 243-18

Guy HOYET
La Maison Royale
70140 Pesmes
Haute-Saône
Tel: (0)3 84 31 23 23
Fax: (0)3 84 31 23 23

Try an American breakfast after taking the waters: Luxeuil is worth a detour and you are in the centre. There is a wooden floor under the rugs in your sitting-room, an open fireplace with big mirror, windows to the street, moulded ceiling. In one room there is striped green-gold wallpaper, white bedspreads... very pretty, very French. Modern touches, too: smoked-glass dining table and black wooden folding chairs. They are a friendly young couple (he is American and works in Paris) with two small children and there's a huge playroom.

Rooms: 1 suite for 4, 2 double, each with bath or shower & wc.

Price: 250-550 Frs for two, including breakfast.

Meals: Wide choice within walking distance.

Open: All year.

From Vesoul N57 N for 30km. In Luxeuil main street, house (black door & flying pennant) is on left 50m before traffic lights.

Map No: 8   MM 242-38

Sophie JOHNSON
13 allées Maroselli
70300 Luxeuil-les-Bains
Haute-Saône
Tel: (0)3 84 40 40 78
Fax: (0)3 84 40 40 78

This fabulously renovated neo-classical house and its stylish owners can be unhesitatingly recommended for an authentic taste of château living. All rooms, with proper period furniture, engravings and family portraits, look out over the fine Directoire-style park. Guests have their own breakfast and sitting-rooms. Madame, as elegant as her house, unintrusively provides for all and Monsieur, whose pride and joy is the park, is pleased to be told that 8 years of painstaking work have been worthwhile.

Rooms: 3 double rooms, 1 suite, all with bath & wc.

Price: 500 Frs for two, including breakfast.

Meals: Auberge 4km.

Open: All year.

From Besançon, N73 to St Vit. Then left through town and right onto D203 to Salans; château in village.

Map No: 12   MM 243-18

Béatrice & Claus OPPELT
Château de Salans
39700 Salans
Jura
Tel: (0)3 84 71 16 55
Fax: (0)3 84 79 41 54

Burgundy

Your room will be under the roof with a lovely view of orchards and meadows and a brook to sing you to sleep. Your hosts are the nicest, gentlest, most generous couple imaginable. Their rather ordinary home — a slightly suburbanised wine merchant's house — is over their delightful art gallery and has a lovely garden at the back where a Wendy house awaits children. And anyone may play the piano in the house or golf just down the road.

Rooms: 1 twin, 1 suite for 4, both with shower & wc.

Price: 240 Frs for two, including breakfast.

Meals: 60 Frs, excluding wine.

Open: All year.

In Lons-le-Saunier towards Chalon/Bourg-en-Bresse. After SNCF station left on D117 toward Maconnay then D41 to Vernantois. Left before church & follow signs to 'Rose Arts'.

Map No: 12   MM 243-30

Monique et Michel RYON
'Rose Arts'
8 rue Lacuzon
39570 Vernantois
Jura
Tel: (0)3 84 47 17 28

This ancient *ferme-auberge* dates from the 1100s. Most of the existing building is 1700s with a long fully-vaulted ground floor. Upstairs, the rooms are thoroughly modern; four of them can house four people. The flower-decked façade overlooks enchanting countryside near arcaded Lons-le-Saunier, birthplace of the composer of the Marseilleise. Madame serves great meals in a cheerful atmosphere; home-produced *fromage blanc* or rhubarb tart are musts. Good value even if the plumbing is noisy.

Rooms: 4 double, 1 twin, each with own shower & wc.

Price: 230 Frs for two, including breakfast.

Meals: 75 Frs, excluding wine (book ahead).

Open: All year.

From Lons-le-Saunier, D117 through Macornay to Géruge; 1st left at entrance to village; La Grange Rouge at end of winding road.

Map No: 12   MM 243-30

Mme Anne-Marie VERJUS
La Grange Rouge
39570 Géruge
Jura
Tel: (0)3 84 47 00 44

This fine C18 *manoir* has a welcoming, comfortable air, an English garden and an impressive terrace. Indoors, guests share the elegant dining, sitting and morning rooms with their relaxed English hosts who know and love the good things their adopted region has to offer: wine, good food, the great Benedictine abbey of Cluny, Romanesque architecture, and more. Roz has a real gift for putting people at their ease. A cushion-filled interior, perfect bathrooms, antique furniture, old fireplaces and homemade goodies for breakfast add up to a great place to stay.

Rooms: 4 double, all with own bath & wc.

Price: 350 Frs for two, including breakfast.

Meals: Good-value restaurant in village.

Open: All year.

Gîtes for 4 people

Two nice big rooms with antique furniture, only let together to members of the same party. They are at the back where the birds sing, the clock chimes and the road can scarcely be heard. You enter through the owners' kitchen/diner, or through your own outside door. This is a typical Burgundy house with its roof sweeping down from the peak and a green flowery face. Madame is sunny too, full of life and lasting beauty. She will serve anything you want for breakfast and Monsieur will give you excellent introductions to local winegrowers.

Rooms: 2 triple, one with wc & handbasin, sharing shower & 2nd wc.

Price: 250 Frs for two, including breakfast.

Meals: Good restaurant 2km.

Open: All year.

From Cluny, D980 towards Montceau-les-Mines. 21km after Cluny, left on D983; after Chevagny turn right onto D303. La Guiche is signposted. In village, left of 'Mairie'.

Map No: 12   MM 243-38

Mrs Roz BINNS
La Roseraie
71220 La Guiche
Saône-et-Loire
Tel: (0)3 85 24 67 82
Fax: (0)3 85 24 61 03

From Beaune N74 towards Chagny, then D981 through Givry/Cluny. Entering Sercy, house on right, 100m after large château.

Map No: 12   MM 243-27

Josette & Pascal BIWAND
Le Bourg
71460 Sercy
Saône-et-Loire
Tel: (0)3 85 92 62 61
Fax: (0)3 85 92 51 28

BURGUNDY

A place to drool over, and the owner, too, is passionate about it. He is a lovely man, bursting with ideas on further restoration; he also cultivates the vines. The bedrooms, in a renovated building near the main 15th-century château, are newly done (the bigger one is a gem, with superb beams and a vast mezzanine) and plain in the way so many are in France. You have a small verandah on which to sit and admire the view. Breakfast is in the château, which is a delightfully lived-in listed monument. Irresistible.

Rooms: 1 triple, 1 quadruple, each with bath or shower & wc.

Price: 390 Frs for two, including breakfast.

Meals: 5 restaurants within 5km.

Open: April to mid-Nov.

Canoe trips on the Loire and forays into the countryside are big attractions here. The unpretentious old farmhouse has a fine stone staircase and solid oak doors. A wood-burning stove provides glowing warmth. The decor in the bedrooms — beige with blue curtains — may seem rather under-designed to some. Monsieur is a nice straightforward person who runs a shop in Marcigny; Madame is calm and hospitable as she serves breakfast in the conservatory. Many guests come again and again and seem like old friends.

Rooms: 1 double, 1 quadruple, each with bath or shower & wc.

Price: 270 Frs for two, including breakfast.

Meals: In Marcigny, 5km.

Open: All year.

From Tournus D14 W towards Cormatin. House is on this road 2km after Martailly-les-Brancion (leave Brancion and La Chapelle on your right).

Map No: 12   MM 243-39

Bertrand & Françoise de CHERISEY
Château de Nobles
71700 La Chapelle-sous-Brancion
Saône-et-Loire
Tel: (0)3 85 51 00 55

From Roanne, D482 and D982 towards Paray-le-Monial. 5km after Marcigny, left for Reffy. Next to church; signposted.

Map No: 12   MM 238-48

M & Mme Daniel CHEVALLIER
Le Cèdre Bleu
Reffy, Baugy
71110 Marcigny
Saône-et-Loire
Tel: (0)3 85 25 20 48/39 68

Very comfortable and delectably quiet, this 300 year-old farmhouse, a former *maison vigneronne*, has been renovated with superb attention to detail — wait till you see the excellent bathrooms. Monsieur is charming, VERY zealous, speaks good English and will share his love of this famous wine-making region with you. When the days are long and warm, breakfast can be taken on the terrace. It's a feast of local produce — jams, honey, bread, cheeses and *pâtés* — which should set you up perfectly for a heady day's visit to the vineyards.

Rooms: 2 double, each with shower or bath & wc.

Price: 270 Frs for two, including breakfast.

Meals: Excellent restaurant nearby.

Open: All year.

The Fachon family encourages you to wander the grounds of this 13th-century château. Tours of the *caves* and the *Route des Vins* are available and woods and gardens are open for walks. One guestroom is in the château, the rest are in the adjacent *maison vigneronne* (in effect the old vine workers' cottages). Madame runs the operation with informal charm (one reader called the atmosphere hilarious) and Monsieur may surprise you with an enormous bottle of cognac at dinner — regional food made with home-grown vegetables.

Rooms: 3 triple, all with bath & wc. Children's room for 7 with bathroom.

Price: 400 Frs for two, including breakfast. Extra bed 90 Frs.

Meals: 90-150 Frs, excluding wine.

Open: All year except January.

Gîtes for 18 people

From Tournus, D14 towards Cormatin. After 12km left onto D163 towards Grévilly. After 200m, follow Grévilly on right. Straight on at T-junction. House 100m on left: outside village, just below church.

Map No: 12   MM 243-39

Claude DEPREAY
Le Pré Ménot
71700 Grévilly
Saône-et-Loire
Tel: (0)3 85 33 29 92
Fax: (0)3 85 33 02 79

From A6 exit at Tournus on D14 through Ozenay towards Marthailly. 600m after Corcelles left at sign 'Caveau'.

Map No: 12   MM 243-39

Marie-Laurence FACHON
Maisons Vigneronnes
Château de Messey
71700 Ozenay
Saône-et-Loire
Tel: (0)3 85 51 33 83/16 11
Fax: (0)3 85 51 33 82
e-mail: chateau-messey@hotmail.com

This cheerful, down-to-earth couple converted the barns into large *chambres d'hôtes* to revitalise their estate. Madame serves traditional home-cooked dinners and will provide a picnic the next day (try the planned walks and Loire canoeing). The pastel rooms with simple bathrooms have parquet floors, country-style beds with good mattresses, old *armoires*, wood-burning stoves and low-level lighting. The house, with its large beflowered terrace and unobtrusive campsite, stands 500m from the road.

Rooms: 3 double, 1 double/twin, 1 triple, all with shower & wc.

Price: 260 Frs for two, including breakfast.

Meals: 80 Frs, including table wine (Burgundy 60 Frs).

Open: All year.

There's a good worn-around-the-edges feel to this authentic old manor house. Madame, with her slightly unorthodox sense of humour (she's "quite a character"), is determined to maintain its personality. You choose: an active holiday — bicycling, walking, horse-riding; or a quiet restorative break — contemplate mountain scenery, stroll around the mature gardens, play the baby grand or browse through the rich collection of local guides and histories in the bibliothèque. Enjoy home-produced fruit and jams.

Rooms: 1 double with bath, shower, wc; 1 suite for 5 with shower, wc, kitchen.

Price: 260 Frs for two, including breakfast.

Meals: Self-catering in suite.

Open: All year.

Gîtes for 12 people

From Roanne, D482 and D982 towards Paray-le-Monial for about 30km. Enter Marcigny; signposted.

Map No: 12   MM 238-48

Maïssa & Alain GALLAND
La Thuillère
71110 Marcigny
Saône-et-Loire
Tel: (0)3 85 25 10 31

From Mâcon, N79 towards Cluny. At Berzé-le-Châtel, N79 on towards Charolles, then D987 to Trambly. Left past church; house on left.

Map No: 12   MM 239-12

François & Florence GAUTHIER
Les Charrières
71520 Trambly
Saône-et-Loire
Tel: (0)3 85 50 43 17

Madame gave up floristry years ago but still has her green fingers. Curiously, the naturalness of the garden and courtyard, with overflowing pots and boxes, contrasts with the kitsch bedrooms (silk flowers, frilly dollies etc). But she is all heart — she may lay a paper heart on your pillow that wishes you *bonne nuit*. She doesn't refuse children but we guess she'd rather you arrived with a little dog under your arm. She or her husband can do winery visits for non-francophones. Ask for one of the larger rooms; the smallest one feels cramped.

Rooms: 1 suite for 4, 1 quadruple, 1 double, all with bath or shower & wc.

Price: 240-280 Frs for two, including breakfast.

Meals: Good choice 3-5km.

Open: All year.

Dominique is sensitive to the needs of travelling families and has invested thought in creating a large family room at the top of the yellow-stone farmhouse. Bathrobes, too, are attentively provided for grown-ups, so everyone feels cared for. There are six rooms available, all sparkling and charmingly simple. Folk return here, not only for the relaxing experience, but also to stock up on the homemade cheeses, local wines and mouth-watering *confitures* that are on sale and served at mealtimes.

Rooms: 2 double sharing shower & wc, 2 twin sharing shower & wc; 2 family suites with shower, wc and kitchen.

Price: 195-325 Frs for two, including breakfast.

Meals: Self-catering in two rooms. Nearby restaurant.

Open: All year.

Gîtes for 15 people

From A6 exit Macon Sud on N79 (Moulins, Cluny) for 7km then exit to Charnay-lès-Macon, La Roche Vineuse. There, towards Sommeré for 2km. House at top of village on left. Bell on wall by gate.

Map No: 12   MM 243-39

Eliane HEINEN
Le Tinailler d'Aléane
Sommeré
71960 La Roche-Vineuse
Saône-et-Loire
Tel: (0)3 85 37 80 68
Fax: (0)3 85 37 80 68

From Tournus, D14 towards Cluny. At Chapaize, D314 towards Bissy-sous-Uxelles. House next to church.

Map No: 12   MM 243-39

Pascale & Dominique de LA BUSSIÈRE
La Ferme
71460 Bissy-sous-Uxelles
Saône-et-Loire
Tel: (0)3 85 50 15 03

Have you ever been cooped up in an hotel without being able to open the windows? Whether you need fresh air or a clear view of the stars, this authentic former charcoal-burner's cottage (the old grate is still perfect for making toast) is an original solution to what has become a major problem. It remains untouched since its last occupants left, unable to cope with the heat, so you can be sure there will be no furnishings in poor taste. An interesting Burnt Sienna colour upstairs and easy access to the roof.

Rooms: Suite for several with ash and natural soap washing facilities.

Price: Free, but bring some thatch.

Meals: Indoor barbecue/grill available.

Open: All year except rainy season.

We were delighted to stumble upon this old farmhouse that combines B&B with a thriving theatre and art gallery. In June and July you can see the local theatre group of actor-winegrowers, *La Mère Folle*, perform in one of the converted barns. Founded in 1981 by Jean-Paul, the group performs and tours regularly. Régine, a musician, helps with productions. Obviously busy, creative people, they still take their B&B business seriously and offer good rooms with comfortable beds and modern decoration in pale wood and original beams.

Rooms: 4 double, 1 twin, all with bath or shower & wc.

Price: 270 Frs for two, including breakfast.

Meals: Choice in village, 3km.

Open: All year.

In town centre, follow signs to 'Sapeurs-Pompiers' (caution fire engines turning); house at end of road on left.

Map No: 12   MM 243-39

Mme Mette-Allue PIROMAN
L'Ancienne Chaumière
Allée des Sapeurs
71999 Fonds-Brulé
Saône-et-Loire
Tel: (0)2 12 34 56 78

From A6 exit Tournus onto D56 towards Lugny. 3km after Chardonnay right on D463 & follow signs to Chambres d'Hôtes/Théâtre Champvent.

Map No: 12   MM 243-39

Régine & Jean-Paul RULLIÈRE
Le Tinailler
Manoir de Champvent
71700 Chardonnay
Saône-et-Loire
Tel: (0)3 85 40 50 23
Fax: (0)3 85 40 50 18

The storm-felled cedar now stands magnificently guard as St Vincent, patron saint of wine-growers. Father and son run the vineyard (1996 Mâcon Gold Medal for Chardonnay), Madame makes jam and cheese and loves spending time with guests, old and young (they have 6 grandchildren). All four bedrooms are big, have warm carpets, clean-cut modern furniture and distinctive colour schemes — two pastel, two strong dark — as well as excellent bathrooms. A supremely comfortable, friendly, relaxing place to stay.

Rooms: 2 double, 1 twin, 1 triple, all with own bath or shower & wc.

Price: 270 Frs for two, including breakfast.

Meals: Self-catering.

Open: All year.

The Ayletts fell in love with a dilapidated (one cold tap and an outside privy) C15 Presbytery, bought it on the spot and set about their high-standard restoration, using old materials. Marjorie's artistry is evident in the elegantly comfortable bedrooms, where rich colours echo the hand-painted tiles in the luxurious bathrooms. Guests can enjoy excellent food, made with organically home-grown produce, in the attractive garden with superb Morvan views. Inside, there is an inglenook fireplace for cooler nights.

Rooms: 2 double, 1 twin, each with bath or shower & wc.

Price: 370-390 Frs for two, including breakfast.

Meals: 120 Frs, including wine.

Open: All year.

From Tournus, N6 towards Mâcon. After 10km, right on D163 to Uchizy; signposted.

Map No: 12   MM 243-39

Mme Annick SALLET
Domaine de l'Arfentière
Route de Chardonnay
71700 Uchizy
Saône-et-Loire
Tel: (0)3 85 40 50 46
Fax: (0)3 85 40 58 05

From Avallon N6 to Saulieu. In centre, left at Hôtel Côte-d'Or onto D26 to La Motte Ternant. In village, follow signs for church.

Map No: 12   MM 243-13

Marjorie & Brian AYLETT
Le Presbytère
La Motte Ternant
21210 Saulieu
Côte-d'Or
Tel: (0)3 80 84 34 85
Fax: (0)3 80 84 35 32

A civilised house and family where you find space, warmth, good taste, intelligent company and a pretty terrace for breakfast (tea, at baying time for the huskies being bred across the lane, is perhaps less peaceful) and so many musical events in summer. Madame is open and at ease. All is harmony in this renovated and not over-furnished manor with its pale colours, old tiles and rugs, modern art and big, soft-textured bedrooms (one more intimate and carpeted). The separate 'little house' should delight the independent.

Rooms: 2 triple, 1 double, 1 cottage for 4, each with bath or shower & wc.

Price: 370 Frs for two, including breakfast.

Meals: Simple place in village, choice in Beaune.

Open: All year.

From A6 Beaune/Chagny exit onto D973 towards Dole & Seurre for 10km. In Corberon house signposted up on left.

Map No: 12   MM 243-28

Chantal & Alain BALMELLE
L'Ormeraie
21250 Corberon
Côte-d'Or
Tel: (0)3 80 26 53 19
Fax: (0)3 80 26 54 01

Soisick is young, fun and informal — you may find yourself waiting for her after the appointed hour — and, though the cats may sneak in under the bedcovers, relaxed animal-lovers enjoy the contrast between this casual attitude and the formal air of the ancient turrets of her pretty château (mostly restored by her). Rooms are comfortable with a lived-in once-elegant look. Dinner, served in the family dining-room, is superb, but do make sure your booking is firm. Lovely gardens, fly-fishing, a games room.

Rooms: 3 double, 1 twin and 1 triple, all with bath or shower & wc.

Price: 360 Frs for two, including breakfast. Extra bed 120 Frs.

Meals: 150 Frs, including wine & coffee (book ahead).

Open: 21 March to 1 November.

From Dijon, N71 towards Châtillon-sur-Seine. Before St Marc-sur-Seine, right on D32 and D901 towards Aignay. Tarperon signposted on D901.

Map No: 7   MM 241-50

Mme Soisick de CHAMPSAVIN
Manoir de Tarperon
21510 Aignay-le-Duc
Côte-d'Or
Tel: (0)3 80 93 83 74

The Dartois are porcelain collectors and fascinating hosts with wide knowledge of local history and archæology and, now that the farm is run by their children, lots of time to share with guests. Theirs is a big, interesting old house in a hamlet of only 80 people surrounded by tranquil countryside where the Seine is but a small stream and the Douix springs spectacularly in a grove near Châtillon. A lived-in, peaceful atmosphere, traditionally-furnished bedrooms, rather dated but adequate shared shower and wc and altogether exceptional value.

Rooms: 1 double & 1 twin, sharing bath, shower & wc

Price: 150 Frs for two, including breakfast.

Meals: Good restaurant 1km.

Open: All year.

This is an endearingly higgledy-piggledy and simple 18th-century house in an attractive hill-top village. The cheerful, plain rooms are lent an artistic flourish by Françoise's hand-decoration of some of the furniture: "neither marble nor satin, but wood and plaster, whiteness and colour" is how she defines her decor. Breakfast features honey from Henri's own hives. You may eat together in the evening, when the needs of a young family allow, and hear about Henri's life as a bee-keeper. He is genuinely fascinating.

Rooms: 1 quadruple, 1 triple, 1 double, 1 twin, all with shower & wc.

Price: 200-220 Frs for two, including breakfast.

Meals: 90 Frs, including aperitif, wine & coffee.

Open: March to November.

From Châtillon-sur-Seine, N71 towards Dijon. At Aisey-sur-Seine, right on D101 to Chemin-d'Aisey; sharp right at church, house on left.

Map No: 7   MM 241-46

Simone & Jean DARTOIS
Chemin d'Aisey
21400 Châtillon-sur-Seine
Côte-d'Or
Tel: (0)3 80 93 22 51

From Nuits-St-Georges N74 towards Beaune. At Corgoloin, D115 to Magny-les-Villers. There, take road leading to Pernand Vergelesses; house almost immediately on right as you leave Magny, going uphill.

Map No: 12   MM 243-16

Françoise & Henri GIORGI
Route de Pernand-Vergelesses
21700 Magny-lès-Villiers
Côte-d'Or
Tel: (0)3 80 62 95 42

Expect a genuine welcome to this modern house with its lovely views over the valley of historic Alesia. Having lived long in Africa, the Gounands came home to build and decorate (slightly garishly) this house, become mayor of the village (Monsieur will describe it all over a *kir*) and offer spotless rooms, new mattresses, high-quality bathrooms to lovers of walking, mediæval villages and wine. Choose Madame's good cooking or your own in the well-equipped, open-sided summer house that Monsieur has designed in the garden.

Rooms: 1 double, 1 twin, each with shower, sharing wc.

Price: 200-220 Frs for two, including breakfast. Extra bed 50 Frs.

Meals: By arrangement 80 Frs, incl. wine & coffee. Self-catering.

Open: Easter to October.

Wooden beams and floors, huge old wooden cupboards, shutters and stone fireplaces all contribute to the warm, relaxed feel of this lovely C18 presbytery. Claude Reny and her husband are Parisian bibliophiles and Claude is an enthusiastic gardener, supplying home-grown salads and always keen to swap horticultural hints. Breakfast, with homemade jam, is served round a large oval table in the *salle à manger*, and ageing bicycles are available for exploring. Monsieur is there in summer and speaks excellent English.

Rooms: 2 double, 1 twin, each with bath & wc.

Price: 380 Frs for two, including breakfast.

Meals: Choice within 6/7km.

Open: May to September.

From Dijon, N71 towards Châtillon-sur-Seine. After Courceau, D6 left and follow signposts. (House is on D19A near junction with D6.)

Map No: 7   MM 243-2

Claude & Huguette GOUNAND
Villa Le Clos
Route de la Villeneuve D19A
21150 Darcey
Côte-d'Or
Tel: (0)3 80 96 23 20

From Arnay-le-Duc N6 towards Châlons-sur-Saône for 1km then left onto D17 towards Beaune. In village, house near church (signpost on D17).

Map No: 12   MM 243-14

Mme Claude RENY
La Cure
21230 Foissy
Côte-d'Or
Tel: (0)3 80 84 22 92

Accompanying a 150-year-old cedar in its beautiful hillside position is a charming *maison de maître*. From its guestrooms white shutters open out to countryside views and a curved double staircase leads down to a kempt lawn. Inside are open fires, antique beds (with antique monogrammed bed clothes!), sympathetic period decorations and an atmosphere of secluded comfort. Madame Bürgi is good-humoured, hospitable and keeps a delightful house while Monsieur, who is Dutch, is friendly and attentive.

Rooms: 3 double with shower & wc; 1 double & 1 twin sharing shower & wc.

Price: 250-380 Frs for two, including breakfast.

Meals: In village.

Open: All year.

Gîtes for 2 people

Leave the nerve-jangling N7 behind for this secluded 19th-century house. Enjoy breakfast in the family's marvellous living-room, seated round the long wooden table, with traditional oak furniture and log fire creating a farmhouse atmosphere. Your hosts, retired farmers, are welcoming and sociable and have years of experience in looking after guests. Add some local colour to your stay by taking advantage of Monsieur's keen knowledge of regional history — he is very erudite and loves his subject.

Rooms: 1 double, 2 twin, all with bath or shower & wc.

Price: 220-260 Frs for two, including breakfast.

Meals: Barbecue possible.

Open: All year.

From Nevers, D977 to Prémery. There, D977 bis towards Corbigny; St Révérien is 15km along; signposted.

Map No: 11   MM 238-22

Bernadette BÜRGI & Florent de BEER
La Villa des Prés
58420 Saint-Révérien
Nièvre
Tel: (0)3 86 29 04 57
Fax: (0)3 86 29 65 22

From Nevers, D978 towards Château-Chinon. At Châtillon-en-Bazois, D945 towards Corbigny; left on D259 towards Mont-et-Marré; farm is 500m along.

Map No: 12   MM 238-35

Paul et Nicole DELTOUR
Semelin
Mont-et-Marré
58110 Châtillon-en-Bazois
Nièvre
Tel: (0)3 86 84 13 94

An engaging 19th-century farmhouse with masses of character under its sweeping roof — exposed beams and genuine old tiles are part of Monsieur's fine renovation job — and a charming, enthusiastic hostess, keen to provide her guests with authentic country hospitality. Rooms are traditionally decorated and comfortable. There is a pleasant living-room with books and games. Breakfast (homemade jams) and dinner are eaten with the family; Madame is Portuguese and will make national specialities if asked — a real treat.

Rooms: 2 double, each with shower & wc.

Price: 290 Frs for two, including breakfast.

Meals: 120 Frs, including aperitif, wine & coffee.

Open: Easter to October.

From Cosne-sur-Loire D114 to Cours & St Loup-des-Bois; veer left on D114: Chauffour is between St Loup and St Vérain: follow signs for 'Musée de la Machine Agricole' then for 'Chambres d'Hôtes'.

Map No: 11   MM 231-27

Elvire & René DUCHET
Chez Elvire
Chauffour
58200 Saint-Loup
Nièvre
Tel: (0)3 86 26 20 22

This unusual farmhouse is a perfect place to unleash the children. You can fish on the huge lake, take out a windsurfer or borrow the owner's small boat and canoes. Rooms look out onto the lake, the surrounding countryside or the courtyard. Breakfast includes home-produced honey and *viennoiseries.* Madame is taking English lessons, but her genuine welcome already transcends the language barrier. A super couple — she is level-headed and he loves to joke.

Rooms: 2 triple, 2 double, all with bath or shower & wc.

Price: 200-275 Frs for two, including breakfast.

Meals: Self-catering.

Open: All year.

From Nevers, D978 to Rouy. There, D132 to Tintury; right on D112 to Fleury (signposted Fertrève) and first right after village: drive up to lake and turn right; signposted.

Map No: 12   MM 238-35

Michel & Marie-France GUÉNY
Fleury La Tour
58110 Tintury
Nièvre
Tel: (0)3 86 84 12 42
Fax: (0)3 86 84 12 42

On château lands, this is functional farmhouse accommodation run by kindly farmers: nothing lavish or luscious but come here with children; they'll adore the little armies of baby ducks that regularly march off in search of shade and the other livestock that roam the farmyard. There are horses to pat (now too old to ride). Farm produce, poultry and eggs are sold on site. The energetic may choose to head for the national mountain bike centre (550km of marked track) and just 3km away you can immerse yourself in watersports.

Rooms: 3 double: one with own shower & wc, two sharing bath & wc.

Price: 250 Frs for two, including breakfast.

Meals: 2 restaurants in St Saulge, 4km.

Open: All year.

Gîtes for 19 people

Come at the right time of year and as far as the eye can see you'll be surrounded by fields of sunflowers. Your modest, friendly hosts clearly enjoy sharing their 1690s house in its 115 hectares of parkland. Immaculately restored, the rooms sport good antique furniture and elegant decor. The Lejaults are happy to suggest activities, from watching the goats being milked to visiting local châteaux. Monsieur is taking English lessons and keen to flex his linguistic muscles with any willing volunteers.

Rooms: 4 double, each with bath or shower & wc.

Price: 270-340 Frs for two, including breakfast.

Meals: Self-catering.

Open: All year.

From Prémery, D38 towards Châtillon-en-Bazois and St Saulge; signposted 'Gîte d'Étape' at junction of D38 and D181 to St Martin.

Map No: 11   MM 238-34

J-Patrick & Marie-Hélène JANDET
Basse-Cour de Saint-Martin
58330 Sainte-Marie
Nièvre
Tel: (0)3 86 58 35 15

From Château-Chinon, D978 through Châtillon-en-Bazois towards Nevers. 4km along (past Alluy), after service station, right on D112 towards Bernière; house on left after 1.5km.

Map No: 12   MM 238-35

Colette & André LEJAULT
Bouteuille
58110 Alluy
Nièvre
Tel: (0)3 86 84 06 65
Fax: (0)3 86 84 03 41

Monsieur likes you to feel you are staying with friends on his manor farm and is an expert guide to things to do and see. And you enjoy the independence of a beautifully-decorated apartment with its own entrance onto a deckchaired garden. Breakfast is DIY with all ingredients provided — a much-appreciated feature, we're told. Charming C19 house with a courtyard framed by long barns and old outbuildings in the rich arable lands of the Loire Valley. Horses, bikes, croquet, badminton and lake swimming (on the estate) all available.

Rooms: Apartment with 2 rooms, one with en-suite bathroom; kitchen.

Price: 300 Frs for two, 500 Frs for four, including breakfast.

Meals: 150 Frs, including wine & coffee; self-catering.

Open: All year.

From Montargis, N7 through Briare towards Cosne-sur-Loire. 2km after Neuvy-sur-Loire; signposted.

Map No: 6   MM 238-20

Bernard & Élisabeth PASQUET
Domaine de l'Étang
58450 Neuvy-sur-Loire
Nièvre
Tel: (0)3 86 39 20 06

Meeting guests with a glass of champagne scores points in many people's books and reflects the Perreaus' *joie de vivre*: they are wonderful, fun-loving folk. You stay in the old farmhouse's big loft where the bright, finely-furnished bedrooms share a large sitting-room. Enjoy the grounds and pool: the picture doesn't do them justice. This dairy and organic vegetable farm also has horses (riding lessons available in July and August). A tremendous place for enjoying the good things in life, including excellent company.

Rooms: 2 twin, 2 double, sharing 2 showers & separate wc's; 1 double with own shower & wc.

Price: 280 Frs for two, including breakfast.

Meals: 100 Frs, including wine. Also self-catering.

Open: All year.

From Nevers D978 towards Château Chinon. 3km before Châtillon right on D10 towards Alluy. In St Gratien left on C3 to La Marquise — 800m on right.

Map No: 12   MM 238-35

Huguette & Noël PERREAU
La Marquise
58340 Saint-Gratien-Savigny
Nièvre
Tel: (0)3 86 50 01 02/06 77
Fax: (0)3 86 50 07 14

In a wonderful setting, this old farmhouse below the château and its annexe further down have been well converted by its young owners who also run a working men's inn. The rooms are modern and comfortable, the whole house has a solid country atmosphere and there is a large garden with games for children. More a guesthouse, perhaps, than a B&B. Madame is an excellent cook and enjoys introducing visitors to the delights of *la cuisine nivernaise*, specialising in chicken dishes. Excellent for families and for those seeking rural simplicity.

Rooms: 2 double & 1 triple room, all with shower & wc.

Price: 220 Frs for two, including breakfast.

Meals: 85 Frs, excluding wine. (Not Sun.)

Open: All year except 20 December to 3 January.

Gîtes for 2 people

From Avallon, D957 to Vézelay, then D958 towards Corbigny to Bazoches: house in village, below castle.

Map No: 12   MM 238-23

Philippe & Nadine PERRIER
Ferme Auberge de Bazoches
58190 Bazoches-de-Morvan
Nièvre
Tel: (0)3 86 22 16 30
Fax: (0)3 86 22 16 30

You can see the river from your beautifully-furnished bedroom in this Burgundian manor-house that has been in the family for 400 years, standing in grand seclusion in its lovely gravel courtyard. The Brunots offer an impressive degree of luxury (including prettily-tiled 'American-style' bathrooms) and genuine hospitality. There is a comfortable guest sitting-room; Madame is an accomplished cook; Monsieur has a superb wine cellar (you might even choose your own wine for dinner). Readers have sent glowing reports.

Rooms: 2 double, 1 twin, each with bath or shower & wc; extra bed available.

Price: 350 Frs for two, including breakfast. Extra bed 100 Frs. (2 nights min.)

Meals: 160 Frs, including wine & coffee.

Open: All year.

From A6, Auxerre-Nord exit on N6 towards Joigny; right on D48, left on D84 towards Brienon for 9km, past turning to Mont-Saint-Sulpice and right down small road by river; house is 0.5km on left.

Map No: 7   MM 237-46

Didier & Françoise BRUNOT
Domaine des Morillons
89250 Mont-Saint-Sulpice
Yonne
Tel: (0)3 86 56 18 87
Fax: (0)3 86 43 05 07

This ancient building so captivated Albert Schmidig that he prefers to be known as Mr Cabalus! Dating from the 12th century, it was an abbey hospice and lodged St Bernard and King Louis VII. There are an art gallery and an excellent coffee shop in a vaulted and pillared room with a huge fireplace. B&B guests have their own breakfast and sitting rooms. There's art everywhere, coir flooring, masses of books. Eccentric, artistic, bearded and slightly shuffling, Mr 'Cabalus' is the perfect gentleman. An exceptional and inimitable place.

Rooms: 1 triple, 1 double, each with shower & wc; 2 triple, 2 double with showers but sharing wc's.

Price: 278-418 Frs for two, including breakfast.

Meals: 80 Frs, excluding wine. Also coffee shop.

Open: All year.

The farm is now run by the children so Henri just works "when he feels like it" and has plenty of time for his guests. These are long-standing local folk with a warm friendly attitude. The bedrooms are delightfully cosy, true to the spirit of an old-fashioned French farmhouse; shower rooms are clean and modern (one behind curtain). Isabelle serves what one reader called a "huge breakfast". A peaceful, rural spot where woods and all things bucolic abound. The village, with its little *auberge* for dinner, is 2km away.

Rooms: 1 double with shower & wc; 2 double sharing shower & separate wc.

Price: 220 Frs for two, including breakfast (less for long stays).

Meals: Auberge in village.

Open: Mid-March to October.

In Vézelay centre, follow main street up to Basilique. House is the last on left before reaching Basilica but next-to-last door (marked).

Map No: 7   MM 238-23

M CABALUS
Cabalus
Rue Saint-Pierre
89450 Vézelay
Yonne
Tel: (0)3 86 33 20 66
Fax: (0)3 86 33 38 03

From Châtillon-sur-Seine, D965 towards Tonnerre and Laignes. At Pimelles, D12 to Cruzy-le-Châtel; at T-junction right towards Nicey, through Cruzy. House signposted after village on right: small road up to farm.

Map No: 7   MM 237-48

Henri & Isabelle CHERVAUX
Les Musseaux
89740 Cruzy-le-Châtel
Yonne
Tel: (0)3 86 75 24 03
Fax: (0)3 86 75 20 50

Simplicity and attention to detail are Madame's keynotes and her harmonious quirky house ('Gothic' windows even in the attic, 'Victorian' panelling, superb old patterned floor tiles) is the warm and friendly central theme. Up two floors, the simply-furnished bedrooms have sloping ceilings, ancient rafters and not one common wall. Breakfast by the old bread oven or outside before learning to 'grow' truffles, choosing the estate wine you'll take home (the cellar is below the house) or setting off for Auxerre. A child-friendly house.

Rooms: 5 double rooms, all with bath or shower & wc.

Price: 270-330 Frs for two, including breakfast.

Meals: Restaurant 2km; Auxerre or Chablis 10km.

Open: All year.

From Auxerre, D965 towards Chablis; after passing under the A6 motorway bridge, 3km on, house on right. DO NOT go to Venoy.

Map No: 7   MM 238-11

François & Françoise CHONÉ
Domaine de Montpierreux
89290 Venoy
Yonne
Tel: (0)3 86 40 20 91
Fax: (0)3 86 40 28 00

Sleeping in a four-poster in the turret of a fortified C12 château, after enjoying a 'mediæval' dinner in a candlelit baronial kitchen/dining-room, is certainly one way to end a day in Burgundy. The mediæval atmosphere, which some have described as strange and extraordinary, is completed by artefacts from throughout the château's history, some dating from the crusades. Madame is a talented cook who is both approachable and passionate about the place. This is a stylish and romantic retreat but not suitable for children under 8.

Rooms: 1 quadruple with own bathroom.

Price: 500 Frs for two, including breakfast.

Meals: 150-250 Frs, excluding wine (100-250 Frs).

Open: All year.

Gîtes for 4 people

From Avallon, N6 towards Saulieu. As you enter Sainte-Magnance, first house on right.

Map No: 12   MM 238-24

Martine & Gérard COSTAILLE
Château Jacquot
RN6
89420 Sainte-Magnance
Yonne
Tel: (0)3 86 33 00 22

Very grand and so very French! The 19th-century manor is set back from the lime-tree-shaded square. Persian carpets on parquet floors, antiques and good, firm beds grace the large, luminous rooms. Well-fitted bathrooms. In winter a wood fire burns in the sitting-room. Madame has taken great pains over her immaculate home; she and her husband put you at your ease in their rather formal surroundings and enjoy talking to guests. "B&B perfection," wrote one reader, "for style, beds, hostess!" Well-behaved children welcome.

Rooms: 1 double/twin with shower & wc; 1 double,1 twin sharing bath & wc.

Price: 280-380 Frs for two, including breakfast.

Meals: 100 Frs, including wine (by arrangement). Restaurant next door.

Open: All year.

From A6, Joigny exit onto D943 towards Joigny then very shortly right onto D89 to Senan. Place de la Liberté is before church on right.

Map No: 6   MM 237-45

Mme Paule DEFRANCE
4 place de la Liberté
89710 Senan
Yonne
Tel: (0)3 86 91 59 89

A hostess after our own heart, Madame is artistic, deeply interested in others, a committed vegetarian, practises yoga, aromatherapy and, what is more, loves jazz and relaxed evenings with guests. She creates a warm, embracing atmosphere in her generous sitting/dining room, with its beams and gold-faced grandfather clock, and serves delicious, mainly organic, meals. The rooms are soberly decorated, not large but comfortable. There is a leafy garden to sit in. Of course people return year after year to bask in the glow.

Rooms: 2 double rooms sharing a bathroom, 1 studio flat with own shower & wc.

Price: 220-290 Frs for two, including breakfast.

Meals: 100 Frs, including wine.

Open: All year.

From Joigny, D943 towards Migennes. At Laroche, left on D181 towards Brion then D47 to Bussy. In village, right on D140 towards Brienon. House 500m on left.

Map No: 6   MM 237-45

Maud DUFAYET
Relais de la Forêt d'Othe
46-48 rue Saint-Julien
89400 Bussy-en-Othe
Yonne
Tel: (0)3 86 91 93 48
Fax: (0)3 86 91 93 48

Cradled among orchards and vineyards, this village house has comfortable, 'no-frills' rooms ideal for children and ground-floor rooms accessible to guests with limited mobility. Some have children's beds (kids can camp in the large, shady garden too). A big dayroom opens onto the guest verandah. Then there's Madame's cooking — breakfasts are so good that guests have been tempted into staying that extra night for another helping. Just down the road is Chablis, where the liquid temptations are well known. Pets by arrangement.

Rooms: 1 double, with shower & wc, in house; 1 double, with bath & wc, in cottage.

Price: 260 Frs for two, including breakfast.

Meals: 90 Frs, incl. wine & coffee (supplement for Chablis). Picnic 40 Frs.

Open: All year.

From Auxerre, N77 to Pontigny. House in village centre, near church.

Map No: 7   MM 237-46

Magda & Philippe GARNIER
Place de l'Eglise
Venouse
89230 Pontigny
Yonne
Tel: (0)3 86 47 75 15
Fax: (0)3 86 47 75 15

"It feels like a wonderful, spiritual home but is not in any way luxurious." A clean and happy 15th-century village house in an ideal spot next to the sublime Basilica in the mediæval town of Vézelay. A stone spiral staircase goes up to the bedrooms; one has a terrace overlooking the Basilica. The owner serves breakfast when you want it in her own dining-room and likes to chat. A special place, for readers have enjoyed its utter Frenchness and Vézelay is a 'must'. Maps and advice for hikers and cyclists.

Rooms: 1 double, 1 twin, sharing shower & wc.

Price: 270 Frs for two, including breakfast.

Meals: In Vézelay.

Open: All year.

From Avallon, D957 to Vézelay. In town, 100m from Basilica — identifiable by turret on house.

Map No: 7   MM 238-23

Monique & Bertrand GINISTY
La Tour Gaillon
Rue Saint Pierre
89450 Vézelay
Yonne
Tel: (0)3 86 33 25 74

Behind its huge castle gates, this 17th-19th-century château contains the Septiers, their toddler, two cats, two friendly dogs and 138 parakeets (that you don't hear). The avian slant is due to Madame's enthusiastic breeding programme but this cosmopolitan couple also pay great attention to their guests whom they just treat as friends in the spare room. The rooms have views over the private woods (badgers to be seen?) and are reached by a sweeping staircase leading up from a ground floor full of knick-knacks and antiques.

Rooms: 2 double with shower and basin each; 2 double without; 2 bathrooms & wc in corridor.

Price: 350 Frs for two, including breakfast.

Meals: 180 Frs, including wine. Book ahead.

Open: All year.

Gîtes for 5 people

From A5 exit Auxerre Nord on N6 towards Auxerre for 1km. Right through Perrigny & St Georges towards Villefargeau. At restaurant 'Relais de la Vallée' left and left again. Château is at end of road.

Map No: 6   MM 238-10

Jacky & Marianne SEPTIER
1 allée du Château
89240 Villefargeau
Yonne
Tel: (0)3 86 41 33 32
Fax: (0)3 86 41 27 25

Feel free to wander in the grounds or settle yourself totally without awkwardness in a corner of this handsome millhouse — it has a most inviting sitting-room. Leigh and Gael's special brand of hospitality is so relaxed that you could fantasise that you own the place. Approached by a private bridge, the house is surrounded by a river, its own lake and rushing water. There's a canoe, (expensive) balloon flights from the garden, a river beach. The big, light rooms have an English country feel and the mill race is noisier than the road...

Rooms: 2 double, 2 twin, 1 triple, 1 suite for 4, all with bath or shower & wc.

Price: 275 Frs for two, including breakfast.

Meals: 125 Frs, including wine & coffee (min. 4 people).

Open: All year.

From Auxerre N6 towards Avallon for 22km. Just before Vermenton village nameplate turn sharp right; signposted.

Map No: 7   MM 238-11

Leigh WOOTTON & Gael ROBERTSON
Le Moulinot
89270 Vermenton
Yonne
Tel: (0)3 86 81 60 42
Fax: (0)3 86 81 62 25

A pair of long low stone buildings behind big blue porch doors, a narrow courtyard in between, the apse of the church looking benignly over the wall and a charming garden with pond and terrace at the back. The hosts are as simple and gentle as their home; they are 'junk-shop' hunters (every bed is different) but they like to keep it uncluttered. The marble bathroom is NOT their doing! A quiet friendly family with two children who adopt stray cats and show a definite desire to do all they can to make your stay restful and fruitful.

Rooms: 1 triple with bath & wc; 1 suite for 5/6 with shower & wc.

Price: 245 Frs for two, including breakfast. Extra bed 90 Frs.

Meals: 90 Frs, including wine & coffee.

Open: All year.

Gîtes for 7 people

From A4 exit on D231 to Villeneuve-le-Comte then right on D96 through Neufmoutiers to Châtres. House in village centre to left of church.

Map No: 6   MM 237-31

Dominique & Pierre LAURENT
Le Portail Bleu
2 route de Fontenay
77610 Châtres
Seine-et-Marne
Tel: (0)1 64 25 84 94
Fax: (0)1 64 25 84 94

Paris – Ile-de-France

A generous farmyard surrounded by beautiful warm stone buildings and set in wide open fields. Cereals, beets and show jumpers — adding a definite touch of elegance to the landscape — flourish. Utter quiet and a genuine welcome, from hosts and labradors alike, out here where Monsieur's family has come hunting for 200 years. Family furniture (the 1900s ensemble is most intriguing though this room has its loo on the floor below) in light-filled rooms and a vast sitting-room for guests with piano and billiards table.

Rooms: 1 triple with shower & wc; 1 apartment: triple room, convertible sofa, mini-kitchen, shower & wc.

Price: 245 Frs for two, including breakfast.

Meals: In walking distance or 4-6km.

Open: All year except Christmas week.

For cat-lovers only — several felines here, plus one labrador, frogs, hedgehogs, rabbits. Home two centuries ago to a family of tax collectors and inn keepers — the bargemen would come to pay their tolls then stay on at the inn — the quiet grounds still go down to the river and lovely towpath walks. The balcony belongs to the 'Champagne' suite, our favourite with its old paintings and wooden floor; the brilliantly Gothic dining-room fireplace once belonged to Alexandre Dumas; your hosts once belonged to the travel industry and are excellent company.

Rooms: 1 suite for 3 with shower & wc, 1 suite for 5 with bath & wc.

Price: 280-340 Frs for two, including breakfast.

Meals: Two good restaurants nearby.

Open: January to October.

From A5 exit 15 on N36 towards Meaux for 200m. Take SECOND right to Crisenoy after TGV bridge, through village then 1.5km to farm (marked on Michelin No106).

Map No: 6   MM 237-31

Philippe & Jeanne MAUBAN
Ferme Vert Saint-Père
77390 Crisenoy
Seine-et-Marne
Tel: (0)1 64 38 83 51
Fax: (0)1 64 38 83 52
e-mail: mauban.vert@wanadoo.fr

From A4 exit 18 onto N3 towards Paris through St Jean then 1st right to Armentières; straight on at junction, past church — house is last but one on right in cul-de-sac.

Map No: 6   MM 237-20

Denise WOEHRLÉ
44 rue du Chef de Ville
77440 Armentières-en-Brie
Seine-et-Marne
Tel: (0)1 64 35 51 22
Fax: (0)1 64 35 42 95

The Art Deco style reigns supreme in this C19 hunting lodge that was exuberantly 'modernised' in the 20s, from the high-windowed, fully-panelled dining-room with its extraordinary dressers and unbelievably mustachioed grandfather to the fabulous bathroom fittings. The original features also include Versailles parquet floors and fine fireplaces: Tae uses her perfect sense of style and colour in decorating around and for them. Quiet spot, well-travelled hosts (especially South America), perfect for Chartres, Paris, Versailles...

Rooms: 2 suites for 5, each with bath & wc.

Price: 420 Frs for two, including breakfast.

Meals: Good restaurants in village.

Open: All year.

The natural air of real farm life. Tractors come and go in the farmyard, the old horse grazes in the field, the four young children play in the sandpit. The Desforges have done an excellent barn conversion. You climb the steep stairs to the lofty raftered dayroom (tea-making equipment, an old dresser, a comfortable sofa) and to the five good-sized bedrooms. They are furnished with grandmother's short-bedded but richly-carved Breton bridal suite, or grandfather's brass bed, old wardrobes and new mattresses. And Madame is delightful.

Rooms: 3 double, 2 twin, all with shower & wc.

Price: 250 Frs for two, including breakfast. Extra bed 60 Frs.

Meals: Choice in Milly 3km. Picnic possible.

Open: All year except mid-Dec to Jan.

From A10 exit 10 to toll gate then right on D27 to St Cyr-sous-Dourdan then continue towards Arpajon — first house on left.

Map No: 6   MM 237-28

Claude & Tae-Lye DABASSE
Le Logis d'Arnières
1 rue du Pont-Rué
91410 Saint-Cyr-sous-Dourdan
Essonne
Tel: (0)1 64 59 14 89
Fax: (0)1 64 59 07 46

From Fontainebleau D837 towards Étampes into Milly centre. 300m after church left on D1 towards Gironville for 3.5km. Farm on right.

Map No: 6   MM 237-30

Sophie & Jean-Charles DESFORGES
Ferme de la Grange Rouge
91490 Milly-la-Forêt
Essonne
Tel: (0)1 64 98 94 21

Only 25 train-minutes (Paris Region express network) from the heart of Paris, in a leafy residential suburb (with the occasional train at the far end of the road), this is a modern, light-filled house decorated with a mix of antique and modern, plus some fascinating oriental treasures, mementoes of years in Indonesia. Your fully-equipped apartment is large and light; Madame is most welcoming. You can really make yourself at home here with your family for a few days. Leave the car and explore Paris at your ease.

Rooms: Apartment for 4 with bathroom & kitchen.

Price: For 3 nights: 389 Frs for two per night, including breakfast. Reduction one week and winter.

Meals: Choice locally.

Open: All year.

From Paris RER line A1 to Le Vésinet/Le Pecq. Madame will fax a plan from station. At No 14, house is right-hand one.

Map No: 6   MM 237-17

Éveline ALBAUT
14 rue Anatole France
78110 Le Vésinet
Yvelines
Tel: (0)1 39 76 19 77
Fax: (0)1 39 76 19 77
e-mail: evelinea@usa.net

Such a soft, quiet woman! She's an art teacher — and definitely an artist — who loves her modern white-walled, white-curtained house under the wooded hillside and fills it elegantly with antiques large and small (she confesses to being a hoarder), as well as her own works in paint and wool. A peaceful feel, a caring hostess who gives you as much time as she has despite her early-morning exits. The big room (with en suite bathroom) is superb; the smaller one excellent value with its own bathroom across the landing. Very convenient for Paris.

Rooms: 2 double (one large, one small), each with bath & wc.

Price: 280 or 380 Frs, including breakfast.

Meals: 80 Frs, including wine & coffee.

Open: All year.

From Paris A13 onto A12 towards St Quentin en Yvelines for 6km then exit on N12 towards Dreux. Exit to Plaisir CENTRE; 1st exit off roundabout towards Plaisir Les Gâtines, 1st left for 400m; right into Domaine des Gâtines: consult roadside plan.

Map No: 6   MM 237-16

Mme Hélène CASTELNAU
7 rue Gustave Courbet
Domaine des Gâtines
78370 Plaisir
Yvelines
Tel: (0)1 30 54 05 15

Amazing! Goats, dogs, exotic fowl and stone boars outside, a collector's paradise and a housemaid's hell inside. This great traveller has amassed carvings and incrustations, inlays and filigrees in brass, lacquer and wood both rough and smooth, large and small, and filled his family mansion. All is exuberance and love of life and beautiful things. He is also very good company. On weekdays his delightful polyglot assistant Taïeb will take excellent care of you. There is also a loo/library and a 3-legged cat.

Rooms: 2 double with own shower & wc; 1 triple, 1 double, sharing bath & wc; 1 triple, 1 suite with bath & wc.

Price: 290-350 Frs for two, including breakfast.

Meals: Three restaurants in village.

Open: All year.

Hazeville is an exceptional experience: from your artist host to his highly aristocratic and refined home (built in 1560); from your rather exotic rooms in the (even older) pigeon-tower to the great farmyard where today the stables house hi-tech artisans rather than cart horses. You will be flooded with history and art, given a generous breakfast on hand-painted china (to match the wall covering) and carefully directed to all the secret treasures of the Vexin. Well-behaved children over 7 welcome.

Rooms: 1 double & 1 twin, both with bath, shower & wc.

Price: 620 Frs for two, including breakfast.

Meals: Wide choice within 5-10km.

Open: Weekends and school holidays.

From N10 north of Rambouillet take D937 then D936 towards Poigny-la-Forêt for 5km. Left on D107 to Poigny. Left up road by church; house is on right.

Map No: 6   MM 237-28

François LE BRET
2 rue de l'Église
78125 Poigny-la-Forêt
Yvelines
Tel: (0)1 34 84 73 42
Fax: (0)1 34 84 74 38

From Rouen, N14 towards Paris. 20km before Pontoise, at Magny-en-Vexin, right onto D983 to Arthies. Left onto D81, through Enfer; château on left.

Map No: 6   MM 237-16

Guy & Monique DENECK
Château d'Hazeville
95420 Wy-dit-Joli-Village
Val-d'Oise
Tel: (0)1 34 67 06 17
Fax: (0)1 34 67 17 82

Flowers everywhere, dried, cut and in the garden... Madame loves gardening. The guestroom is really a suite of two bedrooms and a private *salon* that looks out onto the neatly-tended garden and enormous old cherry tree. Beds and bedding are Ikea-new, there's a lovely old dresser, lots of books (in French) about the region, and a functional shower room. Photos of grandchildren everywhere, and paintings by Philippe's great-uncle. A quiet home and kind hosts, just half an hour from Paris by train. Perfect for a family stopover.

Rooms: 1 double, 1 twin communicating & sharing shower & wc.

Price: 270 Frs for two, including breakfast. Extra person 60 Frs.

Meals: Restaurant 500m.

Open: All year.

South on A16 from Beauvais; pass junction 11 & take slip to N184 dir. Cergy-Pontoise 16km then A15 dir. Rouen. Leave shortly at exit 10; follow signs for Marines; at first lights right for Ennery; 3rd right into village then left on arrival.

Map No: 6   MM 237-17

Claude & Philippe DUBOSCQ
3 rue Georges Lourdel
95300 Ennery
Val d'Oise
Tel: (0)1 30 38 18 72

The end of the road offers a breathtaking view of Notre Dame, buttresses flying in the setting sun. In this air, your skin absorbs the history of Paris, France, Europe through its pores. A few yards along, a great 17th-century doorway opens onto more ancient stones under the utterly Parisian porch. Old stone stairs bring you to a high-ceilinged, family-loved, unpretentious but ancient duplex flat where guests have a breakfast space beside the spiral staircase and a mezzanined, fireplaced room with high windows onto an unexpected green garden — a huge privilege in Paris. Madame is polyglot, active in the city and quietly welcoming.

Rooms: 1 room for 2-4 with bath & wc.

Price: 380 Frs for two, including breakfast.

Meals: Many restaurants nearby.

Open: All year.

Metro: Maubert-Mutualité; RER/Metro: St Michel-Notre Dame. Underground car park: 'Lagrange'.

Map No: 6

Mme Brigitte CHATIGNOUX
Notre Dame/Saint Michel district
75005 Paris
Tel: (0)1 43 25 27 20

From the table you can survey half the rooftops and domes of Paris. The compact living room is attractive with its deep sofas, upright piano and Madame's collection of decorative pill-boxes — altogether a clutter of curiosities that you will enjoy investigating. She likes treating her guests 'properly' and is happy to serve breakfast on fine linen in silver coffee pots. This is the trendy Mosque quarter (do drop into the Mosque tea-room one afternoon), with the colourful, animated Rue Mouffetard and the quieter Jardin des Plantes, once the Paris zoo, now the home of the fantastic Natural History Museum. Madame is quiet, a little shy, and most helpful. She also has a self-contained one-room apartment to let near Place de la République.

Rooms: 1 triple with own shower; 1 double sharing bathroom; both sharing wc.

Price: 270/300 or 350/380Frs for two, including breakfast.

Meals: This is Paris!

Open: All year.

Metro Austerlitz. Car park Rue Censier. 8th floor, lift.

Map No: 6

Madame Lélia COHEN-SCALI
Mouffetard district
75005 Paris
Tel: (0)1 43 36 51 62

A typical little Paris flat in a proudly moulded and bracketed 1900s building in a refreshingly popular yet residential area far from the massed bands of tourists — the famous Mount of Mars or Martyrs (Montmartre) is within walking distance but not so close that you feel harassed by the portraitists waving paint-brushes and sticks of charcoal. The floorboards and ceiling plasterwork are original, as is the wooden fireplace; the décor is as young and lively as Françoise and Hervé themselves: theatrical bits and pieces, ivy growing all over your balcony, a castle scene on the duvet. They really look forward to their foreign guests and are happy to share their love of Paris, French food and good wine with you. You will like their spontaneity, sense of fun — and you may meet their fluffy rabbit, small-scale like the rest.

Rooms: 1 double sharing shower & wc.

Price: 300 Frs, including breakfast.

Meals: Plenty of choice nearby.

Open: All year.

Metro Guy Moquet or Lamarck-Caulaincourt.

Map No: 6

Françoise & Hervé
Rue Coysevox
Montmartre district
75018 Paris
Tel: (0)1 44 85 07 19

Here are intelligence, sobriety and genuine style in one of the smartest of Left Bank streets. You enter a splendid vaulted porch designed in 1830 to take aristocrats' carriages, then mount a magnificent flight of stone steps to the lift. Madame welcomes you calmly into her vast, parquet-floored, high-windowed, sober-tinted apartment — nothing flashy, neither modern gadgets nor antique knick-knacks, just a few good pieces, space and light. Beyond the dining-room, your smaller bedroom gives onto the big, silent, arcaded courtyard. Your multilingual hosts have lived all over the world, have deep knowledge of things of beauty and Monsieur, a retired engineer, still spends his days studying or teaching. Madame is as decided, stylish and genuine as her surroundings and enjoys, in equal parts, renovating her old mill near Chartres and the company of like-minded visitors — she is worth getting to know.

Rooms: 1 twin with bath & wc.

Price: 460 Frs for two, including breakfast.

Meals: Choice within 5 minutes walk; St Germain des Prés is 10 minutes away.

Open: All year.

Metro: Solférino. Car park: Invalides. 3rd floor : lift from street level.

Map No: 6

Mme MARCHAL
National Assembly/Invalides district
75007 Paris
Tel: (0)1 47 05 70 21
or (0)2 37 23 38 19

A narrow old building on a wide tree-lined boulevard where colourful street markets are held: here is a touch of pure Paris. The small flat's delightfully cluttered living-room is 1800s with anachronistic timbers. There are books against every available wall, paintings and objects above and on top of them — from Africa, the Far East, America, they illustrate your hosts' eclectic tastes. Your room is quiet and snug over the inner courtyard. Cynthia is an intelligent, cosmopolitan American, Christian is quintessentially French and deeply informed by a professional life which includes exporting pedigree cattle and touring private châteaux in south-west France. He deals, expertly, in wine, is planning to write historical books and songs, and can guide you through the secret life of night-time Paris. Fun and fascinating.

Rooms: 1 double/twin with bath, shower & wc.

Price: 380 Frs for two, including breakfast.

Meals: Occasionally by arrangement. Varying prices.

Open: All year.

Metro: Edgar Quinet. Many bus lines. Ask owners about private parking.

Map No: 6

Christian & Cynthia de
MONBRISON
Montparnasse district.
75014 Paris
Tel: (0)1 45 38 68 72
Fax: (0)1 45 38 68 72

In a back street off one of the lively shopping districts near the river you find this 17th-century Parisian building and there, behind gently curved double doors, is a city home of charm and elegance. Perceptively, the owners managed to salvage some of the ancient timbers from the renovator's clean sweep and also live happily with one deliriously sloping wrought-iron balustrade (decorative but not structural...). It is warm, white-walled, antique-furnished and not at all imposing, with interesting artwork on the walls. Madame paints, modestly — some of the works are hers — and greatly enjoys her guests. Monsieur is a university professor of literature. Other inmates are plenty of plants and a gentle old cat. The compact guest quarters are nicely private at the end of the corridor — good storage space, pretty quilts, lots of light.

Rooms: 1 twin with hip-bath/shower & wc.

Price: 380 Frs for two, including breakfast.

Meals: Both banks of the Seine beckon.

Open: All year except school holidays.

Metro: Châtelet or Pont-Neuf. Car park: 'Conforama', via Rue du Pont Neuf then Rue Boucher. 3rd floor, lift.

Map No: 6

Mme Mona PIERROT
Châtelet district
75001 Paris
Tel: (0)1 42 36 50 65

It is a privilege to sit in one of Nadine's deep soft chairs in this elegantly high-ceilinged 17th-century timber-frame Paris flat — with those lovely windows onto the pedestrians-only street — and talk about Paris, art and exotic places with her. She is a lively, intelligent, busy Parisienne, juggling expertly with family, friends, profession and guests — you will be drawn into the circle if you stay a while. Her activities as wildlife photographer, writer and purveyor (for friends) of native art by farflung tribes or people nearer to home make for a fascinating and changing display on walls and shelves. You will sleep in complete quiet in the big guestroom whose tall windows give onto the 'turreted' courtyard and, after breakfast in the dining area of the big room, step out into the heart of Paris each morning.

Rooms: 1 double with shower & wc.

Price: 470 Frs for two, including breakfast.

Meals: Paris at your feet.

Open: All year except August.

Metro: Hôtel de Ville or Châtelet. Underground car park "Châtelet". Gentle stairs to 2nd floor.

Map No: 6

Nadine SAUNIER
Châtelet district
75004 Paris
Tel: (0)1 48 87 70 15
Fax: (0)1 48 87 70 15

In a narrow street in the historic centre of lovely old Rouen, just 100m from the Cathedral, stands the C17 family home of Philippe Aunay. He enjoys, in equal measure, sharing, in English, German or Norman, with wry, dry humour, the history of Rouen and the informal comfort of his beautiful (quiet) townhouse. It is a treasure-trove of curios, with huge beams, big windows genuine Norman antiques. Bathrooms are crisply modern. Breakfast is generous and your reception cheerful. Car park a short walk from house.

Rooms: 2 double, 1 twin, with bathrooms (can be used as suite with kitchen facilities); 1 single, sharing a bathroom.

Price: 275 Frs for two, incl. breakfast.

Meals: Vast choice on the spot.

Open: All year.

On cathedral-side embankment: at Théâtre des Arts, take rue Jeanne d'Arc; Rue aux Ours is 2nd on right but NO PARKING. Leave car in Bourse or Pucelle car park, near house, and walk.

Map No: 5   MM 231-23

Philippe AUNAY-STANGUENNEC
45 rue aux Ours
76000 Rouen
Seine-Maritime
Tel: (0)2 35 70 99 68

Normandy

The stern black front door of this solid townhouse hides a light, stylish interior with views across the old town to the spires of Rouen Cathedral. Dominique, a keen and cultured Egyptologist, has a flair for refined decoration — see her paintings, coverings and country furniture. There are rugs on the wooden floor in the sitting-room and French windows lead to a balcony and the garden. A lovely setting for an unhurried feast at her flower-decked breakfast table and a chance to quiz her (her English is excellent) about her latest digs in Egypt.

Rooms: 1 double with bath & wc; 2 double, each with bath, sharing wc.

Price: 260-300 Frs for two, including breakfast.

Meals: 100 Frs, including wine (book ahead).

Open: All year except Oct & Nov.

An area of natural and historical delights: the Forest of Eu, lapping up to the edge of the farm, is 9300 hectares of green space to explore and the Château of Eu is where Louis Philippe and Queen Victoria begat the Entente Cordiale. But come to La Marette for the uncanny silence at night, the birdsong at dawn, and your hosts' radiant smiles at all times. They want you to enjoy the house as it was when their daughters were here: a family atmosphere, the occasional shared shower, masses of human warmth, not an ounce of hotellishness.

Rooms: 1 suite with bath & wc; 1 suite & 1 double, each with wc, sharing shower.

Price: 200-280 Frs for two, including breakfast. Extra bed 100 Frs.

Meals: Choice 4/10/12km. Self-catering.

Open: All year.

On arriving in Rouen, follow signs to Gare SNCF (railway station); take Rue Rochefoucault immediately to right of station; left into Rue des Champs des Oiseaux, across 2 sets of lights, straight across into Rue Vigné then left at fork into Rue Hénault. Black door on left.

Map No: 5   MM 231-23

Mme Dominique GOGNY
22 rue Hénault
76130 Mont-Saint-Aignan
Seine-Maritime
Tel: (0)2 35 70 26 95
Fax: (0)2 35 52 03 52

From A28 exit Blangy-sur-Bresle dir. Le Tréport to Gamaches. There left at lights on D14 to Guerville. There follow signs to Melleville. Just before leaving village, right onto Route de la Marette.

Map No: 6   MM 231-12

Etienne & Nelly GARÇONNET
La Marette
Route de la Marette
76260 Melleville
Seine-Maritime
Tel: (0)2 35 50 81 65
Fax: (0)2 35 50 81 65

You'd never know this venerable Norman farmhouse was built by Monsieur himself: he used old materials, original designs, and was as careful as they both are about getting things right. It has a genuinely good feel to it. Inside there are old beams, lovely furniture (admire the fine *comtoise* clock), spotless guestrooms with good bathrooms and a low, beamed, big-tabled room for breakfast. Then you can take the path hewn out of the cliff face down to the wild rugged beaches, in superb contrast to the domestic cosiness you have just left.

Rooms: 2 double, 1 twin, each with bath or shower & wc.

Price: 300 Frs for two, including breakfast.

Meals: Choice in Fécamp, 3km.

Open: All year except 3 weeks in August.

Gîtes for 4 people

The parrot arrived 5 years ago... and stayed. If you're a golfer you may do the same: you are bang next to the 3rd green. Green is the dominant colour inside, too, thanks not least to the exotic palms. The light, modern house is creature-comfortable and copes well with the transition between 80s daring and 90s pleasing. There is a TV in each room and the sitting area is really the owners' territory, but they are extremely nice people and Madame can give you a yoga lesson. The rooms are comfortable, even a bit plush.

Rooms: 2 twin, 1 double, each with bath or shower & wc.

Price: 280-320 Frs for two, including breakfast.

Meals: Full choice in Dieppe.

Open: All year.

Leave Fécamp by D925; left at signpost to Senneville. In village take bumpy road towards the sea; house is first on left.

Map No: 5   MM 231-8

M & Mme LETHUILLIER
Val de la Mer
76400 Senneville-sur-Fécamp
Seine-Maritime
Tel: (0)2 35 28 41 93

From Dieppe, D75 ('Route du Littoral') W along coast towards Pourville. Once you reach golf course, 1st left, 3rd house on right (signposted).

Map No: 5   MM 231-11

Alain & Danièle NOËL
24 chemin du Golf
76200 Dieppe
Seine-Maritime
Tel: (0)2 35 84 40 37
Fax: (0)2 35 84 32 51

Madame loves to talk (in French) and has a winning smile. Her house is 300 years old; the worn old stones, bricks and flints (less worn!) bear witness to its age as does the fine timberwork inside. Otherwise it has been fairly deeply modernised but the long lace-clothed breakfast table before the log fire (in winter) is most welcoming. The pleasant rooms are good if unremarkable and the only sounds are the occasional lowing of the herd and the breeze blowing in the trees.

Rooms: 1 triple with bath & wc; 1 double with shower & wc; 2 double sharing shower & wc.

Price: 210 Frs for two, including breakfast.

Meals: Auberge 1km.

Open: All year.

Gîtes for 10 people

Madame's welcome is terrific — nothing is too much trouble and her jams are memorable. The garden, her great love, is a wonder almost all year round, an oasis in the town (the road can be noisy but it's all right at night). Her guestrooms are cosy and tempting, all different, reflecting the history of the old house and her collecting flair. There is a dayroom for guests but breakfast is in the pretty family dining-room. Excellent value and a good base for exploring the churches and villages that fill this area.

Rooms: 3 triple, 1 double, each with shower & wc.

Price: 260 Frs for two, including breakfast.

Meals: In village or self-catering.

Open: All year.

From Dieppe N27 towards Rouen for 29km then right on N29 through Yerville & towards Yvetot for 4.5km. Left on D20 to Motteville. Right to Flamanville. In village, Rue Verte is road behind church. Farm is 300m along on left; signposted.

Map No: 5   MM 231-22

Yves & Béatrice QUEVILLY BARET
La Ferme de la Rue Verte
76970 Flamanville
Seine-Maritime
Tel: (0)2 35 96 81 27

From Rouen, D982 towards Le Havre. After passing under Pont de Brotonne, in Caudebec, right onto rue de la République (D131) towards Yvetot; No 68 is 500m on the right.

Map No: 5   MM 231-21

Christiane VILLAMAUX
68 rue de la République
76490 Caudebec-en-Caux
Seine-Maritime
Tel: (0)2 35 96 10 15
Fax: (0)2 35 96 75 25

Close to perfection... not surprising given Janine's bubbling enthusiasm and spritely energy. She is, nevertheless, 'classic' in her dress and appearance and creates a very special breakfast with pewter service and folded napkins. She is deeply intolerant of dust and dirt, so the immensely comfortable bedrooms might even be cleaner than your own. The downstairs sitting-room is vast, about 80m², the staircase is beautifully sculpted, the garden goes down to the river and you are halfway between Giverny and Rouen.

Rooms: 1 double/twin, 1 suite for five, each with bath & wc.

Price: 250-270 Frs for two, including breakfast.

Meals: In village or 6km away.

Open: All year.

Gîtes for 4 people

Exquisite!... and without a whiff of pretension. The Brunets, as delightful as their house, have the lightness of touch to combine the fresh best of modern French taste with an eye for authenticity — in a brand new house. There are recycled château windows, light flooding in from both sides of a classical narrow *maison de campagne*, eye-catching stretches of pine-floored corridor, handsome rugs, a brave mix of old and modern furniture, massive comfort. Gorgeous.

Rooms: 3 twin, 2 double, each with bath or shower & wc.

Price: 450-650 Frs for two, including breakfast.

Meals: In village or 5km.

Open: April to Nov (on reservation in winter).

Gîtes for 8 people

From Evreux, D155 north. 300m after Les Faulx hamlet, right for Heudreville. House in cul-de-sac opposite church.

Map No: 5   MM 231-35

Mme Janine BOURGEOIS
La Ferme
4 rue de l'Ancienne Poste
27400 Heudreville-sur-Eure
Eure
Tel: (0)2 32 50 20 69
Fax: (0)2 32 50 20 69

From A13 exit 14 dir. Vernon/Giverny. Entering Giverny left on Rue Claude Monet. After church, left on Rue Blanche Hoshedé Monet for 1.2km. Left on white arrow then immediately right on track for 800m then left to 'La Réserve'.

Map No: 6   MM 231-36

Didier & Marie Lorraine BRUNET
La Réserve
27620 Giverny
Eure-et-Loire
Tel: (0)2 32 21 99 09
Fax: (0)2 32 21 99 09
e-mail: http//www.giverny.org/hotels/brunet

A pretty little mansion whose small rooms were thrown open to give more light and space but have kept their original ceiling mouldings. The garden is green and flowery, the furnishings eminently comfortable with lots of frilly lamps and ornaments. You climb a steepish staircase to the cosy, welcoming guestrooms (good bathrooms). Madame is delightful. She and her husband are deeply involved in the restoration and running of an ancient water mill, *Le Moulin Amour*. It works and its flour is excellent! Pets welcome but not in bedrooms.

Rooms: One 3-room family suite for 4/5; 1 double; both with bath & wc.

Price: 210 Frs for two; 300 Frs suite for 4, including breakfast.

Meals: Choice 3-7km.

Open: All year.

Their generosity is genuine, their welcome a model for all, their rooms full of fun and individuality, their renovation near-perfect with ancient wonders brought back to the light. As for the food... French Régis makes the cheese and grows the veg and English Nicky is a Cordon Bleu cook. They are young, charming, work like beavers, are always available for guests and really seem to enjoy every minute. Great for children: ride the tractor with Régis, feed his lambs and rabbits. Paradise in an ideal base for exploring Normandy.

Rooms: 2 double, 1 twin, 1 triple, 1 quadruple, all with bath or shower & wc.

Price: 280 Frs for two, including breakfast.

Meals: 120 Frs, including wine & coffee.

Open: All year.

From Le Neubourg D80 towards La Haye du Theil. After La Pyle 2nd left on D631 to Saint-Meslin (& St Nicolas). House is first on right.

Map No: 5   MM 231-34

STOP PRESS!
House sold May 1998

From A13, Le Havre exit, onto D139 towards Pont Audemer. In Fourmetot, left towards Corneville. Farm is 1km from turning on left.

Map No: 5   MM 231-21

Régis & Nicky DUSSARTRE
L'Aufragère
La Croisée
27500 Fourmetot
Eure
Tel: (0)2 32 56 91 92
Fax: (0)2 32 57 75 34

NORMANDY

Just one loo between three bedrooms but we think one loo is a small price to pay for being in such a remarkable old house (rebuilt from nought in the 50s!) — an important site in the Hundred Years War. The rickety wooden bridge across the moat is a good introduction, followed by the affable old goat at the door. Madame has a touch of charming eccentricity and is an excellent hostess. The service is elegant: silver teapot, fruit juice in crystal glasses at breakfast, tea in the afternoon — and the rooms are perfect.

Rooms: 2 double, 1 twin, all with bath or shower; sharing wc.

Price: 350 Frs for two, including breakfast.

Meals: 100 Frs, including wine & coffee.

Open: March to December.

A long drive leads past carefully-tended flowerbeds up to the old *pressoir*, built during the French Revolution and now restored by this exceptional couple — he a gentle ex-sailor who can tell a tale or two, she quiet and engaging. Bedrooms were a labour of love for her — fabrics and papers carefully chosen, flowers cut and dried to match, old trunks and carved *armoires* from family treasure-store. Breakfast on homemade cake to classical music, dine on local specialities with flowers on the table. One of our favourite new discoveries.

Rooms: 2 double, each with shower & wc.

Price: 250 Frs for two, including breakfast.

Meals: 120 Frs, including wine (book ahead).

Open: All year.

From Breteuil, D141 towards Rugles; through forest. At Bémécourt, take left turn; 300m after the traffic lights, right into Allée du Vieux Château.

Map No: 5   MM 231-34

Mme Maryvonne LALLEMAND-LEGRAS
Le Vieux Château
27160 Bémécourt
Eure
Tel: (0)2 32 29 90 47

From Le Havre dir. Paris & Rouen; over Pont de Tancarville on A131 then right on D810 to Pont-Audemer; then D87 through St Germain Village; continue D87 then right into Tricqueville on CV19; signposted.

Map No: 5   MM 231-20

Gaston & Michelle LE PLEUX
La Clé des Champs
27500 Tricqueville
Eure
Tel: (0)2 32 41 37 99

With woods as a backdrop, this delicious family house faces a pastoral meadow and lake and has a manorial double staircase beneath a not-quite manorial elevation: the C18 builder had to sacrifice a floor when he ran out of money! Inside, there are panels, mouldings, parquet floors, flowers all over; Madame is active with gardening, organising seminars (not when B&B guests are here) and caring for two children. The large panelled bedrooms have good beds, old wardrobes and windows onto the gentle world outside. Elegant and restful.

Rooms: 1 quadruple with bath & wc; 1 triple with shower & wc.

Price: 250 or 300 Frs for two, including breakfast.

Meals: Occasionally, 90 Frs, including wine.

Open: All year.

From A13 exit Maison Brulé on N138 towards Bourgthéroulde & Brionne. 8km after Bourgthéroulde left on D83 to Le Gros Theil; on entering village sharp right onto D92 & follow signs for 2km.

Map No: 5   MM 231-22

Béatrice & Patrice NOËL-WINDSOR
Manoir d'Hermos
27800 Saint-Eloi-de-Fourques
Eure
Tel: (0)2 32 35 51 32
Fax: (0)2 32 35 51 32

Madame, tall, sophisticated and immaculate, did all the wallpapering herself and is naturally relaxed and welcoming. She finds it normal that everyone sit at the same big table in the ochre and scarlet breakfast room. There is a family-friendly common room with billiards, table tennis, picnic table, refrigerator. Bedrooms are big and beautifully decorated (*merci Madame!*); *La Jaune* has superb views. No finery, a touch of faded grandeur and all-pervasive warmth characterise this splendid house of friendship.

Rooms: 2 family rooms, 1 double, 1 twin, each with bath or shower shower & wc.

Price: 270 Frs for two, including breakfast.

Meals: Choice in Orbec, 6km.

Open: All year.

From Lisieux, D519 towards Orbec. At Orbiquet, left onto D2 (Calvados)/ D145 (Eure). Go through St Germain-la-Campagne; château on left as you leave village.

Map No: 5   MM 231-32

Bruno & Laurence de PRÉAUMONT
Château du Grand Bus
Saint-Germain-la-Campagne
27230 Thiberville
Eure
Tel: (0)2 32 44 71 14
Fax: (0)2 32 46 45 81

The clean, cool river Epte, which Monet diverted at nearby Giverny for his famous Nympheas, runs at the bottom of the pretty garden. The house is beautifully furnished with family antiques and Madame willingly shares her extensive knowledge of all things Norman (including food); she can also organise painting courses for you. Rooms are stylish and quiet; one has an Art Deco brass bed designed by *Grandpère*. The attic twin is up steep stairs and under sloping ceilings.

Rooms: 2 double, each with shower or bath & wc; 1 twin for young people, with shared bathroom.

Price: 330 Frs for two, including breakfast.

Meals: 130 Frs, including wine & coffee.

Open: 15 March to 15 December.

The listed C15 farmhouse, the pond with black and white swans, the perfect peace, the furniture (each item carefully chosen, some tenderly hand-painted) and, *enfin*, an exceptional hostess who is calm and generous with her time and attention, all make this place special. She cooks a good Norman meal (not always eaten *en famille*) with home-grown organic ingredients and house cider, and your quarters are independent of the house. They also sell good-value wine, should you want to stock up on the way home.

Rooms: 3 double, 2 twin, each with shower & wc.

Price: 250 Frs for two, including breakfast.

Meals: 90 Frs, including aperitif & homemade cider.

Open: All year.

From Dieppe, D915 to Gisors. Cross Gisors then D181 towards Vernon. In Dangu, rue du Gué is beside the river Epte. Look for house with green shutters.

Map No: 6   MM 237-3

Nicole de SAINT PÈRE
Les Ombelles
4 rue du Gué
27720 Dangu
Eure
Tel: (0)2 32 55 04 95
Fax: (0)2 32 55 59 87
e-mail: vextour@com.aol.fr

From Rouen, N15 towards Paris. At Gaillon (about 40km), right on D10 towards La-Croix-St-Leufroy. After about 7km, enter La Boissaye and follow signs for Chambres d'Hôtes.

Map No: 6   MM 231-35

Clotilde & Gérard SÉNÉCAL
Manoir de la Boissière
Hameau la Boissaye
27490 La-Croix-St-Leufroy
Eure
Tel: (0)2 32 67 70 85
Fax: (0)2 32 67 03 18

This Franco-Spanish couple lived in Latin America for over 20 years before retiring to their small manor house in Normandy — spot the mementoes. Monsieur prides himself on having immaculately clean bathrooms — one English guest said she would happily sleep in one! The bedrooms are decorated with good furniture, dried flowers and prints, giving an atmosphere of solid comfort. Enjoy fresh fruit juice and homemade jams over breakfast sitting at the huge olive-wood breakfast table and find time to visit the 11th-century chapel in the village.

Rooms: 1 family room for 4 with bath & wc, 1 double with shower & wc.

Price: 250 Frs for two, including breakfast. Extra bed 50 Frs.

Meals: Auberges 5km.

Open: All year.

They somehow keep going with the farm, although they long for a younger farmer to take over. Any takers? We are delighted to have the Bourgaults in the book for there is something quintessentially *chambre d'hôte* about them and their house. It is unaffected, authentic, low-ceilinged and comfortable. The rooms have a very personal mix of old and new furniture... another traditional B&B touch. Madame bubbles with energy, loves children and gives you the sort of welcome that makes you glow.

Rooms: 1 double, 1 triple, 1 quadruple room, all with bath or shower & wc.

Price: 230-250 Frs for two, including breakfast.

Meals: Choice within 3km.

Open: All year.

From A13 exit 17 for Gaillon then W towards Evreux on D316 through Autheuil, St Vigor & up hill then right for Reuilly. House on road, 200m past town hall (Mairie) on right.

Map No: 5   MM 231-35

Jean-Pierre & Amaia TREVISANI
Clair Matin
19 rue de l'Eglise
27930 Reuilly
Eure
Tel: (0)2 32 34 71 47
Fax: (0)2 32 34 97 64
e-mail: clair-matin@compuserve.com

From Rouen, N138 towards Alençon, through Bernay to Monnai. There, right onto D12; after 2km, follow signs to Chambres d'Hôtes.

Map No: 5   MM 231-32

Gérard & Emilienne BOURGAULT
Les Roches
61470 Le Sap
Orne
Tel: (0)2 33 39 47 39

Utter peace among the cattle-dotted Norman pastures — one woman, her horses, her dog, her cats in a low-lying farmhouse, beautifully rebuilt "from a pile of stones", where old and new mix easily. Barbara calls it "my corner of paradise" and her delight is contagious. The lovely sloping garden is all her own work too. The pastel guestrooms, two upstairs, one with garden access on the ground floor, are attractive and have brand new bathrooms. Come by horse, or walk. Beautiful country and a sociable, interesting woman to welcome you.

Rooms: 2 twin, 1 double, each with bath or shower & wc.

Price: 250 Frs for two, including breakfast.

Meals: 75 Frs, including wine & coffee.

Open: All year.

Real gourmet, organic, vegetarian food is served and vegans are catered for here — rare in the depths of rural France. "We aren't vegetarians but might well convert with this sort of fare," said one reader. The Butlers belong here now, are most knowledgeable about local lore and full of enthusiasm for their project. In the 'guest house', you find sitting and reading rooms (books galore), crawling space for toddlers, bedrooms of character; there's a big garden and mediæval Ticheville is within walking distance. Bayeux and Camembert are driveable.

Rooms: 4 double, sharing 2 showers & 3 wcs. (By spring 1999: 5 rooms, each with shower & wc.)

Price: 260 Frs for two, including breakfast.

Meals: 105 Frs excellent vegetarian meal, excl. (organic) wine (30 Frs). One course 40 Frs.

Open: Easter to October.

From Courtomer, past Mairie then right after last building towards Tellières. 2km from turning, left at crossroads towards Le Marnis.

Map No: 5   MM 231-44

Barbara GOFF
Le Marnis
Tellières-le-Plessis
61390 Courtomer
Orne
Tel: (0)2 33 27 47 55
Fax: (0)2 33 27 29 55

D579 from Lisieux to Vimoutiers then D979 towards Alençon. 5km on, left on D12 towards l'Aigle. In Ticheville: house signposted on left.

Map No: 5   MM 231-32

Jill & Colin KIRK
La Maison du Vert
Le Bourg
61120 Ticheville
Orne
Tel: (0)2 33 36 95 84
Fax: (0)2 33 39 37 78
e-mail: colin.kirk@wanadoo.fr

Although guestrooms are in a converted outbuilding you are unhesitatingly received into a warm and lively family here — the Laignels have 6 children and 8 grandchildren so far — and it feels GOOD. The upstairs room is bigger and lighter, the ground-floor room has a little private garden; both have beams, old wardrobes and mini-kitchens. Meals are taken at the family table, there are fresh flowers everywhere and your hosts have a genuine sense of country hospitality.

Rooms: 1 triple, 1 double, each with shower, wc & mini-kitchen; 1 double sharing shower & wc.

Price: 200 Frs for two, including breakfast.

Meals: 80 Frs, including cider & coffee (by arrangement).

Open: All year.

Gîtes for 6 people

In this good-looking little château that is only one room thick, you enjoy the privilege of being Madame's sole guests. A most interesting old lady — they both travel a lot — she may seem serious, even preoccupied, at first, but she has the loveliest smile. Your room mixes battered school desk with carved *armoire*, marble fireplace with Indian throw; by no means smart (least of all the bedclothes), it is supremely peaceful. You breakfast in the kitchen where superb roof timbers carry an old oil lamp and all is country simplicity.

Rooms: 1 double with bathroom.

Price: 280 Frs for two, including breakfast.

Meals: Not available.

Open: All year.

From Argentan N158 towards Caen. After sign for Moulin-sur-Orne, take next left. House 800m on left; signposted. (3.5km from Argentan.)

Map No: 5   MM 231-31

Janine & Rémy LAIGNEL
Le Mesnil
61200 Occagnes
Orne
Tel: (0)2 33 67 11 12

From Argentan, N26 towards Paris; D113 left towards Fel, then second small road on left after sign for Crennes village.

Map No: 5   MM 231-43

M & Mme LE BOUTEILLER
Château de Crennes
Urou-et-Crennes
61200 Crennes
Orne
Tel: (0)2 33 36 22 11

A fascinating house! An ancestor fled to Scotland in 1789 and returned an Adam fan, hence the fake-marble trompe l'œil and Wedgwood-moulded staircase. A delightful, friendly couple welcome you: she organises chamber music in their big, log-fired drawing-room; he makes top-class Camembert and mows his acres on Sundays. The elegant bedrooms have antiques, books, ancestral portraits, much soft comfort and a loo in a tower. Good walks start 2km away. Eat with the family and belong briefly to this wonderful world.

Rooms: 1 twin & 2 double, each with bath & wc.

Price: 500 (smaller double) or 600 Frs for two, including breakfast.

Meals: 220 Frs, including aperitif, wine, coffee, digestif (book ahead).

Open: All year (by arrangement Dec to end March).

From Verneuil-sur-Avre, N12 SW to Carrefour Ste Anne (24km). Left on D918 towards Longny-au-Perche for 4.5km; left on D289 towards Moulicent. House 800m on right.

Map No: 5   MM 231-45

Jacques & Pascale de LONGCAMP
La Grande Noë
61290 Moulicent
Orne
Tel: (0)2 33 73 63 30
Fax: (0)2 33 83 62 92

These are comfortable, human, sensitive people who like contact and share their quiet sense of humour with each other, with guests and with their children. Guestrooms have cane or brass bedsteads and fresh flowers. Madame spoils you at breakfast and dinner with local honey and Camembert, poultry and rabbit from their own farmyard. Meals are normally taken with the family — most convivial despite limited English. The sitting-room, playroom and kitchen facilities are a bonus.

Rooms: 2 double, each with shower sharing wc; 1 triple, 1 quadruple, each with shower & wc.

Price: 200 Frs for two, including breakfast.

Meals: 90 Frs, including wine & coffee.

Open: All year.

From Argentan, N26 towards L'Aigle and Paris. Left at Silli-en-Gouffern. At Ste Eugénie, last farm on left.

Map No: 5   MM 231-31

Pierre et Ghislaine MAURICE
La Grande Ferme
Sainte-Eugénie
61160 Aubry-en-Exmes
Orne
Tel: (0)2 33 36 82 36
Fax: (0)2 33 36 99 52

You buy into fun, a real unfussy family atmosphere and a most successful mix of things English and French in this converted manor-farm with its pigeon-tower and duck stream. Yours hosts have sheep, dairy cows, 300 apple trees (*Normandie oblige!*) and are thoroughly integrated, as are their two young daughters. Their guestrooms in the old camembert-making dairy are light, soberly furnished with touches of *fantaisie* and Diana's very decorative stencils. Breakfast is superb, dinner an occasion to remember.

Rooms: 1 triple, 2 double, each with bath or shower & wc. Extra beds available.

Price: 250-280 Frs for two, including breakfast.

Meals: 120 Frs, including wine & coffee.

Open: All year.

The Achards are hard-working farmers with a deep knowledge of their milieu — and clear opinions about how to build Europe for all, including farmers, without conflict. They have renovated the old bread oven: two bakings a week produce delicious old-style loaves for breakfast (and sale to discerning bread shops). Madame is as bright as a button, Monsieur more contemplative. Both are down-to-earth, offering simple country rooms (some noisy plumbing!), basic family meals and no frills. It is utterly unpretentious and most relaxing.

Rooms: 2 double, each with shower & basin; 1 twin with basin; all sharing wc.

Price: 200 Frs for two, including breakfast.

Meals: 90 Frs, including coffee.

Open: All year.

From Vimoutiers, D916 towards Argentan. Just outside Vimoutiers take left fork D16 signed Exmes then D26 signed Survie & Exmes.

Map No: 5   MM 231-43

Diana & Christopher
WORDSWORTH
Les Gains
Survie
61310 Exmes
Orne
Tel: (0)2 33 36 05 56
Fax: (0)2 33 36 03 65

From Caen, D9 towards Torigni-sur-Vire. At Caumont l'Eventé, D53 through Sept Vents. After village, take chestnut-lined drive on right and follow 'La Rivière' signs.

Map No: 5   MM 231-28

Geneviève & Raoul ACHARD
Ferme de la Rivière
14240 Caumont l'Eventé
Calvados
Tel: (0)2 31 68 70 44
Fax: (0)2 31 68 41 10

Through the wood and across the stream to the simplest, friendliest house you could imagine. The house is about a century old, the Ameys have that timeless quality of solid country dwellers and will wrap you in blue-eyed smiles. They and their welcome are all unstylish comfort and warmth. The furnishings are 'modern-old', the walls pastel, the curtains lace, the bathroom pink, the towels small. The dinners are reliably Norman and the wisteria blooms. Excellent value.

Rooms: 3 double, each with handbasin, sharing bathroom & separate wc.

Price: 180 Frs for two, including breakfast.

Meals: 80 Frs, including cider & coffee.

Open: All year.

Gîtes for 6 people

A converted mill (no-one knows how old it is) with a delightful bridge and terrace. The guest quarters are in the separate 'Hunting Lodge' where Madame's talented decoration marries things past and designer-colourful present and you have your own dining-room and kitchen. There are nuts to be gathered in the woods, beaches nearby, the stream for entertainment on the spot. Your hosts are sweet and love having families. "My kids spent hours by the shallow stream — not dangerous if they're supervised", said our reader.

Rooms: 1 double with shower & wc, 1 double & 1 twin sharing shower & wc.

Price: 250 Frs for two, including breakfast.

Meals: Restaurants 2-3km. Self-catering.

Open: All year.

From Caen N175 towards Cherbourg/Mt St Michel. Right on D83 towards Cheux for 1.5km then left to Tessel; signposted.

Map No: 5   MM 231-29

Paul & Éliane AMEY
La Londe
Tilly-sur-Seule
14250 Tessel
Calvados
Tel: (0)2 31 80 81 12

From Ouistreham D35 through Douvres & Tailleville. Cross D404. At roundabout entering Reviers, turn right. House on left (NOT first Chambres d'Hôtes).

Map No: 5   MM 231-17

Patricia & Jean-Michel BLANLOT
La Malposte
15 rue des Moulins
14470 Reviers
Calvados
Tel: (0)2 31 37 51 29

It's fun here if you can stand the pace! And don't mind church bells or a bit of traffic. Both Boullots are live wires, he with his horses, she with her artwork and refined food. They love having guests in their ancient house (parts are 12th-century), dining deliciously at the long table, reading in her oh-so-feminine study, playing chess or watching television in the Louis XVI *salon*. Bedrooms are fun too and, if some bits seem lightweight (bathrooms curtained off), remember this is a home not an hotel. Children over 3 welcome (lots of games).

Rooms: 1 quadruple, 2 double, 2 twin, each with bath or shower & wc.

Price: 320 Frs for two, including breakfast.

Meals: 140 Frs, incl. wine & coffee (Tue, Thur, Sat, Sun); pre-booked only.

Open: All year.

Gîtes for 7 people

A handsome square-set château where you can taste the "world's best cider" (dixit Monsieur), admire yourself in innumerable gilt-framed mirrors, luxuriate in a jacuzzi or bare your chest to a hydromassage shower, play the piano, watch pop-up telly, appreciate Monsieur's very dry sense of humour and Madame's superb cooking, and at last lie down in an antique, new-mattressed bed in one of the enormous bedrooms. The period ceilings, tapestries and furniture make this a real château experience; the people make it very human.

Rooms: 2 double and 2 suites, all with bath or shower & wc.

Price: 500 Frs for two, including breakfast.

Meals: 220 Frs, including aperitif, cider or wine, coffee & calvados.

Open: All year.

From Bayeux , D6 to Juvigny then D9 to Caumont-l'Eventé. Opposite Caumont church, D28 towards Balleroy. After 200m, look for Gîtes de France sign on right.

Map No: 5   MM 231-28

Claude & Jeanne-Paule BOULLOT
Le Relais
19 rue Thiers
14240 Caumont-l'Eventé
Calvados
Tel: (0)2 31 77 47 85

From Caen, N158 towards Falaise. At la Jalousie, right on D23; right on D235 just before Bretteville-sur-Laize; signposted.

Map No: 5   MM 231-30

Anne-Marie & Alain CANTEL
Château des Riffets
14680 Bretteville-sur-Laize
Calvados
Tel: (0)2 31 23 53 21
Fax: (0)2 31 23 75 14

Your military historian host is a fascinating talker with strong opinions — you may soon (perhaps despite yourself) share his passion for the dramas that took place here (he organises battlefield tours). This is a superbly-renovated manor, with lovely old courtyard buildings and a great arched gate in warm blond stone. The rooms are big, the furnishings comfortable, the conveniences modern. The yard is home to several tribes of animal, the orchard gives apples for cider, breakfast is French but with gentle Mrs Chilcott's English marmalade.

Rooms: 3 double, 1 twin, all with bath or shower & wc.

Price: 210 Frs for two, including breakfast.

Meals: Full choice Bayeux 1km.

Open: All year.

Gîtes for 8 people

From Bayeux by-pass take D572 towards St Lô. Take 2nd right and follow signs to arched gateway.

Map No: 5   MM 231-17

Lt-Col & Mrs CHILCOTT
Manoir au Pont Rouge
Saint-Loup-Hors
14400 Bayeux
Calvados
Tel: (0)2 31 22 39 09
Fax: (0)2 31 21 97 84
e-mail: chilcott@mail.cpod.fr

At the end of a bumpy unmade road through the woods you come upon an enchanting group of half-timbered buildings round a quadrangle, facing a picture postcard of hills, valleys and pastures. There are gîtes, B&B rooms and the owners' house (so LOTS of people!), all timbers and terracotta — and basic modern comforts among the old stones. Anja is German, Peter is long-exiled English, their baby son is himself. The place breathes their happiness — come and share it, that is what they hope for. Pets by arrangement.

Rooms: 1 triple, 2 double, 1 twin, each with shower & wc.

Price: 260 Frs for two, including breakfast.

Meals: Self-catering.

Open: All year.

Gîtes for 29 people

From Livarot D4 towards St Pierre-sur-Dives for 1km; left on D38 towards Heurtevent & Tortisambert; follow signs for 4km

Map No: 5   MM 231-31

Anja & Peter DAVIES
La Boursaie
Tortisambert
14140 Livarot
Calvados
Tel: (0)2 31 63 14 20
Fax: (0)2 31 63 14 28

The date is precisely 1462; Annick thinks the building (not all of an age) belonged to the Abbaye of Saint Pierre. The old beams are particularly impressive. It is a lovely, green place, in three acres of orchards overlooking the valley of the Auge. The garden is yours and there is fishing for coloured carp in the pond. Good rooms, a charming hostess and lots to do nearby. She often has to be out in the afternoon, by the way, so prefers you to arrive in the late afternoon if possible.

Rooms: 1 double with shower & wc; 2 triple, 1 family room, all with bath or shower, sharing 3 separate wc's.

Price: 250 Frs for two, including breakfast.

Meals: Choice nearby.

Open: All year.

Gites for 10 people

You may sleep like angels; this was a monks' dormitory in the 15th century. The Abbey is right there, floodlit at night, and the whole setting is exquisitely peaceful. The house is beguiling with its stone staircase, exposed beams, old columns and big fireplace. Monsieur, a recently retired breeder of cattle and horses, is quietly contemplative while Madame, a lively grandmother, is bright and attentive — a most pleasant pair of hosts though they don't dine with guests. It is a no-frills, and thoroughly good, place.

Rooms: 1 twin, 2 suites for three, each with shower or bath & wc.

Price: 220-230 Frs for two, including breakfast.

Meals: 85 Frs, including cider/wine & coffee.

Open: All year.

From Lisieux D511 towards St Pierre-sur-Dives. Just before St Pierre D4 left towards Livarot. After 1.5km, right to Berville; signposted.

Map No: 5   MM 231-31

Annick DUHAMEL
Le Pressoir
Berville
14170 Saint-Pierre-sur-Dives
Calvados
Tel: (0)2 31 20 51 26

From Bayeux, N13 west. After 14km, D30 to Écrammeville (2km) and follow signposts (farm is near church).

Map No: 5   MM 231-16

Louis & Annick FAUVEL
Ferme de l'Abbaye
14710 Ecrammeville
Calvados
Tel: (0)2 31 22 52 32
Fax: (0)2 31 22 47 25

It may look like a film set but it is genuine early 17th century. Inside, there is an equally astounding dining-room, added on by one M Swann and resplendently carved, panelled and painted. Two big rooms — *Jaune* and *Verte* — catch the morning sun but the *Saumon* is even better with its heavenly sunset prospect; all are incredible value. Madame, a beautiful lady, made all the curtains and covers. She and her diplomat husband are well-travelled, polyglot, cultured — they help make a stay here as special as any in France.

Rooms: 2 double, 1 twin, each with bath or shower & wc (one downstairs).

Price: 250-280 Frs for two, including breakfast. Extra bed 70 Frs.

Meals: Restaurant 1km away.

Open: All year.

From Caen N13 E towards Lisieux for 25km. At Carrefour St Jean, D50 (virtually straight on) towards Cambremer. 5km from junction, house signposted on right.

Map No: 5   MM 231-31

Christine & Arnauld GHERRAK
Manoir de Cantepie
Le Cadran
14340 Cambremer
Calvados
Tel: (0)2 31 62 87 27

The brass-railed staircase and the drawing room are elegant but graciously pleasing, not grand. The dining-room, with its huge fireplace and modern bar, is relaxed in its yellow and green garb; breakfast crockery is yellow and green, too. Colour is important to Madame and she uses it well. These are genuinely warm folk who welcome guests naturally into their family circle. The biggish, comfortable bedrooms have windows onto wide fields and the 'Norman' dinners have been praised to the skies by our readers.

Rooms: 1 double, 1 triple, 1 quadruple, all with shower or bath & wc.

Price: 240 Frs for two, including breakfast. Extra bed 60 Frs.

Meals: 100 Frs, including wine & coffee.

Open: All year.

From Bayeux N13 towards Cherbourg; through Tour-en-Bessin then left towards Route de Crouay for about 1km. House on right with cartwheel.

Map No: 5   MM 231-16

Catherine & Bertrand GIRARD
Le Relais de la Vignette
Route de Crouay, Tour-en-Bessin
14400 Bayeux
Calvados
Tel: (0)2 31 21 52 83/
(0)6 60 54 52 83
Fax: (0)2 31 45 35 01

You could scarcely find easier, friendlier hosts than Joseph and Marie-Thé. Their farm offers animals and milking for children, table football and volley-ball for teenagers and *pétanque* for all. The Guilberts will join you for a farm supper at the long table in the log-fired (winter), fresh-flowered, guests' day-room — both are full of local lore and advice. They are simple and genuine; so are their rooms and their welcome. This is superb value and the buildings are far enough from the road not to suffer from much traffic noise.

Rooms: 5 rooms/suites for 3 or 4, each with own bath or shower & wc, one with kitchen.

Price: 190 Frs for two, including breakfast. Extra person 30 Frs.

Meals: 75 Frs, including aperitif, wine and coffee. Also self-catering.

Open: All year.

The dining-room is the centrepiece: panelling, old tiles, windows facing both ways, sun pouring in. You eat at separate tables where the views are across the moat, over the formal garden with its swings and profusion of plants, and down to the orangery. Some of the parquet floors are magnificent, as is the whole house, which is littered with wood-carvings and furniture made by Monsieur's father. The bedrooms are, of course, splendid. The US Press Corps camped here in 1944 — sensibly. Pets by arrangement.

Rooms: 5 double, all with bath or shower & wc.

Price: 330 Frs for two, including breakfast.

Meals: Choice 6-10km.

Open: March to December.

From A84/E401 Caen-Rennes motorway exit 42 onto N175 towards Cahagnes for 2km then right following Chambres d'Hôtes signs to farm.

Map No: 5   MM 231-28

Joseph & Marie-Thé GUILBERT
Le Mesnil de Benneville
14240 Cahagnes
Calvados
Tel: (0)2 31 77 58 05
Fax: (0)2 31 77 37 84

From Cherbourg, N13 to Isigny. There, right on D5 towards Le Molay. Left near Vouilly church. Château on right after 500m.

Map No: 5   MM 231-15

Marie-José & James HAMEL
Château de Vouilly
Vouilly
14230 Isigny-sur-Mer
Calvados
Tel: (0)2 31 22 08 59
Fax: (0)2 31 22 90 58

History throbs in every corner of this old farmhouse, in Madame's family for three generations — parts of the building date back to the 11th century when it belonged to *Richard Coeur de Lion*. Rooms are hardly regal now but are perfectly adequate and have small showers. It is at table that the farm comes into its own. The cooking and conviviality are pure *Normandie*. Monsieur sometimes plays harmonica after dinner, there is song and free-flowing *pommeau*. In the morning you may still hear singing as the cows are milked.

Rooms: 3 double, 1 triple, 1 family for 4, each with shower & wc (not all en suite).

Price: 190 Frs for two, including breakfast.

Meals: 75 Frs, including own cider.

Open: All year.

In a lovely setting — flowers everywhere, peaceful walks (itineraries provided) — the farm raises poultry, including geese for *foie gras* (Madame is most knowledgeable about this) and spit-roasting in winter. You are warmly greeted by your youngish hosts, the atmosphere is relaxed and the unremarkable bedrooms are big and clean, with their own entrance, kitchen and sitting-room. But you will come above all for Madame's talented cooking. Children welcome (cots, games and bikes).

Rooms: 2 double, 1 triple (one on ground floor), each with shower & wc.

Price: 195 Frs for two, including breakfast.

Meals: 75 Frs, including cider & coffee (not Sun).

Open: March to October & December.

Gîtes for 7 people

From Bayeux D5 to Molay-Littry then continue on to Tournières. At entrance to village, left (next to 'Boucherie') at their sign.

Map No: 5   MM 231-16

Solange & Pierre ISIDOR
Ferme de Marcelet
14330 Tournières
Calvados
Tel: (0)2 31 22 90 86

From Caen towards Cherbourg then A84 towards Avranches; exit St Martin-des-Besaces onto D53 then left onto D165 towards Brémoy; house is on right, 4km from St Martin.

Map No: 5   MM 231-28

Jacqueline & Gilbert LALLEMAN
Carrefour des Fosses
14260 Brémoy
Calvados
Tel: (0)2 31 77 83 22

NORMANDY

We loved this place — the bucolic setting by the stream, the fine old square house beneath the church, the refined and subtle decoration of the rooms, the books, pictures and antiques and, above all, the alive, lived-in, loving atmosphere. Breakfast is a candlelit feast that can last some time. One room has an ancient but fully usable copper bath, the big (more expensive) room is superb and has its own fireplace for intimate evenings. This Franco-American couple are superb hosts.

Rooms: 3 double, 1 triple, all with bath or shower & wc.

Price: 280 or 360 Frs for two, including breakfast.

Meals: 25 restaurants within 2km. Picnic possible.

Open: All year.

Gites for 6 people

This family really knows about hospitality, serves perfectly delicious regional dinners and will drive you through the secret byways of the area in a pony-drawn trap or take you on night-time discovery walks. The house and decor may lack character but your hosts make up for it in personal warmth and *savoir-vivre* and in the morning you wake to stunning views over the hushed hills of *La Suisse Normande*. The paddock is home to horse and goat, the atmosphere welcoming to all.

Rooms: 2 double, each with own shower & wc.

Price: 200 Frs for two, including breakfast.

Meals: 80 Frs, including cider & coffee.

Open: All year.

From A13 exit 29b on N175 to Troarn. There, right after church on D95 to Bures 2km. Go into village: house is just after church wall (sign).

Map No: 5   MM 231-30

Marie-Catherine LANDON & Michael CASSADY
Manoir des Tourpes
Chemin de l'Église
14670 Bures-sur-Dives, Calvados
Tel: (0)2 31 23 63 47
Fax: (0)2 31 23 86 10
e-mail: mcassady@caen.pacwan.net

From Caen, D562 towards Flers. About 35km on at Le Fresne, D1 towards Falaise. After 4km, house on right; signposted.

Map No: 5   MM 231-30

Roland & Claudine LEBATARD
Arclais
14690 Pont d'Ouilly
Calvados
Tel: (0)2 31 69 81 65

A superbly high-walled fortified farm dated 13th-19th centuries, it has a cat-run garden, a tithe barn and a little watch tower that Madame has transformed into a delightful gîte for two. She is proud of her family home, fine country furniture, friendly boxer dog. One room has a vastly high ceiling and shower in the tower; one looks over the calving field. They are busy farmers so good meals are important... breakfast is endless (*à volonté*). The teenage daughters will even babysit for you if they are free.

Rooms: 2 triple, 1 double, each with shower & wc.

Price: 250 Frs for two, including breakfast.

Meals: 90 Frs, excluding wine (bookings only; not Sun).

Open: All year.

Gîtes for 6 people

The stones of the old farmhouse are utterly authentic, the floorboards, beams and stone fireplaces warmly genuine and the farmyard fowls sound as real in the morning as they taste at dinner (not taken *en famille*). The farm, at a distance from the house, produces cider and vegetables. Lovingly-decorated rooms with hand-sewn curtains; intimate spaces outside with flowers and shrubs. In the evening, your hard-working but welcoming hosts, who have dairy cows, aim to have time for you.

1 family room for 3-4, 2 double, 1 twin, 1 suite for 4, all with own shower & wc.

Price: 230 Frs for two, including breakfast. Extra person 60 Frs.

Meals: 85 Frs, including wine.

Open: All year.

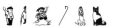

From Bayeux N13 for 30km; exit on D514 to Osmanville and on towards Grandchamp for 5km. Left towards Géfosse-Fontenay; house 800m along on left before church.

Map No: 5   MM 231-15

Gérard & Isabelle LEHARIVEL
Ferme de la Rivière
14230 Géfosse-Fontenay
Calvados
Tel: (0)2 31 22 64 45

From Bayeux, D12 towards Courseulles-sur-Mer and Banville. In village centre, right down rue du Camp Romain to No 24 (don't confuse with other B&B opposite).

Map No: 5   MM 231-17

Arlette & Gérard LESAGE
24 rue du Camp Romain
14480 Banville
Calvados
Tel: (0)2 31 37 92 18

This is a typical old farmhouse, even down to the corrugated iron roof. The guests' wing is in the converted stables where the kitchen/diner has its original stone flags and the manger. The rooms are country-comfortable, nicely decorated, some with balconies onto the farm, apple orchard (and road at the bottom) where all sorts of games await your pleasure — as does Mireille the donkey. Your elderly hosts are friendly and talkative — all their time is for you.

Rooms: 2 double, 1 quadruple, 1 triple, 1 double, all with shower, 2 with own wc, 3 sharing wc.

Price: 200-250 Frs for two, including breakfast.

Meals: Restaurant 500m. Self-catering.

Open: All year.

Madame's son bakes the most delicious bread in the 18th-century oven he has restored. He also produces cakes and *patisseries* of all sorts for afternoon tea. Madame, recently widowed, is a quiet and kindly woman and has created an easy family atmosphere. Ask for 'La Chambre Ancienne', definitely the best, with antique beds and planked floor; the others lack character, though they are big. If you have a spare moment, do take a boat ride in the *Marais* — they'll organise it for you. There is a small camping site on the farm.

Rooms: 2 twin, 1 triple, all with shower & wc. (Extra beds available.)

Price: 230 Frs for two, including breakfast.

Meals: Ferme-auberge 3km.

Open: All year.

From Bayeux, D5 west, through Le Molay Littry, towards Bernesq and Briqueville. Right about 0.75km before Bernesq; Le Ruppaley on this road, signposted.

From Vire centre, D524 towards Tinchebray & Flers; house on right after 2km — signposted.

Map No: 5   MM 231-28

Map No: 5   MM 231-16

Camille & Marcelle MARIE
La Gage
14500 Roullours
Calvados
Tel: (0)2 31 68 17 40

Marcelle MARIE
Le Ruppaley
14710 Bernesq
Calvados
Tel: (0)2 31 22 54 44

Go to great lengths to stay here; the solid beauty of the house, its simplicity, and the serenity of the *Marais* lapping at the edge of the lawn all make it near-perfect. Your hosts, too, are amiable and generous, happy to wait up for you if you arrive late; the rooms are comfortably simple. This is a WWF *Gîte Panda*, a place to learn all about local flora and fauna — binoculars on loan. Stretch your eyes across a luminous landscape of marshes and fields, eat well, enjoy the cider, and sleep in bliss.

Rooms: 1 double, 1 twin, 1 suite for 4, all with bath or shower & wc.

Price: 220 Frs for two, including breakfast.

Meals: 85 Frs, including cider & coffee.

Open: Easter to October.

A measured arrival up the drive to the main house, across the mosaic-floored hallway and up heavy wooden stairs to richly decorated, south-facing rooms. The Masliahs left Paris to renovate this imposing C18 chateau and have accomplished the task with panache. Every rug, curtain, curio and even tap was carefully chosen. Though the rooms are formal, your hosts are not. They happily rise to prepare the odd early breakfast but do try their special brunch after a lie-in. There is no guest sitting-room but you can soak up the sun in your room.

Rooms: 2 triple, 1 twin, each with bath & wc.

Price: 330 Frs for two, including breakfast.

Meals: Restaurant 6km.

Open: All year.

Gîtes for 8 people

From Bayeux, N13 to La Cambe, then D113 south. After 1km, D124 towards St Germain-du-Pert (1.5km).

Map No: 5   MM 231-16

Paulette & Hervé MARIE
Ferme de la Rivière
14230 Saint-Germain-du-Pert
Calvados
Tel: (0)2 31 22 72 92
Fax: (0)2 31 22 01 63

From Caen, N13 to Lisieux then D519 to Orbec then D4 towards Livarot for 6km. Right towards St Martin-de-Bienfaite; first house on right after 1km.

Map No: 5   MM 231-32

Chantal & Didier MASLIAH
Château de la Lande
Cerqueux
14290 Orbec
Calvados
Tel: (0)2 31 32 00 50
Fax: (0)2 31 32 00 15

Well off the busy road, down its own drive, this old stone house, built in 1714, is now a dairy farm. The *salon* is very French and just the place for a quiet read. There are other fine period rooms. The big bedrooms are light and sunny with country furniture (one has a four-poster). The family is charming, hospitable and helpful but not intrusive. Special extras are comfortable garden chairs, a pond for fishing, a horse for riding, paths for walking, homemade yoghurt and cider. Some stay a week.

Rooms: 2 double & 1 suite, all with shower & wc.

Price: 240 Frs for two, including breakfast.

Meals: 110 Frs, including aperitif, wine, cider & coffee.

Open: All year.

A tiny house, a small room but a huge welcome — plus tea-making things and a spare toothbrush. Madame is bright, brave, intelligent and independent. No spring chicken, she still takes one long trip a year, with just a good pair of shoes and a camera for company. So there are tales to be heard. Or you can lounge in the bright-flowered sun-room chairs and admire the wide rolling country beyond this rather unprepossessing village. Excellent value on all counts and it's worth coming just for her.

Rooms: Suite for 3/4 sharing bathroom & wc on landing.

Price: 180 Frs for two, including breakfast.

Meals: 80 Frs, including cider.

Open: March to mid-November.

From Caen, A13 towards Cherbourg then exit for Carpiquet and Caumont-l'Eventé. 500m before Caumont-l'Eventé, left at Chambres d'Hôtes sign into private drive.

Map No: 5   MM 231-28

Alain & Françoise PETITON
La Suhardière
14240 Livry
Calvados
Tel: (0)2 31 77 51 02

From Caen D562 towards Condé-sur-Noireau for 36km. Right towards Château de Pontécoulant & instantly left to Haute Bigne. Signposted in village.

Map No: 5   MM 231-29

Huguette REGNIER
La Haute Bigne
14570 Clécy
Calvados
Tel: (0)2 31 69 72 85

NORMANDY

Falaise was Duke William's home town until he left his native Normandy to conquer other shores and this is a typical Falaise house dating from the 1600s. The large garden is clearly much loved and has a flowery bower with a stone table. Inside you will find some superb pieces of family furniture — country French at its best — as well as crinkly pink lights and little bits of *brocante*. The Thomases are quietly and unobtrusively attentive and you will feel well cared for.

Rooms: 1 suite for 3/4, 1 double/triple, both with shower & wc.

Price: 210 Frs for two, including breakfast.

Meals: Falaise 3km. Barbecue & picnic possible.

Open: All year.

You would never guess the size of 62 Rue Grande from outside: its façade suggests a medium-sized house but it actually stretches deep into the garden where Dorothea and Claude have worked wonders with rose, wisteria and a myriad colourful plants. The two quiet guest suites are in outbuildings; one has an extraordinary wooden spiral staircase which climbs up to huge windows overlooking the light and lusciously rich garden. This polyglot home reflects its owners' polytravels as well as their passion for gardening.

Rooms: Apartment for 2/4 with shower and wc.

Price: 270 Frs for two, including breakfast. Extra person 60 Frs.

Meals: Choice in Orbec.

Open: All year.

From Falaise D63 towards Trun for 3km. 2nd left onto D69 for 1km. At junction, cross over and go round bend. Farm on left; signposted.

Map No: 5   MM 231-30

Alice & Gilbert THOMAS
Ferme la Croix
14700 Villy-lez-Falaise
Calvados
Tel: (0)2 31 90 19 98

Orbec is 19km S of Lisieux on D519. Turn into village — house is on main street next to L'Orbecquoise restaurant.

Map No: 5   MM 231-32

Dorothea VAILLÈRE
62 rue Grande
14290 Orbec
Calvados
Tel: (0)2 31 32 77 99
Fax: (0)2 31 32 77 99
e-mail: www.mairie-orbec.fr

The Valle family has lived at this ancient mill for more than 700 years. The wheel stopped turning in the 1950s but still dominates the enormous dining room and frames as bucolic a view as you could wish for. A grey heron landed just yards from the window while we breakfasted. Perfect peace — with the stream, woods and trees. Françoise and Michel enjoy dining with their guests but can recommend good places in Trouville too. Children will enjoy their two goats, the geese and the elderly dog which keeps you company at breakfast.

Rooms: 2 double, 1 family room, each with bath or shower & wc.

Price: 320-350 Frs for two, including breakfast.

Meals: 100 Frs, excluding wine (approx. 50 Frs).

Open: All Year.

In their restored 18th-century farmhouse surrounded by two open fields, the Vanhouttes welcome an exchange of ideas and cultures. Don't miss the chance to enjoy their company at dinner as well. The food is delicious, with most produce straight from the farm. You are cosseted in your room, too, where the indefatigable Annick, a linen-maker, has made the curtains, padded bedheads, table cloths and even the cross-stitch pictures. Talk to her about how linen is made — she has samples for sale — and to him about cattle or crops.

Rooms: 1 double, 1 triple, each with shower & wc; 1 overflow room.

Price: 230 Frs for two, including breakfast. Extra bed 50 Frs.

Meals: 85 Frs, including wine or cider & coffee.

Open: All year.

From Pont l'Évêque N175 W towards Caen for about 2km then left on D280 towards St Hymer. Mill is signposted.

Map No: 5   MM 231-20

Françoise VALLE
Le Moulin
14130 Saint-Hymer
Calvados
Tel: (0)2 31 64 23 51
Fax: (0)2 31 64 39 72

From St Pierre-sur-Dives D511 towards Falaise and follow signs to Château de Vendeuvre. In front of château, cross bridge and follow signs to farm.

Map No: 5   MM 231-31

Jean & Annick VANHOUTTE
Ferme du Bois de Tilly
14170 Vendeuvre
Calvados
Tel: (0)2 31 40 91 87
Fax: (0)2 31 90 58 13

The most delightful couple live in this delectably ramshackle and unspoiled château with their two small boys and all the guests who come to share the hugely relaxed atmosphere, the big garden, the variegated rooms. The cavernous Mussolini Room has the balcony with views across the heart-shaped lawn, and bath and loo behind a screen. The Colonial Room has pith-helmets and colonial mementoes, while the Hat Room... A very special place — not for the stuffy — and they do amusing 'themed' weekends.

Rooms: 2 double & 1 twin, each with bath & wc (1 screened off); 1 triple, 1 quadruple sharing a bathroom.

Price: 200-260 Frs for two, including breakfast (children half price).

Meals: Choice locally.

Open: All year except Jan & Feb.

Gîtes for 8 people

"A real corker" enthused the inspector. "They are a delight. He has a fine dry wit and loves to chat, about everything — but especially politics. She, too, holds her own and anyone with a smattering of French would enjoy them enormously." They are farmers, and proud of it. The old manor has huge character and a small private chapel; we found the shabbiness and the haphazard decor most endearing. There is even some Art Deco furniture. Wonderful value in a natural and unsophisticated way.

Rooms: 1 triple with bath & wc; 1 triple, 1 double sharing shower & wc.

Price: 180-205 Frs for two, including breakfast.

Meals: Small good-value restaurants locally.

Open: All year.

From Cherbourg, N13 towards Valognes. After 8 miles, right on D119 towards Ruffosses. Cross motorway bridge; signposted.

Map No: 4　　　　　　MM 231-14

Mark & Fiona BERRIDGE
Château Mont Epinguet
50700 Brix
Manche
Tel: (0)2 33 41 96 31
Fax: (0)2 33 41 98 77

From Cherbourg, N13 south; leave at Ste Mère-l'Eglise exit. Go into Ste Mère-l'Eglise & follow signs for Pont-l'Abbé; house signposted on right after 3km.

Map No: 4　　　　　　MM 231-15

Albert & Michèle BLANCHET
La Fière
Route de Pont l'Abbé
50480 Sainte-Mère-l'Eglise
Manche
Tel: (0)2 33 41 32 66

An impressive, creeper-covered 18th-century farmhouse set around a lovely dark-gravel courtyard flanked by old stables and outbuildings (shame about the caged dog). Rooms are rather dark but very comfortable, with homely family furniture. The elderly hosts, who love travelling, are friendly and very accommodating; one has a real sense of being invited into their home. There is a pretty flower garden with tables and chairs and a sandpit.

Rooms: 1 triple, 1 double, with basins & sharing bathroom.

Price: 190 Frs for two, including breakfast.

Meals: In St Lô 5km.

Open: All year.

Amazingly, your beautiful, energetic hostess is a grandmother! She used to help her husband in the fields, too. She now indulges her passion for interior decoration — the bedrooms are a festival of colours, textures, antiques and embroidered linen — and for her visitors; you cannot fail to enjoy staying here as much as they enjoy having you. The great granite fireplace in the sitting/dining room is always lit for the delicious breakfast which includes local specialities. There is a richly-carved, high-backed 'throne' at the head of the long table. A stupendous place.

Rooms: 2 double with shower & wc; 1 twin with bath & wc.

Price: 280 Frs for two, including breakfast.

Meals: Choice in Barfleur 3km.

Open: All year.

Gîtes for 5 people

From Cherbourg, N13 and N174 to St Lô. At St Georges-Montcocq, D191 to Villiers-Fossard. In village, right on C7; house is 800m on right.

Map No: 5   MM 231-27

Jacques & Denise BUISSON
Le Suppey
50680 Villiers-Fossard
Manche
Tel: (0)2 33 57 30 23

From Barfleur towards Quettehous then branch right on D25 towards Valcanville. Take 2nd right and follow signs.

Map No: 4   MM 231-3

Marie-France & Maurice CAILLET
La Fèvrerie
50760 Sainte-Geneviève
Manche
Tel: (0)2 33 54 33 53

In their long, converted Norman farmhouse, Richard and Jay practise perfect hospitality and serve a superb breakfast. Our readers bear witness — "Blissful, a paradise for the children who played in all safety with goats, ducks and rabbits while their parents sipped their white wine (kept in the Clays' fridge) in peace". They feel like personal guests and often become firm friends. The rooms are big and beautifully furnished, the peace complete (even 7am church bells are in keeping), the value hard to beat.

Rooms: 2 double, one with bath/shower & wc, one with shower & wc.

Price: 180 Frs for two, including breakfast.

Meals: Restaurants 5km.

Open: All year.

Gîtes for 12 people

These are solid, earthy, farming folk and Madame, who is a bit shy, has a lovely sunny smile. They encourage guests to visit Sourdeval on a Tuesday to see the cattle market in full swing. The rooms are simple and unpretentious, with candlewick bedcovers, old floor tiles, wooden wardrobes and views across the valley. The family room has two beds or a mezzanine. Guests breakfast at one long table ('new rustic' style) and are welcome to watch the milking. Really good value.

Rooms: Main house: 1 triple, 1 double sharing shower & separate wc. Cottage: family room for 5, shower & wc.

Price: 175 Frs for two, including breakfast. Extra person 70 Frs.

Meals: Choice 5km.

Open: All year.

Gîtes for 2 people

From La Haye-du-Puits, D903 towards Barneville-Carteret. At Bolleville, right on D127 to St Nicolas-de-Pierrepont; left before church; house on right after cemetery.

Map No: 4   MM 231-14

Richard & Jay CLAY
La Ferme de l'Eglise
50250 Saint-Nicolas-de-Pierrepont
Manche
Tel: (0)2 33 45 53 40
Fax: (0)2 33 45 53 40
e-mail: theclays@wanadoo.fr

From Sourdeval D977 towards Vire for 6km. Just before 'end of Manche' sign right towards Le Val. House 2km along on right.

Map No: 5   MM 231-40

Jeanne & Raymond DESDOITS
Le Val
Vengeons
50150 Sourdeval
Manche
Tel: (0)2 33 59 64 16

Madame's delight is her garden — she is deeply knowledgeable about the plant world — with its two froggy ponds, unusual 2-wheel cider press and sheep to do the mowing. Three rooms are in a converted outbuilding (one with corner kitchen at the higher price), two in the enchanting main house but with a separate entrance. The beds are nice old pieces, brass or carved wood; there is lace and pink and granny-style touches, all in keeping with an old farmhouse, and a new conservatory for breakfast when it isn't a terrace morning.

Rooms: 2 quadruple, 1 triple, 2 double, all with shower & wc.

Price: 220 or 260 Frs for two, including breakfast.

Meals: In village or 5km.

Open: All year except a week each in Jan & Oct.

Gîtes for 10 people

Set in attractive farmland and well placed for visitors to enjoy the cultural and social attractions of Valognes, this secluded village house is run by a sweetly hospitable elderly couple. They are very informative on local history and sights, and still keep some sheep. The rooms are not big but comfortable, with new bedding and wallpaper and nice old family furnishings; we definitely preferred the attic room, even if the loo is down a flight of stairs. There is a kitchen specially for guests.

Rooms: 1 double with shower & wc; 1 double with shower, wc on floor below.

Price: 170 Frs for two, including breakfast.

Meals: Self-catering.

Open: All year.

small

From Percy D58 towards Hambye then immediately left on D98 towards Sourdeval for 1.5km. House signposted on right.

Map No: 4   MM 231-27

Daniel & Maryclaude DUCHEMIN
Le Cottage de la Voisinière
Route de Sourdeval D98
50410 Percy
Manche
Tel: (0)2 33 61 18 47/
   (0)6 09 38 21 83
Fax: (0)2 33 61 43 47

From Cherbourg, N13 to Valognes (slow down: signs hard to see entering Valognes), then D902 towards Bricquebec. After 2km, left on D87 to Yvetot-Bocage. At the church, go towards Morville and take first left.

Map No: 4   MM 231-14

Léon & Lucienne DUBOST
Le Haut Billy
Route de Morville
50700 Yvetot-Bocage, Valognes
Manche
Tel: (0)2 33 40 06 74

Definitely a working farm: 40 cows (the high-tech milking shed attracts interest from far and wide; you can watch too) and 800 pigs, with masses of flowers to sweeten the air. The young owners enjoy contact with visitors from other realms. Madame pays special attention to breakfast — her apple tart is delicious — then you can walk directly out into the lovely countryside to see the little chapel or the local château. The rooms are simple, unpretentious and good, one in the house, the other with its own entrance. Small pets welcome in garage.

Rooms: 2 double with own shower and wc.

Price: 180 Frs for two, including breakfast; extra person 50 Frs.

Meals: Good choice 5km.

Open: All year.

Gîtes for 14 people

From Pontorson N175 to Aucey-la-Plaine, then follow signs to Chambres d'Hôtes La Provostière for 3km. Farm is between Pontorson & Vessey.

Map No: 4   MM 231-38

Maryvonne & René FEUVRIER
La Provostière
50170 Aucey-la-Plaine
Manche
Tel: (0)2 33 60 33 67

Great swaying pines, the wild coastline and the sea have guarded this site for over 800 years (the English destroyed the first castle in 1346). Lush lawns and myriad flowers soften the wildness of the landscape. The manor's stern stone façade hides a warm and gentle welcome in rooms with superb fireplaces, good beds, great windows to let in the light and truly personal decoration: pictures, books (breakfast is taken in the library) and antiques. Madame will enthrall you with tales from Norman history and provide detailed maps for hikers.

Rooms: 1 suite for 3, 1 double, each with shower & wc.

Price: 280 Frs for two, including breakfast.

Meals: Auberge within walking distance.

Open: All year.

Gîtes for 6 people

From Cherbourg, D901 to Barfleur. There, D1 towards St Vaast. After signpost marking the end of Barfleur, 2nd right and 1st left.

Map No: 4   MM 231-3

Mme Claudette GABROY
Le Manoir
50760 Montfarville
Manche
Tel: (0)2 33 23 14 21

Only one dog remains but this is still one of the most natural of 'family' houses, very *sympa* the family still descends at weekends. They are an interesting couple, travel a lot and talk well. Jean-Paul is an arbitrator and Brigitte is on the council. Meals (delicious) are taken in the lovely dining-room with huge fireplace. The rooms are good and up to them leads a splendid staircase. The setting of the house is glorious with a lake and a château next door. There are games galore, and it is still a working farm.

Rooms: 2 double, 2 family rooms, all with bath or shower & wc. (Extra beds and cot available.)

Price: 210-225 Frs for two, including breakfast.

Meals: 80 Frs, including cider & coffee; 45 Frs under 12s.

Open: All year.

Ask for the room facing Mont St Michel — it's the nicest... and that view! You can walk there in two hours; or they have bikes for you. In the enclosed courtyard there are passion-fruit and fig trees. The Gédouins have cows and pigs; Annick makes delicious jams; Jean is Mayor — the council meets in his kitchen. Rooms are clean and compact, if short on storage space. There is a warm and kindly welcome, though, and the once-thin walls have now been properly soundproofed. Honey for breakfast, the sea only 500 yards away.

Rooms: 2 double, each with shower & wc.

Price: 200 Frs for two, including breakfast.

Meals: Excellent auberge in village.

Open: All year.

From Avranches, N175 dir. Mt St-Michel. After 12km, 1st right (exit Rennes & Mt St-Michel). After 500m, left on D43 dir. Rennes. At roundabout, D40 dir. Rennes for 5.5km, then D308 left; signposted.

Map No: 4   MM 231-38

Jean-Paul & Brigitte GAVARD
La Ferme de l'Etang
Boucéel, Vergoncey
50240 Saint-James
Manche
Tel: (0)2 33 48 34 68
Fax: (0)2 33 48 48 53

From Mt St Michel, D275 towards Pontaubault. At Montitier, D107 to Servon. There, take D113 left. House on left; signposted.

Map No: 4   MM 231-38

Annick & Jean GÉDOUIN
Le Petit Manoir
21 rue de la Pierre du Tertre
50170 Servon
Manche
Tel: (0)2 33 60 03 44
Fax: (0)2 33 60 17 79

Miles from anywhere, apparently, but pilgrims once rested in this 12th-century farmhouse on their journey to and from the shrine at Santiago. Today's new pilgrims can rest their weary bones at L'Orgerie during their travels in France. Four dogs greet you as you sip your *pommeau* aperitif with delightful hosts and dinner is then taken in the towering dining room with its gallery and huge fireplace. The house has a truly ancient feel but the guestrooms are snug and few will mind the loo being at the end of the corridor.

Rooms: 1 double, 1 twin (family suite), sharing shower & separate wc.

Price: 180 Frs for two, including breakfast.

Meals: 70 Frs, including wine or cider.

Open: All year.

The piecemeal construction, ages, shapes, sizes, of this splendid group of buildings are an historical delight. Mediæval walls shelter from the elements within an elegant 18th-century manor, in thrilling contrast. Furnishings are irreproachably French, as are your hosts: civilisation is the keynote, with panelling, gilt-framed mirrors, plush chairs, engravings and fine china to endorse it. Your apartment has ancient floor tiles, brand new bedding, a loo in a tower. The intelligent and energetic owners are still renovating — hard to believe she's a grandmother!

Rooms: 1 suite for 3 or 4 with shower & wc.

Price: 450 Frs for two, including breakfast. Terms for children.

Meals: Good choice 2-15km.

Open: All year.

Gîtes for 13 people

From Caen N175 SW towards Villedieu/Rennes. At Pont Farcy left on D52 towards Vire for 3km — house signposted on right (DON'T turn to St Vigor).

Map No: 5   MM 231-27

Jacques & Jacqueline GOUDE
L'Orgerie
50420 Saint-Vigor-des-Monts
Manche
Tel: (0)2 31 68 85 58

From Cherbourg, D904 towards Coutances. 3km after Les Pieux, right on D62 towards Le Rozel, then right on D117 into village; house is just after you leave village — signposted.

Map No: 4   MM 231-13

Josiane & Jean-Claude GRANDCHAMP
Le Château
50340 Le Rozel
Manche
Tel: (0)2 33 52 95 08

Perfect for the ferries (6km), yet quietly out in the country, the Guérards' fine stone manor stands majestically on a hill above Cherbourg with views across the valley and out to sea. They have retired from farming and divide their time between grandchildren and guests. The house is not over-modernised and is furnished in very French style with lots of velvet and marble-topped chests. One room has a separate entrance, ideal for early-morning ferry-catchers who can breakfast quietly in a little blue breakfast room.

Rooms: Main house: 1 double, 1 twin, each with bath & wc; outside stairs to triple room with shower & wc.

Price: 210-240 Frs for two, including breakfast.

Meals: Cherbourg 6km.

Open: All year.

Gîtes for 3 people

From Cherbourg, D901 to Tourlaville & towards St Pierre Église. Right at lights towards Château des Ravalet/Hameau St Jean; up hill to 'Centre Aéré', then follow Chambres d'Hôtes signs (3km from lights).

Map No: 4   MM 231-2

Mme GUÉRARD
Manoir Saint Jean
50110 Tourlaville
Manche
Tel: (0)2 33 22 00 86

Remarkable value, even for Normandy, and such likeable hosts. This is a small dairy farm with a large, plain guestroom looking out over the old cider press and the fields: cider has been made here for two centuries — make sure you try it. Breakfast will be straightforward French, with the added bonus of milk fresh from the cows and Madame's homemade jam. The sea is within walking distance (2km), pretty Granville with its fish restaurants is just 5km away or you can easily nip across to the Channel Islands.

Rooms: 1 room for up to four people, with shower & wc.

Price: 175 Frs for two, including breakfast.

Meals: Choice in Granville.

Open: All year.

Gîtes for 10 people

From Granville, D973 towards Avranches. After about 3km, left at Gîtes de France & 'Déchetterie' sign, left after 200m; house on left.

Map No: 4   MM 231-26

Jean-Claude & Lilianne LAISNÉ
Mallouet
50400 Granville
Manche
Tel: (0)2 33 50 26 41

The priest who lived in this former presbytery must have had a pretty grand lifestyle. The house is large and solid with high windows and a fine garden. Madame puts fresh flowers everywhere. There is old country furniture, a log fire and the original *potager* (a stone ember-fired hotplate-cum-simmering-spot) in the big beamed dining room. The bedrooms are just as interesting, with space, light and softness. Madame is dynamic and fun and looks after her guests most attentively.

Rooms: 1 double, 1 triple, each with bath & wc; 1 quadruple, 1 twin sharing bath & wc.

Price: 250 Frs for two, including breakfast.

Meals: Restaurant in village. Picnic possible in garden.

Open: All year.

Inside the stately 16th-century manor, up a twisty stone staircase, along a creaky corridor, is one of the finest B&B suites we know: a half tester, carved fireplaces, a boudoir, rugs, prints and antiques, a claw-footed bath, windows onto lush gardens with ancient trees. The panelled dining-room fills with light, the tiled, be-rugged guest sitting-room is grand yet welcoming, your hosts are lively, cultured and fun: Belgian Yves still partly runs his family business and English Lynne can offer aromatherapy.

Rooms: 1 apartment (D + TW + child's bed) with bath & wc.

Price: 490 Frs for two, including breakfast.

Meals: Good restaurant 3km.

Open: Mid-March to Oct (by arrangement in winter).

From Cherbourg N13 south, exit to Brix & D50 to Sottevast. In village D62 towards Rauville-la-Bigot. 2nd right towards Hameau ès-Adams then 1st left.

Map No: 4   MM 231-14

Françoise & Louis LEBARILLIER
Hameau ès-Adams
50260 Sottevast
Manche
Tel: (0)2 33 41 98 35

From Carentan D903 towards La Haye-du-Puits. At Baupte (5km) right on D69 to Appeville. At Appeville continue on D69 towards Houtteville & take second lane on right — house on left.

Map No: 4   MM 231-15

Yves LEJOUR & Lynne WOOSTER
Le Manoir d'Ozeville
Appeville
50500 Carentan
Manche
Tel: (0)2 33 71 55 98
Fax: (0)2 33 42 17 79

When asked why she chose to open her farmhouse (rebuilt in 1856) to guests, the bright-eyed Madame Poittevin's simple reply is disarming: "*C'est la convivialité*". You cannot fail to be won over by the warmth and friendliness of both the house and your hostess as you chat with her over a leisurely breakfast and sleep soundly in a spotless bedroom where magazines, knick-knacks, carpets and heavy old wardrobes are utterly *famille*. Though dinner is not offered, you can picnic in the garden or cook your own food on the barbecue.

Rooms: 2 double, each with shower & wc.

Price: 198 Frs for two, including breakfast.

Meals: Choice 4-10km.

Open: All year.

From this hillside perch above the village, look across the bay to the mystical outline of Mont St Michel, then *walk* there along the coastal path. The bedrooms are airy and light — try the 'Eisenhower' (yes, he did), or 'Les Tulipes', balconied with super Art Deco furniture. The original tap-making owner left some magnificent basins and fittings. The current owners farm (organically, some miles away), keep a lovely garden and allow guests to use their kitchen. Breakfast is a help-yourself buffet feast.

Rooms: 3 double, 2 twin, each with bath or shower & wc.

Price: 290-450 Frs for two, including breakfast.

Meals: In village or 1-10km. Or self-catering.

Open: All year.

Gîtes for 14 people

From St Lô D972 towards Coutances, through St Gilles; house signposted on left, 4km after St Gilles, on D972.

Map No: 4   MM 231-27

Jean & Micheline LEPOITTEVIN
Saint-Léger
50750 Quibou
Manche
Tel: (0)2 33 57 18 41
Fax: (0)2 33 55 00 01

From Cherbourg, N13 to Valognes then D2 to Coutances then D971 to Granville then D911 (along coast) to Jullouville and on to Carolles and St Jean-le-Thomas (6.5km from Jullouville).

Map No: 4   MM 231-26

André & Suzanne LEROY
Les Hauts
7 avenue de la Libération
50530 Saint-Jean-le-Thomas
Manche
Tel: (0)2 33 60 10 02
Fax: (0)2 33 60 15 40

A typical, 19th-century village house with pleasant, country-style bedrooms, an inviting, armchaired reading corner on the landing and a warm, friendly, welcome. The hosts are smiling, retired farmers, and eager to please. Breakfast is served at the long 10-seater table in the dining-room. There are tennis courts, a swimming pool and restaurants close at hand, and the proximity to Mont Saint Michel is a natural advantage. (When calling to book, better to have a French speaker to hand...)

Rooms: 1 double, 1 triple and 1 twin, all with washbasins, sharing 1 bathroom with wc, 1 shower-room & 1 wc.

Price: 180 Frs for two, including breakfast.

Meals: Auberge next door.

Open: All year.

They have two donkeys and a much-loved horse. They are down-to-earth country folk who welcome you with big smiles, stories and much useful local information. Madame, a delightful and humorous woman, plays the organ in the village church (the adjoining farm is her brother's). Bedrooms have old family furniture (admire *grand-mère's* elaborately crocheted bedcover), good mattresses, simple washing arrangements (curtained off); there is also a roomy big-windowed dayroom with lots of plants and a kitchen in the old cider press.

Rooms: 1 double with shower & wc; 1 twin, 1 triple, each with shower, sharing 2 wc's.

Price: 200 Frs for two, including breakfast.

Meals: Restaurant 1km; choice St Lô 4km; self-catering.

Open: All year.

From Avranches, N175 towards Pontorson. 3km after Precey, right to Servon.

Map No: 4   MM 231-38

M & Mme LESÉNÉCHAL
Le Bourg
50170 Servon
Manche
Tel: (0)2 33 48 92 13

From St Lô D999 towards Villedieu for 3km; right on D38 towards Canisy. House 1km along on right.

Map No: 4   MM 231-27

Marie-Thérèse & Roger OSMOND
La Rhétorerie
Route de Canisy
50750 Saint-Ébremond-de-Bonfossé
Manche
Tel: (0)2 33 56 62 98

Monsieur breeds horses and there is riding available, but only for very experienced riders. The less horsey can enjoy an interesting visit to stables which have produced some great racers (including *La Belle Tière*). The place is a gem, though the guestrooms are up a steep wooden staircase, and Madame cooks all the food, including her own bread and croissants. Meals are served in the beamed dining/breakfast room. The setting is charming, among hills, woods and fields; this would be a delightful place for a winter visit, too.

Rooms: 1 double, 1 twin, each with shower & wc; 1 twin for children.

Price: 180 Frs for two, including breakfast.

Meals: 80 Frs, including wine.

Open: All year.

A solid, welcoming place in good farmhouse style. The old stable block, entirely modernised in the 1970s, is being redecorated this year. With stripped wooden floors and comfortable furnishings, cots in the attic rooms and a kitchenette, the guestrooms are ideal for families. The balcony room is in a league of its own with exposed timbers, country antiques and... even a balcony. Madame "makes a superb soufflé" and offers mouthwatering Norman cuisine. The poetically named Two Estuaries motorway will provide quick access 1km away from 1999.

Rooms: 2 double, 1 twin, 1 family room for 4, all with bath or shower & wc.

Price: 200 Frs for two, including breakfast.

Meals: 83 Frs, including wine & coffee.

Open: All year.

Gîtes for 6 people

Leave Coutances going S on D971 towards Granville and fork quickly left on D7 towards Gavray for 1.5km; then left on D27 to Nicorps. Through village and first right — house on left, signposted.

Map No: 4   MM 231-26

M & Mme POSLOUX
Les Hauts Champs
La Moinerie de Haut
50200 Nicorps
Manche
Tel: (0)2 33 45 30 56

From Avranches, N175 south then D998 to St James. There, D12 towards Antrain. House is on right.

Map No: 4   MM 231-38

François & Catherine TIFFAINE
La Gautrais
50240 Saint-James
Manche
Tel: (0)2 33 48 31 86
Fax: (0)2 33 48 58 17

This young English couple have renovated their square stone Norman house with lots of pine slatting and furniture and fresh wallpaper, and have created a home from home. The soberly-furnished sitting-room has a couple of Spitfire pictures and table football in one corner. Lesley, mother of two small children, is a trained cook and serves international food at separate tables and... Marmite for breakfast alongside her homemade jam. It is peaceful, rural and very welcoming for children. And good for Coutances, Bayeux and the beaches.

Rooms: 2 double, each with shower & wc; 1 single sharing shower & wc.

Price: 225 Frs for two, including breakfast.

Meals: 95 Frs, including wine & coffee.

Open: All year.

This 18th-century château has been renovated and modernised virtually beyond recognition though the farm buildings are genuine. It is set back from the main road, which you can still hear, but the hills and woods behind are lovely. Bedrooms are pastel-papered and simply furnished with brass or wooden beds and mirrored *armoires*. Breakfast is taken at the long family dining table and Madame is eager to help you plan your day. The Botanical Gardens in Avranches are splendid.

Rooms: 1 double with shower & wc; 1 triple & 2 double, each with shower & washbasin, sharing wc.

Price: 200-220 Frs for two, including breakfast.

Meals: In Avranches.

Open: All year.

From Coutances, D972 for 6km towards St-Lô, then right onto D276 towards Belval Bourg for 3km: house on right.

Map No: 4 MM 231-27

Paul & Lesley TROUT
La Guérandière
50210 Belval Bourg
Manche
Tel: (0)2 33 45 21 03 or
UK 01452 840541
Fax: (0)2 33 45 21 03

From Avranches, D973 towards Granville, across Pont Gilbert; 300m after shopping precinct, take 1st drive on left.

Map No: 4 MM 231-38

Eugène & Huguette TURGOT
Le Château
Marcey-les-Grèves
50300 Avranches
Manche
Tel: (0)2 33 58 08 65

Madame is as Norman as this house, where she was born: solidly earthed and used to welcoming strangers with kindness and a strong country accent. She shares her time between family, guests and dairy cows and is extremely proud of her breakfasts. These include fresh farm eggs and are served in the wonderful family dining-room amid photographs, copper pans and old beams. Less characterful, the bedrooms have country furniture, old-style wallpapers and... more photographs. A super person and excellent value.

Rooms: 2 triple, each with bath or shower & wc (one doorless).

Price: 180 Frs for two, including breakfast.

Meals: Restaurants 3km.

Open: All year.

From Cherbourg, N13 past Valognes then right on D2 to St Sauveur-le-Vicomte. There, D15 towards Port-Bail. Farm is on right after about 1km before Château d'Ollonde.

Map No: 4   MM 231-13

Bernadette VASSELIN
La Roque de Bas
Canville-la-Roque
50580 Port-Bail
Manche
Tel: (0)2 33 04 80 27

This, the oldest house (1490s) in beautifully-preserved Bécherel, is as elegant inside as out with long country views at the back. Monique has talent and taste (see her renovation and decor), speaks perfect English, loves people, books and calligraphy; she and Joël are involved in the town's book-promotion activities and she also runs a delicious tea room. The vast, beamed, fireplaced guestroom combines warm ochre, cool blue and Laura Ashley into one of the plushest we know. She's a good cook too!

Rooms: 1 double with bath & wc.

Price: 350 Frs for two, including breakfast.

Meals: 120 Frs, including wine.

Open: All year.

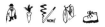

From St Malo N137 S towards Rennes for 43km. At Tinténiac exit, right on D20 to Bécherel. House in town centre, on main square near church.

Map No: 4   MM 230-25

Monique CANET
Le Logis de la Filanderie
3 rue de la Filanderie
35190 Bécherel
Ille-et-Vilaine
Tel: (0)2 99 66 73 17
Fax: (0)2 99 66 79 07
e-mail: http://www.filanderie@aol.com

Brittany

Between St Malo and Mont St Michel, with the sea just 3km away, this is a dairy farm with a neatly-converted stone house. The comfortable rooms include two with mezzanines; the others are smaller. Jean, gentle and bright-eyed, says he's tied to the farm but, "travels through his guests". In cool weather your hostess is up before breakfast to lay the fire in the huge hearth where you can toast bread. They both know and love their Breton music and walks in deep detail. Do let us know how you enjoy it.

Rooms: 5 rooms for 2-4 people, all with shower or bath & wc.

Price: 200-250 Frs for two, including breakfast. Extra bed 80 Frs.

Meals: Choice in Dol-de-Bretagne, 6km.

Open: All year.

Madame wanted us to mention her passion for embroidery; there is much of it about, together with Laura Ashley, flounces, friezes and fantasy... all just within the bounds of good taste. They are a very pleasant couple but you will perhaps see less of them when they create their new outbuilding where guests are to dine and breakfast. So, not very *familiale* but thoroughly caring. Count on Beethoven, *crêpes* and an indoor garden for breakfast. It is in a tiny hamlet.

Rooms: 1 large suite for 5, 1 triple, both with shower & wc. 'Studio' also available.

Price: 260-300 Frs for two, including breakfast. Lovers' night 750 Frs.

Meals: 60 or 100 Frs, excluding wine (60 Frs).

Open: All year.

Gîtes for 4 people

From St Malo N137 S towards Rennes for 15km then exit on N176 towards Mt St Michel for 12km. Exit Dol-de-Bretagne on D80 towards St Broladre for 3km; left on D85 towards Cherrueix; house on right before bridge.

Map No: 4   MM 230-12

Jean & Marie-Madeleine GLÉMOT
La Hamelinais
35120 Cherrueix
Ille-et-Vilaine
Tel: (0)2 99 48 95 26
Fax: (0)2 99 48 89 23

From Rennes, S on new road to Janzé (D163/D41). Here, right on D92 for La Couyère for approx. 6km. House is on right in La Tremblais: yellow gate; signposted. Park behind.

Map No: 4   MM 230-41

Claudine & Raymond GOMIS
La Tremblais
35320 La Couyère
Ille-et-Vilaine
Tel: (0)2 99 43 14 39
Fax: (0)2 99 43 14 39

The 'otter' in the last edition was a coypu! But it is still bucolic here; the beauty of the setting takes you by surprise and the little guesthouse is a dream. In what used to be the bakery, it is just a yard or two from the lake (you can fish), far enough from the main house to feel secluded, snugly romantic and utterly seductive. If your need for intimacy is deep then Catherine will deliver breakfast and dinner (course by course) to your hideaway. But nicer still to join them at table; they are young and delightful.

Rooms: 1 twin/quadruple in cottage with salon, shower & wc.

Price: 240 Frs for two, including breakfast.

Meals: 80 Frs, including wine & coffee.

Open: All year.

Gites for 4 people

Beatrice is a culinary wizard and generous with it: if you are keen you can shop with her and learn from her. She also has boundless energy, enough to take you walking, if you wish. This is a (non-working) mill, with a wheel recently added, so don't expect great bedrooms; they are small and adequate, if a bit dark. The real attractions are the setting, the fishing (borrow their rods), the food and the people. The two teenage sons live here too; nice, quiet lads.

Rooms: 1 double & 1 twin, both with shower and wc.

Price: 250 Frs for two, including breakfast.

Meals: 100 Frs, including wine.

Open: All year.

Gites for 6 people

From St Malo, N137 into St Pierre-de-Plesguen. On church square take D10 towards Lanhelin for 1.5km, then follow signs on right to 'Le Pont Ricoul Chambre d'Hôte'

Map No: 4   MM 230-25

Catherine & François GROSSET
Le Pont Ricoul
35720 Saint-Pierre-de-Plesguen
Ille-et-Vilaine
Tel: (0)2 99 73 92 65
Fax: (0)2 99 73 94 17

From Rennes, D177 towards Redon. After 18km, right onto D776 towards Guer. After 5km, left onto D62 towards Guignen; house is 800m down on left.

Map No: 4   MM 230-39

Claude & Béatrice KRUST
Le Moulin du Bignon
35580 Lassy
Ille-et-Vilaine
Tel: (0)2 99 42 10 04
Fax: (0)2 99 42 08 44
e-mail: claude.krust@wanadoo.fr

The setting of this fine 1620's water-mill, restored in the 19th century, is gorgeous. Monsieur will set the mill-wheel in motion for you. The small guestrooms have stone walls, wooden ceilings, typical Breton furniture, some antiques, satin and lace plus excellent beds and lots of fluffy towels. Madame has 20 years of experience in B&B. Her breakfast ware and linen are most carefully laid out. There is a very pretty garden/orchard and an all-pervading sense of rural peace.

Rooms: 2 double, 2 triple, all with bath or shower & wc.

Price: 350 Frs for two, including breakfast.

Meals: Restaurant 2.5km.

Open: All year, except 1 week in November.

In this big reassuringly solid *malouinière*, built in the 1600s as a privateer's weekend cottage, you are just 300 yards from the sea. The setting is superb, the calm complete, your hosts elegant and civilised. You may meet their beautifully-behaved grandchildren too. The rooms are high, panelled, decorated with ancestors. The monumental staircase leads to your magnificent quarters (big double room, smaller room for children, superb white bathroom). A most agreeable place to stay in every way.

Rooms: 1 suite for 4 with bath & wc.

Price: 400 Frs for two, including breakfast.

Meals: Cancale 4km.

Open: Mid-April to September.

Gites for 5 people

From Cancale D355 towards St Malo. In St Coulomb, follow same road then fork right at church; right (just after school); 1st right (before football pitch), bend left, drive on left (total 1km from village).

From N137 between Rennes and St Malo. In St-Pierre-de-Plesguen, D10 towards Lanhelin: right for 2.5km after sign 'Clos Coq'; signposted.

Map No: 4   MM 230-25

Annie MICHEL-QUÉBRIAC
Le Petit Moulin du Rouvre
35720 Saint-Pierre-de-Plesguen
Ille-et-Vilaine
Tel: (0)2 99 73 85 84
Fax: (0)2 99 73 71 06

Map No: 4   MM 230-12

M & Mme Guy des POMMARE
La Motte aux Chauff
35350 Saint-Coulomb
Ille-et-Vilaine
Tel: (0)2 99 89 07 72

The quiet simplicity of both house and owner are like the utter calm of a balmy summer's morning. Isabelle's talent seems to touch the very air that fills her old family house. There is nothing superfluous: simple carved pine furniture, durries on scrubbed plank floors, palest yellow or mauve walls to reflect the ocean-borne light, harmonious striped or gingham curtains. Starfish and many-splendoured pebbles keep the house sea-connected. The unspoilt seaside village is worth the trip too.

Rooms: 2 double & 1 twin with bath & wc, 2 double with shower & wc (one fully equipped for disabled).

Price: 250-290 Frs for two, including breakfast.

Meals: Choice in village.

Open: All year.

The owner of this fine manor, a talented decorator and flamboyant host, has created something special and wants people of taste to come and have a fantastic(al) time. There is brightly-painted furniture in the bedrooms (a different colour scheme for each), a guests' *salon* and reading room, finely decorated with old rugs, china and dolls, a grand dining-room for candlelit breakfast buffets (separate tables). Pony-and-trap rides along the beach, mountain bikes to take you to pretty little St Briac, St Malo just 8 miles away, complete the picture.

Rooms: 4 double, 1 suite, all with bath or shower & wc.

Price: 350-500 Frs for two, including breakfast. Extra bed 80 Frs.

Meals: Great choice 2.5km.

Open: All year.

From St Malo, N137 towards Rennes. 6km after leaving St Malo, right on D117 to St Suliac. Road leads to main street (Grande Rue) leading down to port (3km from N137 exit to village entrance). House at top on right

Map No: 4   MM 230-11

Isabelle ROUVRAIS
Les Mouettes
Grande Rue
35430 Saint-Suliac
Ille-et-Vilaine
Tel: (0)2 99 58 30 41
Fax: (0)2 99 58 39 41

From St Malo, D168 towards St Brieuc, then D603 towards St Briac-sur-Mer; first left on entering the town and follow signs for 'Camping Municipal'.

Map No: 4   MM 230-11

Jean-François STENOU
Manoir de la Duchée
Saint-Briac-sur-Mer
35800 Dinard
Ille-et-Vilaine
Tel: (0)2 99 88 00 02
e-mail: www.web-de-loire.com

This grand old Breton *longère*, built in the 15th century, has been in the Beaupère family for four generations and is still a working farm. Guests are welcome to eat *en famille*; few will resist *Petits Pigeons, Lardons et Raisins* and local cheeses though the wine may be rather dear. As far as possible, only produce from the farm is used. Rooms are anonymous but comfortable. There are carp ponds for those with interest and a rod and a 9-hole golf course with all the trappings (clubhouse, lessons, socialising). Readers have liked it a lot.

Rooms: 2 twin, 2 double (one with extra bed), all with bath or shower & wc.

Price: 250 Frs for two, including breakfast.

Meals: 80 Frs, excluding wine.

Open: All year.

A fine 15th-century manor that exudes character and history, inside and out. There are monumental fireplaces, a worn spiral staircase, ancestral portraits (including a Marquise among Chinese faces on an embroidered screen), fine furniture. The bedrooms have space, taste, arched doors and good bathrooms. Breakfast is a Breton feast. Madame planted the lovely garden 40 years ago and is still very active in it. Both are elegantly welcoming and their son breeds racehorses on the other half of the estate.

Rooms: 2 twin, each with bath & wc.

Price: 500 Frs for two, including breakfast.

Meals: Lannion 4km.

Open: All year.

dogs only

From Dinan, N176 towards St Brieuc. At Plélan-le-Petit, take D19 (right) to St Michel-de-Plélan. House signposted left, 1km after village.

Map No: 4   MM 230-24

Odile & Henri BEAUPÈRE
La Corbinais
22980 Saint-Michel-de-Plélan
Côtes-d'Armor
Tel: (0)2 96 27 64 81

From Guingamp, N12 W for 25km then Beg ar Chra/Plouaret exit onto D11 to Plouaret then continue D11 towards Lannion for 6km. After Run, D30 left towards St Michel-en-Grève then fourth left: follow signposts.

Map No: 3   MM 230-6

M & Mme Gérard de BELLEFON
Manoir de Kerguéréon
Ploubezre
22300 Lannion
Côtes-d'Armor
Tel: (0)2 96 38 91 46

Once inside this enlarged 1930s house you will understand why it is in this book: the ever-changing light of the great bay shimmers in through the vast expanse of glass whence you can watch the boats come and go, or walk to the beach (10 minutes). Guy chose the house so he could see his small boat at anchor out there (lucky guests may be taken for a sail) and Marie-Clo has enlivened the interior with her talented patchwork and embroidery. It is calm, light, bright; they are attentive hosts and breakfast is seriously good.

Rooms: 2 double, each with sitting area, sea view, shower & wc.

Price: 300 Frs for two, including breakfast.

Meals: Lots of choice in Perros Guirec.

Open: All year.

The sea is at the bottom of the back drive. An extraordinary, somewhat crumbling old château, vast and wonderful guest suites. A lively couple of aristocratic hosts bent on riding, hunting and entertaining you, complete the picture. You breakfast in the upstairs *salon*, or through the low stone arched doorway in the room with the boar's head, downstairs. One suite is pink, another blue and yellow. The beds are canopied, the windows high, the portraits ancestral, the rugs cotton, the atmosphere unreal. There is no other place like it.

Rooms: 3 suites, each with bath or shower & wc.

Price: 400-600 Frs for two, including breakfast. Extra bed 130 Frs.

Meals: Good choice 5km.

Open: May to September.

From Lannion D788 N to Perros Guirec; follow signs to 'Port' then to 'Centre ville par la corniche'; follow round bay for approx. 1km then left at sign 'Nid Vacances'.
(Will fax plan or collect you from railway station.)

Map No: 3/4   MM 230-6

From St Brieuc N12 towards Lamballe exit Yffigniac-Hillion. After Yffigniac left on D80 to Hillion then D34 towards Morieux. 200m after Hillion ends, roadside crucifix on left by château gates.

Map No: 4   MM 230-9

Marie-Clo & Guy BIARNES
41 rue de la Petite Corniche
22700 Perros Guirec
Côtes-d'Armor
Tel: (0)2 96 23 28 08
Fax: (0)2 96 23 28 08
e-mail: guy.biarnes@wanadoo.fr

Vicomtesse Louis du FOU de KERDANIEL
Château de Bonabry
22120 Hillion
Côtes d'Armor
Tel: (0)2 96 32 21 06
Fax: (0)2 96 32 21 06

Janine's love is her vegetarian cooking, Steve's is his sculpture that decorates the rambling, rose-filled garden. Our inspector loved it for its isolation, lack of pretension, and daring to be different. It is the sort of 'alternative' that we like: simple, attractive, comfortable-yet-humble... and interesting. Guests eat at separate tables, tasting, perhaps, the artichoke *aioli* or roasted cherry tomatoes. Use the living-room and garden, browse through the books, make yourself coffee... your hosts are young and easy.

Rooms: 1 family room for 4 with shower & wc; 1 twin, 1 double, sharing bath & wc.

Price: 300-340 Frs for two, including breakfast.

Meals: 100 Frs for 3-course vegetarian meal incl. wine & coffee. Packed lunch 30-40 Frs.

Open: March to November.

Gites for 6 people

From Dinan D766 S for Caulnes approx. 13km then right on D64 to Plumaudan. Here left for Caulnes for approx 150m; 2nd right for Le Plessis; house on right after 2km.

Map No: 4   MM 230-25

Janine & Steve JUDGES
Le Plessis Vegetarian Guesthouse
Le Plessis
22350 Plumaudan
Côtes-d'Armor
Tel: (0)2 96 86 00 44
Fax: (0)2 96 86 00 44
e-mail: janine.leplessis@hol.fr

The estate has been in the family for 600 years and their 'latest' house (C17-C19) is a masterpiece of understated elegance. Ceilings are high, windows generous, guests rejoice in a granite-hearthed, tapestry-walled sitting-room where old books and family portraits remind them this is 'just an ordinary family house'. Madame, dynamic and adorable, loves her visitors. The bedrooms vary in size and character, all are fascinating, we preferred *La Jaune* for its panelling and lovely view. Worth every centime.

Rooms: 3 double, 2 twin rooms, all with bath, shower & wc.

Price: 460-520 Frs for two, including breakfast. Extra bed 100 Frs.

Meals: Crêperie in village; excellent restaurant nearby.

Open: All year.

Gites for 10 people

From St Brieuc, N12 to Guingamp, then D8 towards Tréguier. At Pommerit-Jaudy turn left at the lights.

Map No: 4   MM 230-7

Comte & Comtesse de KERMEL
Château de Kermezen
22450 Pommerit-Jaudy
Côtes-d'Armor
Tel: (0)2 96 91 35 75
Fax: (0)2 96 91 35 75

A long low Breton house built on hard Breton granite, guarded by a soft Breton spaniel and kept by a relaxed and friendly Breton woman whose family has owned it for generations (she lives in the little house). There is old wood everywhere — ceilings, wardrobes, beams, beds; there are gingham cloths, floral curtains and lace cushions. Breakfasts and evening meals (these must be requested) are cooked on a wood-fired range and served on attractive rough pottery at separate tables in the guests' dining-room.

Rooms: 3 double, 1 twin, 1 triple, 1 double + bunks, all with bath or shower & wc.

Price: 235-255 Frs for two, including breakfast (booking essential).

Meals: 85 Frs, including wine & coffee (not Sun).

Open: All year.

From Dinard, D168 to Ploubalay and D768 to Plancoët. There, D19 to Saint-Lormel. Turn left opposite school at far end of village then follow signs for 1.5km.

Map No: 4   MM 230-10

Évelyne LEDÉ
La Pastourelle
Saint-Lormel
22130 Plancoët
Côtes-d'Armor
Tel: (0)2 96 84 03 77
Fax: (0)2 96 84 03 77

Sheer delight for lovers of the utterly personal, even eccentric. In this miniature museum of a house, the infectiously vibrant Rhona will introduce you to her wiggly Chinese sofa, her husband's regimental drum, the 18th-century looking glass in your room and other cherished household gods. A home like no other, a remarkable garden (climb up to the second terrace with a drink and a book), a supremely comfortable bed (with view of a fine bathroom through the glass door), a generous and elegant breakfast, a 10-minute walk to the beach. Unforgettable.

Rooms: One double with own bath, shower & wc.

Price: 250 Frs for two, including breakfast.

Meals: Wide choice within walking distance.

Open: All year.

From Dinan central square, take rue de Lehon, through Porte St Louis, follow road down, bear left below ramparts, straight across into rue de Coëtquen.

Map No: 4   MM 230-25

Rhona LOCKWOOD
55 rue de Coëtquen
22100 Dinan
Côtes-d'Armor
Tel: (0)2 96 85 23 49

A quiet country place with genuine farming folk, nice, simple and direct who offer gentle piped music and Breton pancakes for breakfast in the big traditional dining room. Madame collects dolls and other items of folklore. Great carved mirror-fronted wardrobes are standard here, the beds are firm and comfortable, the bathrooms modern. You will feel well looked after and there is a kitchen annexe for self-catering.

Rooms: 2 double, 1 triple, each with bath or shower and wc.

Price: 210 Frs for two, including breakfast.

Meals: Choice in Yffiniac 4km. Self-catering.

Open: All year.

Gites for 25 people

After the French Revolution, priests would be hidden here en route to Jersey. Hang expense and hide in this wonderful house. Old, old stones are combined with rich, deep-piled carpets, Christine's extraordinary mediæval-inspired art, and the family heirlooms. There are even hydro-massage baths, among the many little luxuries. Bedrooms are vast; one has gilt chairs, a four-poster AND a *lit bateau*... very modern-mediæval; another has a painted bathroom ceiling. Expect a smiling, gracious welcome from a naturally hospitable couple.

Rooms: 2 double, 1 twin, 1 triple, each with bath & wc.

Price: 590-750 Frs for two, including breakfast. Extra adult 150 Frs.

Meals: Choice within 5km.

Open: All year.

From N12 exit Yffiniac (NOT 'Yffiniac Gare') into village. Go 1km then left towards Plédran, through La Croix Orin: Le Grenier is down hill on left, 3.5km from Yffiniac centre.

Map No: 4   MM 230-23

Marie-Reine & Fernand LOQUIN
Le Grenier
22120 Yffiniac
Côtes-d'Armor
Tel: (0)2 96 72 64 55
Fax: (0)2 96 72 68 74
e-mail: oliloqui@cybercom.fr

From St Brieuc N12 E dir. Rennes for 12km then NE on D786 dir. Le Val André for 8.5km. In Planguenoual D59 dir. Lamballe; house signposted after 2.5km.

Map No: 4   MM 230-9

Jean-Yves & Christine MARIVIN
Manoir de la Hazaie
22400 Planguenoual
Côtes-d'Armor
Tel: (0)2 96 32 73 71
Fax: (0)2 96 32 79 72

Enter the enclosed courtyard and you will discover the charms of this 17th-century grey stone presbytery with its blue shutters and climbing roses. Walled gardens and an orchard for picnics complete the peaceful, private mood. Rooms are finely furnished. The biggest is high and stylish, and the style is reflected in its amazing bathroom. The cosy attic rooms have great character, low beams and small shower rooms (not for taller people). Madame has itineraries for your deeper discovery of her area — plan 2 or 3 days if possible.

Rooms: 1 double and 2 twin, all with bath or shower & wc.

Price: 300 Frs for two, including breakfast; terms for longer stays (exc. July & Aug).

Meals: 125 Frs, including wine & coffee.

Open: All year.

Gites for 6 people

The Robinsons lovingly gutted this solid stone house in an active farming village (early-morning rural activity on their road) then John hung his admirable collection of watercolours. The old stones and beams set the tone for the open ground-floor living area that is reserved for guests. The guestrooms have firm beds, floral drapes, lace curtains; the garden is a triumph of British talent and Breton weather. John is eagerly chatty, Sue is quieter; they both enjoy their multinational evenings. Dinan is 10km away.

Rooms: 2 double, 3 twin, each with bath or shower & wc. Extra beds available.

Price: 280-300 Frs for two, including breakfast.

Meals: 90 Frs, excluding wine.

Open: All year except February.

From Guingamp N12 towards Morlaix, then Louargat exit. From Louargat church, D33 to Tregrom (7km). House in village centre, opposite church (blue door in wall).

Map No: 3   MM 230-6

Nicole de MORCHOVEN
Le Presbytère Tregrom
22420 Plouaret
Côtes d'Armor
Tel: (0)2 96 47 94 15

Plouer is beside the N176. Take Plouër exit, do not enter village: instead, go straight on towards La Hisse on D12. House on right after 2.5km.

Map No: 4   MM 230-11

John & Sue ROBINSON
La Renardais, Le Repos
22490 Plouër-sur-Rance
Côtes-d'Armor
Tel: (0)2 96 86 89 81
Fax: (0)2 96 86 99 22

Exposed to the wild Breton elements, this fortified Bishop's seat, now a vegetable farm, offers fine walks in its grounds and a luxurious interior where marble fireplaces, gilt mirrors and antiques abound. Madame's *salon* is classically French while she, a young mother, is warmly direct and not at all grand. Rooms are big and richly decorated, the tower room deliciously different, more 'rustic', with its timbers and mezzanine, and breakfast a Breton feast to linger over in good company.

Rooms: 2 double, 1 twin, 1 triple and 2 suites for 3-4 people; all with private bathrooms.

Price: 550 Frs for two, including breakfast.

Meals: 250 Frs, including wine & coffee (on reservation).

Open: All year.

Modern houses have a hard time getting into this book but this one sailed in. Clad in red cedar, open-plan to provide space for six children, its wood, metal and glass are in perfect harmony; only the best materials are used and every tiny detail has been taken care of, e.g. plain white covers on beds, Eastern-style cushions and wall hangings on plain walls. The beds and towels are superb, shower-pressure just right. Breakfast is *un peu brunch*, as carefully thought out as the house. Lovely people and an exquisite, serene house.

Rooms: 1 double/twin, 1 double + bunks, each with shower & wc.

Price: 280 Frs for two, including breakfast.

Meals: Within walking distance.

Open: All year.

From Guingamp, D8 to Plougrescant. In Plougrescant, right after the church (leaning spire) and right again 200m along.

Map No: 4   MM 230-7

Vicomte & Vicomtesse de ROQUEFEUIL
Manoir de Kergrec'h
22820 Plougrescant
Côtes-d'Armor
Tel: (0)2 96 92 59 13
Fax: (0)2 96 92 51 27

From Dinan N176 W dir. St Brieuc for about 12km. Exit right to Plélan-le-Petit. Follow signs to 'Centre/Mairie'; at 'Mairie' right towards St Maudez then 2nd right.

Map No: 4   MM 230-24

Martine & Hubert VIANNAY
Malik
Chemin de l'Étoupe
22980 Plélan-le-Petit
Côtes-d'Armor
Tel: (0)2 96 27 62 71

BRITTANY

There are stained glass scenes from the life of Joan of Arc whose descendants (*Maid* of Orleans?) are said to have lived here, there are period murals, gilded mouldings, elaborate fixtures and fittings in stupendous quantity, none uncomfortably new. The dining-room is great fun — expect porcelain, silver and homemade cake at breakfast. Generous bedrooms have unusual angles and furnishings; Madame, an ex-journalist, loves doing B&B and her warm-hearted attention proves it; the bassets will walk with you in the fine garden.

Rooms: 4 double, 2 twin, each with bath & wc. Extra bed 120 Frs.

Price: 380-480 Frs for two, including breakfast.

Meals: 180 Frs, excluding wine (80 Frs max.).

Open: All year.

Sleep in the old cider-press; father still brews his magic for the family and guests' use. But the two most memorable things here are, first, Marie-Christine's radiant and passionate smile as she talks about her native Brittany, its myths, its pathways and its soul; and, secondly, the sympathetic use of wood on floor, ceilings and walls. Breakfasts are enormous, perhaps with Breton music in the background. It is quiet and cosy, the setting is lovely and Marie-Christine is delightful.

Rooms: 2 triple, each with shower & wc.

Price: 250 Frs for two, including breakfast.

Meals: Good crêperie in Brasparts.

Open: All year.

Gîtes for 15 people

From Quimperlé D22 NE towards Pontivy for 6km; château on left — take care turning in!

Map No: 3 — MM 230-34

Monique & Michel BELLIN
Château de Kerlarec
29300 Arzano
Finistère
Tel: (0)2 98 71 75 06
Fax: (0)2 98 71 74 55

From Morlaix D785 S towards Quimper for about 35km. 800m before Brasparts, turn right (on bend) & follow signs.

Map No: 3 — MM 230-19

Marie-Christine CHAUSSY
Garz ar Bik
29190 Brasparts
Finistère
Tel: (0)2 98 81 47 14
Fax: (0)2 98 81 47 99

This neat old farmhouse has kept watch over the bay for generations. Typically Breton, the entrance is guarded by a religious statue and, as you would expect, the *Bretonne* room has proper Breton furniture while the *Romantique* room has a canopied bed with bunches of roses. There are flowers everywhere, indoors and out, on the walls, on the balconies, in the garden, in the rustic, flagstoned dining-room where you have breakfast. A peaceful house, charming hosts and just five minutes walk from the sea.

Rooms: 2 double (one on ground floor), each with shower & wc.

Price: 250 Frs for two, including breakfast.

Meals: Choice in Douarnenez.

Open: All year.

Gîtes for 12 people

small

From Douarnenez, D7 towards Locronan. House is before village, on first road on left after sign for 'la plage du Ris'; signposted.

Map No: 3   MM 230-17

Henri & Henriette GONIDEC
Lanévry
Kerlaz
29100 Douarnenez
Finistère
Tel: (0)2 98 92 19 12

Madame is a darling — quiet, serene and immensely kind — and really treats her guests as friends. The long, low, granite house has been in the family for all of its 300 years, enjoying the peace of this wind-blown, bird-sung spot just five minutes walk from the sea and that gorgeous coastal path. Most of the building consists of gîtes; the *chambres d'hôtes* are squeezed into the far end — definitely small, impeccably simple, like the dining-room. With charming Port Manech and some handsome beaches nearby, it is a wonderful holiday spot.

Rooms: 2 double, 3 twin, all with shower & wc.

Price: 240 Frs for two, including breakfast.

Meals: In village: walking distance.

Open: All year.

Gîtes for 14 people

From Pont Aven, D77 towards Port Manech: right just before the signpost Port Manech, and 1st left. Signposted 'Chambres d'Hôtes'.

Map No: 3   MM 230-33

Yveline GOURLAOUEN
Kerambris
Port Manech
29920 Nevez
Finistère
Tel: (0)2 98 06 83 82

Squarely planted in its Breton soil, this is without doubt a family house open to guests not a purpose-converted undertaking. The children now run the farm and the Gralls have time for visitors. After a blissful night (warm traditional decor, excellent mattresses, neat modern bathrooms) and a bucolic awakening to birdsong in the fields, come down to Madame's homemade *crêpes* or *far breton* at their square Breton table beside the deeply-carved sideboard. Family antiques, family warmth, peace and unity that reassure and relax.

Rooms: 2 double, 1 twin, each with shower & wc.

Price: 200-250 Frs for two, including breakfast.

Meals: Restaurant 2.5km.

Open: All year.

The verandah is a modern appendage on this 19th-century house but the welcome inside is timelessly genuine. Your hosts are relaxed and friendly without being effusive. Monsieur gave up farming because he preferred dealing with guests! They have mixed ancient and modern in their furniture and decor and the whole house is comfortable without being exciting, unless you count the electrically-operated double mattress. Breakfast is more like brunch with cheeses and meats and cake... and you are so near the sea.

Rooms: 1 double/twin, 1 suite for 4, both with own bath & wc.

Price: 360 Frs for two, including breakfast.

Meals: Good choice within walking distance.

Open: All year.

Gîtes for 10 people

From St Pol-de-Léon D10 W to Cléder (8km). There, right towards coast (Theven-Kerbrat); leave road to Château de Traonjoly on left; turn left 2km after Cléder; signposted.

Map No: 3   MM 230-4

François & Marceline GRALL
Kernévez
29233 Cléder
Finistère
Tel: (0)2 98 69 41 14

From St Pol de Léon D10 to Plouescat. Just after town name sign right towards 'Plages' & Pen-Kear. Signposted.

Map No: 3   MM 230-4

Marie-Thérèse & Raymond LE DUFF
Pen-Kear
29430 Plouescat
Finistère
Tel: (0)2 98 69 62 87
Fax: (0)2 98 69 67 33

A beautiful house set in woods 3km from the sea, it contains some brilliant examples of Old Breton furniture — a *lit clos* (big carved wooden box with doors concealing a small double bed), dresser, chests, wardrobes; and Madame is one of the most attractive, humorous people we know. Her highly-qualified son makes barrels for Breton *eau-de-vie* on the premises. The living room is light and generous, like its owner; bedrooms have more old pieces, pretty fabrics, parquet throughout and one of the showers behind a curtain.

Rooms: 2 double, 1 twin, all with shower & wc.

Price: 250 Frs for two, including breakfast.

Meals: Town very near.

Open: All year.

Gites for 6 people

The view across fields and wooded hills is perfectly wonderful. Your quarters are in a converted outbuilding and each smallish room (older children only, who can sleep alone) gives onto the long terrace where chairs await. There is a big verandah room for breakfast (with *crêpes* or croissants), where a richly-carved Breton wardrobe takes pride of place. Rooms and bathrooms are impeccable. Madame is efficient, full of information about Breton culture, and very purposeful. Small pets welcome.

Rooms: 4 double, 2 twin, all with shower & wc.

Price: 250 Frs for two, including breakfast.

Meals: 85 Frs, including wine & coffee. Self-catering.

Open: All year.

From Douarnenez D765 towards Audierne for 2km (Pouldavid is a suburb of Douarnenez). 500m after lights, right (beside No46) onto C10 following signs for Chambres d'Hôtes.

Map No: 3   MM 230-17

Mme Marie-Paule LEFLOCH
Manoir de Kervent
Pouldavid
29100 Douarnenez
Finistère
Tel: (0)2 98 92 04 90

From Quimper, D765 towards Quimperlé. At Saint-Yvi left towards Kervren; at very end of lane (2km).

Map No: 3   MM 230-33

Odile LE GALL
Kervren
29140 Saint-Yvi
Finistère
Tel: (0)2 98 94 70 34

The setting is out of this world so what matter the newness of the house? You can boat on the lake, walk by the babbling stream through the woods, sit on the bank and gaze across the valley to the distant hills, or barbecue in the orchard. The sense of welcome comes naturally to this serene retired couple who are happy to share their truly privileged environment in a quiet hamlet. The rooms are perfectly adequate, the atmosphere incomparable.

Rooms: 1 triple, 1 double, both with shower & wc.

Price: 230 Frs for two, including breakfast.

Meals: Choice 5km. Barbecue possible.

Open: All year.

Gîtes for 6 people

From Quimperlé D790 towards le Faouët 9km. Left to Querrien. There follow signs towards Mellac & Belle Fontaine. 1st left to Kerfaro. There left after stone house. Last house in lane.

Map No: 3   MM 230-34

Renée & Yves LE GALLIC
Kerfaro
29310 Querrien
Finistère
Tel: (0)2 98 71 30 02

A haven is what guests call this exquisitely renovated house (ancient stones set off by plain white walls) with its own chapel. Big, beamed guestrooms with antique furniture, modern beds and 4-star bathrooms, relaxed and knowledgeable hosts who want to communicate their feel for 'real' Brittany (Peter hunts treasure), serve refined dinners made with home-grown organic vegetables and organise fungus-hunting holidays. Work up your appetite on miles of canal towpath or by visiting the beautiful unsung Breton hinterland.

Rooms: 2 double, 1 twin, 1 family room for 4, all with own bath/shower & wc.

Price: 260-295 Frs for two, including breakfast.

Meals: 120 Frs, including wine & coffee (by arrangement).

Open: Easter to October.

From Brest N165 towards Quimper for 45km; left on N164 to Carhaix Plouguer. At 'Districenter' on N164 follow signs to Prevasy; right at triangular green, straight on to house.

Map No: 3   MM 230-20

Peter & Clarissa NOVAK
Manoir de Prevasy
29270 Carhaix
Finistère
Tel: (0)2 98 93 24 36

Uncomplicated folk leading a simple farming life (visitors can watch the 30 cows being milked as long as they don't disturb the old gals), the Oliers are real weatherbeaten Bretons who have converted an outhouse into three good basic rooms (restfully plain white walls) and a comfortable dayroom. Madame serves a Breton breakfast in her dining-room; Monsieur may offer you a bunch of flowers. Their smile is a great gift. There are walks across two valleys from the house; beaches and ports are 10km away.

Rooms: 1 double, 1 triple, 1 twin/quadruple all with own shower & wc.

Price: 250 Frs for two, including breakfast. Extra person 80 Frs.

Meals: Good choice 5km. Kitchen facilities.

Open: All year.

This rural haven lies between *Armor*, the land by the sea and *Argoat*, the land of woods. It is a Breton house with Breton furniture, a huge brass pot once used for mixing *crêpes*, and naturally hospitable Breton owners. They love children who may explore the dairy farm. Madame is welcoming and chatty (in French), Monsieur has a reassuring earthy calmness. One of the large, light, country-style rooms has just been redone in sunny yellow. Copious breakfasts include those *crêpes* and home-grown kiwi fruit in season.

Rooms: 3 double and 1 twin, all with shower & wc.

Price: 250 Frs for two, including breakfast.

Meals: Restaurant 4km.

Open: All year.

From Douarnenez D765 towards Audierne. On entering Confort-Meilars, 1st left and follow signs for 2.5km.

Map No: 3   MM 230-17

Anne & Jean OLIER
Kerantum
29790 Mahalon
Finistère
Tel: (0)2 98 74 51 93

From Scaër, D50 direction Coray-Briec; after 3km, left at 'Ty Ru' and follow signpost for Kerloaï.

Map No: 3   MM 230-19

Louis & Thérèse PENN
Kerloaï
29390 Scaër
Finistère
Tel: (0)2 98 59 42 60
Fax: (0)2 98 59 05 67

On the fascinating, desolate heath of the Monts d'Arée, Kreisker is a sensitive, utterly Breton conversion: all local stone, slate roofs and giant slabs of schist from the old floors. Inside there is scrubbed wood, more stone, ethnic rugs, fresh cotton and pretty china. The independent room has a lovely blue/grey-clothed brass bed and a fine bathroom. After the feast that is breakfast, your ears ringing with Madame's knowledgeable talk of Breton culture, go forth and explore this ancient land.

Rooms: 1 double with bathroom.

Price: 230 Frs for two, including breakfast.

Meals: Crêperies and restaurants 3-15km.

Open: All year.

Gîtes for 8 people

The young couple who have converted this old Breton weavers' house are active, artistic (he has briefly set his darkly expressive painting aside) and fun. They have four school-age children, three guestrooms and a small *auberge* serving all sorts of *crêpes* and meats grilled on the open fire. The rooms have clever layouts, lovely colour schemes and fabrics; the quadruples both have two beds on mezzanines — superb. All is gentle and soft; there are animals and swings for children's delight — and more *crêpes*.

Rooms: 2 quadruple, 1 double, all with bath or shower & wc.

Price: 250-350 Frs for two, including breakfast.

Meals: About 130 Frs, including wine.

Open: April to mid-November.

From Morlaix, D785 towards Quimper. At La Croix Cassée, D42 to Botmeur; house is on right on leaving village towards La Feuillée.

Map No: 3   MM 230-19

Marie-Thérèse & Jean-Bernard SOLLIEC
Kreisker
29690 Botmeur
Finistère
Tel: (0)2 98 99 63 02

From St Brieuc N12 towards Morlaix, exit 'Plouigneau' towards Plougonven. There towards Plourin-lès-Morlaix for 5km. House on right; signposted.

Map No: 3   MM 230-5

Charlick & Yolande de TERNAY
La Grange de Coatélan
29640 Plougonven
Finistère
Tel: (0)2 98 72 60 16

Gill, a senior member of the Quilters' Guild and much-appreciated teacher of patchwork, and Clive, a retired banker and accomplished cook (try his excellent 4-course dinners), are friendly, humorous hosts, enjoying their year-round flowering garden in the balmy Breton air. Their house (a resurrected ruin) has soft furnishings, soft cats, a nice mix of old and new. Their welcome includes good simple rooms with non-matching beds and informed help on what to see in the adopted country they so love.

Rooms: 1 twin, 1 family room for 4, both with shower or hip bath & wc; 1 twin sharing bathroom.

Price: 220-270 Frs for 2, including breakfast.

Meals: 95 Frs, including kir, wine & coffee.

Open: All year.

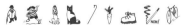

The Balsans have renovated their old farmhouse to within an inch of its life, but lovers of all things clean and efficient will delight in the order brought about by its restoration. The dayroom is large and light, with a lovely fire and large french windows leading onto the patio and garden. Rooms lead off a long, white passage upstairs and are extremely comfortable. The sea is 500 yards away, historic towns are close and so are the mystical standing stones of Carnac. Homemade Breton cakes and jams for breakfast.

Rooms: 3 double, 2 twin, all with shower & wc.

Price: 300-320 Frs for two, including breakfast.

Meals: Good choice 1km.

Open: All year.

From Morlaix, D785 towards Pleyben for 23km. Left on D764 towards Huelgoat for 7km. Right on D36 towards Châteauneuf-du-Faou. Laz is on the D36 after Châteauneuf; house at end of village on left. (Secure parking.)

Map No: 3   MM 230-19

Gill & Clive THOMPSON
Les Deux Aiguilles
3 Grand'Rue
29520 Laz
Finistère
Tel: (0)2 98 26 87 23

From Carnac town take Avenue des Druides towards Beaumer. At crossroads left on Chemin de Beaumer. Impasse de Beaumer is 2nd on left.

Map No: 4   MM 230-35

Marie-France & Daniel BALSAN
L'Alcyone
Impasse de Beaumer
56340 Carnac-Plage
Morbihan
Tel: (0)2 97 52 78 11
Fax: (0)2 97 52 13 02

Madame, an elegant and wonderfully French country lady, serves generous breakfasts ('a little different every day') in her pretty beamed dining-room by the great fireplace and the grandfather clock. It used to be a farmhouse, still has a pond where you can do some desultory fishing and is just 20 minutes from those little harbour towns, the beaches and the ferry to Belle Ile. Inside the old walls, the B&B conversion is fairly standard but each room has its own private outside area and such restful views all round.

Rooms: 5 double/triple, each with shower & wc.

Price: 240 Frs for two, including breakfast.

Meals: Good restaurants nearby. Self-catering.

Open: All year.

The house feels much older than its twenty years because of the old timbers and doors used to build it — an excellent job. The bedrooms are smart, almost snazzy, with their orange, pink and green-clothed walls and antiques though the double room and bed are small by modern standards. Your hosts are keen to communicate their love and knowledge of this area. Their house is just 150m from the estuary and there are beaches, sailing, golf courses within easy reach; standing stones and dolmens too.

Rooms: 1 double with shower & wc, 1 twin with bath & wc.

Price: 400 Frs for two, including breakfast.

Meals: Many possibilities locally.

Open: All year.

From N24 Baud exit onto D768 towards Auray for 16km. At first Pluvigner roundabout left onto D16 towards Locminé for 4km then turn right and follow signs.

Map No: 4   MM 230-36

Marie-Claire COLLET
Kerdavid-Duchentil
56330 Pluvigner
Morbihan
Tel: (0)2 97 56 00 59

From Vannes, N165 towards Lorient; left at Auray on D28 to St Philibert; right on D781. After 500m, left at Le Congre then first left into Rue des Paludiers then left into Rue des Peupliers. House at end on right — no signs!

Map No: 4   MM 230-36

Joël & Mylène CUZON du REST
Lann Kermane
13 rue des Peupliers
56470 Saint-Philibert
Morbihan
Tel: (0)2 97 55 03 75
Fax: (0)2 97 30 02 79

The situation is heavenly, cradled in a quiet hamlet 200 yards from the river in a particularly lovely corner of Brittany. The people are delightful: Philippe pots and teaches aikido, Martine looks after old folk and young Melissa, both have lots of time for their guests. The two big, superbly-converted, uncluttered attic rooms have been decorated with flair in subtle pastels and fitted with good shower rooms. Guests have their own sitting/breakfast room and kitchen. Birds sing. The cat is one of the best ever. The welcome is genuine.

Rooms: 2 twin, each with shower & wc.

Price: 220 Frs for two, including breakfast.

Meals: Wide choice in St Nicolas, 3km. Guests' kitchen.

Open: Easter to October; otherwise by arrangement.

From Pontivy, D768 towards Lorient. Exit for Port-Arthur/St Nicolas-des-Eaux to St Nicolas. Right immediately after bridge and follow signs for 3km (Chambres d'Hôtes and Poterie).

Map No: 4   MM 230-35

Martine MAIGNAN & Philippe BOIVIN
Lezerhy
56310 Bieuzy-les-Eaux
Morbihan
Tel: (0)2 97 27 74 59
Fax: (0)2 97 27 74 59

A beautiful setting among the fields, Carnac minutes away, beaches and coastal pathways close. Kerimel is a handsome group of granite farm buildings. The bedroom is a beauty: plain walls, some panelling, pale blue covers and curtains, old stone and beams plus modern comfort. (More rooms to come soon.) The dining-room is cottage perfection: dried flowers hanging from beams over wooden table, tiled floor, vast blackened chimney, stone walls. Gentle, generous people... "We talked of flowers", wrote one guest.

Rooms: 1 double/twin + single with shower & wc. 4 more planned for summer 1999.

Price: 290 Frs for two, including breakfast. Extra bed 90 Frs.

Meals: Good place 3km away.

Open: All year.

From N165 exit for Quiberon/Carnac on D768 for 4km then right to Ploemel. There D105 W towards Erdeven; house signposted on right after 1.5km.

Map No: 4   MM 230-35

Babeth & Pierre MALHERBE
Kerimel
56400 Ploemel (Carnac)
Morbihan
Tel: (0)2 97 56 84 72
Fax: (0)2 97 56 84 72

In the heart of rural Brittany where you feel the clock stopped 50 years ago, a forgotten peace descends, your pace slows, *la tranquillité* sets in. This welcoming couple has converted an old farmhouse and its barns into a wonderful holiday spot, a place full of warmth, laughter and the happiness of being there. The weekly international barbecue with guests and locals is highly appreciated, the 3 acres of garden give space for all (there are 7 gîtes and a pool too); it is ideal for families.

Rooms: 1 twin with shower & wc, 1 two-room suite for 4 with shower & wc.

Price: 250 Frs for two, including breakfast.

Meals: In village or good choice 5km.

Open: All year.

Gîtes for 28 people

Antiques and old lace in a pretty 16th-century château. It has a totally 'Breton mansion' *salon* with velvet curtains and high-back chairs; silver coffee pots and freshly squeezed orange juice at breakfast; 3000 rosebushes in the big garden. An amazing place; the bedrooms are stunning too. The Belordes, retired teachers, bought back the family seat after decades of 'alien owners'. Her father was in London with de Gaulle; she loves the English, enjoys cosmopolitan conversation, offers candlelit champagne dinners (supplement...). Expensive but special.

Rooms: 1 suite for 4, 1 double, 1 twin, all with bath & wc.

Price: 500-800 Frs for two, including breakfast.

Meals: 250 Frs, including aperitif, wine & coffee. Picnic possible.

Open: All year.

From Pontivy D764 towards Josselin for 5km; straight on through C4 (Noyal-Pontivy/St Thuriau) crossroads; 100m after crossroads, right to Pennerest.

Map No: 4   MM 230-22

Peter & Pat ROBERTS
Pennerest
56920 Noyal Pontivy
Morbihan
Tel: (0)2 97 38 35 76
Fax: (0)2 97 38 23 80

From Nantes leave A83 ring-road on D85 past airport. At T-junction at 'Champ de Foire' left through Pont St Martin & follow signs to Le Plessis.

Map No: 9   MM 232-28

M & Mme BELORDE
Château du Plessis
44860 Pont-Saint-Martin
Loire-Atlantique
Tel: (0)2 40 26 81 72
Fax: (0)2 40 32 76 67
e-mail: http://www.chateaux-france.com/-plessis.fr

Such is the owners' commitment to the faithful restoration of this 17th-century château (500 hours work on the walnut panelling) that the heating is underfloor to dispense with radiators and only period furniture has been added — Monsieur is an avid auction-goer. This produces a feeling of Renaissance nobility that extends everywhere except to the bathrooms, which are reassuringly modern. The charming Calonnes produce a Muscadet from the surrounding vineyards, served as an aperitif at about seven before you sally forth for dinner.

Rooms: 5 double with bath or shower & wc.

Price: 470 or 670 Frs for two, including breakfast.

Meals: Wide choice within 5 minutes.

Open: April to October; by arrangement in winter.

Gîtes for 10 people

The typical long low 18th-century house in its vineyard setting is perfect for a quiet escape. The friendly, unobtrusive Desbrosses particularly enjoy the company of foreign visitors who may use their library and drawing-room with its deeply comfortable chairs around an imposing fireplace. Madame is an artist and potter — the strong colours are her (successful) choice, guestrooms are individually styled and dinner is served on matching blue and yellow plates. You will be taken very good care of at La Mozardière.

Rooms: 1 suite, 1 double, both with shower & wc.

Price: 270 Frs for two, including breakfast.

Meals: 95 Frs, including wine.

Open: All year.

From Nantes N249 towards Poitiers then N149 towards Clisson. Just before Le Pallet right to Monnières then left on D76 towards Clisson. Château 1km along on left.

Map No: 9   MM 232-29

Annick & Didier CALONNE
Château Plessis-Brezot
44690 Monnières
Loire-Atlantique
Tel: (0)2 40 54 63 24
Fax: (0)2 40 54 66 07

From Nantes D937 towards La Roche. At Rocheservière D753 to Legé. In village centre towards Challans. Left just after 'Le Paradis' restaurant. Signposted 'Richebonne'.

Map No: 9   MM 232-40

Christine & Gérard DESBROSSES
La Mozardière
Richebonne
44650 Legé
Loire-Atlantique
Tel: (0)2 40 04 98 51
Fax: (0)2 40 26 31 61

It is all rather endearingly formal, with breakfast at 9am sharp and a touch of old-fashioned primness about table manners. But your graceful, cultivated hosts always dine with you, creating an authentic taste of life with the French country aristocracy; dress for it, and enjoy a game of billiards afterwards. Inevitably, the bedrooms are magnificent. The château has its own lake and 100 hectares of magnificent parkland... all within the Brière Regional Park where water and land are inextricably mingled and wildlife abounds.

Rooms: 2 double, 1 twin, all with own bath or shower and wc.

Price: 450-500 Frs for two, including breakfast.

Meals: Candlelit dinner 220 Frs, incl. aperitif, wine & coffee.

Open: All year.

Gîtes for 10 people

A fine welcome awaits you at this young couple's farmhouse out in the sunflower fields. Francette has put her considerable flair into turning the top of the house, previously empty space, into an attractive communal sitting area and two delightful rooms, all white walls, local furniture, old tiled floors, exposed stone and pretty yet unfussy decor. There is a little flower garden, a shop selling René's duck preserves (served at breakfast too), delicious dinners and a peaceful night guaranteed.

Rooms: 1 room for 4/5, 1 double, both with shower and wc.

Price: 280 Frs for two, including breakfast. Extra person 40 Frs.

Meals: 95 Frs, incl. wine (bookings only). Picnic possible outside.

Open: All year.

From N165 exit 15 for La Roche-Bernard towards La Baule to Herbignac. Here, fork left on D47 towards St Lyphard for 4km; house on right.

Map No: 4   MM 232-13

François & Cécile de la MONNERAYE
Château de Coët Caret
44410 Herbignac
Loire-Atlantique
Tel: (0)2 40 91 41 20
Fax: (0)2 40 91 37 46

From Nantes ringroad towards Bordeaux then D937 through Rocheservière and on for 4.5km. At first crossroads after town right on D84/D94 to Ferme des Forges. Signposted on left.

Map No: 9   MM 232-40

Francette & René PEAUDEAU
La Ferme des Forges
44650 Legé
Loire-Atlantique
Tel: (0)2 40 04 92 99
Fax: (0)2 40 26 31 90

These are the sweetest people! They really do 'treat their guests as friends'. Madame is bright and sparkling with a smiling open face, very proud to show you her decorated books, musical scores and hats; Monsieur is a retired farmer, less chatty but equally friendly. The house is warm (log fire in winter), cosily country-furnished and the rooms are soft and welcoming (but mind your head on the way up) with great attention to detail. Breakfast at the long table, served in pretty little baskets.

Rooms: 2 triple, each with shower & wc; 1 triple sharing bath & separate wc.

Price: 248 Frs for two, including breakfast.

Meals: Good restaurant 3km. Self-catering in summer.

Open: All year.

Gîtes for 4 people

From Rennes N137 towards Nantes for 63km. Exit at Nozay on N171 towards Blain for 8km. At bottom of hill, left at roadside cross; signposted.

Map No: 4   MM 232-15

Yvonne & Marcel PINEAU
La Mercerais
44130 Blain
Loire-Atlantique
Tel: (0)2 40 79 04 30

The Arnaults, retired farmers, are a quiet, welcoming couple who may offer you a glass of homemade rosé in their wine cellar under the old windmill. They are real country people, their traditional ivy-clad farmhouse, set among vineyards and wheat fields, has an authentic country interior — not falsely pretty but muted, practical and clean — and they enjoy the contact with guests. There are many craft and cultural events in the area, including the Artichoke Fair in Coutures in September.

Rooms: 2 triple with washbasins, sharing a bathroom & separate wc.

Price: 190 Frs for two, including breakfast.

Meals: Wide choice within 10km.

Open: February to October.

The Loire Valley

From Saumur, D751 to Coutures, through Gennes. 2km after Coutures, left on rue des Alleuds, following signs to Chambres d'Hôtes.

Map No: 10   MM 232-32

Marcel & Thérèse ARNAULT
Fredelin
49320 Coutures
Maine-et-Loire
Tel: (0)2 41 91 21 26

This handsome, airy manor has elegance in its very stones — though the (genuine) beams in the dining-room look strangely anachronistic — and a wonderful riverside garden looking up to the village across the water. The panels, cornices, mouldings, subtly-muted floor tiles add grace, the traditional French *salon* furnishings bring softness. In these formal surroundings Madame, relaxed and communicative, adores having guests. Monsieur is jovial and loves fishing! Fine bedrooms, superb bathrooms.

Rooms: 3 double, 1 twin room, each with bath & wc.

Price: 360-400 Frs for two, including breakfast.

Meals: 130 Frs, excluding wine.

Open: Easter to 31 October.

A dream for fans of neo-Gothic — the interior is worthy of Hollywood. The everyday sitting-room is wildly mock mediæval while the drawing-room was taken whole from an 18th-century château. This was once a properly self-sufficient country estate and there are the remains of a chapel, dovecote and mill (you can swim in the river). Any proper château has a Bishop's Room: you can sleep in this one. An elegantly warm welcome from lovely people who fill this house with friends and family and might even play bridge with you.

Rooms: 2 triple, 1 double, each with bath or shower & wc.

Price: 350 Frs for two, including breakfast.

Meals: 120 Frs, including wine & coffee.

Open: Easter to 31 October.

From Angers, N162 towards Lion d'Angers. At Grieul (20km) right on D291 to Grez-Neuville. At church, rue d'Ecluse towards river.

Map No: 5   MM 232-19

Jacqueline & Auguste BAHUAUD
La Croix d'Etain
2 rue de l'Ecluse
49220 Grez-Neuville
Maine-et-Loire
Tel: (0)2 41 95 68 49
Fax: (0)2 41 18 02 72

From Angers, N23 north. At Seiches-sur-Loir, D74 towards Châteauneuf/Sarthe for 5.5km. Chateau is on right as you leave Montreuil village.

Map No: 5   MM 232-20

Jacques & Marie BAILLIOU
Château de Montreuil
49140 Montreuil-sur-Loir
Maine-et-Loire
Tel: (0)2 41 76 21 03

This solid old manor is a truly French family house: the energetic Bastids have a health-food shop in town, four lovely children and an open and genuinely welcoming attitude. The reception rooms, of generous proportions, are furnished with antiques and heirlooms but not imposing. The pleasant guestrooms are altogether simpler (two shower rooms are simply curtained off) and the big bosky garden is a good barrier against the road. Children love the neighbour's menagerie too. On request, all diets can be catered for at breakfast.

Rooms: 1 suite, 1 triple, 1 double, 1 twin each with bath or shower & wc.

Price: 250-350 Frs for two, including breakfast.

Meals: Wide choice in Saumur.

Open: All year (by arrangement in winter).

From Saumur centre N147 towards Angers. Cross Loire & railway, straight on for 200m to Renault garage then left on Ave des Maraîchers towards St Lambert. House on RH corner of junction with Rue Grange Couronne (300m from Saumur station by Rue Choudieu).

Map No: 10   MM 232-33

Catherine & Emmanuel BASTID
La Bouère Salée
Rue Grange Couronne
49400 Saint-Lambert-des-Levées,
Saumur
Maine-et-Loire
Tel: (0)2 41 67 38 85/
      (0)2 41 51 12 52

Once the servants' quarters of the château, it is in a quiet, deep and secluded valley, right on the GR3 (the long-distance path) and the Loire Valley walk. The bedrooms are under the high exposed roof beams, elegantly and discreetly done and with good antiques. Matching wallpaper and fabrics (flowery English?), and impeccable bathrooms and loos. Breakfast is beautifully served, with linen table napkins, silver tea-pot etc; it is refined but relaxed, and you can picnic in the garden if you wish.

Rooms: 1 double, 1 twin/triple, both with shower & wc.

Price: 320 Frs for two, including breakfast.

Meals: Wide choice in the area.

Open: Easter to November. By arrangement in winter.

From Saumur D751 W along Loire for 15km. In Gennes D69 S towards Doué-la-Fontaine up hill, past church & police station. At roundabout take road past Super U — drive to house is 500m along on left.

Map No: 10   MM 232-32

Annick & Jean-Baptiste BOISSET
Le Haut Joreau
49350 Gennes
Maine-et-Loire
Tel: (0)2 41 38 02 58

Overhanging trees shade the grassy approach to this rambling 19th-century château in 4 hectares of mature gardens. A wonderful woman greets you, a gentle artist and nature-lover with a very sure and personal approach to interiors, both house and human. It all feels warm and authentic, offering timeless comfort and silence in the lush green surroundings; one reader said "magical". The woodwork has been stripped back, walls are cloth-covered in rich colours, the furniture is old but not wealthy, the light pours in and you simply bask in harmony.

Rooms: 1 double, 1 triple & 1 suite for 5, all with bath or shower & wc.

Price: 320-440 Frs for 2; suite 720 Frs for 5, including breakfast. Extra bed 90 Frs.

Meals: Saumur 9km.

Open: All year (by arrangement in winter).

The cheerful, cosy sitting-room with its open fire immediately sets the tone — this is a charming, friendly house run by an equally welcoming young couple who have small twin sons and guest-loving dogs. Many readers have praised the hospitality shown to both young and old and the "remarkable" food — vegetarians catered for — served in the lovely light dining-room. The rooms, up steep stairs, are delightful (the 'family' room rather more ordinary) with showers behind curtains, 2 separate shared wc's and French towels (i.e. smaller than ours).

Rooms: 2 double, 2 twin, all with shower & sharing 2 separate wc's.

Price: 220 Frs for two, including breakfast.

Meals: 120 Frs, including wine & coffee.

Open: Mid-April to October.

From Saumur, N147 towards Longué. At la Ronde, D767 towards Vernantes; left on D129 towards Neuillé. 1km before Neuillé take Fontaine Suzon road; signposted.

Map No: 10   MM 232-33

Mme Monique CALOT
Château du Goupillon
49680 Neuillé
Maine-et-Loire
Tel: (0)2 41 52 51 89

From Angers, N162 towards Laval. At Le Lion-d'Angers, D770 towards Candé. After 1.5km left by big roadside cross; signposted.

Map No: 5   MM 232-19

M & Mme Patrick CARCAILLET
Le Petit Carqueron
49220 Le Lion d'Angers
Maine-et-Loire
Tel: (0)2 41 95 62 65

A fine house that the energetic young owners are still renovating, it has views across the little river that runs at the bottom of the garden and on into the countryside. The large, old-furnished, modern-bathroomed, arched-windowed bedrooms in the main house are lovely. One has a *pantalonnière*, a chest of drawers specially designed for trousers. The little cottage with its half-timbered entrance and spiral stair to the sleeping platform is delicious. You will be well cared for here in country peace.

Rooms: 2 triple with bath or shower & wc; 1 cottage for 2/3 with shower and kitchen.

Price: 270-300 Frs for two, including breakfast.

Meals: Choice 3-7km. Barbecue and picnic in garden.

Open: All year (by arrangement in winter).

From Angers N160 towards Cholet. Exit at Mûrs-Erigné & on towards Chalonnes for 3km. Signposted on right.

Map No: 10   MM 232-31

Philippe & Anita CATROUILLET
Les Roches
49610 Mozé-sur-Louet
Maine-et-Loire
Tel: (0)2 41 78 84 29

The design of this farm makes you want to sing — all is curvy harmony with virtually no farm mess to spoil it. Yet these farmers work hard, growing fields of lupins, hollyhocks and thyme for seed production: there is scent in the air. Your hosts' wing (other family members live on the farm too) has been renovated with simple good taste; each room has a personal touch and there are landing chairs for guests to watch farmyard life go by. Martine is most likeable, young, dynamic and conscious of what B&B enthusiasts really want.

Rooms: 1 double with shower & wc; 1 double, 1 twin, each with own shower, sharing 2 wc's (one behind curtain).

Price: 220 Frs for two, including breakfast.

Meals: Restaurants 3 or 7km.

Open: All year.

Gîtes for 18 people

From Angers, N260 towards Cholet, then D748 towards Poitiers. After Brissac, D761 towards Poitiers. Continue for 2km; house signposted on left, at end of avenue of chestnut trees.

Map No: 10   MM 232-32

Jean-Claude & Martine COLIBET
La Pichonnière
49320 Charcé
Maine-et-Loire
Tel: (0)2 41 91 29 37 (mealtimes)

Original is the word for this 200-year-old house in its little village. Design buffs will be thrilled by its curious fenestration (half a curvy-glazed triangle in your bathroom) and extraordinarily complicated dining table. Everyone will love the big peaceful garden, the deep-seated, welcoming sitting-room and the well-decorated, simply furnished bedrooms. English Claire is an amusing and knowledgeable hostess who organizes golfing tours; French Eric loves sharing the cooking and includes vegetarian specialities.

Rooms: 1 triple, 2 double, 1 twin, all with hip-bath/shower & wc.

Price: 260 Frs for two, including breakfast. Extra bed 100 Frs.

Meals: 90 Frs, excluding wine (40 Frs).

Open: April to October.

From Laval N162 through Château Gontier & 16km towards Angers. Right on D78 to St Martin-du-Bois. Past 'Tabac' then 1st left. House along on right.

Map No: 5   MM 232-19

Claire DIGARD & Eric PAJAK
La Pigeonnerie
18 rue du Prieuré
49500 Saint-Martin-du-Bois
Maine-et-Loire
Tel: (0)2 41 61 33 52

The countryside may not be the most spectacular but the house is utterly peaceful in its little hamlet and Monsieur will guide beginners in the art of billiards if they wish. Madame is shy but kind, welcoming and properly proud of her pretty, unfussy rooms where pastel colours, tiled floors and oriental rugs sit well under old rafters and stones. Breakfast, with homemade jams, can be in the garden on fine mornings and you can picnic there too or bicycle down to the banks of the Loire.

Rooms: 2 double, 1 triple, all with shower & wc.

Price: 250 Frs for two, including breakfast.

Meals: 90 Frs, including table wine & coffee.

Open: All year.

From Angers N761 towards Brissac & Doué. At les Alleuds left onto D90 towards Chemellier. After 3km hamlet on left.

Map No: 10   MM 232-32

Eliette EDON
49320 Maunit-Chemellier
Maine-et-Loire
Tel: (0)2 41 45 59 50

The château, partly in bad repair but endearingly so, has been in the family since 1757 and has an intimate family atmosphere that belies the imposing exterior. Your hosts are both excellent, smiling company. The guestrooms have an engaging air of faded grandeur. The suite (summer only) has white walls and Mexican rugs. Dine at a long table on wooden settles by the fireplace where copper pans adorn the wall. The River Loir is 2km away. Peace, real atmosphere in great walking, boating and cycling country. A wonderful place.

Rooms: 3 double, 1 family suite, each with bathroom.

Price: 450-550 Frs for two, including breakfast.

Meals: 135 Frs, excluding wine.

Open: All year.

Racine was appointed Prior here by his uncle but was removed by the bishop; the incident inspired *Les Plaideurs*. Rooms are in a converted priory outbuilding, each one a two-floor suite, well-but-simply furnished. The main house has a friendly family kitchen and a dining-room with stacks of books and a pianola in the fireplace. The old chapel is now a garden room for breakfasts and there's a big garden with a swimming pool. Your hosts are lovely people, interesting and educated. We love the area too... and its wines.

Rooms: 2 suites for 4, each with bath & 2 wc's; 1 twin with bath & wc.

Price: 400 Frs for two, including breakfast. Extra person 100 Frs.

Meals: 120 Frs, including aperitif, wine & coffee.

Open: March to November.

From Paris, A11, Durtal exit then D859 towards Châteauneuf for 2km, then D68 to Baracé. Entrance to château on right as you enter village.

Map No: 5   MM 232-20

Michel & Lucia FRANÇOIS
Château de la Motte
49430 Baracé
Maine-et-Loire
Tel: (0)2 41 76 93 75

From Angers N23 W dir. Nantes for 13km. Go through St Georges and on for about 1.5km then left after a garage. Go on past château then house is on left. Park outside and walk through gate.

Map No: 10   MM 232-31

Bernard & Geneviève GAULTIER
Prieuré de l'Epinay
49170 Saint-Georges-sur-Loire
Maine-et-Loire
Tel: (0)2 41 39 14 44
Fax: (0)2 41 39 14 44

The town is old and intriguing. The house was a rich man's residence in the 17th century; the Suite Blanche has beams, tiles, mirrors, fireplaces, carved Anjou *armoires*. Other rooms are big too, but less stunning, and maintenance may be needed. But the glorious living-room with its mystifyingly high-level door, high beamed ceiling and old built-in cupboards is worth the visit by itself. Monsieur restores antiques — his house speaks well of his trade. Madame is pleasant and efficient and restoration continues.

Rooms: 2 suites, 2 triple (1 with kitchenette), all with bath or shower & wc (very occasionally sharing).

Price: 290 Frs for two, including breakfast.

Meals: Choice in town or self-catering.

Open: March to October.

A big old house protected from the encroaching town by the flood lands it overlooks so views are across open fields. Its heavy furniture is old-fashioned elegant and if a degree of clutter disguises the antiqueness, the lived-in feel is comforting and guests have space and independence with their own sitting area. In the attractive breakfast/dining-room, the huge television and the stone fireplace vie for supremacy. Your retired hosts are unintrusive — Monsieur has a nice dry sense of humour — and welcome children.

Rooms: 2 double, 1 twin, 1 family room for 3/4; all with shower & wc.

Price: 230 Frs for two, including breakfast.

Meals: In village: son's restaurant.

Open: All year.

From Saumur, D147 towards Poitiers. In Montreuil-Bellay, Place des Augustins is parallel to, and on the left of, Rue Nationale.

Map No: 10   MM 232-33

Monique & Jacques GUÉZÉNEC
Demeure des Petits Augustins
Place des Augustins
49260 Montreuil-Bellay
Maine-et-Loire
Tel: (0)2 41 52 33 88
Fax: (0)2 41 52 33 88

From Angers, N162 towards le Lion d'Angers for about 7km then right on D768 towards Montreuil centre & immediately right on Ave d'Europe for about 2km to end of built-up area then left into Rue Espéranto; signposted.

Map No: 5   MM 232-19

Jean-Louis & Suzanne HUEZ
Le Plateau
Rue Espéranto
49460 Montreuil-Juigné
Maine-et-Loire
Tel: (0)2 41 42 32 35

The atmosphere is relaxed, the piano in the small dining-room is for everyone to play, the furniture is English pine within utterly French walls, the rooms are friendly and comfortable, especially the new one under the roof with its beams, stripped pine floor and good views through low roof windows. Vanessa is happy for guests to join in, be it feeding animals (there are boisterous spaniels too) or filling their own flasks — one French guest even asked to dig the garden. Wonderful for children.

Rooms: 3 triple rooms, each with shower or bath & wc.

Price: 250 Frs for two, including breakfast.

Meals: 85 Frs, including wine & coffee.

Open: All year.

Gîtes for 4 people

An old farmhouse on the family estate transformed from tumbledown dereliction to rural idyll to house this charming, cultured, artistic, unpretentious couple and their four beautifully-behaved children — the place exudes age-old peace and youthful freshness. Rooms are decorated with flair and simplicity — white walls, sea-grass flooring, good fabrics. A perfect retreat for music and nature lovers — join Tuesday choir practice at the château, take singing lessons with a sister; fish, boat, walk in the unspoilt countryside. A very special place.

Rooms: 1 twin, 1 double, 1 triple, each with bath or shower & wc.

Price: 250-320 Frs for two, including breakfast.

Meals: 120 Frs, including aperitif, wine & coffee.

Open: All year.

From La Flèche, D308/D938 towards Baugé. There, follow sign for Tours & Saumur; right at traffic lights on D61 to Vieil-Baugé. Signposted after 2km.

Map No: 5   MM 232-21

John & Vanessa KITCHEN
La Chalopinière
49150 Le Vieil Baugé
Maine-et-Loire
Tel: (0)2 41 89 04 38
Fax: (0)2 41 89 04 38
e-mail: chalop@infonie.fr

From Angers towards Lion d'Angers. At Montreuil Juigné right on D768 towards Champigné. 500m after crossroads at La Croix de Beauvais right up drive to La Roche & Malvoisine.

Map No: 5   MM 232-29

Patrice & Regina de LA BASTILLE
Malvoisine
49460 Ecuillé
Maine-et-Loire
Tel: (0)2 41 93 34 44/
         (0)6 80 57 54 84
Fax: (0)2 41 93 34 44

The austerity of the façade is misleading; within all is warm, cosy and easy. It is a family home, and a delightful one — full of character with big but cosy bedrooms and bathrooms, four-posters, antiques and beautiful decoration. Downstairs are the sitting-room, billiards room/library and big family kitchen — all comfortable and informal. You feel very much in the countryside although only 2km from the town centre. It is a treat to stay in one château while exploring others.

Rooms: 2 suites, 3 doubles, 1 triple, 1 twin, each with bath or shower & wc.

Price: 300-450 Frs for two, including breakfast. Extra bed 100 Frs.

Meals: 200 Frs, including wine. Not June-Sept: barbecue 120 Frs.

Open: All year except Dec & Jan.

The house is only 8 metres thick, but behind is a large barn-enclosed courtyard, two large towers, a 300-year-old oak and a covered terrace for lounging. The Migons couldn't be nicer and their house is a labour of love. The bedrooms — big, north-facing windows with shutters — are pretty, elegant, comfortable. The dining-room fireplace has spits, the furniture is antique and you see the beams. The games room has two billiards tables, a piano, a set of drums (Monsieur plays bass guitar). Fear not: *Drain* is old French for 'oak'.

Rooms: 4 doubles, each with bath or shower & wc.

Price: 400-500 Frs for two, including breakfast.

Meals: Wide choice within 15km.

Open: All year.

From Saumur D947 E towards Chinon. Château is on right just after Gratien Meyer wine cellars. (2km from Saumur centre.)

Map No: 10   MM 232-33

Andrea MICHAUT
Château de Beaulieu
Route de Montsoreau
49400 Saumur
Maine-et-Loire
Tel: (0)2 41 67 69 51
Fax: (0)2 41 50 42 68
e-mail: chbeaul@club-internet.fr

From A11 exit 20 on D923. Cross Loire to Liré on D163. There, right on D751 to Drain then left on D154 towards St Laurent-des-Autels. Gateway to drive about 4km along on left.

Map No: 9   MM 232-29

Brigitte & Gérard MIGON
Le Mésangeau
49530 Drain
Maine-et-Loire
Tel: (0)2 40 98 21 57

These are straightforward farming people (with a couple of lively kids) who have been badly hit by BSE. You breakfast in their very plain farmhouse kitchen which is alive with family and the desire to please. The attic has been recently converted to house the guestrooms where great old roof timbers share the space with nice new rustic-style beds and old *armoires*. It is all very simple and clean-cut with discreet plastic flooring, plain pastel walls and sparkling new shower rooms.

Rooms: 2 triple, 1 twin, each with shower & wc; extra room with handbasin.

Price: 220 Frs for two, including breakfast. Extra bed 70 Frs.

Meals: Choice 5km.

Open: All year.

A fine house set proudly on the Loire embankment: the view is unbeatable but the road is busy. Guests have a cobble-floored kitchen/diner whence the original stone stairs lead up to the main house and four well-furnished double-glazed rooms (that view!). There are two super new rooms in the old stables in the courtyard. We loved the architecturally-correct dog kennel too! Young and lively, Claudine is always full of ideas to keep you busy and interested — take one of her mystery tours or book her traditional Songs-of-the-Loire dinner.

Rooms: 1 double & 1 suite for 4, each with shower, wc & kitchenette; 2 triple, 1 double, 1 twin, each with shower & wc.

Price: 290-340 Frs for two, including breakfast.

Meals: 120 Frs, including wine & coffee. Self-catering.

Open: All year.

From Angers N23 to Seiches-sur-le-Loir; right on D766 towards Tours for 9km; right into Jarzé on D59 towards Beaufort-en-Vallé. House on left 700m after Jarzé.

Map No: 5   MM 232-20

Véronique & Vincent PAPIAU
Le Point du Jour
49140 Jarzé
Maine-et-Loire
Tel: (0)2 41 95 46 04
Fax: (0)2 41 95 46 04

From Angers, D952 towards Saumur. House is on left hand side of road (signposted) as you enter St Mathurin-sur-Loire.

Map No: 10   MM 232-32

Mme Claudine PINIER
Verger de la Bouquetterie
118 rue du Roi René
49250 Saint-Mathurin-sur-Loire
Maine-et-Loire
Tel: (0)2 41 57 02 00
Fax: (0)2 41 57 31 90

This is different and not for the stuffy or formal. Joyce, an appropiately relaxed and welcoming aromatherapist, has a fully organic kitchen garden, cooks good veggie food, receives art, yoga and meditation workshops (lovely meditation room) and generally invites guests to 'come and join in'. The old farm has been here since the 17th century in its soft, leafy stand of poplars; there are beams everywhere so take care crossing the threshold to your bedroom late at night. Old it feels, New Age it sings. Small camping site too.

Rooms: 1 triple, 1 double, sharing bath & wc.

Price: 250 Frs for two, including breakfast.

Meals: Vegetarian 75 Frs, including wine & coffee.

Open: All year.

Gîtes for 7 people

Madame's delight is to renovate and decorate her wonderful house and make sure guests love it too. Monsieur is an artist; his Venus emerges from one of the bathroom walls. In a quiet wooded spot, the house is all dormers and balconies and Victorian extravaganza; the little tower, once dovecote and chapel, is older. Furnishings are a study in disorganised elegance, masses of antiques, *brocante* and modernities — great fun. There are relaxation sessions, billiards, piano, fishing and coffee-roasting on the spot. Good food, too.

Rooms: 1 suite for 5, 4 double, all with bath & wc.

Price: 340 Frs for two, including breakfast. Extra bed 85 Frs.

Meals: 110 Frs, including wine & coffee.

Open: All year.

From Le Mans N23 to La Flèche. There D37 to Fougeré then N217 towards Baugé for 1.5km. House behind poplars on left.

Map No: 5   MM 232-21

Joyce RIMELL
La Besnardière
Route de Baugé
49150 Fougeré
Maine-et-Loire
Tel: (0)2 41 90 15 20

From A11 left onto A85 towards Tours. Exit at Longué on D938 towards Baugé for 5km. Right on D62 towards Mouliherne. House is 5km along on right.

Map No: 5   MM 232-33

Françoise & Michel TOUTAIN
Le Prieuré de Vendanger
49150 Le Guédeniau
Maine-et-Loire
Tel: (0)2 41 67 82 37/
    (0)6 12 63 03 74
Fax: (0)2 41 67 82 43

The Viviers have lovingly preserved their typical old Segré farmhouse with its long deep roof and curious *outeau* openings (some might have put modern dormers). The living-room has great beams, a big brick fireplace, the old bread oven glazed in at the back of it, exposed stone walls... and new country furniture. Rooms are deliciously rustic too: crochet, terracotta, pine, sloping ceilings. Madame virtually lives in her kitchen, making jams and pastries just for you. The woods are full of birdlife.

Rooms: 2 quadruple, 1 double, all with bath or shower & wc.

Price: 200-230 Frs for two, including breakfast. Extra bed 80 Frs.

Meals: Choice 2-5km. Picnic in garden.

Open: All year.

Gîtes for 10 people

Madame, a history teacher, is a great source of local knowledge (old slate mines, model villages, river trips...). The converted farm building, in the grounds of the Château du Teilleul, has a big, convivial, cedar-panelled sitting-room. The bedroom, charmingly decorated and beamed with a sloping roof, has the bath behind a bookcase/bar and its own loo in the corridor. This splendid home, littered with heirlooms, has been called "homely if chaotic, with super conversation and ambience". Four lovely children too.

Rooms: 1 twin with own bath & basin in room, wc down corridor.

Price: 280 Frs for two, including breakfast.

Meals: 100 Frs, including wine & coffee.

Open: All year.

From Angers N162 towards Le Lion d'Angers; follow signs to Rennes then take D863 towards Segré for 3km. Left at Chambre d'Hôte sign. House 1km along on left.

Map No: 5   MM 232-19

Jocelyne & François VIVIER
Les Travaillères
49220 Le Lion d'Angers
Maine-et-Loire
Tel: (0)2 41 61 33 56
Fax: (0)2 41 61 30 66

Take D923 from St. Sauveur towards Segré. Driveway is on right, 200m after village.

Map No: 5   MM 232-19

Marie-Alice & Michel de VITTON
Le Domaine du Teilleul
49500 Saint-Sauveur-de-Flée
Maine-et-Loire
Tel: (0)2 41 61 38 84
Fax: (0)2 41 61 38 84

The history-laden château (Henry III is buried here) with its mullioned windows, rare covered wooden gallery and 500-year-old lime tree, has just changed hands: the enthusiastic new owners are hard at work rejuvenating the décor. *Aliénor* is a fine room with vast fireplace, beams, window-seat and inside shutters — the brown 60s bathroom in amusing contrast; *Henri Plantagenet* is charmingly round in its tower (pink 60s bathroom); *Richard Cœur-de-Lion* is tiny with cramped washing facilities. Masses of character throughout. Do visit Fontevraud Abbey.

Rooms: 1 quadruple, 1 double, 1 twin, each with bath or shower & wc.

Price: 340 or 240 Frs for two, including breakfast.

Meals: Good choice nearby.

Open: All year.

On every pillow a cotton nightcap, in every room a religious book. The kitchen garden grows botanical throwbacks and plants for witches' brews. The house looks like a museum but feels like a (very refined) home. It is fascinating, compelling, utterly seductive. The rooms are all different and close to perfection. Your host is endlessly inventive: breakfast is 'as our country forebears ate' with cheese, cold meats and wine. Dinners are based on 17th-century aristocrats' recipes with lots of spices... and much more than space will allow.

Rooms: 2 suites for 3, 1 double, all with own bath & wc.

Price: 640-1120 Frs for two, including (superb) fork breakfast.

Meals: 240 Frs, including aperitif, good wine & coffee.

Open: All year.

From Saumur, D947 towards Chinon. At Montsoreau, D947 towards Loudun. Entrance to château 4km after Fontevraud; signposted.

Map No: 10   MM 232-33

Véronique de CASTELBAJAC
Château de la Roche Martel
86120 Roiffé
Vienne
Tel: (0)5 49 98 77 54
Fax: (0)5 49 98 98 30

From Tours by-pass Chinon then towards La Devinière, past La Devinière/La Roche Clermault & on to Bournand. Go to war memorial, turn left then 1st left for 100m. House on left, grey gate.

Map No: 10   MM 232-33

Christian LAURENS
Château de Bournand
86120 Bournand
Vienne
Tel: (0)5 49 98 77 82
Fax: (0)5 49 98 97 30

A fine château next to the River Mayenne and, thanks to surrounding park and farmland, surprisingly quiet although just off the road. There is a large, formal sitting-room and, across the central hallway with its grand piano and staircase, an elegant dining-room with separate tables for breakfast. The house has been much added to since it came into the family 400 years ago but every object, antique and picture tells a story. Bedrooms are a suite with a double four-poster and river views and a tiny double with two single four-posters.

Rooms: 1 twin, 1 suite, each with bath & wc.

Price: 350 or 400 Frs, including breakfast. Extra bed 100 Frs.

Meals: Choice in town.

Open: All year.

Three peacocks wander the garden, ducks and geese paddle in the enchanting pond, cows graze in the fields and apples are transformed into cider. When you walk into the house you walk into another world. It is a beam-lover's delight and the amazing oak staircase takes off in several directions. There are nooks and crannies, odd angles and crooked lines; terracotta tiled floors, big windows, half-timbered walls, a canopied bed, antiques here for over 150 years. Madame is bright, energetic, down-to-earth and blessed with a laugh that sings.

Rooms: 2 double, 1 triple, 1 family room, each with shower or hip bath & wc.

Price: 230 Frs for two, including breakfast. Extra bed 50 Frs.

Meals: 75 Frs, excluding wine (approx. 50 Frs).

Open: All year.

In Château-Gontier N162 N towards Laval. Château entrance is 50 metres after last roundabout as you leave the town.

Map No: 5   MM 232-19

Brigitte & François d' AMBRIÈRES
Château de Mirvault
Mirvault-Azé
53200 Château-Gontier
Mayenne
Tel: (0)2 43 07 10 82
Fax: (0)2 43 07 10 82

From Laval N162 S dir. Château-Gontier for 14km then left through Villiers-Charlemagne to Ruille-Froid-Fonds. In village left on C4 for Bignon. Signposted.

Map No: 5   MM 232-19

Claudette DAVENEL
Villeprouvé
53170 Ruille-Froid-Fonds
Mayenne
Tel: (0)2 43 07 71 62

The house is indisputably French, the owners Franco-British, the breakfast 'Scandinavian' and the squirrels on the green sward red. In this haven of quiet, Denis and Patricia will fascinate you with tales of their days as foreign correspondents. Guests enjoy good beds, their own cosy sitting-room with the old bread oven, a complete kitchen and a lovely path down to the stream. After visiting villages, walking the trails, dreaming in the rolling country, return to good conversation and real hospitality.

Rooms: 2 double/twin, each with bath & wc.

Price: 320 Frs for two, including generous breakfast.

Meals: Auberge in village; good restaurant nearby; guest kitchen.

Open: All year.

Hard to beat! The atmosphere is elegant yet relaxed and supremely friendly, the rooms are exquisite, the hospitality utterly natural, the noble horse and love of beautiful things inform house and hosts. In this lovely mediæval village, your hosts run one of only six carriage-driving schools in France. As well as fine dinners there are superb pony-and-trap picnics — a treat not to be missed. It is peacefully off the beaten track and genuinely civilised.

Rooms: 2 double, 1 triple, all with own shower and wc.

Price: 330-385 Frs for two, including breakfast.

Meals: 150 Frs, incl. wine & coffee. Picnics available.

Open: All year.

On N12 from Mayenne towards Alençon; after 5km, left on D34 towards Lassay. In Montreuil-Poulay, left on D160; house is 700m along.

Map No: 5   MM 231-41

Denis & Patricia LEGRAS-WOOD
Le Vieux Presbytère
53640 Montreuil-Poulay
Mayenne
Tel: (0)2 43 00 86 32
Fax: (0)2 43 00 81 42
e-mail: 101512.245@compuserve.com

From Sablé-sur-Sarthe, D309 (D27) towards Angers. On entering St Denis, 1st left at Renov'Cuire sign. House is 100m along, signposted.

Map No: 5   MM 232-20

Martine & Jacques LEFEBVRE
Le Logis Du Ray
53290 Saint-Denis-d'Anjou
Mayenne
Tel: (0)2 43 70 64 10
Fax: (0)2 43 70 65 53

Old stones, indeed, as they say in French and readers have loved the "real character of the place". It is an enchanting 15th-century manor with staircase tower to the upstairs bedroom, bread oven and a fine dining-room where breakfast is served to the chiming of the church clock. This is the Nays' old family home, well restored and really lived in (they have two small sons). They weave baskets, make music, will teach you French and radiate enthusiasm. A wonderful atmosphere in delectable countryside.

Rooms: 1 double, 1 triple, both with bath or shower & wc.

Price: 220 Frs for two, including breakfast.

Meals: In village or 3km.

Open: All year.

Gîtes for 6 people

From Laval, N157 towards Le Mans. At Soulgé-sur-Ouette, D20 left to Evron then D7 towards Mayenne. In Mézangers; signposted.

Map No: 5   MM 232-8

Léopold & Marie-Thérèse NAY
Le Cruchet
53600 Mézangers
Mayenne
Tel: (0)2 43 90 65 55

An exceptional and engaging couple; Thérèse is vivacious and conversation at their table is the very heart and soul of this marvellous place. Everything is homemade at dinner, from *paté* to *potage* to *patisserie*...all *Normand* and attractively presented. Breakfast is a feast at which you help yourself to freshly-squeezed juice, eggs, cheese and buckets of coffee. The bedrooms are average-sized, decorated with Japanese grass paper and a few antiquey bits and bobs. Good people, and one or two sons may also be there.

Rooms: 1 triple, 2 double, 1 twin, each with shower or bath & wc.

Price: 220 Frs for two, including breakfast.

Meals: 90 Frs, including aperitif, wine & coffee.

Open: April to November.

From Fougères N12 east towards Laval for 15km when farm signposted on right.

Map No: 5   MM 232-6

Maurice & Thérèse TRIHAN
La Rouaudière
Mégaudais
53500 Ernée
Mayenne
Tel: (0)2 43 05 13 57
Fax: (0)2 43 05 71 15

Mansion house and B&B on the grandest of scales gracefully combined in a splendid château in the heart of the town. The surrounding park with its formal, box-lined French garden and wild, romantic 'English' garden creates a sylvan setting. The hosts are exquisitely courteous and the rooms large and light, each one decorated in individual style. You will find an easy mix of luxury and comfort in the cavernous bathrooms, marble fireplaces and beautiful original panelling, some of it delicate blue against striking yellow curtains and bedspreads.

Rooms: 3 double, 1 suite, each with bath & shower & wc.

Price: 650-750 Frs for two, including breakfast.

Meals: Full choice in Laval.

Open: All year except Dec & Jan.

  50 Frs

So French a château! Nothing overwhelming, just loveliness and peace. Surrounded by farmland and woods, on the edge of a village with a big garden, it is ideal for families. Guests who swear they never sleep beyond 6am arrive sheepishly for breakfast at 10am. The interior is gratifyingly untidy in corners, just as one would expect of a real family home, with much unselfconscious good taste. Dinner happens at one big table where the wine flows unstinted and all nations communicate happily. "Super folk", "Delightful", say our readers.

Rooms: 2 suites, with bath or shower & wc; 2 separate wc's.

Price: 270-320 Frs for two, including breakfast. Extra bed 80 Frs.

Meals: 100 Frs, including wine & coffee.

Open: All year.

Gîtes for 5 people

In Laval centre follow signs to 'Mairie' then to 'Le Bas du Gast' — opposite 'Salle Polyvalente' and 'Bibliothèque'.

Map No: 5   MM 232-7

M & Mme François WILLIOT
Le Bas du Gast
6 rue de la Halle aux Toiles
53000 Laval
Mayenne
Tel: (0)2 43 49 22 79
Fax: (0)2 43 56 44 71

From Le Mans, N23 towards La Flèche. At Cerans-Foulletourte, D31 to Oizé; left onto D32; signposted on right.

Map No: 5   MM 232-22

Alain DAVID & Nicole DUBOIS
Château de Montaupin
72330 Oizé
Sarthe
Tel: (0)2 43 87 81 70
Fax: (0)2 43 87 26 25

A group of low buildings in a picture of a place by a 3-acre, tree-reflecting pond full of fish, frogs and ducks with a view up to a hilltop village — peace and space for all. There are games (croquet, table-tennis, *pétanque*), a boat and even a sauna. The rooms are smallish, well-fitted, with separate entrances and mixed modern and old furnishings. Madame, grandmother to ten, loves to have guests and to feed them. Breakfast, outside or in the dining-room, includes cheese and cold meats. Dinner is an important event, so indulge!

Rooms: 2 triple, 2 double, 1 twin, all with shower & wc.

Price: 270-330 Frs for two, including breakfast.

Meals: 90 Frs, including wine & coffee.

Open: March to mid-Nov.

The whole atmosphere is deliciously casual and shambolic and dinner, with masses of home-produced ingredients, is a large, gregarious affair that may last some time — wonderful for lovers of French family cooking. The guestrooms and their shower rooms, in converted outbuildings, may show signs of the passing of time... and the family cats, but you will enjoy the Langlais, a lively, active couple with children and a farm to run who still find time to handpaint lampshades, take you to watch the milking or search for freshly-laid eggs.

Rooms: 2 double, 1 twin, 1 triple, plus 1 suite in 'La Petite Maison', all with shower & wc.

Price: 230-260 Frs for two, including breakfast.

Meals: 100 Frs, including wine & coffee.

Open: All year.

Gîtes for 6 people

From Le Mans D304 to Grand Lucé and La Chartre. Left on D305 through Pont de Braye. Left on D303 to Lavenay & follow signs (2km).

Map No: 5   MM 232-24

Monique & Jacques DÉAGE
Le Patis du Vergas
72310 Lavenay
Sarthe
Tel: (0)2 43 35 38 18
Fax: (0)2 43 35 38 18

From Alençon south on N138. After 4km, left onto D55, through Champfleur towards Bourg-le-Roi; farm signposted 1km after Champfleur.

Map No: 5   MM 231-43

Denis & Christine LANGLAIS
Garencière
72610 Champfleur
Sarthe
Tel: (0)2 33 31 75 84

A warm, open-armed welcome is guaranteed in this square house on the town square. The big rooms are square too, with original mouldings and lovely tiles in the hall. The skylit landing (in fact a 'bridge' between two parts of the building) is fun. The decor and furnishings are mostly recent, functional, coordinated pastel and plush — comfortable and unintrusive. You will find it noisy in the front, quieter at the back. Claude is bear-like, while Dianne is brisk and efficient.

Rooms: 1 double, 1 triple, 1 quadruple, each with bath or shower & wc; 1 double with washbasin & shared bathroom.

Price: 260 Frs for two, including breakfast.

Meals: Good eating places very near.

Open: March to September.

From Le Mans, N138 towards Tours. House in town centre, set back from town square.

Map No: 5   MM 232-23

Dianne & Claude LE GOFF
22 rue de l'Hôtel de Ville
72500 Château-du-Loir
Sarthe
Tel: (0)2 43 44 03 38

A fairytale cottage: mellow old stone, white shutters, green ivy, a large leafy garden and a 12th-century castle round the corner (this used to be the castle's servants' quarters). Green-eyed Michèle is modern, intelligent and interested in people; she and Michel share the hosting. The suite is three gentle Laura Ashley-inspired interconnecting bedrooms that look onto garden or endless fields. Stay a while and connect into the gentle hills, woods, streams and châteaux. Guests can be as independent as they like (separate entrance).

Rooms: One 3-room suite for 5 with bathroom and separate wc.

Price: 250 Frs for two, including breakfast. Extra person 120 Frs.

Meals: Occasionally 70-90 Frs, excluding wine.

Open: April to October.

From Le Mans, N138 towards Tours. After Dissay/Courcillon, left onto small road on the bend & follow signs to 'Chambres d'Hôtes'.

Map No: 5   MM 232-23

Michèle LETANNEUX & Michel GUYON
La Châtaigneraie
72500 Dissay-sous-Courcillon
Sarthe
Tel: (0)2 43 79 45 30

THE LOIRE VALLEY

A house of great character and charm, it has memories of the English occupation during the 100 Years War and a turret turned into a bedroom for children — a little stone nest with exposed stone walls, old tiled floor, narrow windows and fireplace. Madame is an utterly delightful hostess (and regional cook) and the atmosphere of the house is one of simple, unaffected hospitality. 20-mile views across the beautiful Sarthe countryside from all rooms, space, parquet floors and period furnishings.

Rooms: 1 triple with shower, 1 double with separate (occasionally shared) bath, both sharing wc. One room has extra beds for children.

Price: 230-300 Frs for two, including breakfast. Extra bed 80 Frs.

Meals: 85 Frs, including cider & coffee.

Open: All year.

From Mamers, D3 towards Le Mêle for 6km. Do not go into Aillières. Farm on left.

Map No: 5   MM 231-44

Marie-Rose & Moïse LORIEUX
La Locherie
Aillières
72600 Mamers
Sarthe
Tel: (0)2 43 97 76 03

A jewel, in rolling parkland, with sheep grazing under mature trees, horses in the paddock, swans on a bit of the moat, deer, boar... Your hosts are the nicest, easiest of aristocrats, determined to keep the ancestral home alive in a dignified manner. Bedrooms: antique furniture on parquet floors, good rugs, modern beds, bathrooms and loos in turrets, cupboards, alcoves. Downstairs: an elegant dining-room with family silver, sitting-room with log fire, family portraits, and small book-lined library. Hunting trophies on walls; timeless tranquillity.

Rooms: 1 suite for 3, 2 double, 1 twin, each with bath or shower & wc.

Price: 450-550 Frs for two, including breakfast.

Meals: 195 Frs including wine; 'Dîner Prestige' 320 Frs.

Open: All year.

From Alençon N138 S towards Le Mans for approx. 14km. At La Hutte left on D310 for 10km then right on D19 through Courgains then left on D132 to Monhoudou; signposted.

Map No: 5   MM 232-10

Michel & Marie-Christine de MONHOUDOU
Château de Monhoudou
72260 Monhoudou
Sarthe
Tel: (0)2 43 97 40 05
Fax: (0)2 43 33 11 58

Such an easy, friendly person, such a lovely old house (parts are 14th-century) with a plain façade hiding a beautifully-decorated interior, bedrooms with masses of personality, a large garden and a properly-concealed pool. The rooms are in renovated outbuildings and thus independent, while convivial meals are shared in the dining-room — and delicious they sound too. Madame is passionate and fascinating about local village history and culture. Sit and listen with delight under the big tree.

Rooms: 1 double, 1 triple, 1 suite for 4/5 with small kitchen, all with own shower & wc.

Price: 250-300 Frs for two, including breakfast.

Meals: 90 Frs, excluding wine. Self-catering suite.

Open: All year.

Muriel is a perfectionist and has let loose her considerable decorative flair on this miniature Italian villa where Marie de Médicis used to take the waters. The fine garden still has a hot spring. The interior is unmistakably French in its careful colours, lush fabrics and fine details — fresh flowers too. Carved wardrobes and brass beds grace some rooms. The suite is a wonderful 1930s surprise and has a super-smart bathroom. You will be thoroughly coddled in this very stylish house.

Rooms: 1 suite, 1 quadruple, 2 double, 2 twin, all with bath or shower & wc.

Price: 400 Frs for two, including breakfast.

Meals: 200 Frs, including wine & coffee.

Open: All year.

From Le Mans, D147 to Arnage, then D307 to Pontvallain. House in town centre; signposted.

Map No: 5   MM 232-22

Mme Michèle VIEILLET
Place Jean Graffin
72510 Pontvallain
Sarthe
Tel: (0)2 43 46 36 70

Macé is 3km north of Blois along N152 towards Orléans. Go into village & follow signs. House is 500m on right before church.

Map No: 6   MM 238-3

Muriel CABIN-SAINT-MARCEL
La Villa Médicis, Macé
41000 Saint-Denis-sur-Loire
Loir-et-Cher
Tel: (0)2 54 74 46 38
Fax: (0)2 54 78 20 27

A fine family house on the edge of this village in the lovely Cher valley, set against a steep hillside with fields and woods above. Madame is a most amiable lady with a nice sense of humour, living with her cats and Gigi, the Heinz 57 dog. Her son looks after the horses. The bedrooms are comfortable, light and medium-sized with traditional French family decor. The sitting-room manages to be both big and cosy, with an open fireplace — a real family room where friends and family relax for a drink and a smoke.

Rooms: 4 double, all with bath or shower & wc, 1 double sharing bathroom.

Price: 260 Frs for two, including breakfast.

Meals: Good restaurant nearby.

Open: All year except 2 weeks in March.

Oh the rarity of a Loire-side house! Forget the main road above (one reader said the house was perfect and the road inaudible), it is exceptional to sit on a grassy bank by a C16 house (originally a towing stage) and watch the mighty river go by. Françoise is an attentive and enthusiastic hostess who always dreamed of having guests and making cake and jam for them. Three rooms are on the top floor, three in converted outbuildings; they are nicely done with long beds and new bathrooms. Breakfast is a feast and the place is full of personality.

Rooms: 4 triple, 1 double, 1 twin, all with shower or bath & wc.

Price: 320-450 Frs for two, including breakfast.

Meals: Wide choice in Blois 5km.

Open: April to mid-Oct & 1-10 Nov or by arrangement.

From Blois, D956 to Contres, then D675 for St Aignan. At Noyers-sur-Cher, right before intersection of D675 and N76: Rue de la Mardelle is the last street before the level crossing.

Map No: 11   MM 238-15

Mme CHOQUET
La Mardelle
68 rue de la Mardelle
41140 Noyers
Loir-et-Cher
Tel: (0)2 54 71 70 55

From Blois centre (old bridge), N152 towards Tours for 5km. House is last on left in Blois.

Map No: 6   MM 238-3

Françoise & Yves COSSON
Le Vieux Cognet
4 Levée des Grouëts
41000 Blois
Loir-et-Cher
Tel: (0)2 54 56 05 34
Fax: (0)2 54 74 80 82

The C13 chapel is still used on the village feast day and the manor house, somewhat newer (C16), drips with history... which the modern decor manages to respect. The sitting and dining-rooms are huge, the bedrooms are smallish and cosy. One has a large stone fireplace, stone floor, painted beams and very successful Laura Ashley fabrics. The setting is superb: high up and overlooking the Cher Valley. Fine mature trees shade the garden, and you can put you horse in the paddock. A stunning place — and you'll like your hosts, too.

Rooms: 1 suite, 2 double, each with bath or shower & wc.

Price: 300-380 Frs for two, including breakfast.

Meals: Wide range locally.

Open: All year.

St Georges is on N76 between Chenonceau & Montrichard. In town centre, turn up hill following signs to 'La Chaise'. There, continue up Rue du Prieuré. No 8 has heavy wooden gates.

Map No: 10   MM 238-14

Danièle DURET-THERIZOLS
Prieuré de la Chaise
8 rue du Prieuré
41400 Saint-Georges-sur-Cher
Loir-et-Cher
Tel: (0)2 54 32 59 77
Fax: (0)2 54 32 59 77

What a delightful couple: welcoming, sensitive and fun! So eager to make real contact that they have taken English lessons and will 'brief' guests at length on where to go. Madame rightly calls her C18 farmhouse *le petit trésor caché* — it has that serendipity touch. Its shutters open onto a garden (with over 100 sorts of flower) which rambles down to the small River Cisse and water meadows; its rooms are pretty, cosy, quiet; the sitting/dining-room is beamed and book-lined. Fires in winter, breakfast outside in summer — a dream of a place.

Rooms: 2 double, 2 twin, all with bath or shower & wc.

Price: 340 Frs for two, including breakfast.

Meals: Choice locally.

Open: March to December.

Leave N152 Blois/Tours road towards Onzain opposite bridge to Chaumont. Left immediately after underpass (chemin du Roy). After 2.5km, right. Left at stop sign. House 100m on left.

Map No: 5   MM 238-14

Martine LANGLAIS
46 rue de Meuves
41150 Onzain
Loir-et-Cher
Tel: (0)2 54 20 78 82/
      (0)6 07 69 74 78
Fax: (0)2 54 20 78 82

This 18th-century house stands in 7 acres of woodland that cut out all sight of the nuclear power station. A good place to rest after château-visiting exertions: one owner went through Revolution, Restoration, Napoleon, 3 prisons, 3 death sentences... and then died in his bed. Traditionally furnished bedrooms are light and sunny. There are nice old things everywhere. Madame is most interesting and keeps animals for the two of her five children still here. Perfect for Chambord, and for walks in the Sologne.

Rooms: 1 quadruple, 1 triple, 1 double, all with shower & wc.

Price: 270 Frs for two, including breakfast.

Meals: 2 restaurants in village.

Open: All year.

The picture-framing workshop is where Madame is found; her jovial husband farms outside town and will serve your breakfast. The rooms are light and simple, with understated good taste and subdued shades of off-white, grey and blue. There are beams, floors of polished parquet or tiles, billiards in the sitting-room and a kitchenette for you. The garden at the back is charming, the miniature trees at the bottom screening outbuildings. A 16th-century townhouse, but you feel you are in the countryside.

Rooms: 3 triple, 1 double/twin, 1 suite each with bath or shower & wc.

Price: 280-350 Frs for two, including breakfast.

Meals: Choice in Mer.

Open: All year except Jan.

Leave N152 Orléans-Blois road in Mer and park by church. House is short walk up main shopping street: entrance in picture-framing shop on left. (Instructions for car access given on arrival.)

Map No: 6   MM 238-3

From Orléans, D951 towards Blois. On entering St Laurent, follow signs to 'Chambres d'Hôtes'.

Map No: 6   MM 238-4

Catherine & Maurice LIBEAUT
L'Ormoie, 26 rue de l'Ormoie
St Laurent-des-Eaux
41220 St Laurent-Nouan
Loire-et-Cher
Tel: (0)2 54 87 24 72

Joëlle & Claude MORMICHE
9 rue Dutems
41500 Mer
Loir-et-Cher
Tel: (0)2 54 81 17 36
Fax: (0)2 54 81 70 19

"A little gem of a B&B" with its sweeping farmyard, its pond and such a welcome. You can see for miles across fields filled with larksong and cereals. It is peaceful, pretty and a place for picnics. The owners are a smiling couple who give you their time but do not invade your space. Their rooms have gentle colours, soft materials and firm mattresses. The furniture is simple and rustic, the bedrooms and bathrooms are deeply raftered, the old farmhouse breathes through its timbers.

Rooms: 1 double with shower & wc; 2 double sharing bath & wc.

Price: 230-250 Frs for two, including breakfast. Extra bed 90 Frs.

Meals: 75 Frs, including wine.

Open: All year.

Up two flights of a spiral staircase, in the attic (fear not, Monsieur will carry your bags), the bedroom feels not unlike sleeping in a church with unexpectedly comfortable beds, lots of books, and good shower on the floor below. There are reminders of pilgrimage and religion everywhere — indeed, the little prayer room is your sitting-room — but they don't intrude. So close to the great cathedral... we are delighted to have discovered this slightly eccentric and welcoming place. Your host is a charmer and enjoys a chuckle.

Rooms: 1 twin room with shower & wc.

Price: 250 Frs for two, including breakfast.

Meals: Choice at your doorstep.

Open: All year.

On arriving from Dreux by N154 follow signs for IBIS Centre and park as you reach Hotel IBIS (Place Drouaise) then walk 20m along Rue de la Porte Drouaise and on Rue Muret to No 80 (approx. 100m car to house).

Map No: 6   MM 231-48

From Vendôme D957 towards Blois for 6km. Right at sign to Crucheray & Chambre d'Hôte. House 4km from turning; signposted.

Map No: 5   MM 238-2

Élisabeth & Guy TONDEREAU
Les Bordes
41100 Crucheray
Loir-et-Cher
Tel: (0)2 54 77 05 43
Fax: (0)2 54 77 05 43

Jean-Loup & Nathalie CUISINIEZ
Maison JLN
80 rue Muret
28000 Chartres
Eure-et-Loire
Tel: (0)2 37 21 98 36
Fax: (0)2 37 21 98 36

A large courtyard full of roses and fine gravel opens out in front of the old farmhouse and separate small guesthouses. They are charmingly decorated and well heated. In each case, there are a sitting-room (sofa-bed) and corner kitchen on the ground floor and the bedroom is upstairs. Children can play in the delightful garden behind the main house. Madame delivers fresh bread in the morning and guests do their own breakfast — she is welcoming but prefers to allow guests their privacy.

Rooms: 1 double, 1 family room for 4, each with shower and wc.

Price: 250 Frs for two, including breakfast. Extra bed 70 Frs.

Meals: Self-catering.

Open: All year.

Gîtes for 7 people

The furniture and decoration of this fine old farmhouse are in truly impeccable taste. Bedrooms with exposed timbers and excellent beds overlook the garden. There's an attractive *salon* and prettily-presented breakfasts. The Lothons are proud of their home with its refined, rather exclusive air — Monsieur is an antiques dealer, Madame a gentle hostess — and they thoroughly enjoy guests. Groups taking both rooms can have their own cooking and laundry facilities (supplement).

Rooms: 1 triple, 1 double, each with bath & wc.

Price: 380 Frs for two, including breakfast.

Meals: Choice 5km.

Open: All year.

Gîtes for 4 people

From Chartres, D921 towards Illiers Combray. After 5.5km, at le Pont Tranchefêtu, right towards St Georges-sur-Eure. After level crossing, left towards Chauffours. Farm is on left after village.

Map No: 6   MM 231-47

Denis & Catherine HASQUENOPH
Bailleau le Pin
3 rue des Gémeaux
28120 Chauffours
Eure-et-Loire
Tel: (0)2 37 26 89 15
Fax: (0)2 37 26 81 65

From Houdan, D61 towards Bourdonné; right on D115 to Dannemarie. There, follow D101 to Faverolles. In village, signposted La Cour Beaudeval Antiquités.

Map No: 6   MM 231-48

Mireille & Jean-Claude LOTHON
La Cour Beaudeval
28210 Faverolles
Eure-et-Loire
Tel: (0)2 37 51 47 67

These amiable, elderly, hard-working farmers are renovating their house; they lead a sociable life and their grandchildren are often around. The low-beamed bedrooms are modest but comfortable. The house has that relaxing lived-in air, the welcome is genuine, so what matter if the French is sometimes hard to follow? Expect meals, eaten *en famille*, to be just that: i.e. good, honest, family fare that readers have found excellent. The farm buildings include a gîte. A good stopover.

Rooms: 2 double with own bathrooms.

Price: 230-240 Frs for two, including breakfast.

Meals: 75 Frs, including wine.

Open: All year.

Gîtes for 18 people

Michel grows poppies for use in pharmaceuticals — a rare expertise of which he is very proud. Géraldine's lively manner and easy welcome into her delightful family relieve the dreariness of the ever-flat Beauce. The farm is set round a quiet, tidy courtyard where rabbits and hens lead their short lives, the good guestrooms are light and pleasantly if simply furnished, the bathrooms brand new. "Remarkable value. Real people. They've got it just right," said one reader, but don't expect designer decor or gourmet food at these amazing prices.

Rooms: 2 triple, 1 double, 1 twin, all with shower & wc.

Price: 170 Frs for two, including breakfast.

Meals: 55 Frs, including wine & coffee.

Open: All year.

Gîtes for 5 people

From Dreux, N12 to Houdan; D115 to Boutigny; D101 towards Prouais; farm is between the two villages, signposted 'Chambres d'Hôtes'.

Map No: 6   MM 231-48

Serge & Jeanne-Marie MARÉCHAL
La Ferme des Tourelles
11 rue des Tourelles, La Musse
28410 Boutigny-Prouais
Eure-et-Loire
Tel: (0)2 37 65 18 74/
    (0)6 08 06 29 98
Fax: (0)2 37 65 18 74

From A10, Allaine exit on D927 towards Châteaudun. At La Maladrerie, D39 to Loigny. Signposted opposite church.

Map No: 6   MM 237-39

Géraldine & Michel NIVET
8 rue Chanzy
28140 Loigny-la-Bataille
Eurer-et-Loire
Tel: (0)2 37 99 70 71

They are delightful! Virginie beautifully French, Richard a gentle American/European, their son a toddler. The old family house with its tall windows and fine proportions feels properly lived in — deep comfortable armchairs by the marble fireplace under crystal chandeliers. The top floor has been converted into five good rooms with sound-proofing, US-size beds, masses of hot water, mix 'n match colour schemes... and not much decoration for the moment! They are easy, fun and intelligent; and Virginie loves cooking.

Rooms: 1 triple, 3 double, 1 twin, all with shower & wc.

Price: 280 or 330 Frs for two, including breakfast.

Meals: Simple dinner: 70 Frs, including wine & coffee (Sun & Mon only; book ahead).

Open: March to October.

From A11 exit Ablis on N10 towards Chartres. Exit almost immediately Ablis/Prunay-en-Yvelines. Right to Prunay. There left on D168 to Esclimont, Bleury & Ecrosnes. In Ecrosnes right & immediately left to Jonvilliers for 2.5km. White château gates straight ahead.

Map No: 6   MM 240-16

Virginie & Richard THOMPSON
Château de Jonvilliers
17 rue d'Épernon
28320 Jonvilliers-Ecrosnes
Eure-et-Loire
Tel: (0)2 37 31 41 26
Fax: (0)2 37 31 56 74
e-mail: reservations@chateaudejonvilliers.com

"One of the best nights I have ever spent in a *chambre d'hôte*". Our inspector loved it, largely because of the Vasseurs. Only 15 minutes from Chartres, it is totally quiet in a blanket of fields. Bruno works out there single-handedly but is no typical farmer; he went to the Lycée in London, so conversation can be in either language. Dinner is unforgettable — try the goat cheese — and breakfast is orgiastic with farm-laid eggs. Deeply comfortable bedrooms, simple sitting/dining-room, children, relaxed but refined people.

Rooms: 2 double, 1 twin, each with bath or shower & wc.

Price: 260-280 Frs for two, including breakfast. Extra person 70 Frs.

Meals: 90 Frs, including wine & coffee.

Open: All year.

Gîtes for 6 people

From Chartres N154 N for Dreux. Shortly after leaving Chartres, left on D133 for Fresnay and follow signs for 'Chambres d'Hôtes' to Levéville (also spelt Levesville).

Map No: 6   MM 231-48

Nathalie & Bruno VASSEUR
Ferme du Château
Levéville
28300 Bailleau l'Évêque
Eure-et-Loire
Tel: (0)2 37 22 97 02
Fax: (0)2 37 22 97 02

Eulogies for these people have reached us. A beautiful painted sign leads to the well-restored old house which still retains a certain quaintness. Three cosy, white rooms and one very large ground-floor room, all with excellent bedding. Madame is matronly and trusting and the house has a warm family atmosphere, with old pieces of furniture. Birdsong soothes your ear and wheat fields sway before your eye as you rest in the pretty garden. Your hosts can teach you lots about the various bird species. In summer there is a children's pool.

Rooms: 1 double, 1 triple, 2 quadruple, all with shower & wc en suite or on landing.

Price: 255 Frs for two, including breakfast.

Meals: Choice 7km.

Open: All year except November.

White walls, terracotta floor tiles, beams, silver on the table, a lovely inlaid cupboard, long pink/green/white curtains, several animal objects — all in the dining-room. Agnès, who left Paris for country calm, is keen on hunting and horses... and it shows. You are very likely to eat game for dinner. Upstairs, the corridor is white with green doors and dark beams. The bedrooms are brilliantly done, small but cosy, with steeply sloping roofs — no good for the over-stretched; the suite is larger.

Rooms: 1 double, 1 twin, 1 suite for 4, each with bath or shower & wc.

Price: 300-350 Frs for two, including breakfast.

Meals: 100 Frs, excluding wine (60-80 Frs).

Open: All year.

From Châteaudun, N10 towards Chartres. At Bonneval, D17 to Moriers; there, D153 to Pré-St Martin; signposted.

Map No: 6   MM 237-39

Bernadette & Jean-Baptiste
VIOLETTE
Le Carcotage Beauceron
8 rue Saint-Martin
28800 Pré-Saint-Martin
Eure-et-Loir
Tel: (0)2 37 47 27 21

From Orléans N60 E to Châteauneuf-sur-Loire then right onto D11/D83 to Vannes. Go through village — house approx. 1km after village on right.

Map No: 6   MM 238-6

Agnès CELERIER NOULHIANE
Domaine de Sainte-Hélène
Route d'Isdes
45510 Vannes-sur-Cosson
Loiret
Tel: (0)2 38 58 04 55
Fax: (0)2 38 58 28 38

Looking for traditional French farmhouse atmosphere? Le Bangin has it all — from its ivy-covered stone walls to cosy bedroom quilts. Not over-renovated, it has a slightly dilapidated character, even down to one splendid old bathtub. The same authentic approach applies to Madame's cooking, which draws inspiration from her wonderful kitchen garden. Rediscover the true taste of home-grown fruit, vegetables and free-range eggs and, a rare treat nowadays, there's homemade soup every evening. Lawn tennis too.

Rooms: 5 double, each with washbasin, all sharing 2 bathrooms and 2 wc's.

Price: 180 Frs for two, including breakfast.

Meals: 80 Frs, including wine & coffee (book ahead).

Open: All year except Christmas to New Year.

From Châteauneuf-sur-Loire, N60 to Bellegarde. There, D44 towards Lorris. 1km beyond Beauchamps-sur-Huillard, right following signs.

Map No: 6   MM 237-42

Mme DHUIT
Le Bangin
Beauchamps-sur-Huillard
45270 Chatenoy
Loiret
Tel: (0)2 38 26 10 17

This vast estate by the Loire boasts a private hunting reserve (long-stay guests may visit it). Trees and garden surround the manor. The interior is carefully decorated and the rooms have lovely old furnishings. Breakfast in the *salon* (games and hi-fi) or on the flowered terrace. The young hosts — he is a vet, she looks after the house, their small children and you — make it feel friendly despite the grand appearance. They themselves live in another house just nearby. Children welcome. Don't miss the canal bridge at Briare.

Rooms: 3 double, all with shower or bath & wc; 1 suite for 3 with bathroom & kitchen.

Price: 250, 270 or 340 Frs for two, including breakfast.

Meals: Briare 1km. Self-catering in suite.

Open: All year.

Gîtes for 2 people

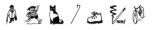

From A6, Dordives exit onto N7 to Briare then D952 towards Gien. Signposted by the nurseries, midway between Briare and Gien.

Map No: 6   MM 238-8

Mme Bénédicte FRANÇOIS
Domaine de la Thiau
45250 Briare
Loiret
Tel: (0)2 38 38 20 92
Fax: (0)2 38 67 40 50

The canal that flows gently past this handsome old village house imparts a special calm. There's a village bar next door (don't worry, it now closes at 10pm) and a garden with a self-contained cottage with thoughtfully-equipped kitchen and open fire. The loft bedroom in the main house with its exposed beams is particularly appealing. Your hosts are kind, well-educated and welcoming. Do walk to the great 19th-century canal bridge over the Loire in Briare — a stupendous and handsome alliance of engineering and nature.

Rooms: 2 double, 1 suite, all with shower & wc.

Price: 270 Frs for two, including breakfast.

Meals: 120 Frs, including wine & coffee.

Open: All year.

Gîtes for 4 people

From Châteauneuf-sur-Loire D952 to Gien then towards Poilly-lez-Gien and on D951 to Châtillon-sur-Loire; signposted.

Map No: 6   MM 238-8

M et Mme Gilbert LEFRANC
La Giloutière
13 rue du Port
45360 Châtillon-sur-Loire
Loiret
Tel: (0)2 38 31 10 61

The privilege of sleeping beneath that unsurpassed cathedral is priceless. Add the company of an articulate, professional couple and the old stones of a 15th-century guesthouse to enclose you and it's a gift! In the main room those old stones are crumbly in places where ancient walls, timbers, niches, cupboards have been exposed in all their mixed-up glory. This room is where you have breakfast. Bedrooms are wonderful too. All is character and intelligence. The Brouste family live on the other side of the quiet courtyard.

Rooms: 2 suites for 3/4 each with bath & wc; 2 double with bath or shower & wc.

Price: 350 Frs for two, including breakfast.

Meals: Full choice within walking distance.

Open: All year.

In the centre of Bourges, at the foot of the cathedral. Park in yard if space permits.

Map No: 11   MM 238-30

Marie-Ange & Joël BROUSTE
Les Bonnets Rouges
3 rue de la Thaumassière
18000 Bourges
Cher
Tel: (0)2 48 65 79 92
Fax: (0)2 48 69 82 05
e-mail: www.oda.fr/aa/les-bonnets-rouges

The Chambrins are quiet country folk with tanned faces, clear eyes and much gentle reality. Nice touches, such as great swathes of creeper outside and dried flowers and an old iron cot inside give character to this simple old farmhouse set among the sunflower fields. The kitchen-cum-breakfast room, with its carved dresser, is small and intimate. The rooms are comfortable though not huge but there is a nice guests' sitting area on the landing with books.

Rooms: 2 double, 1 twin, each with shower & wc. Extra bed 80 Frs.

Price: 200 Frs for two, including breakfast.

Meals: Choice 3-10km.

Open: All year.

Gites for 5 people

In the lovely countryside by the upper reaches of the mighty Loire, where the sweet Sancerre grape grows, stands this 15th-century manor-house, with its spiral staircase in the stone turret — all the rage in the 1480s. The large guestrooms (one especially so), with huge beams and tiled floors, are modern. The amiable, down-to-earth hosts will help out by cooking you a meal on the first night, if you ask. Do try the *pain d'épices* (gingerbread) in the morning (cooked breakfast on request).

Rooms: 1 suite for 4 with shower & wc; 2 double, 1 triple, each with bath or shower & wc. Extra beds available.

Price: 300 Frs for two, including breakfast.

Meals: 80 Frs, excluding wine.

Open: Easter to 31 October.

From Bourges, N144 to Levet; then D28 towards Dun-sur-Auron. After 2km turn right. House 300m from junction.

Map No: 11   MM 238-31

Marie-Jo & Jean CHAMBRIN
Bannay
18340 Saint-Germain-des-Bois
Cher
Tel: (0)2 48 25 31 03
Fax: (0)2 48 25 31 03

From Bourges, N151 and D955 towards Sancerre. Left on D86 to Briou. After 0.7km, left to Vauvredon.

Map No: 11   MM 238-20

Raymond & Simone CIROTTE
Manoir de Vaudredon
Briou-de-Crézancy-en-Sancerre
18300 Sancerre
Cher
Tel: (0)2 48 79 00 29

The stables of this big farmhouse have been brilliantly redesigned as guest quarters, using pale wood to clothe the space with architectural features such as a 2.5-storey staircase and sliding shutters. Contemporary fabrics are perfectly married with lacey linen and crocheted covers. The house is full of light, the garden, where guests have a terrace, has an abundance of green and flowery things. Meals sound delicious and Madame quietly and graciously looks after you.

Rooms: 3 double, 2 twin, all with bath or shower & wc (2 on ground floor).

Price: 260 Frs for two, including breakfast.

Meals: 90 Frs, excluding wine.

Open: Mid-Feb to mid-Nov.

From Sancerre, D958 towards Bourges. At les Salmons, left on D93 to Montigny. Take D44 for 5km; signposted.

Map No: 11   MM 238-19

Elizabeth GRESSIN
La Reculée
18250 Montigny
Cher
Tel: (0)2 48 69 59 18
Fax: (0)2 48 69 52 51

An easy, natural couple, each with a different history, who have come together (he's already a grandfather) in this rustic haven where the garden flows into woods and fields, where deer roam and birdlife astounds and where they have their new family. The house reflects their past: interesting bits from journeys to distant places; Indian rugs and Moroccan brass trays in the pleasant ground-floor guestrooms. Plus lots of old farmhouse stuff, nothing too sophisticated. Return after contemplating Bourges and meditate in God's garden.

Rooms: 2 triple, 1 quadruple, all with shower & wc; duplex for 4/5 with bath & wc.

Price: 235 Frs for two, including breakfast. Extra bed 65 Frs.

Meals: 70 Frs, excluding wine.

Open: All year.

From Bourges D944 towards Orléans. In Bourgneuf left and immediately right and follow signs 1.5km.

Map No: 11   MM 238-18

Jean MALOT & Chantal CHARLON
La Grande Mouline
Bourgneuf
18110 Saint-Eloy-de-Gy
Cher
Tel: (0)2 48 25 40 44

THE LOIRE VALLEY

A *ferme-auberge* is a good window onto rural life. This one is typical, with a big open fireplace, long oak tables and meals based on local seasonal produce — plus hunting trophies on the walls. Guests have a small breakfast room and a little sitting room. A good place to experience a farm lifestyle among convivial folk, knowledgeable about the area — Monsieur is an expert on *la chasse* — and with a keen interest in Romanesque art and architecture. Bedrooms are a cut above average, with good fabrics and comfy beds.

Rooms: 2 double, each with shower & wc.

Price: 230-250 Frs for two, including breakfast.

Meals: 80 Frs, excluding wine. Book ahead.

Open: All year except Sept & Jan.

The 1940s manor-house is furnished entirely in Art Deco style and houses an eclectic collection of modern art. Monsieur paints and runs an antique shop. Guests find original art and good beds in the rooms, can learn how to make a proper French garden and may breakfast whenever they want. Dine, upon request, with the spontaneously hospitable, down-to-earth hosts (both called Claude) in a congenial Bohemian atmosphere. Their sense of fun and hospitality will seduce you utterly — until the small hours.

Rooms: 2 double and 1 twin, all with own bath, shower, wc.

Price: 350-400 Frs for two, including breakfast.

Meals: 150-200 Frs, including aperitif, wine & coffee.

Open: All year.

From Bourges, N144 to Levet and D940 towards Lignières. 3km before Lignières, right on D129 to la Celle-Condée.

Map No: 11   MM 238-30

Alain & Élisabeth MANSSENS
Ferme-Auberge de Pont Chauvet
18160 La Celle-Condé
Cher
Tel: (0)2 48 60 22 19

From St Amand-Montrond, D951 towards Sancoins and Nevers. At Charenton Laugère, D953 towards Dun-sur-Auron; house is 300m along on left.

Map No: 11   MM 238-31

M & Mme Claude MOREAU
La Serre
18210 Charenton Laugère
Cher
Tel: (0)2 48 60 75 82

This early 20th-century house stands in 125 hectares of wheat and maize — and its quiet, leafy front garden. The Proffits are typical farmers: busy with work and children but friendly hosts. Guests lodge in a separate 'modern rustic-style' wing where bedrooms are plainly furnished and comfortable and they have their own large long-tabled living-room where Madame will join them for (slightly basic?) meals if they wish. She is open and most helpful, especially about what to do and see.

Rooms: 1 double, 2 twin, all with shower & wc.

Price: 230 Frs for two, including breakfast.

Meals: 80-90 Frs, excluding wine.

Open: All year.

Like so many water mills, this place is just a delight to look at and the ground-floor double has its own door to the stream-side terrace — the soothing sound of water should drown out any overhead floorboard creaks. Pretty rooms all, with antiques and lace, a good sitting-room with wonderful beam structure in the former milling area (look out for graffiti on the stone walls) and breakfast feasts. The owners have done a sensitive restoration, are genuinely interested and caring and have a flexible approach to your needs.

Rooms: 1 double, 1 triple, 1 suite for 4, each with shower & wc.

Price: 230 Frs for two, including breakfast.

Meals: 95 Frs, including kir, wine & coffee.

Open: All year.

From Bourges, N151 towards la Charité. At St Germain-du-Puy, D955 towards Sancerre. At Les Aix-d'Angillon, 2nd right towards Ste Solange & follow Chambre d'Hôte signs for 4km.

Map No: 11   MM 238-19

Odile & Yves PROFFIT
La Chaume
18220 Rians
Cher
Tel: (0)2 48 64 41 58
Fax: (0)2 48 64 29 71

From Loches N143 S dir. Châteauroux for 16km. On entering Fléré, village square is on right — Moulin clearly signed at bottom of square.

Map No: 10   MM 238-26

Danielle AUMERCIER
Le Moulin
36700 Fléré-la-Rivière
Indre
Tel: (0)2 54 39 34 41

THE LOIRE VALLEY

Teacher and hurdy-gurdy player involved in the summer folk festival, Solange Frenkel has converted an 18th-century *grange* (barn) into one of the friendliest *chambres d'hôtes*. In the remote rural area where George Sand held her salons and consorted with Chopin, it has high ceilings, huge beams, a vast fireplace in the sunken cosy living-room 'pit' and pretty bedrooms with garden entrances. You can have unlimited breakfast while Lasco the Labrador waits patiently to take you walking. One reader simply wrote, "The best".

Rooms: 1 double, 1 twin, each with bath or shower & wc.

Price: 270 Frs for two, including breakfast.

Meals: By arrangement 85 Frs, including wine.

Open: All year.

From Bourges, N144 towards Montluçon. At Levet D940 towards la Châtre. At Thevet-St-Julien, D68/D69 towards St Chartier. After 2km, left; after 1km, left again. Signposted.

Map No: 11   MM 238-41

Solange FRENKEL
La Garenne
36400 Thevet-St-Julien
Indre
Tel: (0)2 54 30 04 51

These environment-passionate people — courageously agin' huntin' in France's royal hunting grounds, nature photographer (wonderful pics of local fauna) and bird-knower (binoculars for ornithologists) — are quiet and serious. Their elegant house has an amazing mound of fallen and resuscitated judas tree for spring splendour, great-grandmother's solid Second Empire furniture and amusing sculptural plastic works created by father and son. The Brenne nature reserve is all here: take Alain's accompanied walks in spring and autumn.

Rooms: 2 double, each with bath or shower & wc.

Price: 260-280 Frs for two, including breakfast.

Meals: Choice in Le Blanc.

Open: All year (book ahead).

From Argenton-sur-Creuse, N151 towards Poitiers. At Le Blanc, D975 towards Martizay; then D27 towards Rosnay. After 2km right to Les Chézeaux; signposted.

Map No: 10   MM 238-38

Annie & Alain JUBARD
Les Chézeaux
36300 Le Blanc
Indre
Tel: (0)2 54 37 32 17

A brave and endearing young English couple who came to farm in France, with their rabbit-eared sheep (they now have two small children too), invite you to drive 2km through wild woods for a taste of rural French tranquillity. Their house still has old beams, terracotta tiles and stone fireplace. Rooms are big, pale-floored, simply-furnished, supremely peaceful. Alison will take good care of you and Robin may tell you tales of shearing French sheep and settling into this 'other' land. Argenton, 'Venice of the Indre', is a must.

Rooms: 1 double with bath & wc; 2 double, 1 triple, sharing a bathroom & separate wc.

Price: 240-270 Frs for two, including breakfast.

Meals: 80 Frs, including wine & coffee (book ahead).

Open: April to December.

A20 from Châteauroux; exit 16 to Tendu taking 1st left into village. Pass Mairie then fork left at church towards Chavin & Pommiers. House 2km up track.

Map No: 11   MM 238-40

Robin & Alison MITCHELL
La Chasse
36200 Tendu
Indre
Tel: (0)2 54 24 07 76

Monsieur is the most naturally hospitable man you could imagine. He is energetic and creative: he built that tower himself to extend his house without just adding another square bit, dug his own swimming pool, installed two good rather mod-furnished rooms in the old bakery — one still has the bread oven — and has a third more traditional room in the main house under the rafters. Meals are taken in his simple farmhouse kitchen with its elegant grandmother clock and his lively (French) conversation. We've had rave reviews!

Rooms: 1 quadruple, 1 double, each with shower & wc (1 fully fitted for disabled); 1 quadruple with basin, separate wc, sharing shower.

Price: 250 Frs for two, including breakfast.

Meals: 80 Frs, including wine & coffee (bookings only).

Open: All year.

From La Châtre, D940 towards Guéret for 4km then right to Le Montet; signposted.

Map No: 11   MM 238-41

M Gabriel PESSEL
Le Montet
36160 Pouligny-Saint-Martin
Indre
Tel: (0)2 54 30 23 55

Your charming, talented, partly-Parisian hosts — one a window-dresser, the other a theatre hair-and-make-up artist — have created a stylish home of simple sophistication in a relaxed atmosphere. The elegant, well-proportioned rooms have canopied beds, subtle colour schemes (*Les Mûriers* just avoids being blackberry-lurid) and good tiled bathrooms. The sitting-room has white walls, matting on old tiles, good country antiques and an old fireplace. Enjoy the lime-tree-shaded garden and your hosts' genuine hospitality.

Rooms: 1 double, 1 twin, each with shower & wc; 1 suite for 5 with bath & wc.

Price: 300 Frs for two, suite 550 Frs, including breakfast. Extra bed 100 Frs.

Meals: 110 Frs, including kir, wine & coffee (bookings only). Restaurant in village.

Open: Mid-June to mid-Sept (winter weekends by arrangement).

From Loches, N143 S dir. Châteauroux for 16km. Go through Fléré; 1km after village, right on D13a for Cléré-du-Bois; signposted.

Map No: 10   MM 238-26

Claude RENOULT
Le Clos Vincents
36700 Fléré-la-Rivière
Indre
Tel: (0)2 54 39 30 98
Fax: (0)2 54 39 30 98

This wonderful, uniquely atmospheric house — some say spartan, even primitive, others say austerely sober 17th-century — has been bought by a young, energetic, artistic mother who loves its simple authenticity as we do. No slick hotel bathrooms — one bath behind thick curtains, a loo in a cupboard, so as not to spoil the history of the room. The staircase is open-tread and uneven: it's original! The cool china blue *salon* speaks of calm intellectual pursuits. There is ancient peace here which Madame hopes to share with those who appreciate such rare treasures.

Rooms: 2 double, 1 twin, all with bath or shower & wc.

Price: 360 Frs for two, including breakfast.

Meals: Good choice 1-5km.

Open: Easter to 31 October.

Gîtes for 16 people

From Chinon, D749 towards Bourgueil. Little road to Montour is first on left; house easily found behind imposing gates. (2km off D749, 8km from Chinon.)

Map No: 10   MM 232-34

Mme Valérie ARBON
Manoir de Montour
37420 Beaumont-en-Véron
Indre-et-Loire
Tel: (0)2 47 58 43 76
Fax: (0)2 47 58 43 76

An imposing lodge set in a big 'English' garden and surrounded by forest, it has a harmonious, almost mellow feeling despite being built recently — but in C17 Angevin style with old materials from the château next door. An unusual and refreshingly natural place, it reflects the family's plan to return to country simplicity. They are relaxed and relaxing, chatty and creative, as proved by the delightful, carefully-designed and decorated bedrooms and living-dining area with their terracotta tiles and scrubbed rafters. Children over 10 welcome.

Rooms: 2 twin, each with shower & wc.

Price: 320 Frs for two, including breakfast.

Meals: In village.

Open: All year, except 20 December to 5 January.

From Tours, N152 towards Saumur. At St Patrice, D35 to Bourgueil. There, D749 to Gizeux then D15 to Continvoir. In village, left on D64; signposted.

Map No: 10   MM 232-34

Michel & Claudette BODET
La Butte de l'Épine
37340 Continvoir
Indre-et-Loire
Tel: (0)2 47 96 62 25
Fax: (0)2 47 96 62 25

Madame loves flowers — she won 2nd prize in a _gîtes fleuris_ competition for her glorious summer garden — and hates winter. She is relaxed and pleased to make you feel at home in her pretty farmhouse (sunflowers grow in all the surrrounding fields). Rooms, predictably flower-themed and fresh-flower decorated, are smallish but bright and cheerful, the guests' dayroom opens onto the terrace and the family dining-room is most welcoming. Try not to miss the spectacular maze created every summer with cereal crops at Reignac.

Rooms: 1 double, 1 twin, 2 triple, each with bath or shower & wc.

Price: 240-260 Frs for two, including breakfast.

Meals: 85 Frs, including wine & coffee. Picnic hamper 60 Frs.

Open: All year.

From Tours N143 dir. Loches, through Cormery and on for 10km. Here, see Massy-Ferguson garage on left and turn left for Azay-sur-Indre/Chambre d'Hôte; house 700m along, signposted.

Map No: 10   MM 238-14

Marie-Agnès BOUIN
La Bihourderie
37310 Azay-sur-Indre
Indre-et-Loire
Tel: (0)2 47 92 58 58
Fax: (0)2 47 92 22 19

The *Suite Empire* has two BIG single beds, one made for Oncle Vincent with matching wardrobe and chest of drawers, the other, brass-knobbed and not matching the cane chair... and Madame is very proud of her fine linen. This is such a French family house; you sleep in family-furnished rooms (two showers are behind curtains) or the newly-done cottage, wander through a fabulous rose garden, discover their favourite wine-growers and craftsmen. They love having guests and opening doors onto unknown bits of the Loire area.

Rooms: 2 double, 1 twin, with shower or (separate) bath, all sharing wc. 1 cottage for 3 with shower & wc.

Price: Rooms 240-260 Frs; cottage 300 Frs for two, including breakfast.

Meals: Auberge 50m away.

Open: All year.

From Chinon, D16 to Huismes. In village go under arch between church and large house, then 1st street on left & 2nd house on right.

Map No: 10   MM 232-34

Anne & Jean-Marc BUREAU
Le Clos de l'Ormeau
37420 Huismes
Indre-et-Loire
Tel: (0)2 47 95 41 54
Fax: (0)2 47 95 41 54

A simple old farmhouse with character and atmosphere. Monsieur quietly gets on with his gardening. Madame is charming and clearly delights in her role as hostess. Now retired, they are both active in their community, caring and unpretentious. Traditionally furnished, the rooms have subtle, well-chosen colour schemes and the bathroom is new and clean. Breakfast is served in the dining-room with homemade jams and crusty bread. The house backs onto the gardens of the château, is surrounded by chestnut trees and wonderfully quiet.

Rooms: 1 triple, 1 twin, 1 suite for 5, all with bath or shower & wc.

Price: 230 Frs for two, including breakfast. Extra bed 70 Frs.

Meals: Auberge 300m.

Open: All year.

Gîtes for 10 people

From Tours D29 to Beaumont-la-Ronce. House signposted in village.

Map No: 5   MM 232-24

Michel & Andrée CAMPION
La Louisière
37360 Beaumont-la-Ronce
Indre-et-Loire
Tel: (0)2 47 24 42 24

A modern house (1980s) in old style (C18 Loire), with modern comforts (heating and bathrooms) and old materials (beams, stones), carved chests and contemporary sculptures: these ex-Parisians clearly have a gift for marrying old and new, city sophistication and country earthiness. A place of warmth and luxury, superb rooms, beautiful furniture, a long and spectacular vineyard-to-Vienne River view. Madame is humorous, cultured and happy to guide you round the estate. Guests have their own sitting and utility rooms.

Rooms: 1 suite for 3/4 in main house; 2 double in pool-side cabin; all with bath or shower & wc.

Price: 450 Frs for two, 580 Frs suite for three, including breakfast.

Meals: In Ile Bouchard 4km.

Open: All year.

Gîtes for 4 people

An elegant dressed-stone house, a well-converted stable block, the inimitable limpid light of the Loire Valley on the edge of a quiet little village. The guests' quarters have ancient beams, some stone walls and new floors, space to sit or cook, even a little terrace. The uncluttered, sizeable rooms have the same happy mix of old and new with some fine pieces of furniture. You will be welcomed by a couple who are proud of their house and want you to like it too. "Very clean, very friendly, very good food."

Rooms: 2 triple, each with bath & wc; 1 double with shower & wc.

Price: 220-270 Frs for two, including breakfast.

Meals: 85 Frs, including aperitif, wine & coffee. Self-catering too.

Open: All year.

From Chinon, D21 to Cravant-les-Coteaux. Continue towards Panzoult; house is on left after 2km.

Map No: 10　　　　　MM 232-35

Marie-Claude CHAUVEAU
Domaine de Beauséjour
37220 Panzoult
Indre-et-Loire
Tel: (0)2 47 58 64 64

From Chinon D749 towards Bourgueil for 6km. Left towards Savigny-en-Véron & follow signs to 'Camping'. House 1km after campsite on right.

Map No: 10　　　　　MM 232-34

Marie-Françoise & Michel CHAUVELIN
Cheviré
11 rue Basse
37420 Savigny-en-Veron
Indre-et-Loire
Tel: (0)2 47 58 42 49

Bruno, a philosopher and former teacher, is as casually refined and interesting as the house. The roomy and engagingly shabby bedrooms have large windows over the park, big, old-fashioned baths, fireplaces and rugs. Use the charming sitting/dining-room with its stone-tiled floor, pretty blue-and-white curtains, fireplace and cosy armchairs, or play in the 100-hectare park with its fine old cedars... "rather like a Gainsborough". The estate makes *foie gras*, so not for the squeamish.

Rooms: 1 double, 1 twin, each with bath & wc.

Price: 480 Frs for two, including breakfast.

Meals: In village or Tours (5km).

Open: April to November.

From Tours D751 SW towards Chinon for 5km. In Ballan-Miré, right at lights just before level crossing. Signposted — entrance opposite golf course.

Map No: 10   MM 232-35

Monsieur Bruno CLÉMENT
Château du Vau
37510 Ballan-Miré
Indre-et-Loire
Tel: (0)2 47 67 84 04
Fax: (0)2 47 67 55 77

In the lesser-known and lovely Loir valley you have a little old house in the garden all to yourselves. It has a kitchen and a bathroom downstairs, two little bedrooms up a steep staircase, all recently renovated, and its own piece of flower-filled garden for intimate breakfasts. Or you can join Madame. She is friendly and dynamic, very involved in the local music festival and tourist activities so an excellent advisor for guests, and also a great maker of jams. It's not luxurious, but homely, quiet and welcoming.

Rooms: 2 double in cottage with one bathroom.

Price: 280 Frs for two, 480 Frs for 4, including breakfast.

Meals: 100 Frs, including wine & coffee

Open: All year.

Gîtes for 4 people

From Tours/La Membrolle N138 towards Le Mans. At Neuillé-Pont-Pierre D68 to Neuvy-le-Roy. House on road through village: blue front door, opposite turning to Louestault.

Map No: 5   MM 232-23

Ghislaine & Gérard de COUESNONGLE
20 rue Pilate
37370 Neuvy-le-Roi
Indre-et-Loire
Tel: (0)2 47 24 41 48

Worth every penny. The owners are a likeable, cosmopolitan couple with gentle voices and masses of energy. They are proud of their smart château with its listed garden (stupendous trees), lavishing tremendous civilised care on it and its occupants. The décor is superb with lovely materials, subtle colour schemes, fine furniture and attention to origins. One 'monastic' room (plain walls, old tiles, exposed brick and timber) contrasts pleasingly with the plushness elsewhere. Good company, PLUS a heated outdoor swimming pool!

Rooms: 2 suites for 3, 2 double, 2 twin, all with bath & wc.

Price: 590-750 Frs doubles, 790-1050 Frs suites, for two, including breakfast.

Meals: Choice within walking distance.

Open: All year.

Troglodytes once lived here — the cave with its original fireplace now houses preserves and pans while the pretty little creeper-covered old house (illustrated) in its secluded and steeply sloping garden has become a gentle 20th-century retreat from the crowds visiting the châteaux. Madame, relaxed and welcoming, is most knowledgeable about her beloved Loire Valley. She has installed two excellent rooms in an outbuilding, one with a superbly carved Norman bridal bed (doves and sheaves meaning peace and prosperity).

Rooms: 2 double, each with shower & wc.

Price: 270 Frs for two, including breakfast.

Meals: Wide choice within 5km.

Open: Easter — September.

From Tours N152 towards Blois for 4km. At St Georges left and follow signs 1km to château.

Map No: 10   MM 232-36

Christine & Jacques DESVIGNES
Château de Montgouverne
37210 Rochecorbon
Indre-et-Loire
Tel: (0)2 47 52 84 59
Fax: (0)2 47 52 84 61

From Saumur D751 towards Chinon to Montsoreau (10km) then D751 straight on through Candes & St Germain-sur-Vienne. 500m on, at the Goujon Frétillant restaurant, turn right and follow signs for 1.5km.

Map No: 10   MM 232-34

Anne DUBARRY
7 La Vallée des Grottes
37500 Saint-Germain-sur-Vienne
Indre-et-Loire
Tel: (0)2 47 95 96 45

High on a cliff above the Loire, it looks over the village and across the vineyards and valley to a château. Only 4 years old but done in *Tourangeau* style with reproduction furniture, the house is immaculate and meticulous: one room is in Louis XIV style, plus orangey carpet and flowery paper. There is a big dining/sitting area with tiled floor and rugs, an insert fireplace and views over the large sloping garden... under which there is a troglodyte dwelling. Mountain bikes to borrow, giant breakfasts... great value for the Loire.

Rooms: 1 suite, 2 double, each with bath & wc.

Price: 245-280 Frs for two, including breakfast.

Meals: Wide choice locally & in Tours.

Open: All year.

Richelieu is an unusual and historic little town. The Lawrences have set up their English-language and music schools in a long C17 townhouse with studios on the street side and a beamed entrance through to a sunny courtyard garden (hibiscus and banana trees) and the main house. The big rooms are softly decorated, beds are canopied with attractive fabrics chosen with flair and imagination and have good lighting. Tim and Marion are welcoming, considerate hosts and provide bountiful breakfasts.

Rooms: 1 double, 2 quadruple, all with own bath or shower & wc.

Price: 290 Frs for two, including breakfast. Extra bed 90 Frs.

Meals: Wide choice within 200m. Picnic and barbecue possible.

Open: All year.

From Tours A10 N towards Paris; cross River Loire then leave exit 20. Follow signs to Rochecorbon. In village left at lights then right up steep narrow lane; signposted.

Map No: 10   MM 232-36

Mme Jacqueline GAY
7 chemin de Bois Soleil
37210 Rochecorbon
Indre-et-Loire
Tel: (0)2 47 52 88 08
Fax: (0)2 47 52 88 08

A10 motorway, Richelieu exit. After entering Richelieu, take 2nd left. House 300m down on right.

Map No: 10   MM 232-46

Marion & Tim LAWRENCE
L'Escale
30 rue de la Galère
37120 Richelieu
Indre-et-Loire
Tel: (0)2 47 58 25 55

Elegance is the word here, for both house and hostess. They are undeniably French, refined and expect appreciation of their ageless quality. The rooms have huge character (antiques, lovely linen, soft fabrics) but are full of surprises. One (up a steep stair) has a tent-like loo, another deep purple curtains and a theatrical bathroom. The suite, in an annexe, has a Mediterranean light to it and the second bedroom is a jaw-dropping reproduction of an old *Tourangelle* kitchen: fireplace, simple table, 4 chairs and an enclosed bed. Inimitable!

Rooms: 2 double & 1 twin room, each with bath or shower & wc; 1 suite with bath en-suite, wc downstairs.

Price: 280-350 Frs for two, including breakfast.

Meals: Good choice in town.

Open: 1 February to 31 December.

The Pallais Restaurant opposite has a Michelin star! People come to this tiny village and stay in this unassuming B&B, just for that. But there is more: Natacha, a busy young mother, is sweetly attentive, her husband is grounded here in his family goat-cheese business (almost 200 goats 3km away) and le Grand Pressigny (10km) has a superb prehistory museum. The fairly basic guestrooms (French cheap n' cheerful) are in a separate wing with a good dayroom and real disabled facilities in one room.

Rooms: 4 double, each with shower & wc.

Price: 250 Frs for two, including breakfast. Extra bed 80 Frs.

Meals: Two restaurants in village, one starred, one simple 'family'.

Open: All year.

From A10, Ste Maure exit, D760 to l'Ile-Bouchard & D757 to Richelieu. There, rue du Collège to junction of rue Jarry and place des Religieuses.

Map No: 10   MM 232-46

Mme Marie-Josephe LE PLATRE
Les Religieuses
24 place des Religieuses
37120 Richelieu
Indre-et-Loire
Tel: (0)2 47 58 10 42

From Châtellerault D725 through La Roche Posay & Preuilly sur Claise. 1km after Preuilly left on D50/D41 to Le Petit Pressigny. House in centre opposite Restaurant Dallais.

Map No: 10   MM 232-48

Bernard & Natacha LIMOUZIN
La Pressignoise
37350 Le Petit Pressigny
Indre-et-Loire
Tel: (0)2 47 91 06 06

Yet another easy-going, happy family — dogs, cats, children — that will sweep you inside with real warmth. Malvina has all the time in the world for guests... a great skill. Bedrooms are upstairs in a barn, under the roof, with low beams, sloping ceilings, but lots of light. The floors are parquet, the walls creamy-limed, the beams scrubbed, the furniture simple but attractive, and there is a small kitchen for you. The sitting/dining-room has more beams, a fireplace, heavy oak table, and there is a fenced-in pool behind the barn.

Rooms: 2 twin, 1 triple, each with shower & wc.

Price: 250-290 Frs for two, including breakfast.

Meals: 100 Frs, including wine.

Open: All year.

Gîtes for 14 people

Susanna is a special person: calm, cultivated, full of knowledge and taste. You will enjoy her company, log fires and books. Her background is Anglo-Irish-American-Scottish — so are her guestrooms, beautifully low-key and elegant with muted decor, nice bits of furniture and modern bathrooms. The finely-restored high-ceilinged main room has a relaid 17th-century tiled floor of great beauty. The style is perfec yet without pretension. A Romanesque arch stands in the garden and the churc tower stands protectively over it.

Rooms: 2 triple, 1 twin, 2 double, all with bath or shower & wc.

Price: 290-330 Frs for two, including breakfast.

Meals: 140 Frs, including aperitif, wine & coffee.

Open: All year.

From Loches N143 S towards Châteauroux. After Perrusson (approx. 2km), right onto D41 to Verneuil. Left in village; signposted.

Map No: 10   MM 238-26

Malvina & Olivier MASSELOT
La Capitainerie
37600 Verneuil-sur-Indre
Indre-et-Loire
Tel: (0)2 47 94 88 15
Fax: (0)2 47 94 70 75
e-mail: captain@creaweb.fr

From Tours N143 towards Loches for 15km. In Cormery, cross bridge & take, very quickly, 3rd left. House 100m up on left (signposted).

Map No: 10   MM 232-36

Susanna McGRATH
Le Logis du Sacriste
3 rue Alcuin
37320 Cormery
Indre-et-Loire
Tel: (0)2 47 43 08 23
Fax: (0)2 47 43 05 48
e-mail: sacriste@creaweb.fr

Their file overflows with readers' praise — for Andrew's superb cooking, Sue's fabulous welcome, the setting, the decor, the fun. They really are delightful. Their deliciously watery home, a carefully restored mill on an island, is all ups and downs, nooks and crannies, big rooms and small, character and variety with skilful use of stencils and sponging. Plus a restful shady garden, private sandy beach and the added temptation of 300 paperbacks. Not really suitable for young children because of the water.

Rooms: 2 double, 2 triple, 1 twin, all with bath or shower & wc.

Price: 300-340 Frs for two, including breakfast.

Meals: 130 Frs, including wine & coffee.

Open: All year except Dec & Jan.

Small, dark and dynamic, she has boundless energy for her very full life which includes running a boutique, keeping house and garden immaculate, cooking fantastic dinners, and still finding time for guests — her lack of English does NOT prevent her communicating. Her elegant yet comfortable house has huge character and a serene mood. Under high, sloping, limed beams, on creamy yellow floors, the guest bedrooms and sitting area are big, light and glow with good pastel taste. The beautiful garden has a fish pond. Perfection?

Rooms: 1 suite, 1 double, each with bath & wc.

Price: 360 Frs for two, including breakfast. 2 nights min. April-Aug.

Meals: 130 Frs, including aperitif, wine and coffee.

Open: All year.

From Loches, N143 towards Châteauroux; pass Perusson then left at sign to St Jean-St Germain; house is last over the bridge on the left.

Map No: 10   MM 238-14

Andrew PAGE & Sue HUTTON
Le Moulin
Saint-Jean-Saint-Germain
37600 Loches
Indre-et-Loire
Tel: (0)2 47 94 70 12
Fax: (0)2 47 94 77 98

From Tours N143 S towards Loches. In Cormery left on D17 to Azay-sur-Indre. There, right up hill towards church; signposted.

Map No: 10   MM 238-14

Danièlle PAPOT
Le Prieuré
37310 Azay-sur-Indre
Indre-et-Loire
Tel: (0)2 47 92 25 29 or
       (0)6 80 07 18 26

The house had lost most of its original features but Michelle has created a cosy atmosphere with an open fireplace and lots of antiques and ornaments. Chatty, energetic and direct, she is a keen gardener and her garden, full of hidden corners, is a riot of foliage and flowers, with plenty of shade in summer. Rooms are immaculate and stylish, e.g. blue stripey wallpaper, prints, a brass bed, white table lamps. The Indre valley is charming; Balzac lived and wrote here; Alexander Calder lived and created here. Children over 12 welcome.

Rooms: 2 triple, 1 double, 1 suite for 4, each with shower & wc.

Price: 335-380 Frs for two, including breakfast.

Meals: Wide choice 10 minutes drive.

Open: Mid-March to mid-Nov.

A working goat-farm producing its own delicious cheese. Sleep in the pigsty (or is it the stable block?), swim in their beautiful pool then carouse over dinner in the lovely old room in the main house with its large open fireplace; the meal, very much *en famille*, starts after the evening's milking. The atmosphere around the table, the unusual and lovely setting and the easy good nature of your hosts make the fairly basic rooms utterly acceptable. Bits of the house are 13th century.

Rooms: 2 double, 1 twin, 1 quadruple, each with shower & wc.

Price: 230 Frs for two, including breakfast. Extra bed 60 Frs.

Meals: 80 Frs, including aperitif, wine & coffee.

Open: March to December.

From Azay-le-Rideau D84 E towards Artannes. Hamlet of Sablonnière is 6km along; house clearly marked on left in centre of hamlet.

Map No: 10　　　　　　MM 232-35

Mme Michelle PILLER
Les Tilleuls
16 rue de la Sablonnière
37190 Saché
Indre-et-Loire
Tel: (0)2 47 26 81 45
Fax: (0)2 47 26 84 00

Château-la-Vallière is 33km NW of Tours. From Château-la-Vallière take D34 S towards Langeais — first right then right again, past ruined castle: house at top of track.

Map No: 5　　　　　　MM 232-22

Gérard & Martine RIBERT
Vaujours
37330 Château-la-Vallière
Indre-et-Loire
Tel: (0)2 47 24 08 55

Rarely does one see so masterly a renovation. Foncher is memorable for the genuine mediæval atmosphere of the great square drawing room — old worn flagstones, monumental fireplace, low low doors, no curtains (not authentic)... and, in contrast, furniture from France, Africa, Vietnam. It is magical. One bedroom has a brick-and-timber wall, a great plain wooden bed, lace bedcovers; the other a marble washstand and a monkish mirror. Your hosts are excellent, cosmopolitan company. This really is special so book early.

Rooms: 1 suite for 3/4 with bath & wc.

Price: 650 Frs for two, 925 Frs for 3/4, including breakfast.

Meals: Choice in Villandry.

Open: April to September.

Eric was the first Frenchman to join the Campaign for Real Ale! He is a charming, artistic Anglophile, with a sense of fun and a real interest in people. The four downstairs rooms have their own terraces, stone beams and fireplaces. All rooms have magnificent bath or shower rooms and a stylish use of colour while the white panelled dining-room has attractive blue and white fabrics and a crystal chandelier over the big oval table. Smallish cosy sitting-room with wooden fireplace. History, culture, peace — magical.

Rooms: 1 suite of 2 twins, 2 triple, 1 twin, 3 double, all with bath or shower & wc.

Price: 580 Frs for two, including breakfast. Min. 2 nights.

Meals: In village or wide choice 10km.

Open: April to November.

Gîtes for 4 people

From Tours D7 to Savonnières. There, right across bridge then immediately left. House 3km along on right.

Map No: 10   MM 232-35

Michel & Marie-Françoise SALLES
Manoir de Foncher
37510 Villandry
Indre-et-Loire
Tel: (0)2 47 50 02 40
Fax: (0)2 47 50 09 94

From Savonnières left at Hôtel Faisan towards Ballan and up hill about 1km. House on left (signposted).

Map No: 10   MM 232-35

Eric & Christine SALMON
Prieuré des Granges
15 rue des Fontaines
37510 Savonnières
Indre-et-Loire
Tel: (0)2 47 50 09 67
Fax: (0)2 47 50 06 43

The lovely symmetry envelopes you, glazed fanlights on each arm of the cross look through onto trees, the welcome is utterly open-armed. Christian, a lively, amusing, naturally hospitable host, deals in Asian objects — the eclectic furnishings tell fascinating tales — and opens his house to walkers, yoga students (big light dojo on the top floor), gentle therapy groups as well as B&B guests. Expect lots of laughter and good imaginative cooking. It is warm, human, harmonious and unforgettable.

Rooms: 2 twin with shower & wc; 2 double with shower & basin, sharing wc.

Price: 270 Frs for two, including breakfast.

Meals: 110 Frs, including wine & coffee.

Open: All year.

Gîtes for 16 people

Writing a novel? Then that L-shaped room with stone fireplace and old desk is ideal for you. But all the rooms are large, light, old-tiled, well-bathroomed and the newly-restored outbuilding has a fine family room in the old hayloft. A calm, homely atmosphere is cultivated by these educated farmers who have the gift of working hard yet apparently having all the time in the world for you. Breakfast includes goat cheese and *saucisson* from the village and Madame cooks delicious, wholesome country dinners.

Rooms: 1 twin, 3 double, 1 suite, 1 family room, all with bath or shower & wc.

Price: 240-270 Frs for two, including breakfast.

Meals: 100 Frs, including wine & coffee.

Open: All year (except Christmas).

From Chinon cross River Vienne & take D749 then D760 to Ile Bouchard. After entering town, 2nd right and follow signs.

Map No: 10   MM 232-35

Christian VAURIE
La Commanderie
16 rue de la Commanderie
37220 Brizay, Indre-et-Loire
Tel: (0)2 47 58 63 13
Fax: (0)2 47 58 55 81
e-mail: http://www.touraine-com/lacommanderie

From A10, Ste Maure-de-Touraine exit onto D760, then D59 towards Ligueil. Go through Sepmes. Farm is on left as you leave village; signposted.

Map No: 10   MM 232-35

Anne-Marie & Joseph VERGNAUD
La Ferme les Berthiers
37800 Sepmes
Indre-et-Loire
Tel: (0)2 47 65 50 61

I have a weakness for water-mills (and this one is close to the château of Montrésor). Recently converted in stylish and simple good taste, with plain beige wool carpets, attractive lined curtains and co-ordinated colour schemes. Good linen and towels too, and coconut matting on the landing up a plain wooden staircase. Welcoming and very warm, with lots of original features... and quiet flows the water beneath the dining-room. Madame is as educated as she is travelled and her family has been in the château since the 17th century.

Rooms: 1 double, 1 twin, 2 triple, each with bath or shower & wc.

Price: 280-330 Frs for two, including breakfast. Extra bed 80 Frs. Under 4s free.

Meals: Choice within 5km.

Open: All year.

Gîtes for 10 people

From Loches D760 to Montrésor. In village, left towards Chemillé and mill is on left; signposted.

Map No: 10   MM 238-14

Sophie & Alain WILLEMS
Le Moulin de Montrésor
37460 Montrésor
Indre-et-Loire
Tel: (0)2 47 92 68 20
Fax: (0)2 47 92 74 61

The humble bee reigns royal on this bee farm where several honeys and other bee products are made — the small shop in the courtyard is a hive of activity. Charline welcomes you with an uplifting smile and, while Jacky actually does the bee-tending, is excellent at explaining (in French) the arcana of bee-keeping over breakfast in the separate guest building. If the decor is a little garish and synthetic in the velux-windowed bedrooms, the warmly human and relaxed atmosphere draws a veil over critical eyes. Great for children too.

Rooms: 2 double, 1 twin, each with bath or shower & wc. (Extra beds available.)

Price: 230 Frs for two, including breakfast. (Children under 5 free.)

Meals: Restaurant in St Savin. Barbecue available.

Open: Mid-February to mid-October.

Poitou –
The Atlantic
Coast

From Chauvigny, N151 towards St Savin. 2km before St Savin, left to Siouvre; signposted.

Map No: 10   MM 233-10

Charline & Jacky BARBARIN
Siouvre
86310 Saint-Savin
Vienne
Tel: (0)5 49 48 10 19
Fax: (0)5 49 48 46 89

You will be mollycoddled by these delightful people. One bedroom (full wheel-chair access) is in a converted woodshed, with beams, pretty curtains, blue and yellow tiled floor and view over the large, rambling garden with its frog pond (hence *Grenouillère*). Two rooms are upstairs in a separate house across the courtyard where Madame's mother, a charming lady, lives. Pleasant, comfortable rooms, and the buildings are most attractive. Meals can be served on the shaded terrace and you can mess about in the small rowing boat.

Rooms: 2 triple, 2 double, each with bath or shower & wc.

Price: 210-280 Frs for two, including breakfast. Extra bed 70 Frs.

Meals: 90 Frs, including wine (children 50 Frs).

Open: All year.

From Tours N10 S towards Châtellerault for 55km. In Dangé-St-Romain, right at 3rd traffic lights; cross river; keep left on little square; house 100m along on left; signposted.

Map No: 10   MM 232-47

Annie & Noël BRAGUIER
La Grenouillère
17 rue de la Grenouillère
86220 Dangé-Saint-Romain
Vienne
Tel: (0)5 49 86 48 68
Fax: (0)5 49 86 46 56

Come and experience the daily life of farmers in a small hilltop village with a fine 12th-century church. After 20-odd years of B&B, your hosts still enjoy their guests enormously. He, a jovial retired farmer (the son now runs the farm), knows his local lore; she smiles quietly and gets on with her cooking in the big homely kitchen. Up the superb old solid oak staircase, bedrooms are clean and bright with good beds, curtained-off showers and separate loos. A warm and generous welcome is assured plus masses of things to do and see.

Rooms: 3 double, one with extra bed for child, each with shower & wc.

Price: 205 Frs for two, including breakfast.

Meals: 75 Frs, including wine.

Open: All year.

From Loudon, follow signs for Thouars then take D60 towards Moncontour. At Mouterre-Silly, find the church; house is 50m along towards Silly, signposted 'Chambres d'Hôtes'.

Map No: 10   MM 232-45

Agnès & Henri BRÉMAUD
Le Bourg
86200 Mouterre-Silly
Vienne
Tel: (0)5 49 98 09 72
Fax: (0)5 49 22 33 40

The G.R.48 path goes past the house — this is a great place for walkers. Your delightful hosts, much involved in local life, are a friendly family with three children. Deby's brother (the sheep farmer) and parents (antique-dealers) also live on the estate. Guests are in the main family house which is comfortable and attractive, with interesting and original antiques, prints and good fabrics in the bedrooms. The sitting-room is cosy, the dining-room elegant. A wonderful place for nature lovers. One reader simply said "Outstanding".

Rooms: 2 double, 2 twin, 1 suite for 4/5, all with bath or shower & wc.

Price: 320 Frs for two, including breakfast.

Meals: 95 Frs, including wine & coffee (book ahead).

Open: All year.

Gîtes for 14 people

Vivaldi would have delighted in this fine C18 coaching inn, attractively converted by M Flambeau and his vivacious English wife. The rooms are named after the seasons, 'Summer' has a brass four-poster and 'Winter' a white canopied bed. The 'Four Seasons' suite is in progress. The bathrooms are beautifully tiled to match the bedrooms. On the main square of a quiet village, it has a charming courtyard and a large garden planted with mature trees: an oasis of peace and greenery. Baby-sitting available

Rooms: 1 suite, 1 quadruple, 3 double, each with bath or shower & wc.

Price: 250-290 Frs for two, including breakfast.

Meals: 95 Frs, including wine & coffee.

Open: All year.

From Chauvigny, D54 to Montmorillon then D727 towards la Trimouille. House is on right 10km along this road: signposted.

Map No: 10   MM 233-11

Richard & Deby EARLS
La Boulinière
Journet
86290 La Trimouille
Vienne
Tel: (0)5 49 91 55 88
e-mail: jr-earls@interpc.fr

From Poitiers N149 W towards Nantes for 14km. At Vouillé left on D62 to Latillé. House is the largest in main village square. (Poitiers-Latillé 24km.)

Map No: 10   MM 233-7

Yvonne FLAMBEAU
La Demeure de Latillé
1 place Robert Gerbier
86190 Latillé
Vienne
Tel: (0)5 49 51 54 74
Fax: (0)5 49 51 56 32

The fortified farmhouse is set in highly roamable parkland. The guestrooms, slightly squeezed into the converted stables, are furnished with high old beds and family pieces. The conversion was almost all Pierre-Claude's own work as was the replacement of the courtyard laurel by a coyly naked lady in a bower! After a game of *pétanque*, he regales guests with family history over candlelit dinners in the vast family kitchen while Chantal cooks to her own excellent recipes. Well-placed for ancient Fontevraud and modern Futuroscope.

Rooms: 3 double, 1 room for 3-6, 1 room for 2-4, each with shower & wc.

Price: 200 Frs for two, including breakfast.

Meals: 110 Frs, including wine & coffee.

Open: All year.

Gîtes for 10 people

A large and elegant 18th-century house in the centre of Chauvigny, just 20km from the Futuroscope. The exterior and hall are typically French, the numerous rooms are full of antique furniture and there are flowers everywhere. Although this is just a B&B there can be a lot of people about. The owners have now retired here and, with their assistant, are glad to share their knowledge of the area's history and culture with visitors. From the peaceful walled garden there are fine views of the castle up above.

Rooms: 4 double, 1 triple and 1 single; all with bath or shower & wc.

Price: 230-300 Frs for two, including breakfast.

Meals: 80 Frs, including wine.

Open: February to November or by arrangement.

Gîtes for 12 people

From Saumur, D947 to Candes, then D147 to Loudun. There, D14 to Monts-sur-Guesnes; left at post office — signposted.

Map No: 10   MM 232-46

Pierre-Claude & Chantal
FOUQUENET
Domaine de Bourg-Ville
86420 Monts-sur-Guesnes
Vienne
Tel: (0)5 49 22 81 58
Fax: (0)5 49 22 89 89

From Poitiers, N151 towards Le Blanc. On entering Chauvigny, second left turn after church.

Map No: 10   MM 233-9

Jacques & Claude de GIAFFERRI
La Veaudepierre
8 rue du Berry
86300 Chauvigny
Vienne
Tel: (0)5 49 46 30 81/41 41 76
Fax: (0)5 49 47 64 12

Dannie is a gem, who actually looks forward to the start of each season and the flood of guests — her enthusiasm knows no bounds! She cooks magnificent traditional family dinners and makes sure everyone gets on well; her rooms are decently big with polished parquet floors, good old family furniture, good fabrics (all curtains and bedspreads handmade). She and her husband inherited the old family house: it is solid 19th-century, set back off the road just outside beautiful mediæval Chauvigny, in a lovely part of the Vienne valley.

Rooms: 1 suite for 6, 3 triple, 1 quadruple, each with shower & wc.

Price: 260 Frs for two, including breakfast.

Meals: 70 Frs, including wine & coffee.

Open: All year.

Gîtes for 3 people

From Châtellerault D749 S for 26km. 2km before Chauvigny, in hamlet of Les Barballières — house on left, signposted.

Map No: 10   MM 233-9

Dannie HERVÉ
La Louisière
1 route des Courlis, Les Barballières
86300 Bonnes
Vienne
Tel: (0)5 49 46 53 58
Fax: (0)5 49 01 86 54

An utterly delightful couple who just cannot do enough for you. Monsieur, who once resuscitated cars for a living, now takes much more pleasure in reviving tired travellers. Their house is on the old ramparts and the pretty garden looks directly out over the boulevard below (quiet enough at night). The two rooms are neat, with good beds and old *armoires*. One has big-flower wallpaper, the smaller one is plain blue; both have space. Breakfast in high-backed chairs at the long table in the converted stables beneath the old hay rack.

Rooms: 2 twin rooms, each with shower or bath & wc.

Price: 230 Frs for two, including breakfast. Extra bed 70 Frs.

Meals: Restaurants in village.

Open: All year.

From Châtellerault D725 towards Parthenay for 30km. In Mirebeau right opposite 'Gendarmerie', straight across lights then immediately left into rue Jacquard.

Map No: 10   MM 232-46

Jacques & Annette JEANNIN
19 rue Jacquard
86110 Mirebeau
Vienne
Tel: (0)5 49 50 54 06

The château started life as a mediæval fortress and was 'finished' in the 18th century. Behind a great carved screen brought from another stately home, the first-floor *salon* runs superbly the full length of the house. Here guests can sit, read, write, dream. Good rooms with loads of personality are perfectly fitting; Madame's hand-painted tiles adorn the bathrooms, her laughter accompanies your breakfast. Monsieur tends his trees, makes jam and knows all there is to do in the area. A great couple.

Rooms: 2 suites, 1 double, all with bath or shower & wc.

Price: 350-370 Frs for two, including breakfast. Extra bed 100 Frs.

Meals: Nearby inn.

Open: All year.

Gîtes for 4 people

From A10 Futuroscope exit. At roundabout towards Neuville, at 2nd r'about D62 towards Neuville for 5km. At Quatre Vents r'about D757 to Vendeuvre. Just after entering Vendeuvre left on D15 to Chéneché. 800m after entering Chéneché, Labarom is signposted on right.

Map No: 10   MM 232-46

Eric & Henriette LE GALLAIS
Château de Labarom
86380 Chéneché
Vienne
Tel: (0)5 49 51 24 22/
(0)6 80 46 17 66
Fax: (0)5 49 51 47 38

This pretty château in its large park is an old family seat with period pieces, family trees and portraits. Madame has a twinkly brightness and will greet you like a long-lost friend in intelligent if slightly impeded French; Monsieur is a genial, English-speaking field sportsman; they have 11 grandchildren. Rooms and washing arrangements are also rather eccentric and other-worldly: all antiques, alcoves, showers in cupboards. Your hosts will gladly discuss visits to Loire châteaux, Futuroscope and other delights.

Rooms: 1 triple, 1 double, each with shower; 1 single with basin; 1 bathroom, 2 wc's for all, one on another floor.

Price: 250 Frs for two, including breakfast.

Meals: 90 Frs, including wine & coffee.

Open: All year.

From Loudun, D759 towards Thouars. After 7km, left on D19 to Arçay, 1km along — château is on right behind big gates as you enter village (no signs).

Map No: 10   MM 232-45

Hilaire & Sabine LEROUX de LENS
Château du Puy d'Arçay
86200 Arçay
Vienne
Tel: (0)5 49 98 29 11

Hidden away in wooded Poitou, this 18th-century manor is uniquely stylish, blending sumptuous fabrics, beautiful antiques, beams, stone and rough-plastered walls to achieve a mood of intimate luxury — a must for the sophisticated, discerning traveller. Each suite has its own entrance and the entrance to the main house is a large, book-lined hall. Breakfast when you like in dining-room, bedroom or terrace. Andrea, vivacious and casually elegant, used to breed horses but now concentrates on caring for her guests.

Rooms: 2 suites, each with bath, shower & wc.

Price: 650 Frs for two, including breakfast.

Meals: Good choice within 15km.

Open: April to October, otherwise by arrangement.

From Loudun D61 E towards Richelieu for 12.5km. At La Polka right on D24, through Maulay and towards Monts-sur-Guesnes for another 4km. Then right on D66. After 500m right into drive to house: Boufray 1km.

Map No: 10   MM 232-46

Andrea de MONTAL
Boufray
86200 Maulay
Vienne
Tel: (0)5 49 22 77 77
Fax: (0)5 49 22 57 04

Sweep up the driveway to this lovely old farmhouse where 5 generations of Picards have lived. Overlooking the chestnut-treed garden are the generous bedrooms where good furnishings include handsome wardrobes. Sunlight streams into the huge sitting-room with its magnificent fireplace, beams, white walls and terracotta-tiled floor. Breakfast in the yellow dining-room or on the leafy terrace. The quiet, welcoming hosts are busy cereal farmers but will do anything to help you enjoy yourselves.

Rooms: 2 double, 1 twin, each with bath or shower & wc.

Price: 260 Frs for two, including breakfast. Children 60 Frs.

Meals: In village or Richelieu.

Open: All year.

Gîtes for 6 people

From Richelieu, D7 towards Loudun. After 4km, right onto a drive with lime trees on both sides.

Map No: 10   MM 232-46

Jean & Marie-Christine PICARD
Le Bois Goulu
86200 Pouant
Vienne
Tel: (0)5 49 22 52 05

The guest house — a converted barn — is older than the main house and has been very nicely done. There is a superb cobbled terrace the full length of the building where you can sit on balmy evenings gazing across the wide landscape and listening to the music of the wind in the poplars. Muted colour schemes in the largish rooms harmonise with ethnic rugs. Madame has one young son, is frank, sociable and very good company. With a nature reserve on the doorstep this is a little-known corner waiting to be discovered.

Rooms: 4 triple, 1 double, all with bath & wc.

Price: 270 Frs for two, including breakfast. Extra bed 70 Frs.

Meals: 95 Frs, including wine & coffee.

Open: All year.

The main house used to be the château stables; the 'cottage' used to be the pig-sty! The whole estate is still shared by Madame's family (her brother does B&B in the orangery), and most welcoming they are, kind, knowledgeable and helpful. Monsieur is a true bibliophile and vastly erudite, with a living-room full of books, pictures, treasures and a sense of history. The rooms are just as soft and comfortable with their old furniture and pale walls. The cottage has its own little garden and a (disused) 3-hole alcove for hens' nests.

Rooms: Main house: 1 twin with shower & wc. Cottage: 1 quadruple with hip-bath/shower & wc.

Price: 310 or 330 Frs for two, including breakfast.

Meals: 130 Frs, including wine & coffee; children 3-10, 50 Frs.

Open: All year.

From Châtellerault D749 to Vouneuil-sur-Vienne. In church square follow Chambre d'Hôte signs. Last house in hamlet on right. Caution: 'Chabonne' is the name of the house — the village of Chabonne is 2 km away.

Map No: 10   MM 232-47

Florence & Antoine PENOT
Chabonne
86210 Vouneuil-sur-Vienne
Vienne
Tel: (0)5 49 85 28 25

From A10 Poitiers Nord exit on N10 towards Limoges for 7km. Left to Bignoux & follow signs to Bois Dousset/Les Godiers.

Map No: 10   MM 233-9

M & Mme Philippe RABANY
Les Godiers
86800 Lavoux
Vienne
Tel: (0)5 49 61 05 18

Elegant and sophisticated is the feel. This fine château is soberly but immaculately decorated with a mix of antique and modern furniture. The dining-room has a remarkable carved wooden fireplace with doors and drawers for plate-warming. The finely-proportioned bedrooms are full of character, the suite has windows on three sides onto the peaceful, unspoilt park. Madame is small, dark and loquacious; Monsieur is tall, blond and reserved; together they are delicious hosts who will do anything for you.

Rooms: 1 suite, 2 double, 1 twin, 1 triple, each with bath or shower & wc.

Price: 290-500 Frs for two, including breakfast.

Meals: Supper tray 60 Frs, excluding wine (60 Frs).

Open: All year.

Gîtes for 7 people

50 Frs

This working sheep farm lies in unspoilt, rolling, stream-run country where fishing competitions are held. All the farm produce is organic: don't miss the chance to try Madame's Limousin specialities — lamb, chicken cooked in honey, vegetable pies — round the family table. The Salvaudons are educated, intelligent farmers — he energetic and down-to-earth, she gentle and smiling — committed to the natural way ("there's more to the Vienne than the Futuroscope"), who like swapping travellers' tales and sharing simple values.

Rooms: 1 triple, 1 double, with showers and basins; shared wc.

Price: 190 Frs for two, breakfast included.

Meals: 80 Frs, including wine & coffee.

Open: All year.

Gîtes for 6 people

From Poitiers N147 S towards Limoges. At Fleuré, right on D2 towards Gençay for 4km. Château entrance signposted on left.

Map No: 10   MM 233-9

M & Mme REBILLARD
Château de la Guillonnière
86410 Dienné
Vienne
Tel: (0)5 49 42 05 46
Fax: (0)5 49 42 48 34

From Poitiers, D741 to Civray. There, D148 east and D34 to Availles. There D100 towards Mauprévoir. After 3km, signposted.

Map No: 10   MM 233-20

Pierre & Line SALVAUDON
Les Ecots
86460 Availles-Limousine
Vienne
Tel: (0)5 49 48 59 17

The guest quarters are decorated with a wonderful flair for fabrics and colours — mats and tablecloth match crockery; bathrooms match bedrooms. It's smart yet utterly welcoming, as befits a converted bakery — the largest room, finely renovated with exposed beams, stones and thick white curtains, houses the old bread oven. Monsieur, his daughter or their friendly housekeeper will happily chat (he in perfect English) in the pleasant sitting area about all the things in the cultural treasure-chest that is the Poitou.

Rooms: 1 room for 3/4, 2 twin, all with bath, shower & wc.

Price: From 350 Frs for two, including breakfast.

Meals: Self-catering. Restaurants 2-8km.

Open: Mid-Feb to October (by arrangement in winter).

It is SO French, this former orangery in the fine château park — not stilted but utterly natural. The stone-flagged *salon* has a wonderful jumble of 10 French chairs, bits of ancient furniture, pictures, ornaments and lamps. The dining-room has traditional elegance. There are statues here and there about the house. Bedrooms are large, bursting with character; bathrooms too. The family is lively, natural and fun with many interests and lots to tell you. The occasional *fleur-de-lys* pattern marks the aristocratic connection.

Rooms: 2 double, 1 twin, 1 suite, all with own bathrooms (one on separate floor).

Price: 350 Frs for two, including breakfast. Terms for children.

Meals: 70 Frs, including wine & coffee (book ahead). Forest inn 4km.

Open: All year.

From A10 or N10 take Rocade Est (ringroad) round Poitiers, exit on D3 to Montamisé then right on D18 for 2km. Château on right.

Map No: 10   MM 233-8

M & Mlle VAUCAMP
Château de Vaumoret
Rue du Breuil Mingot
86000 Poitiers
Vienne
Tel: (0)5 49 61 32 11
Fax: (0)5 49 01 04 54

From A10, Poitiers Nord exit, N10 towards Limoges. After 7km, left to Bignoux; follow signs to Bois Dousset.

Map No: 10   MM 233-9

Vicomte & Vicomtesse Hilaire de
VILLOUTREYS de BRIGNAC
Logis du Château du Bois Dousset
86800 Lavoux
Vienne
Tel: (0)5 49 44 20 26
Fax: (0)5 49 44 20 26

Madame Chollet is justifiably proud of her house which has a charming old-world atmosphere and is good value in this rather touristy area. Idyllic location, with views out to the Sèvre Niortaise River — very quiet in the evenings when the day-trippers have gone. There is a small boat available and Monsieur, who is very knowledgeable about the utterly fascinating *Marais* area, will escort guests on boat trips (at reasonable rates). Families welcome, but preferably without toddlers.

Rooms: 1 double, 1 triple each with own shower & wc.

Price: 250-280 Frs for two, including breakfast. Extra person 80 Frs.

Meals: Restaurants within walking distance.

Open: All year.

A former *coin Protestant*, and the *Marais Poitevin* is near: do visit it. Your hosts make a delightful partnership — she teaches, he does the cooking. One reader especially enjoyed the way he did his pigeons. He pops in and out of the kitchen to chat while cooking dinner, so the atmosphere is very 'family'. Much of the food is home-produced, too. Guests are free to use the big dining-room and sitting-room and the pleasant bedrooms are up two flights of stairs in the attic. Excellent value in an easy and attractive village house.

Rooms: 1 triple with curtained-off shower & wc; 2 double sharing shower & wc.

Price: 200 Frs for two, including breakfast.

Meals: 80 Frs, including wine.

Open: Easter to mid-October.

From Coulon centre D23 towards Irleau. At end of village, immediately left along bank of River Sèvre which is Rue Élise Lucas.

Map No: 10   MM 233-5

Ginette & Michel CHOLLET
68 rue Élise Lucas
79510 Coulon
Deux-Sèvres
Tel: (0)5 49 35 91 55/42 59

From A10 exit 32 onto D7 towards Mougon for 1km then left on D5 dir. La Mothe St Héray for 7km then right for Prailles; sign on left on entering village — continue up & turn right to house.

Map No: 10   MM 233-6

Michel & Marie-Claude DUVALLON
Le Colombier des Rivières
79370 Prailles
Deux-Sèvres
Tel: (0)5 49 32 84 43

The picture tells it all — moat, keep, drawbridge, dreams. Up two spiral stone flights is "the biggest bedroom in France" — solid granite windowsills, a giant fireplace, a canopied bed and the shower snug in the former *garde-robe* (water closet). Breakfast under the 5-metre guardroom vault, your feet on the original C14 flagstones. The old stones are exposed, the furniture sober and sparse and the fires always laid, just like olden times. Pippa is eager and attentive — flowers, bubbly, fishing in the moat, all on the house!

Rooms: 2 connecting doubles, each with shower & wc (only let to same party).

Price: 550 Frs for two, 650-850 Frs for four, including breakfast.

Meals: Restaurant 3km; choice 9km.

Open: All year.

From A10 exit 29 onto N147 then N149 W to Parthenay. Round Parthenay northbound, continue N149 towards Bressuire; 7km N of Parthenay, right at sign for château.

Map No: 10   MM 232-44

Nicholas & Philippa FREELAND
Château de Tennessus
79350 Amailloux
Deux-Sèvres
Tel: (0)5 49 95 50 60
Fax: (0)5 49 95 50 62
e-mail: http://www.wfi.fr/tennessus

The family snapped the house up after the Revolution; it has only changed hands once since the 15th century. Come not for the rooms but for the idyllic setting. It is all slightly shambolic and faded in a way that quite won us over: utterly 'family', and they serve splendid dinners, enjoying the conversation and perhaps a game of bridge as well. Children would love the enormous park and the boat. Monsieur uses a limpid and charming French; Madame smokes *Gauloises* and speaks with a husky voice — a most likeable pair.

Rooms: 1 triple, 2 double, 1 twin, each with bath or shower & wc; 2 double sharing shower & wc.

Price: 200-400 Frs for two, including breakfast.

Meals: 100 Frs, including wine & coffee.

Open: All year.

From A10 exit 'Poitiers Sud' on N10 dir. Angoulême then right on N11 dir. Niort for 14km. From Lusignan D950 to Melle and on towards Brioux for 3km then right on D301 to St Romans. House in village, near church.

Map No: 10   MM 233-17

François RABANY
Le Logis
79500 Saint-Romans-lès-Melle
Deux-Sèvres
Tel: (0)5 49 27 04 15
Fax: (0)5 49 29 18 37

A dream... a fine house with its own boat to drift you deep into the *Marais*, or *Venise Verte* (odd name). The old *maison de maître*, in the village, has a glorious walled garden with over 70 varieties of iris. Monsieur is a doctor; Liliane, bright and enthusiastic, is a local guide. The bedrooms: parquet floors, photos of the *Marais*, regional furniture, in one a four-poster with views of the water. Downstairs: books, a chess table, more parquet. Rabelais lived in the Abbey, a stone's throw away. Very special.

Rooms: 3 double, 1 triple, 1 twin, each with bath or shower & wc.

Price: 320-350 Frs for two, including breakfast. Extra bed 50 Frs.

Meals: In village.

Open: All year.

From Fontenay-le-Comte N148 dir. Niort for 9km then right on D15 to Maillezais. There, follow signs for L'Abbaye. House on left, signposted.

Map No: 10   MM 233-4

Liliane BONNET
69 rue de l'Abbaye
85420 Maillezais
Vendée
Tel: (0)2 51 87 23 00
Fax: (0)2 51 00 72 44

A solidly reliable address, this 18th-century village house just yards from the beautiful cloisters of the Royal Abbey where Eleanor of Aquitaine was born and her mother buried. The rooms are recently converted, simply and with subdued rustic good taste (one is very big), and look over the walled garden. The dining-room is in the old stable block and there is a small sitting-room in the former wash-house where Christine will make up a fire if it's cold. She and her parents, who live in the main house, are most welcoming,

Rooms: 2 triple, 1 double, 1 twin, each with shower & wc.

Price: 260-280 Frs for two, including breakfast.

Meals: 75 Frs, incl. aperitif, wine & coffee; 45 Frs under 10s. Book previous day.

Open: April to October.

From Niort N148 NW towards Fontenay-le-Comte for 20km. After Oulmes right to Nieul-sur-l'Autize; follow signs to Abbey — house just before it on left.

Map No: 10   MM 233-5

Christine CHASTAIN-POUPIN
Le Rosier Sauvage
1 rue de l'Abbaye
85240 Nieul-sur-l'Autize
Vendée
Tel: (0)2 51 52 49 39
Fax: (0)2 51 52 49 46

At the very end of the lane, just yards from the river, Massigny is a secret corner of marshy Vendée. The rooms are as handsome as you'll find: Jean-Claude teaches cabinet-making and his delight in wood is evident. Add beds for deep sleep, unfussy fabrics, papers and painted beams for æsthetic satisfaction, a guest sitting-room with two carved *armoires* and a lovely copper tub for plants, and all you need is to dine with these friendly, open people and share their wide-ranging conversation. Remarkable value.

Rooms: 2 double, each with shower & wc.

Price: 220 Frs for two, including breakfast.

Meals: 80 Frs, including wine.

Open: All year.

From A83 exit at Fontenay-le-Comte onto D938ter and go SW towards La Rochelle for 6km, then right at small sign for Massigny.

Map No: 10   MM 233-4

Marie-Françoise & Jean-Claude NEAU
Massigny
85770 Velluire
Vendée
Tel: (0)2 51 52 30 32

This charming traditional house beside a river on the edge of the village is owned by the equally delightful and welcoming Ribert family. It was completely renovated five years ago and the big, light, airy rooms with their stripped doors and traditional furniture are full of fresh flowers from the secluded walled garden. Excellent breakfasts (cooked if requested) and dinners are eaten in the family room or in a larger dining-room, depending on the number of guests. Lots to do in the area; they have plans for canoes on the river.

Rooms: 5 triple rooms, all with own bath or shower & wc.

Price: 260 Frs for two, including breakfast. Extra person 70 Frs.

Meals: 90 Frs, including wine & coffee.

Open: March to December.

From Fontenay-le-Comte, D938ter for 13km then right on D25. Le Gué-de-Velluire is 4.5km on.

Map No: 9   MM 233-4

Christiane RIBERT
Le Logis
5 rue de la Rivière
85770 Le Gué-de-Velluire
Vendée
Tel: (0)2 51 52 59 10
Fax: (0)2 51 52 57 21

A fine family house — formerly a cognac-making 'château' — with beautiful mature gardens, set in excellent walking country and forest. Immaculately restored by the owners, émigrés from Paris, the house is well decorated, beautifully furnished, sparklingly clean; Madame's food is excellent and everything is done properly, without fuss. Just relax and enjoy the nearby River Dordogne and the sea. Readers have praised the place and the convivial dinner party atmosphere in the evenings.

Rooms: 2 twin, 1 triple, 1 quadruple, each with shower & wc .

Price: 270 Frs for two, including breakfast.

Meals: 1,00 Frs, including wine.

Open: All year except October.

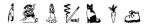

You enter a grand old château: dark walls, weapons on the walls, fine antiques and lots of light: it's just one room thick. Your hosts, a delightful couple of elderly characters, are addicted to receiving guests and "won't stop till they have to". Bedrooms are decorated and furnished with taste and flair, the plumbing is somewhat old-fashioned and the open-fired original kitchen a superb place for (occasional) breakfasts. Artists and musicians love the long thin house and its fine gardens, and there is so much to do in the area .

Rooms: 1 suite with bath & wc; 2 twin, sharing shower & wc.

Price: 280 or 320 Frs for two, including breakfast.

Meals: Neighbouring farm; restaurants 5-12km.

Open: March — November.

From A10 Mirambeau exit onto D730 to Montlieu-la-Garde; then N10 towards Angoulême. After Pouillac, first left after (closed) petrol station; signposted after 800m.

Map No: 10   MM 233-39

Denise & Pierre BILLAT
La Thébaïde, Pouillac
17210 Montlieu-la-Garde
Charente-Maritime
Tel: (0)5 46 04 65 17
Fax: (0)5 46 04 65 26

From Saintes, N137 towards la Rochelle. After 10km, D119 to Plassay; house on right as you enter village — signposted.

Map No: 10   MM 233-15

Alix & Jacques CHARRIER
Le Logis de l'Epine
17250 Plassay
Charente-Maritime
Tel: (0)5 46 93 91 66

"She welcomed us like family and sent us home with produce from her vineyard." Behind a fine old exterior, this small château exudes light, harmony, colour and elegant informality inside with its spiral stone stairs and painted beams. The well-furnished bedrooms have soft colours and gentle wallpapers; both airy and warm. You can have breakfast in your room. At dinner, refined food with estate wines is served at individual tables. Mother, who paints, and daughter, who speaks good English, are doing a good job.

Rooms: 2 double, 3 twin, all with bath or shower & wc.

Price: 500-650 Frs for two, including breakfast.

Meals: 160 Frs, excluding wine (book when reserving room).

Open: Easter to September.

From A10, exit 27 at Mirambeau then D730 towards Royan. Château is between Lorignac and Brie-sous-Mortagne; signposted at D730/D125 junction.

Map No: 10   MM 233-26

Mme Sylvie COUILLAUD
Château des Salles
17240 Saint-Fort-sur-Gironde
Charente-Maritime
Tel: (0)5 46 49 95 10
Fax: (0)5 46 49 02 81

We know why people come back again and again: the Deschamps just love doing B&B and it shows. Madame delights in cooking delicious meals for her guests and Monsieur enjoys talking English. They have enlarged their dining-room to take a bigger table and their generosity is legendary (they once delayed a friend's party to dine with late-arriving guests), so what matter a slightly unkempt façade? Huge wardrobes dominate the bright-papered bedrooms, beds and bedding are traditional French, and the best room has three lovely windows.

Rooms: 1 double, 2 suites, each with bath or shower & wc.

Price: 230-250 Frs for two, including breakfast.

Meals: 90 Frs, including aperitif, wine & coffee.

Open: Easter to 30 October.

From St Jean d'Angély, D939 towards Matha. 3km after crossroads to Varaize, D229 towards Aumagne. House 0.8km on left.

Map No: 10   MM 233-17

Eliane & Maurice DESCHAMPS
La Clé des Champs
17770 Aumagne
Charente-Maritime
Tel: (0)5 46 58 23 80
Fax: (0)5 46 58 23 91

Jenny loves cooking and writing, John is building a boat to sail across the Atlantic in, together they have lovingly restored their *Charentais* farmhouse and delight in having guests. The atmosphere is convivial and you are welcome to socialise and dine *en famille*. Or feel free to go your own way (separate guest entrance). The beautifully-landscaped garden, with its pretty windmill (let separately), has an English feel — and a croquet lawn — but the 'sense of place' remains unmistakably French. And pretty St Savinien is a painters' delight.

Rooms: 1 room for 2-4 with bath & wc.

Price: 260 Frs for two, including breakfast.

Meals: 85 Frs, including wine & coffee (book ahead).

Open: All year except Christmas.

This old farmhouse — built in 1600, renovated in 1720 — stands in a garden of mature trees that goes right down to the River Boutonne for peaceful walks and shallow swimming. Guests have a big dayroom with comfortable chairs, games and a full-size French billiards table. The clean, fresh bedrooms have good beds and large *armoires*. Indeed, the whole place has a totally French country feel to it: you might be staying with your favourite granny. There are good bike trails and you can visit the one and only place in France that produces angelica.

Rooms: 1 double/twin with shower & wc; 1 double, 1 twin sharing bath & wc.

Price: 260 Frs for two, including breakfast.

Meals: 90 Frs, including wine & coffee (not Sun).

Open: All year.

From bridge in St Savinien D14 along river, under railway bridge, left onto D124 signed Bords. After 2km, 2nd left after 'Le Pontreau' sign; house 200m on right.

Map No: 10   MM 233-16.

John & Jenny ELMES
Le Moulin de la Quine
17350 Saint-Savinien
Charente-Maritime
Tel: (0)5 46 90 19 31
Fax: (0)5 46 90 28 37

From Gendarmerie in St Jean d'Angély, D127 towards Dampierre-Antezant. In Antezant, first right.

Map No: 10   MM 233-16

Pierre & Marie-Claude FALLELOUR
Les Moulins
17400 Antezant
Charente-Maritime
Tel: (0)5 46 59 94 52
Fax: (0)5 46 59 94 52

Your hosts moved south on retirement to enjoy the balmy climate here — guests respond to it as willingly as do all those flowers and... pumpkins. Country-style rooms have big pieces of furniture in smallish spaces, good mattresses and smallish towels. The area is flat — where else could those millions of oysters bed down for their short lives? — but lovely beaches are just 10 minutes away, there are forests for walking or bicycling, birdlife for hours of watching and fortified Brouage on the Ile d'Oléron to visit.

Rooms: 1 double with bath & wc; 1 double with shower & wc.

Price: 230 or 280 Frs for two, including breakfast.

Meals: Full choice in Marennes 3km.

Open: All year except October.

Gîtes for 5 people

Madame's *galettes* are famous in the area — enjoy them, and other specialities, in the warm and homely dining-room where the television is blessedly hidden in a cupboard. The Forgets are a sweet, welcoming couple who have made great efforts with their nice French country furniture, pretty curtains and scattered treasures. The rooms are named after flowers in a genuine country family atmosphere. There are bikes for rent, swings to play on, wonderful cookery weekends. One guest found "Food, drink and company all excellent".

Rooms: 1 double, 1 triple, 1 family room, each with bath or shower & wc; 1 twin, 1 double, sharing shower & wc.

Price: 210-250 Frs for two, including breakfast.

Meals: 85 Frs, including wine and coffee.

Open: All year.

Take D123 towards Ile d'Oléron. At Marennes, right towards Château de la Gateaudière then follow signs.

Map No: 9   MM 233-14

Jean & Jacqueline FERCHAUD
11 rue des Lilas
La Ménardière
17320 Marennes
Charente-Maritime
Tel: (0)5 46 85 41 77

From Saintes, N150 towards Niort. After 6km, D129 towards Ecoyeux; signposted (red & white).

Map No: 10   MM 233-16

Henri & Marie-Andrée FORGET
Chez Quimand
17770 Ecoyeux
Charente-Maritime
Tel: (0)5 46 95 92 55
Fax: (0)5 46 95 92 55

One of our most special places, run by a charming, indefatigable mother/daughter team. Pretty, old-style rooms, harmonious colour schemes, lovingly-collected antiques and *brocante*, fine old linen everywhere. Find peace in the guests' library or climb up to the pulpit for your dose of telly. Outside, admire the museum of dolls and costumes, roam the huge gardens, take up archery, enjoy the swimming pool area... there's lots more to discover and so much space for everyone, as well as outstanding country cooking.

Rooms: 1 double/twin, 1 twin, 4 double (1 on ground floor), all with shower & wc.

Price: 370-420 Frs for two, including breakfast.

Meals: 110 Frs, including wine & coffee.

Open: All year.

From A10, exit 34 for St Jean-d'Angély. There, left on N150 towards Niort. House signposted just after St Denis-du-Pin.

Map No: 10   MM 233-16

Michèle & Florence FRAPPIER
Domaine de Rennebourg
Saint-Denis-du-Pin
17400 Saint-Jean-d'Angély
Charente-Maritime
Tel: (0)5 46 32 16 07
Fax: (0)5 46 59 77 38

Standing in peaceful, flat country, the prettily-furnished modern house is in pleasing contrast with its all-green cloak and army of bucolic ducks amongst the flowers. Breakfast copiously on the lawn, play croquet, but please don't feed the fowl or bring a dog. More flowers and chocolates complete the attractively traditional rooms with their big windows onto the fine view. Breakfasts include regional *brioche*. Madame is a charming, if slightly formal, hostess. And the beaches are ten minutes away.

Rooms: 2 double, 1 twin, 1 single, all with hand-basins. Shared bathrooms.

Price: 340 Frs for two, including breakfast (2 nights min).

Meals: Auberge 8km; otherwise 12km.

Open: June to mid-September.

From La Rochelle, N11 towards Poitiers. After Zone Commerciale de Beaulieu, D9 towards Luçon. After St-Xandre village, D202 to Sauzaie. There, take road for Usseau; 50m along, right into rue du Château: 2nd house on left.

Map No: 9   MM 233-3

Mme Annick LANGER
Aguzan, Rue du Château
La Sauzaie
17138 Saint-Xandre
Charente-Maritime
Tel: (0)5 46 37 22 65

You are clearly in a family home NOT a guesthouse here — the big antique wardrobes were Madame's mother, the lacy covers on the lovely old boat beds (*lits bateau*) are even older, the well-furnished, old-fashioned atmosphere is so comfortable. Madame keeps a good home-produced table; Monsieur organises outings to distilleries and quarries; both enjoy their guests, especially those who help catch escaping rabbits. They are kindly farmers, really worth getting to know — stay a few days, even if the plumbing is a touch noisy.

Rooms: 1 triple on ground floor, 1 suite for 2-4, both with shower & wc.

Price: 240-270 Frs for two, including breakfast.

Meals: 85 Frs, including wine.

Open: All year.

This is 5-star B&B! Agathe and Philippe both knew La Loge as children but never imagined they might one day own the 19th-century village house. They've transformed the place with sensitivity and flair and now everything about it feels just right. Big, comfortable bedrooms and lots of homegrown fruit and vegetables at dinner. The peace is almost monastic, especially under the 300-year-old oak trees in the garden. La Loge is ideal for families.

Rooms: 2 double, 1 twin each with bath, shower and wc.

Price: 260 Frs for two, including breakfast. Extra person 60 Frs.

Meals: 90 Frs, including wine & coffee.

Open: Mid-April to September.

From A10, Saintes exit onto N137 towards Rochefort-la-Rochelle. After about 11km, D119 to Plassay. House on left on entering village.

Map No: 10   MM 233-15

Michelle & Jacques LOURADOUR
La Jaquetterie
17250 Plassay
Charente-Maritime
Tel: (0)5 46 93 91 88

From A10 exit 26 to Pons then D142 to Jonzac. There D134 through Ozillac and Fontaines d'Ozillac. On leaving village, signposted (5km).

Map No: 10   MM 233-28

Agathe & Philippe PICQ
La Loge
17130 Chaunac
Charente-Maritime
Tel: (0)5 46 70 68 50
Fax: (0)5 46 70 62 41

The owners have lavished love, money and time on this superb farmhouse where they settled on returning to France after years in Africa. A delightful, interesting couple. Anne-Marie is a talented artist whose stylish painted furniture and co-ordinated colour schemes adorn the house. Good breakfasts and dinners are eaten with your hosts in the dining-room or by the swimming pool. The gardens are landscaped, the terrace paved, flowers bloom and the bedrooms are big. Quiet children over 6 welcome.

Rooms: 3 double, each with bath & wc.

Price: 350 Frs for two, including breakfast. Extra person 80 Frs.

Meals: 120 Frs, including aperitif, wine and coffee.

Open: All year.

A rarity in France: hosts who, although happy to cook meat, are really keen on vegetarian food. Marie-Christine is an enthusiastic professional musician but not at all precious about it: she encourages people to play at musical evenings and welcomes music groups. Bit by bit she and her husband are re-doing the house, collecting old linen and tiles, exposing beams, buying old furniture. The rooms are in the barn, duplexes with tiled floors and pretty stone-walled showers. A dear old house with a very special atmosphere.

Rooms: In house: 1 with 2 double beds, shower, wc. In cottage: 1 with 2 doubles & 2 singles, sharing shower, wc, kitchenette.

Price: 250-270 Frs for two, including breakfast. Extra person 60 Frs.

Meals: 80 Frs meatless organic dinner, including wine.

Open: All year.

From Saintes N150 west for 5km then fork right on N728 for 29km. Right on D118 to St Sornin. In village centre take Rue du Petit Moulin opposite church door.

Map No: 9   MM 233-15

M & Mme PINEL-PESCHARDIÈRE
La Caussolière
10 rue du Petit Moulin
17600 Saint-Sornin
Charente-Maritime
Tel: (0)5 46 85 44 62
Fax: (0)5 46 85 44 62

From Surgères D939 towards la Rochelle for 7km. Through Le Cher (past church & cemetery) then 2nd right after church — house 400m on right.

Map No: 10   MM 233-15

Marie-Christine RAFFIN
Les Ormeaux
17290 Chambon
Charente-Maritime
Tel: (0)5 46 27 83 95

Once a modest inn for train travellers it still overlooks the station, now attractive and lived in. Their brochure says: 'La Font Bétou is one of those very rare places in the world that does not pretend but just is.' They are both ex-market researchers, Gordon from London, Laure from Paris, and thoroughly enjoy people. Laure cooks (rather well) because she loves it. The annexe has the rooms, pretty ones, but you can use your hosts' sitting-room or lounge by the pool and the kitchen door is always open.

Rooms: In house: 1 double, 1 twin, sharing bath & wc. In cottage: 1 double, 1 twin, each with shower & wc.

Price: 270-300 Frs for two, including breakfast.

Meals: From 100 Frs, including aperitif, wine & coffee.

Open: All year except January.

A village farmhouse, well restored, with lots of exposed beams and a huge fireplace. Big bedrooms, with names like *Agatha Christie* and *Picardie*, look over the quiet garden. Your hosts, who retired here from Picardy about five years ago, are very enthusiastic about this beautiful region and love to chat with guests about the best places to explore. We have heard of "breakfasts on the sunlit terrace with homemade jams". A new restaurant has opened in the village: great-value meals and good atmosphere. Older children welcome.

Rooms: 3 double, 1 twin each with own shower & wc.

Price: 260 Frs for two, including breakfast. Extra bed 70 Frs.

Meals: In village.

Open: April to mid-November.

From Angoulême N10 S for 45km then left onto D730 through Montlieu-la-Garde towards Montguyon. 2km after Orignolles, right to house.

Map No: 10   MM 233-39

Laure TARROU & Gordon FLUDE
La Font Bétou
17210 Orignolles
Charente-Maritime
Tel: (0)5 46 04 02 52
Fax: (0)5 46 04 02 52

From Saintes N137 towards Rochefort for 6km then left onto D127 to St Georges. Rue de l'Eglise is in village centre. House on left.

Map No: 10   MM 233-15

Anne & Dominique TROUVÉ
5 rue de l'Église
17810 Saint-Georges-des-Coteaux
Charente-Maritime
Tel: (0)5 46 92 96 66
Fax: (0)5 46 92 96 66

The old house stands proudly on its wooded hill. Rooms, in a well-converted stable-block overlooking the garden and the pool-and-waterfall feature, are done with thoughtful taste, antiques and good, tiled shower rooms. Madame, busy with her successful horse breeding (gorgeous foals in summer), always has time to tell guests what to see in the area, arrange cognac-distillery visits or invite you to relax in a hammock after a game of badminton. Monsieur is most sociable and offers a local aperitif to guests of an evening.

Rooms: 1 double & 1 twin, each with shower & wc.

Price: 250-300 Frs for two, including breakfast.

Meals: Restaurant nearby. Self-catering possible.

Open: All year.

Gîtes for 8 people

An exquisitely French neo-Gothic château which Béatrice inherited and lovingly protects from the worst ravages of modernisation (good bathrooms, separate loos). She, a primary school teacher, and Christopher, a philosphy teacher, like eating with their guests. Sleep between old linen sheets, sit in handsome old chairs and wallow in a superb bathroom. The sitting-room has a most unusual window over the fireplace — whither the smoke? This is a gem, perfect for those who definitely do not want a hotel.

Rooms: 1 family suite, 2 double, 1 twin, each with bath or shower, sharing 2 wc's on guestroom floor + 1 downstairs.

Price: 280 Frs for two, including breakfast.

Meals: 65 Frs, including wine (book ahead).

Open: All year.

From Angoulême, N141 to la Rochefoucauld and D13 towards Rochechouart. After about 5km, D62 left towards Chasseneuil and D162 to St Adjutory.

Map No: 10   MM 233-31

Sylviane & Vincent CASPER
La Grenouille
16310 Saint-Adjutory
Charente
Tel: (0)5 45 62 00 34

From A10 exit 36 E to Pons, Archiac & Barbezieux (D732/D700/D731); continue D731 towards Chalais for 12km. After Passirac, 1st right at roadside cross and up leafy drive.

Map No: 10   MM 233-29

Mme Béatrice de CASTELBAJAC
Le Chatelard
Passirac
16480 Brossac
Charente
Tel: (0)5 45 98 71 03
Fax: (0)5 45 98 71 03

This interesting house has an old-fashioned, well-lived-in, much-loved air to it. The bedrooms have parquet floors, old-style wallpaper, nice old beds (new mattresses) and built-in cupboards. Madame's regional cooking is highly appreciated and dinner is worth coming back for. A conservatory is being built to seat more people round a bigger table where your hosts hope to stay and chat a while if not too busy serving you. Their huge and lovely Pyrenean sheepdog, and occasional grandchildren, extend the same warm welcome.

Rooms: 2 triple, each with basin & shower; 2 double, 1 twin, with basins, sharing shower. ALL sharing one wc.

Price: 180-220 Frs for two, including breakfast.

Meals: 75 Frs, including wine & coffee.

Open: All year.

With Alexander fresh from music-publishing, they took on her family farm and have worked hard to make a go of it. It now produces venison and ostrich meat: if you want to try some, ask for dinner; you will be offered a glass of *pineau* too. There are wallabies and llamas, of course, and sheep, chickens, dogs and cats; it is a perfect place for family holidays, which the Everitts encourage. Breakfast in the oak-and-stone kitchen. Bedrooms are newly-converted in a farm building, clean and fresh, one small, one big.

Rooms: 1 quadruple, 1 triple, each with bath or shower & wc.

Price: 240-260 Frs for two, including breakfast.

Meals: 80 Frs, excluding wine (40 Frs).

Open: All year.

Gites for 4 people

From A10, Pons exit on D700 towards Barbezieux Archiac. After Echebrune, D148 (1st left) towards Lonzac-Celles. Right onto D151, then follow signpost 'Le Chiron'.

Map No: 10   MM 233-28

Micheline & Jacky CHAINIER
Le Chiron
16130 Salles-d'Angles
Charente
Tel: (0)5 45 83 72 79
Fax: (0)5 45 83 64 80

From Poitiers D741 S dir. Confolens for 50km. 10km after Pressac, left on D168 for St Germain-de-Confolens; signed after 2km.

Map No: 10   MM 233-20

M & Mme EVERITT
Le Pit
Lessac
16500 Confolens
Charente
Tel: (0)5 45 84 27 65
Fax: (0)5 45 85 41 34

Brenda and Kit have been doing B&B in this corner of the Charente for six years. They are delightful hosts and, although English, have an impressive list of regular French and Belgian guests and... 330 thimbles (*les dés*)! Their thoroughly-renovated farmhouse is run with irreproachable efficiency. Rooms and bathrooms are sparklingly clean and all overlook the pretty garden with its pool. Brenda keeps a diary of dishes served so if you too, should return, she'll ensure you sample something different, and equally good.

Rooms: 2 double, 1 triple, 1 family room, one with own shower & wc, 3 with bath or shower but sharing wc.

Price: 215 or 240 Frs for two, including breakfast.

Meals: 75 Frs, including aperitif & wine.

Open: All year.

Deep inside the splashy fen you will find this riverside hideaway with its exclusive eye-level views of waders and water birds from all windows; you can even feed the swans from your bed. Guests enjoy complete privacy here — for some reason, nobody else comes. One eau-de-nil room flows sweetly into another and the sploshing of water is a soothing backdrop. Potentially superb fresh fish dinners, on a self-caught, self-baked, self-serve basis, are always accompanied by a bottle of local *Entre Deux Eaux*, a rare treat.

Rooms: 1 double waterbed with sunken bath & gravity wc.

Price: 25 feet of caulking felt for two; DIY instant breakfast.

Meals: Self-service main course (lines provided).

Open: All year except St Peter's Day and neaps.

From Angoulême N10 exit Mansle. Cross River Charente. First left D61 to Fontenille. Just before the village, left and follow signs to Chambres d'Hôte. 400 metres to house.

Map No: 10   MM 233-19

Brenda & Kit JOLLEY
Les Dés
Les Morices, Fontenille
16230 Mansle
Charente
Tel: (0)5 45 20 39 72

From Aigues-Douces, follow river downstream to third confluence. There take small River O (also spelt Eau) upstream to first bridge. Boat is just visible on left bank beside pillar.

Map No: 10   MM 233-23

Vice-Amiral Odon TREMPE-LINEAU
Les Eaux Vives
16999 Vallée de l'O
Charente
Tel: (0)5 12 34 56 78

The Monts d'Ambazac provide lovely hiking over hills and vales, through woods and open spaces (itineraries at La Bezassade). Andrée spent her childhood here and returns each summer when the garden blooms, as it did for her mother. The guest suite with its small *salon* has nice old rustic furniture and details such as thick towels and pretty sheets. Sit in the absolute peace of the garden; dine on Limousin specialities (*pâtés* and stews) with home-grown vegetables, or local potato *pâté* for vegetarians. Superb hospitality.

Rooms: 1 independent suite for 2 (+ 2 children) with shower & wc.

Price: 220 Frs for two, including breakfast.

Meals: 80 Frs, including wine & coffee (book 24 hrs ahead).

Open: 25 June to August.

From A20 exit 24.2 (Bessine-sur-Gartempe) onto D27 E to Bersac (9km) then D28 to Laurière (4km); continue towards St Goussand for 3km then right to La Bezassade.

Map No: 11   MM 239-2

Andrée & Robert CHANUDET
La Bezassade
87370 Laurière
Haute-Vienne
Tel: (0)5 55 71 58 07 (summer)/(0)3 21 99 30 41 (winter)

Limousin – Dordogne

A demure little house built in the 1700s for the farm manager and his family, it is in a wonderful wooded setting, something of an idyll. There is a flagstoned, beamed and chimneyed sitting-room with books, ancient dresser and old photos... and a bread-oven still occasionally used; a roped wooden staircase leads to the rooms, planked and pine-clad, not unlike a boat. The kindly Desmaisons are passionate about the area and will point you towards fabulous walks. You can use the barbecue, make picnics, and you breakfast in your own quarters.

Rooms: 1 double, 1 twin, sharing shower & wc on floor below.

Price: 300 Frs for two, including breakfast. Extra person 50 Frs.

Meals: Barbecue + hotplate; auberge 10km.

Open: May to September.

There once stood a forge here, producing cannon balls. They now produce *patés, confits* and *rillettes...* and keep ducks, horses, a pig, dogs, a cat and two children (3 and 6); the latter are very much part of life here and the atmosphere is easy and *familiale*. Nothing fancy about the bedrooms — they are cosy and comfortable. A huge sitting-room with enormous hearth, stone walls, tatty sofa, and the nicest possible people. Stay for dinner; most ingredients are home-grown or raised. Boating on the lake. Guests love it all.

Rooms: 3 double, each with shower & wc.

Price: 240 Frs for two, including breakfast. Extra bed 70 Frs.

Meals: 90 Frs, including wine.

Open: All year.

From A20 exit 41 onto D82 towards Glanges. Cross railway line then 1st right onto D120 & follow signs for 5km.

Map No: 11   MM 239-14

Anne-Marie & Jean-Luc
DESMAISON
Lancournet
87380 Glanges
Haute-Vienne
Tel: (0)5 55 00 81 27
Fax: (0)5 55 00 81 27

From A20 exit 40 to Pierre-Buffière then W across river onto D15 then D19 dir. St Yrieix-la-Perche for 18km. At La Croix d'Hervy, left on D57 for Coussac-Bonneval. Mill on left after approx. 4km.

Map No: 10   MM 239-13

Valérie & Renaud GIZARDIN
Moulin de Marsaguet
87500 Coussac-Bonneval
Haute-Vienne
Tel: (0)5 55 75 28 29

Go through your own entrance, covered in wisteria and rose, to your own kitchen area and stairs up to the rather appealing bedroom with its white walls, off-white carpet and sea-grass wallpaper. The other bedroom is useful for overflow. You have your own living-room too, with an open fire. (It can all be let as a gite.) Néline is a wonderful hostess. The house is lovely, splashed with colour and imaginative gestures, and the 2½-acre garden makes further demands upon a willing pair of owners.

Rooms: 1 double/twin, 1 twin, sharing shower, wc & small kitchen (same group only).

Price: 250 Frs for two, including breakfast. Extra bed 100 Frs. Reduction 2 nights.

Meals: Self-Catering.

Open: All year.

Gites for 4 people

The atmosphere is more traditional than the photo suggests, lively yet restful. Michel's modern sculptures add magic to the garden and his work is everywhere: handmade door handles, towel rails, shelf supports, etc... mainly in brass and steel. Bedrooms and bathrooms are biggish and the house glories in an extravagant use of materials: opulent floor-length curtains, off-white material instead of wallpaper and a tented ceiling of it in the day-room (all Madame's work). The living and dining-rooms have a working-studio feel.

Rooms: 2 double, each with shower & wc.

Price: 280 Frs for two, including breakfast.

Meals: 85 Frs, including wine & coffee.

Open: April to December.

From Limoges, D941 to St Léonard then D39 towards St Priest; after 5km right towards Lajoumard; first left and follow signs.

Map No: 11   MM 239-14

Mme Néline JANSEN de VOMÉCOURT
La Réserve
Bassoleil
87400 Saint-Léonard-de-Noblat
Haute-Vienne
Tel: (0)5 55 56 18 39

From Eymoutiers, D30 towards Chamberet. House in village of La Roche, 7km beyond Eymoutiers.

Map No: 11   MM 239-15

Michel & Josette JAUBERT
La Roche
87120 Eymoutiers
Haute-Vienne
Tel: (0)5 55 69 61 88

Real farmers who like to be as self-sufficient as possible, so meals are home-grown and nourishing. The four rooms share a living-room with kitchen, but dine with your hosts if you can: they are completely unpretentious and very agreeable. Two rooms are on the ground floor, two in the roof, with pine-clad sloping ceilings, white walls and roof windows. The farm is surrounded by woods (superb walking), and children love helping to milk the goats and collect the eggs. Adults do too.

Rooms: 3 double, 1 triple, each with own shower & wc.

Price: 240 Frs for two, including breakfast.

Meals: 85 Frs, including wine.

Open: All year.

A glorious touch of eccentricity here. The house, once 12th-century, is now entirely 16th/17th and in the family for generations. You may share a bath or creep down a floor for the loo, but one room is authentic Charles X and all are deeply evocative. The main house has a spectacular stone staircase with Egyptian vases pillaged from a Pharaoh's tomb, huge bedrooms and modern bathrooms. The great dining hall has wood panelling. Monsieur, who plays jazz on those two pianos, runs his own model train museum.

Rooms: In gatehouse: 1 double with shower, 2 double sharing bathroom, all 3 sharing wc; in main house: 1 triple, 1 suite, each with bath & wc.

Price: 300-350 Frs for two, including breakfast.

Meals: 100 Frs, including wine & coffee; 100 Frs ferme-auberge next door (closed Mon).

Open: All year.

From A20, exit 41 to Magnac Bourg then D215 (between Total service station & Brasserie des Sports) SW then follow signs 4km to La Chapelle.

Map No: 11   MM 239-13

Patrick & Mayder LESPAGNOL
La Chapelle
87380 Château-Chervix
Haute-Vienne
Tel: (0)5 55 00 86 67
Fax: (0)5 55 00 70 78
e-mail: lespagno@club-internet.fr

From Limoges, D979 towards Eymoutiers; Fougeolles is on left just before entering Eymoutiers, signposted Chambres d'Hôtes.

Map No: 11   MM 239-15

Jacques et Frédérique du MONTANT
Fougeolles
87120 Eymoutiers
Haute-Vienne
Tel: (0)5 55 69 11 44

Great for vegetarians and all lovers of good home cooking, based on homegrown vegetables and fruit plus, for the carnivorous, delicious homemade *pâtés* and *rillettes*, duck, pigeon and rabbit: Madame simply loves to cook (try her tomato jam too). The old farmhouse (1760), with its magnificent wooden staircase and all the original beams and timber framing, has lovely country antiques, functioning fireplaces, a garden full of toys, and... excitement on an Ultra Light(!). Wonderful French value with most interesting hosts.

Rooms: 2 quadruple, 1 triple, 1 double, all with own shower sharing 3 wc's: one on same floor, 2 on ground floor.

Price: 200 Frs for two, including breakfast.

Meals: 80 Frs, including wine & coffee.

Open: All year.

Gîtes for 6 people

Eight centuries ago Knights Templar farmed here; four centuries ago Henri IV hunted wolves here; the same family has always owned these 750 acres and pilgrims have always passed through on the way to Compostela — such is the tapestry of history that your intelligent, sociable hosts weave for you beneath the Aubusson or across the grand dinner table. All rooms are properly period furnished, but pay the extra for the superb suite and enjoy its mighty bathroom (shower rooms smaller).

Rooms: 1 suite for 4, 1 double, 1 twin, each with bath or shower & wc.

Price: 320, 350 or 400 Frs for two, including breakfast.

Meals: 100 Frs for two, excluding wine (50 Frs).

Open: April to October.

In Bellac follow signs to Limoges; just before leaving Bellac right on D3 towards Blond. 4 km to Thoveyrat. House signposted on left.

Map No: 10   MM 233-22

Daniel & Bernadette MORICE
Thoveyrat
87300 Bellac
Haute-Vienne
Tel: (0)5 55 68 86 86

From A20 exit 24 onto D27 to Bersac; continue towards Laurière then left after railway bridge and follow signs 3km to château.

Map No: 11   MM 239-1

Eric & Annie PERRIN des MARAIS
Le Château du Chambon
Le Chambon
87370 Bersac-sur-Rivalier
Haute-Vienne
Tel: (0)5 55 71 47 04
Fax: (0)5 55 71 51 41

LIMOUSIN – DORDOGNE

"Still a secret for everyone" is the motto of this lovely but unsung region of farms and forests. Here you find the old stone farmhouse of La Borderie, emblematically and literally at the end of the road — the last of the hamlet's five houses. Such deep-country quiet is rare. Marc, Maryse and their four children, "generous and affectionate hosts", share the pleasures of an area whose history, folk festivals and walks they know intimately (ask about their special themed weekends). Children love the room with the mezzanine.

Rooms: 2 double, each with shower & wc; 1 twin sharing a bathroom.

Price: 190 or 250 Frs for two, including breakfast.

Meals: 90 Frs, excluding wine.

Open: All year.

If something quaint, quirky and creative appeals, do drop in on this 18th-century house on the edge of town. The bouncy dog, the exquisite patchwork quilts that contrast with fading wallpaper and cluttered terrace (with stunning views of the 12th to 15th-century Château de Boussac), and the jolly, genuine hostess who lives in amiable confusion, all add up to a totally French experience. Perfectly acceptable clean rooms — ask for one with a view. A good place for exploring countryside and towns.

Rooms: 2 double, 1 suite, all with bath or shower & wc.

Price: 250 Frs for two, including breakfast. Extra bed 70 Frs.

Meals: 70 Frs, including wine (by arrangement).

Open: March to October.

From Royère-de-Vassivière, D8 towards Bourganeuf. Just before you reach Le Compeix, right to 'La Borderie'; signposted.

Map No: 11   MM 239-15

Marc & Maryse DESCHAMPS
La Borderie
Saint-Pierre-Bellevue
23460 Royère-de-Vassivière
Creuse
Tel: (0)5 55 64 96 51

From A71 exit 10 onto D94 W by-passing Montluçon (15km) then right onto D916 through Domérat, Huriel, Trégnat to Boussac. In Boussac, butcher's shop to left of Mairie; turn into Rue des Loges by butcher's shop.

Map No: 11   MM 238-42

Françoise GROS & Daniel COLSENET
La Courtepointe
3 rue des Loges
23600 Boussac
Creuse
Tel: (0)5 55 65 80 09

An Egyptian belly-dancer mannequin is your first encounter in this remarkable house. Abandoned for 150 years, its park overgrown, its beams sagging, it became Marie's mission. She is painstakingly unravelling the building's history and restoring its fabric. The *salon* has a great fireplace, massive beams, a carpet on the concrete floor. Up the spiral staircase are swish bathrooms and beds; the C15 room is quieter, away from the road, with a wafer-brick fireplace. Idiosyncratic, old... and heroic. Pond swimming.

Rooms: 2 double, each with bath, sharing wc.

Price: 250 Frs for two, including breakfast.

Meals: In village and beyond.

Open: All year.

On winter weekends, you can learn to make *foie gras*! The house's strangely suburban look belies its deeply rural nature, though La Borde once housed missionaries — the present dining-room was their chapel. The place is now run in true *chambres d'hôtes* spirit: relaxed and practical (shower rooms through saloon doors). Hosts always dine with their guests and most of the meal will be home-produced, including that *foie gras* on Sundays. There is a games room upstairs and masses of space outside for children. A real French family house.

Rooms: 2 double & 3 twin, all with own shower & wc.

Price: 280 Frs for two, including breakfast.

Meals: 70 Frs, including wine & coffee.

Open: Easter to mid-September.

From A71 exit 10 on D94 W dir. Guéret skirting Montluçon to join N145 after 12km; continue towards Guéret for 40km then left on D990 to Jarnages. Here, first right after bridge — house on right.

Map No: 11   MM 239-4

Marie & Georges LOMBARDI
Château de Jarnages
2 Grande Rue
23140 Jarnages
Creuse
Tel: (0)5 55 81 89 55

From Brive, N20 towards Uzerche about 18km, then left through Sadroc to St Bonnet; here, D156 towards Perpezac-le-Noir. Farm is 1km on left.

Map No: 11   MM 239-26

Nadine BUGE
La Borde
19410 St Bonnet-l'Enfantier
Corrèze
Tel: (0)5 55 73 72 44
Fax: (0)5 55 73 72 44

Knowledgeable guides to local life and lore, the Greenwoods have made every effort to integrate. Their restoration of this small farmhouse shows respect for the original beams and stones, now married comfortably with elements from their English background. A small stream runs through the garden with a splash pool, a cloak of peace drapes itself over all, there's stunning countryside to explore on foot, a wealth of history and architecture all around, and canoeing is possible on the Dordogne.

Rooms: 1 double & 1 twin room sharing bath, shower & wc.

Price: 180 Frs for two, including breakfast.

Meals: 80 Frs, including wine & coffee.

Open: All year.

A delightfully renovated village house. Jacquie is half-French and Ian half-Hungarian so it's all very cosmopolitan. Both speak fluent French (as well as English) and are a mine of information about the locality and its people, history and flora. A professional chef, Ian produces food of superb quality and amazing variety, complemented by wines from his own cellar. Dinner (and pre-dinner drinks) taken *en famille* are occasions for stimulating conversation — not a time for shrinking violets. Well-behaved children welcome.

Rooms: 3 twin, each with bath or shower & wc.

Price: 160-190 Frs for two, including breakfast.

Meals: By arrangement 80 Frs, including wine & coffee.

Open: All year.

From Beaulieu-sur-Dordogne, D940 towards Tulle. After 5km, in Laroche de Nonards, left opposite bar towards Nonards & Puy d'Arnac. House is 400m on right.

Map No: 11   MM 239-39

Paul & Jean GREENWOOD
Le Marchoux
19120 Nonards
Corrèze
Tel: (0)5 55 91 52 73
Fax: (0)5 55 91 52 73

From Tulle N120 to Forgès. Left into Place de la Mairie and park in church square behind.

Map No: 11   MM 239-27

Ian & Jacquie HOARE
La Souvigne
1 impasse La Fontaine
19380 Forgès
Corrèze
Tel: (0)5 55 28 63 99
Fax: (0)5 55 28 65 62

From their house bordering the Dordogne river this affable farming couple raises beef cattle and grows walnuts. In functional cleanliness you can share the family's sitting-room and feel integrated with the life of the farm. The new modern extension is furnished with period pieces and set in the garden full of old trees. Everywhere the atmosphere is family, farming and friends. Ask about their stretch of private beach on the river where you can swim, fish and take out a canoe. This is now a conservation area.

Rooms: 1 quadruple, 1 triple, 1 double & 1 twin, all with own shower & wc.

Price: 250 Frs for two, including breakfast. Extra bed 50 Frs.

Meals: Self-catering or good choice 2km.

Open: All year.

Gîtes for 11 people

Here we have an English gent who has been designated a local pall bearer and coach of the village football team. What more proof do you need of the Lardners' integration into their chosen corner of France? Their beautifully-restored farmhouse is surrounded by rolling, wooded hillsides. Numerous walks nearby and visits to local farms can be arranged (many of the farmers are the Lardners' friends). Breakfast is served on the kitchen table and regional suppers in the dining-room, the latter with very good wine. Excellent value.

Rooms: One twin with bath & wc (extra room for children).

Price: 190 Frs for two, including breakfast.

Meals: 85 Frs, including wine & coffee.

Open: All year.

Gîtes for 2 people

From Tulle, N120 to Argentat then D12 along River Dordogne towards Beaulieu; past Monceaux to Saulières (6km from Argentat).

Map No: 11   MM 239-27

Marie-Jo & Jean-Marie LAFOND
Saulières
Monceaux-sur-Dordogne
19400 Argentat
Corrèze
Tel: (0)5 55 28 09 22

From Argentat, N120 towards Tulle then left onto D921 towards Brive. Pass sign to Albussac; 300m on, left to Le Prézat, through hamlet; house is on right with English lawn.

Map No: 11   MM 239-27

Anne and Jim LARDNER
Le Prézat
19380 Albussac
Corrèze
Tel: (0)5 55 28 62 36
Fax: (0)5 55 28 62 36

Live like royalty! This fairytale château is being restored with devotion and sensitivity by an English couple in love with France. The living-room is baronial with an enormous open fire and even the bedrooms (palatial in size and quality of decor, bathrooms to scale) have fireplaces ready for logs. There are fresh flowers in all the rooms and a suite in the tower. Vast and varied grounds include open pasture, wooded hillside, a moat and a small lake. Pool and a choice of *salons* for more gentle relaxation. Children over 14 welcome.

Rooms: 2 double with own bathrooms.

Price: 520-620 Frs for two, including breakfast.

Meals: 150-200 Frs, including wine & coffee.

Open: All year except Christmas.

One reader who stayed a week wrote that "The room, the food, the setting, the view were all superb". Madame, a "hostess with the mostest", presides over brilliant, non-vegetarian, dinner parties (she will organise a day's cookery course if you stay a while) in her *ferme-auberge*. Other messages are: the hospitality is magnificent, the atmosphere relaxed and the decor traditional French rustic. Madame now shares her responsibilities with her daughter-in-law and they make an excellent team.

Rooms: 1 double, 1 triple, 1 quadruple all with shower & wc.

Price: 240 Frs for two, including breakfast (min. 2 nights).

Meals: 110 Frs, including wine & coffee.

Open: March to November.

Gîtes for 5 people

From Tulle D940 towards Beaulieu for about 30km; château is on left turn (opposite cemetery) off D940 (do not go up hill into Nonards village); signposted.

Map No: 11   MM 239-39

Joe WEBB
Château d'Arnac, Nonards
19120 Beaulieu-sur-Dordogne
Corrèze
Tel: (0)5 55 91 54 13
Fax: (0)5 55 91 52 62
e-mail: www.chateau.mcmail.com

From Bergerac, D32 towards St Alvère. After 10km, look for signpost 'Périgord — Bienvenue à la Ferme'.

Map No: 10   MM 234-4

Marie-Jeanne & Marie-Thérèse
ARCHER
La Barabie — D32
Lamonzie-Montastruc
24520 Mouleydier
Dordogne
Tel: (0)5 53 23 22 47
Fax: (0)5 53 22 81 20

Diana, a passionate cook, is happy for people to come into her marvellous great kitchen (EXCEPT when she's cooking), to enjoy her company and the views from all four sides of this very finely converted old millhouse. There is an island for loners, a dream of a garden round the mill-pond* (all John's work), a well-hidden swimming pool and superb, light, airy rooms with pretty soft furnishings, lacy linen and bathrooms across the corridor. A thoroughly English picture in a very French frame.
*Children over 12 welcome.

Rooms: 1 double, 1 twin, each with bath or shower & wc.

Price: 600 Frs for two, including breakfast.

Meals: 200 Frs, excluding wine.

Open: All year.

A genuinely picturesque old farmhouse with a 13th-century tower (built by the English) and a genuinely French country hostess to greet you at Lapeyère. Madame, who retired from farming some time ago, is proud of her home with its rustic atmosphere and simple style. Upstairs from the kitchen, the two guestrooms, with screened-off bathroom, are old-fashioned but perfectly comfortable. Wonderful for a family which enjoys a bit of character. Small pets are welcome. Best to ring at mealtimes.

Rooms: 2 connecting double rooms, each with own wc, sharing shower room. Apartment also available.

Price: 200 Frs for two, including breakfast.

Meals: Two restaurants 2.5km.

Open: 1 March to 31 October.

Gîtes for 5 people

From Périgueux, N21 towards Limoges. About 2 km on, right over bridge towards airport. Left at next roundabout onto D5 towards Hautefort. 1.5km after Tourtoirac, left towards La Crouzille. Cross the Auvezère. 1st drive on right.

Map No: 10   MM 233-44

John & Diana ARMITAGE
Le Moulin de la Crouzille
Tourtoirac
24390 Hautefort
Dordogne
Tel: (0)5 53 51 11 94
Fax: (0)5 53 51 11 94

From Bergerac, N660 towards Port de Couze to Beaumont. Take D676 towards Villeréal; house is 500m on left after Nojal.

Map No: 15   MM 235-9

Mme Georgette BERTHOLOM
Lapeyère
24440 Sainte-Sabine
Dordogne
Tel: (0)5 53 22 31 07

Madame is a refined, well-travelled, lively lady who enjoys having visitors, especially English — she worked in England some time ago. Now she shares this handsome country manor (of 17th and 18th-century origin) and its fine garden with her guests, whom she likes 'to welcome as friends'. Her freshly-papered, painted, floral-curtained drawing room is full of fine antiques and flowers from the garden. You can picnic and barbecue, play table tennis and *pétanque* outside. This is a house with no set rules and lots of charm.

Rooms: 2 double with own bathrooms (3 in 1999).

Price: 320 Frs for two, including breakfast.

Meals: Barbecue available.

Open: Easter to end October.

Staying in this charming watermill as guests of Robert and Stuart is a delight. Restful views over an idyllic mill landscape of a deep, willow-dotted meadow, green lawns, stream coursing under the house, and a reedy spring-fed lake, can be enjoyed from all the immaculate, though small, rooms. Tables for breakfast are set out on a pretty little terrace covered with vines. Outside and inside everything is lovingly tended, and nearby is the unspoilt village of Paunat with its huge church and peace, perfect peace. Small pets on request.

Rooms: 3 double, 2 twin, 1 triple, all with bath or shower & wc.

Price: 364 Frs for two, including breakfast.

Meals: Good choice in nearby towns.

Open: All year.

From Bergerac, N21 south for 11km, then left on D14 to Issigeac, then D21 towards Castillonnes. At Monmarves; signposted. Turn into green gate.

Map No: 15   MM 234-8

Annie de BOSREDON
Le Petit Pey
Monmarves
24560 Issigeac
Dordogne
Tel: (0)5 53 58 70 61

From Le Bugue D703 towards Limeuil then left on D31 through Limeuil. At crossroads D2 towards Ste Alvère; after 100m fork left; house is on left 2km along, below the road.

Map No: 10   MM 233-43

Robert CHAPPELL & Stuart SHIPPEY
Le Moulin Neuf
Paunat
24510 Sainte-Alvère
Dordogne
Tel: (0)5 53 63 30 18
Fax: (0)5 53 73 33 91

Would you like to be the guests of charming, genteel farmers? Sleep in high old beds in large, square, elegantly-papered rooms furnished with antique sofas on polished floorboards and supplied with luxurious views? Bask in the company of a warm, gentle, caring person who is always ready to laugh? Yes? Then come to this beautiful 19th-century manor set in 50 hectares of parkland. It has been in the family for five generations and is now even lovelier than it is in the photo. A rare find!

Rooms: 1 double, 1 suite for 5, each with shower & wc; 2 double sharing shower & wc.

Price: 240 Frs for two, including breakfast.

Meals: Auberge 1km.

Open: Mid-May to September.

The family's converted barn is tucked away in a charming rustic hamlet. Madame is proud of her regional cuisine (she'll teach you!), using the finest ingredients, many home-produced — including vegetables, nuts, honey, preserves, fruits and free-range chickens. This area is charged with history — from ancient caves to stately châteaux — and you can add spice to sightseeing with a sprinkling of local folklore, available courtesy of Monsieur who acts, if requested, as a willing and knowledgeable guide on walks and visits.

Rooms: 2 triple rooms with showers and wash-basins behind screens, sharing a wc.

Price: 230 Frs for two, including breakfast.

Meals: 70 Frs, including wine & coffee.

Open: All year.

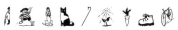

From Thiviers N21 to Sorges; right at sign to 'Mairie'; continue out of town. Right at crossroads, left at 'Chambres d'Hôtes' sign to Poux.

Map No: 10   MM 233-43

Mme Annie DELAIRE
Domaine de Poux
24420 Sorges
Dordogne
Tel: (0)5 53 05 02 02

From Angoulême D939 south. After Dignac D23 to Villebois-Lavalette, D17 to Gurat then D102 towards Vendoire for 2km then left into hamlet.

Map No: 10   MM 233-30

André & Pierrette DURIEUX
Le Bouchaud D17
24320 Vendoire
Dordogne
Tel: (0)5 53 91 00 82

We loved this place, especially the breakfast room with its limed walls, white tablecloths and white-striped chair covers — bright and rustic. Bedrooms, also with limed stone walls, are simply furnished (as are bathrooms) with good taste and African throws. The cool, overflowing stone plunge pool in the green and pleasant garden is unforgettable. Delightful, energetic Jane offers imaginative food ("excellent", "superb"), early supper for children AND creative writing courses, all in this lovely tranquil spot.

Rooms: 2 double, 1 twin each with shower & wc; 1 double, 1 twin sharing shower & wc.

Price: 275-300 Frs for two, including breakfast.

Meals: 95 Frs, excluding wine (45 Frs).

Open: All year.

Gîtes for 6 people

From Ribérac towards Verteillac for 2km. At La Borie right on D99 for 4km, continue through Celles then 4km to right turning marked Pauliac. House signposted in hamlet.

Map No: 10   MM 233-41

Jane & John EDWARDS
Pauliac
Celles
24600 Ribérac
Dordogne
Tel: (0)5 53 91 97 45
Fax: (0)5 53 90 43 46
e-mail: pauliac@infonie.fr

A lovely, homely farming couple with such enthusiasm for their natural, healthy home-produced food! They give you an insight into rural France, love having you at their own table where French gastronomic tradition is deeply respected and Monsieur serves his own liqueurs. The setting is blissfully peaceful, the new Périgord-style house was built with old stones and beams, the bedrooms are old in style — so much so that three have shower and loo behind screen or curtain only. Tours in a horse-drawn buggy can be arranged.

Rooms: 3 twin, 1 double, all with shower & wc; 1 double & 1 single sharing shower & wc.

Price: 210 Frs for two, including breakfast.

Meals: 80 Frs, including aperitif, wine, coffee & digestif.

Open: 1 March to 30 November.

From Périgueux, N89 towards Brive then D710 towards Cahors-Fumel. At 'le Périgord en Calèche' sign, turn right. It is the first house.

Map No: 15   MM 235-9

Jacqueline & Robert
MARESCASSIER
Le Bourg
24550 Mazeyrolles
Dordogne
Tel: (0)5 53 29 93 38
Fax: (0)5 53 29 93 38

The roof timbers in the bedrooms are wild! And you can visit the prune ovens. There are also dairy cows and a productive vegetable garden — meals consist of succulent regional dishes and are eaten with the family. Madame will diligently turn the pages of her dictionary to find the *mot juste* in English; one reader says it's "huge fun but don't talk while the weather report is on". Rooms are traditional country French (one screened-off shower) and the house is altogether an excellent and welcoming stopping place.

Rooms: 2 double, 1 triple all with bath or shower & wc (1 ground-floor room).

Price: 200 Frs for two, including breakfast. Half-board 360 Frs for two.

Meals: 80 Frs, including wine.

Open: All year.

Gîtes for 5 people

In a particularly beautiful setting, this small isolated community is all calm and simplicity. The *auberge* is three fairly grand unspoiled old buildings; a stream bounds the pretty courtyard — it feels rather mediæval. Rooms are small, white, patchwork-quilted. The restaurant is superb with its big fireplace; food is light and vegetable-orientated though menus are occasionally repeated. The guests' dayroom gives onto a minstrels' gallery. Relaxed, well-travelled, cultivated owners to finish the picture. Children over 12 welcome.

Rooms: 2 double, 1 suite for 4, each with bath or shower & wc.

Price: 330 or 370 Frs, including breakfast.

Meals: 100 Frs, excluding wine (carafe 36 Frs).

Open: April to mid-November.

From Beaumont-du-Périgord, D660 5km towards Montpazier; second farm on right after sign for Petit Brassac .

Map No: 15   MM 235-5

Gilbert et Reine MARESCASSIER
Petit Brassac
Labouquerie
24440 Beaumont-du-Périgord
Dordogne
Tel: (0)5 53 22 32 51

From Montignac D65 south for 6km then left on minor road towards Valojoulx. House in centre of hamlet to left of Mairie.

Map No: 10   MM 233-44

Yvonne MILLIEZ & Astrid VAN EECKHOUDT
La Licorne
Valojoulx
24290 Montignac-Lascaux
Dordogne
Tel: (0)5 53 50 77 77
Fax: (0)5 53 51 19 04

This is one of the most famous châteaux in the region, on top of a hill just outside the mediæval town of Sarlat. The rooms are off the main spiral staircase, with the superb dining-room at its base. You can choose whether you take breakfast at the long table in here, surrounded by 17th-century Perigordian furniture, or outside on one of the terraces or turreted patios. The Comtesse will even bring it to your room — as you recline in a four-poster canopied bed with marble fireplace and stunning panoramic views.

Rooms: 1 double, 1 quadruple, both with bath, shower & wc.

Price: 750 Frs for two, including breakfast.

Meals: Highly-recommended restaurant 5km away.

Open: April to October.

Gîtes for 10 people

"Wow!, wrote the inspector "What a beautiful house", ... and immensely friendly hosts too. Set in pretty grounds with a lake overlooking a wooded valley, it has been lovingly restored to a sophisticated standard, with lots of Laura Ashley and superb bathrooms, 4 of them behind magnificent curtains. Pictures, antiques, tapestries, harmonised colours, comfortable sofas, three superb 'public' rooms for guests, a playroom: elegance yet homeliness... almost a château-hotel, but much friendlier and far better value.

Rooms: 2 twin, 2 double, 1 extra child's room, each with bath or shower & wc.

Price: 350-500 Frs for two, including breakfast.

Meals: 150 Frs, including wine.

Open: All year.

From Sarlat S on D57 towards Beynac then very quickly right onto D25 towards Le Bugue for 4km; then right at Ventojols & La Métairie signs — 800m then right for 400m of drive.

Map No: 10   MM 235-6

From Sarlat D47 towards Les Eyzies for 8km. Château signposted on left.

Map No: 10   MM 235-6

Comte & Comtesse de MONTBRON
Château de Puymartin
24200 Sarlat-la-Canéda
Dordogne
Tel: (0)5 53 59 29 97
Fax: (0)5 53 29 87 52

Michel & Martine PINARD-LEGRY
La Metairie Haute
Lasserre
24200 Sarlat, Dordogne
Tel: (0)5 53 30 31 17
Fax: (0)5 53 59 62 66
e-mail: http://www.arachnis-asso-fr/dordogne/vitrines/plegry/htm

The well-kept gardens that surround this renovated 18th-century manor-house give a sense of blissful peace. Guests sleep in a big separate building. White walls contrast with wooden beams in the spotless rooms, which have excellent beds and central heating. Breakfast is served until late and the Rubbens enjoy chatting to their guests. The service is excellent and well-behaved children are tolerated!

Rooms: 1 triple with bath & wc; 1 double with shower & wc in hall; 2 double sharing bath & wc in hall.

Price: 380 Frs for two, including breakfast.

Meals: Restaurant in village, 2km.

Open: From Easter to October.

From Périgueux, D939 to Brantôme. There, D78 & D83 towards Champagnac-de-Belair; D82 & D3 to Villars and 'Grottes de Villars'. Left to Lavergne; signposted.

Map No: 10   MM 233-32

Mme Eliane RUBBENS
L'Enclos
Lavergne
24530 Villars
Dordogne
Tel: (0)5 53 54 82 17

In the Périgueux-Sarlat-Bergerac triangle, rustic charm envelopes the converted 18th-century barn, farm buildings and log cabin nestling among oaks and pines where woodland paths beckon. Main-house rooms and log cabin are equally attractive. Madame, eager for guests to be happy, provides a raft of activities: boules, badminton, swings, a solar-heated pool. Breakfast and dinner are healthy family fare with local fruit and veg in season. The new conservatory has a summer kitchen so guests can be as independent as they like.

Rooms: 1 double, 1 suite for 5 in house, 1 suite for 3 in log cabin, all with bath or shower & wc.

Price: 250-300 Frs for two, including breakfast. Extra person 100 Frs.

Meals: 100 Frs, including wine & coffee. Self-catering.

Open: All year.

Gîtes for 4 people

From Le Bugue D703 towards Pezuls for 10km then left towards Vaudunes for about 1.5km across first junction; house is on right.

Map No: 10   MM 235-5

Xavière SIMAND
La Maison des Bois
Maison-Neuve
24510 Paunat
Dordogne
Tel: (0)5 53 22 75 74
Fax: (0)5 53 22 75 74

The Bells came from South Africa to this tiny hamlet among the acorns and walnuts of Périgord to bring up their young son far from violence and pollution. With its steep roofs and dark stone, the old house is quaint and inviting. Inside, it is furnished in all simplicity with old iron beds, mats on tiled floors, pictures and, in the huge open-plan living-kitchen, an open hearth and a closed stove. A relaxed, bohemian atmosphere — he an artist, she a happy cook — makes this house perfect for the young (and the young at heart).

Rooms: 1 double, 1 triple, 1 double + bunks, 1 suite for 3, all with bath or shower & wc.

Price: 220 Frs for two, including breakfast.

Meals: 90 Frs, including walnut aperitif, wine & coffee.

Open: All year.

Gîtes for 16 people

From Brive, N20 S for 10km then N140 dir. Gramat/Rocamadour for 21km; D36 left to Rignac; at church, left then 1st right; cont. D36 dir. Lavergne for 50m; left for Pouch by green bottle bank. 2km: first house, signed.

Map No: 16   MM 235-6

Gavin & Lillian BELL
Pouch
46500 Rignac
Lot
Tel: (0)5 65 33 66 84
Fax: (0)5 65 33 71 31

Definitely the 'French experience' — staying with friendly farming people who are always ready for a drink and a chat (in French) — this is a real farm run by hard-working people who enjoy having guests. Use the peaceful terrace where your hosts are happy for you to sit all day over your breakfast, revelling in the setting, the views and the garden. Inside, the decor is in keeping with the farmhouse, with curtained-off bathrooms. No dinner but lots of homegrown wine and aperitif, as well as *gâteau de noix* with their own honey.

Rooms: 2 double, 1 triple each with own shower & wc.

Price: 240 Frs for two, including breakfast.

Meals: Good choice within 5 km.

Open: All year.

Gîtes for 6 people

From Cahors D8 west for 10km. Just before Flaynac right at Chambres d'Hôtes sign then right and right again.

Map No: 16   MM 235-14

M & Mme Jean FAYDI
Flaynac
46090 Pradines
Lot
Tel: (0)5 65 35 33 36

We have been flooded with praise for the Hauchecornes' welcome and their care and concern in looking after their guests. Organic jams, made by Gisèle, are served for breakfast at the kitchen table or on the terrace. They had a restaurant for many years, where she was the chef; now they have time for visitors. This is a rustic house, with big grounds (containing 5 gîtes) and a pool. Gisèle has created a dear little children's bedroom in the old *pigeonnier*: two beds (one on a platform above the other) and pictures of clowns.

Rooms: 2 double, each with shower & wc; 1 children's room.

Price: 250 Frs for two, including breakfast; 90 Frs per child in tower room.

Meals: 85 Frs, including wine & coffee.

Open: All year.

Gîtes for 25 people

From Gourdon D673 towards Fumel then left on D6 to Dégagnac. In town square take road to SNCF station. After football ground on left take 2nd right. At top of hill right to La Franquette.

Map No: 16   MM 235-10

Gisèle & Alain HAUCHECORNE
La Franquette
Montsalvy
46340 Dégagnac
Lot
Tel: (0)5 65 41 51 57
Fax: (0)5 65 41 51 57

Your hosts are entertaining people who like to chat while cooking, dine with their guests and enjoy good wine and company. The old stone barn has been attractively converted into cosy B&B rooms with antiques, deep armchairs and restful colours. There's a warm sitting-room, which the owners (who live in the unconverted farmhouse) share with their visitors, and a cool pool outside. Anthony, who deals in wine, is English, powerfully articulate, and enthusiastic; his aristocratic French wife is genteel and charming.

Rooms: 3 double, 2 triple, 1 quadruple, all with bath or shower & wc.

Price: 300-350 Frs for two, including breakfast.

Meals: 125 Frs, including wine & coffee.

Open: All year (book ahead, esp. in winter).

Gîtes for 2 people

From Figeac centre N140 towards Decazeville. Outside town left on D2 towards Montredon for 3km then right on D210 towards Lunan then follow signs.

Map No: 16   MM 235-11

Anthony & Dominique NIELSON de LAMOTHE
Liffernet Grange
Lunan
46100 Figeac
Lot
Tel: (0)5 65 34 69 76
Fax: (0)5 65 50 06 24

This sensitively-restored old mill, with parts dating back 400 or 600 years to the Templars, is set in colourful gardens beside a river where you may fish for trout. The bedrooms, with cream-painted or bare stone walls and tapestries over bedheads, have glimpses of river and garden below (double-glazing should you have to shut out the sounds of running water). Monsieur is an artist and his paintings of typical local houses are on view; Madame, a keen cook, includes several vegetarian dishes on her menu; their welcome is superb.

Rooms: 4 double & 1 twin, all with shower & wc.

Price: 270-390 Frs for two, including breakfast.

Meals: 110 Frs, including wine.

Open: Mid-March to mid-November.

From Gramat, N140 towards Figeac; after 500m, left onto a small road leading to the mill.

Map No: 16   MM 235-6

Gérard & Claude RAMELOT
Moulin de Fresquet
46500 Gramat
Lot
Tel: (0)5 65 38 70 60/
       (0)6 08 85 09 21
Fax: (0)5 65 38 70 60

The C17 farmhouse and barn, built in the famous champagne-hued Lot stone, have been restored by the Scotts to look like the old characters they are. But they have modern comforts too and those stunning views over two valleys (when the trees are bare). The bedrooms are smallish but the pool (solar-heated, salt-purified) and sunbeds beckon you out. Very friendly hosts who want you to have a good time. Breakfast is served any time, anywhere, and dinner is fun, friendly, relaxed and informal. Pool-house kitchen and fridge for picnic lunches.

Rooms: 1 double with bathroom; 1 double & 1 single sharing bathroom.

Price: 250-300 Frs for two, including breakfast.

Meals: 100 Frs, incl. aperitif, wine & coffee (book ahead). Barbecue.

Open: All year (please telephone).

Gîtes for 16 people

By-pass Cahors dir. Toulouse; at roundabout onto D653 towards Agen; at fork turn right onto D656. Pass Villeseque, Sauzet, Bovila then take 3rd left on straight stretch; signposted.

Map No: 15   MM 235-13

Peter & Zoé SCOTT
Mondounet
46800 Fargues
Lot
Tel: (0)5 65 36 96 32
Fax: (0)5 65 31 84 89
e-mail: scotsprops@aol.com

Madame, small, neat, well-dressed, very French and attractive, is starting again having lived most of her life in Provence. Her house is a fine *maison de maître*, the ground floor of which is her domain and classically French in style. Upstairs is for guests, and reached by a separate entrance. There is a big dayroom with books, board games and light cane furniture. The bedrooms have plain, painted walls and a light, uncluttered feel, plus long views down the valley. Historic villages and lovely countryside.

Rooms: 2 double, 1 twin, each with bath or shower & wc.

Price: 236-266 Frs for two, including breakfast.

Meals: 80 Frs, including aperitif, wine & coffee.

Open: All year.

Ann knows her design — she and Alain have clearly enjoyed doing the conversion using interesting paint techniques. There are lovely gardens and three acres of ancient trees around the château. It has salmon-coloured shutters, open fires, lots of high windows, brightly-coloured walls, palm trees, polished wooden floors, some Empire furniture. The superb bedrooms are very plush and new-mattressed, one with a Rice Bed from Ann's native South Carolina. Dinner is delicious and your hosts are gregarious yet efficient.

Rooms: 1 duplex for 5 with 2 bathrooms; 4 double, each with bath or shower & wc.

Price: 480-690 Frs for two, including breakfast. Third person in duplex 200 Frs; other extra beds 100 Frs.

Meals: 130 Frs, including wine & coffee. Picnic baskets available.

Open: All year.

From Agen N21 N for 6km then fork left on D13 to Montpezat. In village turn right to church (Eglise St Jean). After passing church on right take 1st left and follow signs.

Map No: 15   MM 234-16

Madeleine GASQUY
Pince-Guerre
47360 Montpezat d'Agenais
Lot-et-Garonne
Tel: (0)5 53 95 07 71

From A62 exit 6 towards Aiguillon. Take 2nd right, D642, towards Buzet. Château on right, signposted, shortly before Buzet.

Map No: 15   MM 234-16

Ann & Alain Doherty GELIX
Château de Coustet
47160 Buzet-sur-Baïse
Tarn-et-Garonne
Tel: (0)5 53 79 26 60
Fax: (0)5 53 79 14 16
e-mail: ccoustet@easynet.fr

Ten hectares of parkland provide scope for walks from your door — and space even for a free-range 8,000-chicken farm. Despite its size, the C17 château is a comfortable, informal home and is ideal for children. Rooms are big — even grand — with views over the garden to meadows and woods beyond. Private pool and billiards table. Breakfast — with home-produced breads and the inevitable eggs — and dinner are very much *en famille*. Madame has two sons, is a most friendly hostess and obviously enjoys her guests.

Rooms: 1 double, 1 twin, 1 suite, all bath or shower & wc.

Price: 280-350 Frs for two, including breakfast.

Meals: 100 Frs, including wine & coffee. Children 60 Frs.

Open: All year.

An elegant family mansion with a friendly, homely atmosphere and even a frisky spaniel which has to be restrained from joining guests on walks. Light and cheerful bedrooms have pretty wallpaper, brass beds, roomy bathrooms. There are fine oak floors, lovingly polished and decorated with rugs, and a wonderful elm staircase. The old-fashioned sitting-room is furnished with antiques and formal chairs. Your hosts are active and charming. Outside there are pool, verandah and basket chairs for relaxing over a drink. Small dogs welcome.

Rooms: 2 double, 1 twin, 1 suite for 2-4 people, all with bath or shower & wc.

Price: 360-390 Frs for two, including breakfast (less 40 Frs winter).

Meals: By arrangement 95 Frs, including wine & coffee.

Open: All year (book ahead to be sure).

From Marmande, D933 towards Casteljaloux. Château on right; signposted.

Map No: 15   MM 234-16

M & Mme de LA RAITRIE
Château de Cantet
Samazan
47250 Bouglon
Lot-et-Garonne
Tel: (0)5 53 20 60 60

From Villeneuve-sur-Lot, N21 towards Bergerac. At Cancon, D124 towards Monbahus. Left after 150m; signposted.

Map No: 15   MM 235-9

Francis & Simone LARRIBEAU
Chanteclair
47290 Cancon
Lot-et-Garonne
Tel: (0)5 53 01 63 34
Fax: (0)5 53 41 13 44

You're part of the family here but you really need to be the sort of person who enjoys large, scatty tribes. Madame, artistic and energetic, reigns over a happy, rather chaotic household with people constantly coming and going. Children are free to roam the house and garden without parents worrying about their messing anything up. The dining-room and bedrooms have a certain style, with big wrought-iron beds, lots of space, wooden floors and some stone walls. There are paintings everywhere. The motorway is only just within earshot.

Rooms: 1 twin, 2 double, each with bath or shower & wc.

Price: 250 Frs for two, including breakfast.

Meals: 75 Frs, including wine & coffee.

Open: All year.

This old farm is near three famous *bastides* (strongholds) and there's a château thrown in for the view. The good bedrooms and a sitting-room with log fires and country furniture are in their own converted pigeon tower (hawks and owls nest in the holes on the outside); highchair, bottle-warmer and games are kept on hand for children; a fine swimming pool for all. The farm grows tobacco, maize and sunflowers. Madame has an infectious energy (her affable husband is quieter) and they both speak fluent English. Our readers are enthusiastic.

Rooms: 2 double, each with shower & wc, 1 with mini-kitchen.

Price: 260-280 Frs for two, including breakfast.

Meals: 100 Frs, including wine.

Open: All year.

Gîtes for 8 people

From Bordeaux, A62, Damazan exit. Enter Damazan; right at Renault garage on D108 towards Buzet/Nirac. 'Balous' on right after 200m.

Map No: 15   MM 234-16

Mme Françoise SAVY-TAQUET
Château Balous
47160 Damazan
Lot-et-Garonne
Tel: (0)5 53 79 42 96

From Villeneuve-sur-Lot, D676 to Monflanquin and D272 towards Monpazier. House is opposite 'Dordogne' sign 1.5km after crossroads to Dévillac.

Map No: 15   MM 235-9

Michel & Maryse PANNETIER
Colombié
47210 Dévillac
Lot-et-Garonne
Tel: (0)5 53 36 62 34
Fax: (0)5 53 36 04 79

The sophisticated young owners of Le Petit Verdus clearly want their guests to experience the best of château life. The atmosphere at table is formal; you'd certainly dress for dinner here. Monsieur is in the wine business so there's an extensive *grand cru* wine list. The bedrooms, reached by a beautiful spiral staircase, are immaculate and satisfy the appetite whetted by the fine drive up. After a hearty breakfast you can explore the vast park, discover the old railway line, now a fine cycle path, or play tennis on the clay court.

Rooms: 1 double with shower & wc, 1 suite for 4 with bath & wc .

Price: 450 Frs for two, including breakfast.

Meals: 160 Frs, including aperitif & coffee, excluding wine (30 Frs).

Open: February to December.

Gîtes for 5 people

From Bordeaux D936 towards Bergerac then D671 towards Créon; after Loupes, just beyond Château Landereau (on left), right towards Château Seguin. At crossroads right to Le Petit Verdus: 2nd white gate on right.

Map No: 15   MM 234-7

Aquitaine

Karin & Stéphane AURIOL
Château le Petit Verdus
Lorient
33670 Sadirac
Gironde
Tel: (0)5 56 23 71 23
Fax: (0)5 56 30 69 28
e-mail: auriol@quaternet.Fr

A hard-working young couple in a C18 château, without quite enough money to make it over-stylish; but they have three good and very big bedrooms, a stone entrance hall, a wrought-iron balcony terrace for a glass of (their own dry white Semillon) château wine, and bantams everywhere. It is relaxed and easy — even busy — with three young children, and deer in the woods. Breakfast is on the terrace, wine-tasting in the magnificent *salle de dégustation*. The small pool is for evening dippers rather than sun-worshippers.

Rooms: 3 triple, each with shower & wc.

Price: 300 Frs for two, including breakfast.

Meals: Choice in Bourg, 2km.

Open: All year except February & 1 week in August.

Tradition has deep roots her; you sense it in the ancient walls. The *Girondin* farmhouse has stood for three centuries, the vines are mature, the wine superb; the lovely linen and lace bedcovers are family heirlooms, the family itself, all three generations, is busy, lively, full of character. Madame's eagle eye for detail, her spotless care of the stone-walled, old-furnished guestrooms, her attention to your every need and her beautiful breakfast table in the cosy family dining room make it special indeed (though she's sometimes away).

Rooms: 2 double, 2 twin, 1 triple, all with bath or shower & wc.

Price: 300-320 Frs (+4.40 Frs tax) for two, including breakfast.

Meals: 90 Frs, excluding wine (35-120 Frs): book ahead. Self-catering.

Open: February to December.

From A10 exit 40a or 40b through St André-de-Cubzac W onto D669 through Bourg towards Blaye and very soon right on D251 dir. Berson for 1km; signed on right up lane/drive.

Map No: 10   MM 233-38

M & Mme BASSEREAU
Château de la Grave
33710 Bourg-sur-Gironde
Gironde
Tel: (0)5 57 68 41 49
Fax: (0)5 57 68 49 26

From Libourne, D243 towards Saint-Emilion. 3km before Saint-Emilion, D245 towards Pomerol; signposted.

Map No: 10   MM 234-3

Claude et Jacqueline BRIEUX
Château Millaud-Montlabert
33330 Saint-Emilion
Gironde
Tel: (0)5 57 24 71 85
Fax: (0)5 57 24 62 78

Parts of this priory are 12th-century, when it provided rest for pilgrims. Its charming hostess sees that her 20th-century guests are also refreshed. The serenity of the setting and Susie's warm personality are worth coming for (she does personal development workshops). Lie in a hammock under the walnut tree, let the fan-tail pigeons coo you into a blissful siesta, the nightingales serenade your dawn. No routine — breakfast served whenever it suits, candlelit dinners on request. The lower price is for travellers not using garden or pool.

Rooms: 2 triple, 2 double; 1 single — 3 with shower, bath & wc; 2 sharing shower & wc.

Price: 350-480 Frs for two, including breakfast

Meals: 160 Frs, including wine & coffee.

Open: All year.

Gîtes for 6 people

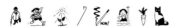

There are five comfortable guestrooms in this generous 18th-century mansion, built on the foundations of a mediæval château in a place loaded with history. It surveys vineyards (the fulsome Côtes de Blaye are here), fields and forest. The large, quiet, sunny rooms have their own entrance, kitchen and living-room. In summer, guests may share a thoroughly French dinner with the Chartiers who breed horses. Well-organised, 'no-nonsense' hospitality and Monsieur will arrange vineyard tours for you.

Rooms: 3 triple with en suite shower & wc; 1 triple with separate shower & wc.

Price: 190-230 Frs for two, including breakfast.

Meals: Summer only: 90 Frs, inc. wine. Self-catering; restaurants nearby.

Open: All year.

From Bordeaux D936 towards Bergerac through St Quentin-de-Baron. Exactly 1km after village, house signposted on right.

Map No: 15   MM 234-7

Susie de CASTILHO
Le Prieuré
33750 Saint-Quentin-de-Baron
Gironde
Tel: (0)5 57 24 16 75
Fax: (0)5 57 24 13 80

From A10, Exit 38 on D132 and D115 to St Savin. There, D18 to St Mariens. Left just before village; signposted.

Map No: 10   MM 233-38

Daniel & Yvonne CHARTIER
Château de Gourdet
33620 Saint-Mariens
Gironde
Tel: (0)5 57 58 05 37

Madame was an interior designer and her house is straight out of *Maisons et Jardins*. Walls taken back to the original stones and a plethora of stripped woodwork marry well with a catholic mix of features and flourishes. This is THE area for wine buffs and Monsieur, who used to be a wine merchant, will happily share his knowledge at wine tastings. The pool was specially built for guests. The food is simple but delicious and in warm weather is served on the terrace overlooking the large garden.

Rooms: 2 double, 1 twin, each with bath or shower & wc.

Price: 320 Frs for two, including breakfast.

Meals: From 120 Frs, including wine.

Open: All year.

Visitors eat round a 10ft-diameter table made from an outsize wine barrel, in a C19 barn with beams, cantilevered gallery and a magnificent two-storey fireplace. Antoine teaches cookery yet loves to whip up regional feasts in his own sensational stainless steel kitchen then serve rather special wines from his contacts in the trade. Children have a sandpit, climbing frame and pool (and the company of Claire and Antoine's three young children). Canoeing, canal trips, fishing, riding and cycling are available locally.

Rooms: 4 double, 1 twin, each with bath and/or shower & wc.

Price: 280 Frs for two, including breakfast.

Meals: 100 Frs, including wine. Barbecue available.

Open: All year.

From A62 exit 4 onto D9 to La Réole. There, D670 then D668 towards Monségur. At roundabout onto D21 for St Sève. Through village, down hill, right after bridge into lane to house; signed on left.

Map No: 15   MM 234-11

Paul & France CHAVEROU
Domaine de la Charmaie
33190 Saint-Sève
Gironde
Tel: (0)5 56 61 10 72
Fax: (0)5 56 61 27 21

From A62 exit 4 for La Réole. At junction with D9 left towards Bazas-Grignols then 1st left 250m after bridge — La Tuilerie signed for remaining 3km.

Map No: 15   MM 234-11

Claire & Antoine LABORDE
La Tuilerie
33190 Noaillac
Gironde
Tel: (0)5 56 71 05 51
Fax: (0)5 56 71 05 51

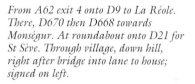

Good country folk, the Lanneaus live in a large 18th-century *maison paysanne* in the Médoc wine area. They do B&B as a family — parents and daughter — because they love having people. The more appealing room is the small 1900s former grape-pickers' cabin in the garden. The other is a newly-converted outbuilding. Both have independent entrances and modern pine furniture. Come and visit at grape harvest time. The largest natural lake in France and the useful ferry to fashionable Royan are near. No children.

Rooms: 2 double with bath or shower & wc.

Price: 270 Frs for two, including breakfast.

Meals: 3 restaurants in village.

Open: All year.

Food and wine buffs will love it here. Madame, a keen cook who includes vegetarian and diabetic food on her menu, was making *paté/terrine* when we arrived; Monsieur is a wine expert. Their early 19th-century farmhouse, set in an area of fields and vineyards, is simply but attractively furnished and the beamed, wallpapered guestrooms are big and comfortable. The dining-room is decorated in art deco style with modern pictures. The Levys do Sunday lunches for non-guests and are booked weeks, even months in advance.

Rooms: 1 double, 2 triple, each with bath, shower & wc.

Price: 320 Frs for two, including breakfast.

Meals: 110-185 Frs, excluding wine.

Open: January to September.

From Bordeaux, N215 towards Le Verdon. After about 80km, right to St Vivien; in village, go towards Grayan (rue Général de Gaulle): approx. 800m on right.

Map No: 9   MM 233-25

Pierre & Marguerite LANNEAU
Mirambeau
50 rue du Général de Gaulle
33590 Saint-Vivien-de-Médoc
Gironde
Tel: (0)5 56 09 51 07

From Libourne, D670 through Sauveterre, then left on D230 to Rimons. At Rimons sawmill on the right, take first left; signposted.

Map No: 15   MM 234-12

Dominique & Patrick LÉVY
Grand Boucaud
Rimons
33580 Monségur
Gironde
Tel: (0)5 56 71 88 57
Fax: (0)5 56 71 88 57

The New Hebrides, Brazil, New Zealand, the Sahara... Michèle has lived in them all; it is enough to make one feel parochial. But her family has been here for five generations and they built this hacienda-style house where the old farm crumbled away. Yes, there is imitation zebra and tiger-skin upholstery in the living-room but some good memorabilia too... African sculpture etc. Bedrooms are traditional, with fine views across oceans of vines. Their own wine comes with dinner and the nearby ferry comes from Blaye.

Rooms: 1 double with bath & wc; 1 twin with shower & wc.

Price: 290 or 300 Frs for two, including breakfast.

Meals: 150 Frs, including aperitif, wine & coffee.

Open: All year.

From Bordeaux Rocade (by-pass) exit 9 onto D1 to Castelnau then N215 through St Laurent. 4km after St Laurent right for St Sauveur & Vertheuil. Through village leaving abbey on right, down over level crossing, white house approx. 1km on left.

Map No: 10   MM 233-37

Michèle TARDAT
Cantemerle
9 rue des Châtaigniers
33180 Vertheuil-Médoc
Gironde
Tel: (0)5 56 41 96 24
Fax: (0)5 56 41 96 24

"The whole place is special! The furniture is astounding, the house captivating. I love it." The inspector was obviously moved. The house (1610) and contents have been accumulated by Colette's family for 14 generations (portraits from C12 onwards). The bedrooms are spectacular: antique beds with canopies and drapes, strong colours, wonderful old furniture; two have open fireplaces. Dining-room and salon are handsome, too: antiques, terracotta tiles and huge stone fireplace. Colette is elegant, attentive, helpful and hugely resourceful.

Rooms: 3 double, each with bath or shower & wc.

Price: 240-280 Frs for two, including breakfast.

Meals: 80 Frs, including wine.

Open: All year.

From Dax D947 for Pau/Orthez for 10km. Stay on D947, ignoring sign for Mimbaste and take NEXT right onto D16 then follow discreet little blue and white signs to house.

Map No: 14   MM 234-26

Colette DUFOURCET-ALBERCA
Maison Capcazal de Pachioü
40350 Mimbaste
Landes
Tel: (0)5 58 55 30 54
Fax: (0)5 58 55 30 54

Madame is a gem, gracious and charming, her husband more reserved; but you'll delight in this miniature chateau. Madame teaches yoga, paints, is a long-distance walker and a committed vegetarian — she does dinner for 3-day guests. Children can freely roam the 20 hectares of parkland — they love it. The rooms are large and properly decorated, some with herringbone parquet floors. We think the smaller ones give better value. High ceilings, old prints, a glimpse of the Pyrenees and the call of a peacock outside... glorious!

Rooms: 1 double, 1 twin, each with shower & wc; 2 large doubles with bathrooms en-suite.

Price: 300 Frs for two (500 Frs for the larger doubles), including breakfast.

Meals: Vegetarian dinner 80 Frs, incl. wine & coffee. Restaurant 1km.

Open: April to October (other times by arrangement).

From A10 or A63 motorways: exit St Geours-de-Maremne to Orist and on to Monbet (10km).

Map No: 15   MM 234-30

M & Mme Hubert de LATAILLADE
Château du Monbet
40300 Saint-Lon-les-Mines
Landes
Tel: (0)5 58 57 80 68
Fax: (0)5 58 57 89 29

Béatrice, direct and talkative with a great sense of humour, is also a stained-glass artist (see one of the bathrooms). Her jams show character, too: green tomato, watermelon and vanilla, carrot marmalade. The bedrooms: antiques, books, one with sofa and armchairs, one with black ceiling, and lots of unusual touches. One bathroom has carpeted walls and ceiling (sic). The *salon* is elegant, with grand piano; the dining-room is in pale woods, pale yellows and creams. Bring your horse; the stable awaits. Children over 10 welcome.

Rooms: 1 double, 1 triple, each with bath or shower & wc; 1 double/twin, 1 twin, each with shower, sharing separate wc.

Price: 200-280 Frs for two, including breakfast. Extra person 80 Frs.

Meals: 80 Frs, including wine & coffee.

Open: May to October.

From Mont-de-Marsan D38 NW towards Morcenx. Once out of Mont-de-Marsan follow discreet signs for Chambres d'Hôtes (5/6km from city centre).

Map No: 15   MM 234-22

Béatrice & Philippe de MONREDON
Lamolère
40090 Campet-Lamolère
Landes
Tel: (0)5 58 06 04 98
Fax: (0)5 58 06 04 98

In a matchless setting, the house stands proud on its hill with spectacular vistas to the Pyrenean green. Madame welcomes you with gracious formality to her superbly restored 18th-century farmhouse with its exposed timbers and generous open-plan living area. This is her dream spot — found after a long search — and you probably won't want to leave it either. Breakfast and dinner are eaten with your hosts on their terrace, looking out over the ever-changing foothills of those stunning mountains — soft in the morning mist, bright in the sun and snow.

Rooms: 3 double, 2 twin, all with shower & wc.

Price: 280 Frs for two, including breakfast.

Meals: 90 Frs, including wine.

Open: All year.

Basque Country – The South West – Pyrenees

STOP PRESS
No longer doing B & B

This grand 18th-century village house and its owners are quiet, elegant, sophisticated. Don't miss dinner, the chance to talk with your hosts about the region, or delve into their extensive library (she binds books). They have completely renovated the house since finding this sleepy village in the foothills of the Pyrenees. The bedrooms are light and airy with interesting old furniture. *La Rose* is very chic and *La Verte* is a dream — enormous, beautifully furnished, with views out to the mountains and a 'waltz-in' bathroom! Readers are ecstatic.

Rooms: 2 double with own shower or bath & wc.

Price: 270 Frs for two, including breakfast.

Meals: 90 Frs, including wine & coffee.

Open: All year.

This 16th-century Basque farmhouse in a superb listed village has had new life breathed into it by its French/Irish owners who revel in sharing their home with guests. Dinners around the enormous oak dining table are lively; local dishes, like *daube* (a thick stew) and *garbure* (soup with *confit de canard*), often grace the menu. The rooms are big, light and airy, with exposed wafer bricks, beams and hand-stencilling. An excellent breakfast is served on the terrace in warm weather and Gilbert will teach you to play *pelote basque* — wildly.

Rooms: 1 triple, 3 double, 1 quadruple all with own bath or shower & wc.

Price: 280-330 Frs for two, including breakfast.

Meals: 120 Frs, including wine.

Open: All year (check ahead).

From Navarrenx D2 towards Monein to Jasses. There D27 towards Oloron Sainte Marie. In Lay-Lamidou turn left then first right; 2nd house on right.

Map No: 15 MM 234-34

Marie-France DESBONNET
64190 Lay-Lamidou
Pyrénées-Atlantiques
Tel: (0)5 59 66 00 44

From A64 junction 4 towards Urt/Bidache then right on D123 to La Bastide Clairence. House is on left in main street.

Map No: 14 MM 234-29

Valerie & Gilbert FOIX
Maison Marchand
64240 La Bastide-Clairence
Pyrénées-Atlantiques
Tel: (0)5 59 29 18 27
Fax: (0)5 59 29 14 97
e-mail: valerie.et.gilbert.foix@wanadoo.fr

Come for the calm, the views from the terrace over lush greenness, the forest and the river at the bottom of the field (with an occasional heron). Nicole, a cheerful, lively hostess, was a hairdresser, Jean-Marie has an agricultural background and they create an easy, informal mood. The bedrooms (dull, rear views) have plain walls, country antiques, built-in formica cupboards, beams, pretty country fabrics. Superb Basque dishes with fresh farm produce served in the attractive dining-room. Children over 7 welcome.

Rooms: 2 double, 1 twin, each with bath or shower & wc.

Price: 240 Frs for two, including breakfast.

Meals: 75 Frs, including wine.

Open: All year except January.

Liliane is a great character, blunt, fun and immensely competent, and you have to like dogs to come here — she has six. She also likes gardening, happily, for the garden is huge. And she enjoys reading, cooking and music. *Voilà*... not a dull person. She has filled the old farmhouse with collections of favourite things — spinning tops and antique cameras, for example. Bedrooms are big and cosy with pretty cushions, lamps, rugs — somehow they hang together in an easy, attractive way. Lovely food to cap it all.

Rooms: 1 double, 1 triple, each with shower & wc.

Price: 325 Frs for two, including breakfast. Extra bed 75 Frs (under 12s) or 150 Frs.

Meals: 150 Frs, excluding wine (from 50 Frs).

Open: All year (book ahead).

From Bayonne A64 towards Pau. Leave at exit 5 and follow Chambres d'Hôtes signs. House about 3km from exit 5.

Map No: 14   MM 234-29

Nicole & Jean-Marie LAPLACE
Maison Huntagneres
64520 Guiche
Pyrénées-Atlantiques
Tel: (0)5 59 56 87 48/
(0)6 80 70 64 90

From A64 exit to Peyrehorade. There, follow signs for Hastingues & Sames (keeping south of river). In Sames follow signs for Bidache and for Le Lanot.

Map No: 14   MM 234-30

Liliane MICKELSON
Le Lanot
64520 Sames
Pyrénées-Atlantiques
Tel: (0)5 59 56 01 84

Two super women, mother a homeopathic nurse, daughter a naturopath/beautician, both lovers of animals and all things natural. The lovely old farmhouse has an air of homely chaos and a typical beamed and stone-walled dining-room; bedrooms, in a converted outbuilding, are small and functional. But you come here for the vast Pyrenees — so close you can almost touch them — and the superb walking, so what matter the small sleeping spaces? There are (off-season) fitness courses for adults and pony-rides for small children.

Rooms: 5 twin, 1 double, each with bath or shower & wc.

Price: 295 Frs for two, including breakfast.

Meals: 80 Frs, excluding (table) wine (10 Frs).

Open: All year.

From A64 exit 11 dir. Tarbes then S on D218 to Gomer & Chaperot; join D145 to Mirepeix & Nay then right to Arros-de-Nay. Then follow signs for 'Centre de Remise en Forme' and Haut-de-Bosdarros (about 20km in all).

Map No: 15   MM 234-39

Béatrice de MONTEVERDE
Ferme Loutarès
64800 Haut de Bosdarros
Pyrénées-Atlantiques
Tel: (0)5 59 71 20 60
Fax: (0)5 59 71 26 67

The brand new old-style Basque house was designed by Monsieur; his subtle use of pastels, fabrics and simple furniture makes for delightful bedrooms which all have a fine view of the stunning Rhune mountain range. Hall, living and dining areas have a touch of Morocco, where your hosts used to live and big windows facing the mountains. They are wonderful people, open and easy to talk to; he can educate you in the finer aspects of the *corrida*, she can be counted on to dissuade you! He cooks too.

Rooms: 4 double, each with shower, two sharing wc, two with own wc.

Price: 250-300 Frs for two, including breakfast.

Meals: From 100 Frs, including wine.

Open: All year except December & January.

From A63, exit 2 dir. Urrugne/Col d'Ibardine. At roundabout, 3rd exit dir. Col d'Ibardine. At next roundabout, 2nd exit then next left for 500m; follow signs for Maison Haizean.

Map No: 14   MM 234-33

Murielle NARDOU
Maison Haizean
Chemin Rural d'Acharry Ttipy
64122 Urrugne
Pyrénées-Atlantiques
Tel: (0)5 59 47 45 37
Fax: (0)5 59 47 45 37

All the cosily-decorated rooms have steep stairs up to a mezzanine (ideal for children), lovely views over the valley of the Cize, and doors onto the large, communal balcony. There is an open-plan sitting-breakfast area where you can also make your lunch. Madame is a genteel country lady who has spent time in California and now lives here with her brother, the retired shepherd, and her other brother, the priest. Dine in the main house with these interesting people and taste the shepherd brother's *Soupe du Berger*.

Rooms: 3 quadruple, 1 triple, 1 twin, each with bath or shower & wc.

Price: 240 Frs for two, including breakfast. Extra person 60 Frs.

Meals: 80 Frs, including aperitif & wine.

Open: All year.

Gîtes for 18 people

From St Jean-Pied-de-Port D428 towards St Michel and follow signs.

Map No: 14   MM 234-37

Jeanne OURTIAGUE
Ferme Ithurburia
64220 Saint-Michel
Pyrénées-Atlantiques
Tel: (0)5 59 37 11 17

She is passionate about her garden, lovingly developed by generations of nurserymen into a collector's paradise of old evergreens, magnolia, azalea, rhodedendron, benches discreetly placed for quiet reading... and the Pyrenees as a backdrop. The word for these Béarn houses is 'sturdy', with solid old furniture and traditional decoration. There are modern touches too: colourful wallpapers in the bedrooms and small but modern bathrooms. Madame is smartly dressed and very on the ball... doing nearly all the work herself.

Rooms: 2 twin, 1 double, 1 for 3 or 4, each with shower & wc.

Price: 295 Frs for two, including breakfast. Extra person 60 Frs.

Meals: 90 Frs, excluding wine (from 15 Frs carafe).

Open: All year.

Gites for 10 people

From A64 exit 7; right for Salies '<5 tonnes' then take next right signed to Le Guilhat for 1.8km. La Closerie on left beside Despaux nurseries.

Map No: 14   MM 234-30

Marie-Christine POTIRON
La Closerie du Guilhat
64270 Salies-de-Béarn
Pyrénées-Atlantiques
Tel: (0)5 59 38 08 80
Fax: (0)5 59 38 08 80

Marie-Luce and Jean-Vincent have created three guestrooms in one of their barns. They are deliberately functional and clean, if unmemorable; they have small shower rooms but the beams and the great views out of the large windows give them that special something. So, too, do your hosts. Marie-Luce will happily give children a guided tour of her farm — to the ducks and geese, chickens and rabbits — some of whose relatives will doubtless be served at the good honestly-priced dinner. Lourdes is 13km away.

Rooms: 1 double, 1 triple, 1 twin, all with own shower & wc.

Price: 200 Frs for two, including breakfast.

Meals: 70 Frs, including wine & coffee.

Open: All year.

From Lourdes D937 towards Pau ('par Bétharram'). In St Pé-de-Bigorre right between church and Mairie. House 4km out at top of hill; signposted.

Map No: 15   MM 234-39

Marie-Luce & Jean-Vincent
ARRAMONDE
Ferme Campseissillou
65270 Saint-Pé-de-Bigorre
Hautes-Pyrénées
Tel: (0)5 62 41 80 92

The Bolacs, warmly gracious and very French, shop at good auction houses and it shows: each bedroom has some special pieces and three have 4-posters canopied with acres of flowers. After a buffet breakfast in the guest quarters, dip into the well-stocked library then, after day exploring the Bread Basket of France (this area is, in fact, more Gers than Pyrenees), dip into the swimming pool before sharing a remarkable-value regional dinner (including home-grown salads, vegetables and herbs) in the dining-room.

Rooms: 1 suite, 1 triple, 1 twin, 1 double, each with bath, shower & wc.

Price: 300 Frs for two, including breakfast.

Meals: 100 Frs, including aperitif, wine & coffee.

Open: All year but booking essential in winter.

From Tarbes D935 N for 40km. In Castelnau, château is 0.5km from centre; well signposted.

Map No: 15   MM 234-31

Claudie & Xavier BOLAC
Château du Tail
65700 Castelnau-Rivière-Basse
Hautes-Pyrénées
Tel: (0)5 62 31 93 75
Fax: (0)5 62 31 93 26

Neither airs nor graces, just good solid value. Josette is a keen decorator and her husband an artisan in wood, as you can see. The house lay abandoned for 35 years but now has a peach/ochre salon, a yellow/blue dining-room, a gorgeous kitchen floor and a billiards room with huge fireplace. The hall is vast, and in stone. Bedrooms and bathrooms are large, superbly done with antiques, a mix of simple and rich fabrics, good linen and have views over the handsome park and pond. Good-value people too.

Rooms: 2 quadruple, 1 double, each with bath & wc.

Price: 320 Frs for two, including breakfast. Extra person 80 Frs.

Meals: 100 Frs, including wine.

Open: All year.

Madame is heavenly, a person of enormous grace; her *domaine* is an oasis of calm where peace reigns and you may find a lifelong friend, sharing her delight in playing the piano or golf (good golf course 3km). Built during the Napoleonic Wars, the house has a coolly elegant hall, big, airy bedrooms and superb bathrooms while fine furniture and linen sheets reflect her pride in her ancestral home. A beautifully-presented breakfast is further enhanced by civilised conversation. Come to unwind — you may never want to leave.

Rooms: 1 double, 1 triple, 1 quadruple, all with bath & wc.

Price: 250 Frs for two, including breakfast.

Meals: Restaurant 2km.

Open: All year.

From Pau NE on D943 through Morlaas & Lembeye towards Maubourguet. 2km before Maubourguet left on D59 to Sombrun; through village: house on outskirts on left.

Map No: 15   MM 234-31

Josette BRUNET
Château de Sombrun
65700 Sombrun
Hautes-Pyrénées
Tel: (0)5 62 96 49 43
Fax: (0)5 62 96 01 89
e-mail: http://www.sudfr.com/chateaudesombrun

From A64 exit 16 to Lannemezan; there, D117 towards Toulouse for 5km. In Pinas, at church take road towards Villeneuve. House on right after 1km.

Map No: 15   MM 234-40

Mme Marie-Sabine COLOMBIER
Domaine de Jean-Pierre
Route de Villeneuve
65300 Pinas (Lannemezan)
Hautes-Pyrénées
Tel: (0)5 62 98 15 08
Fax: (0)5 62 98 15 08

The Hindu greeting *namaste* for a name, star-spangled, moonstruck beams and furniture — there are exotic touches here. Architecture buffs will like the impressive barn with walls containing sections of the original earth construction. The Fontaines have spent two years restoring their lime-rendered C18 farmhouse, polishing wooden floors and creating a balance between traditional and modern. The guestrooms both have doors leading to semi-secluded corners of the garden. In cold weather, enjoy the comfortable *salon's* huge open fire.

Rooms: 1 quadruple with bath & wc, 1 triple with shower & wc.

Price: 270 Frs for two, including breakfast.

Meals: 95 Frs, including wine.

Open: All year.

From A64 exit 16 onto D939 through Lannemezan to Galan. From village square/church, take Rue de la Baïse towards Recurt — house 500m on left.

Map No: 15   MM 234-40

Jean & Danièle FONTAINE
Namaste
13 rue de la Baïse
65330 Galan
Hautes-Pyrénées
Tel: (0)5 62 99 77 81

Cedar and sequoia shade this imposing 400-year-old house. The large bedrooms, with old, uneven, stained wooden floors and curtained 4-posters, have regal titles and modern bathrooms. Buffet breakfast and formal dinner are at separate tables set with silver, linen and candelabras. Besides restoring house and garden (including a French-style kitchen garden), Monsieur's passions are computers (games for children), music (he has an excellent CD collection) and receiving guests. Rafting and canoeing close by.

Rooms: 3 double, 1 triple, all with bath or shower & wc (one behind curtain).

Price: 320 Frs for two, including breakfast.

Meals: 130 Frs, including aperitif, wine & coffee.

Open: All year.

children

From Pau D938/937 for 31km towards Lourdes. In St Pé, facing 'Mairie', take road to its right — house 50m up on right.

Map No: 15   MM 234-39

Christian PETERS
Le Grand Cèdre
6 rue du Barry
65270 Saint-Pé-de-Bigorre
Hautes-Pyrénées
Tel: (0)5 62 41 82 04
Fax: (0)5 62 41 85 89
e-mail: grand.cedre@sudfr.com

The rooms are indeed in the chateau's converted stables and are furnished so simply that there's almost a monastic feel. Carefully-chosen Indian dhurries and furniture spirited out of the château where Madame grew up add an extra dash of style. Breakfast is served in the kitchen, dinner in the dining-room and Madame is a delightful, unbusinesslike, charmingly scatty hostess who unleashes an endearing giggle. There is a huge guests' dayroom and one room especially equipped for wheelchair users.

Rooms: 1 triple, 1 double, 2 twin, all with shower or bath & wc.

Price: 290 Frs for two, including breakfast.

Meals: 80 Frs, including wine & coffee.

Open: All year.

Tostat is 13km north of Tarbes on D8. House is in village centre.

Map No: 15   MM 234-36

Catherine RIVIÈRE D'ARC
Les Écuries du Château
65140 Tostat
Hautes-Pyrénées
Tel: (0)5 62 31 23 27/19 83

Steve owned a restaurant in London and cooks beautifully; Kris has been in the theatre; he and Steve are a creative couple and most engaging company. Their remote mill, in this region of small, scattered farms, has been restored with great taste; the stream running round the house attracts lots of wildlife and the gardens ramble through quiet patios. Inside, you find white walls, exposed timbers, simple, natural wood furniture and oriental rugs that impart a stylish warmth. Ideal for their occasional meditation workshops too.

Rooms: 1 double & 1 triple sharing shower & wc; 2 triple with own shower & wc.

Price: 225 Frs for two, including breakfast.

Meals: 80 Frs, including wine & coffee.

Open: All year.

From Toulouse N117 to Boussens then D635 to the edge of Aurignac and D8 towards Samouillan, then D96; signposted.

Map No: 15   MM 235-37

Stephen CALLEN & Kris
MISSELBROOK
Le Moulin
Samouillan
31420 Aurignac
Haute-Garonne
Tel: (0)5 61 98 86 92
Fax: (0)5 61 98 86 92

Conspicuously set in flat farmlands, the Carrière family seat, designed by Guillaume Cammas who also 'did' the Toulouse Capitole, has a magnificent hall, hung with family portraits, whence you sweep up to the vast *salon* for your aperitif. The affable and disarmingly unpretentious Baroness is happy to describe the many paintings and antiques while serving her guests. Guestrooms are high-ceilinged with more pictures, books, silk screens, views. Make sure you are expected as the entrance gate is locked.

Rooms: 4 double, each with bath or shower & wc; 2 extra beds available.

Price: 400 Frs for two, including breakfast.

Meals: 130 Frs, including wine & coffee.

Open: Easter to October.

In an area with few places to stay, this *auberge* has simple, rustic, comfortable rooms with curtained shower rooms and lovely views. Much of the almost entirely wooden house dates from 1769 and has the non-perpendicular features you might expect. On the outskirts of a pretty hamlet, it uses some of its produce for the food, which is excellent value and typically includes vegetable soup, homemade *pâté* and big country omelettes. Vegetarian fare too. Annie and her family are helpful, if a little reserved.

Rooms: 1 quadruple, 1 triple, each with shower & wc.

Price: 220 Frs for two, including breakfast.

Meals: From 65 Frs, including wine & coffee.

Open: All year.

From Toulouse, D1 towards Aéroport Cornebarrieu; stay on D1 until St Paul then D87 right to Larra.

Map No: 15   MM 235-26

Baronne Brigitte de CARRIÈRE
Château de Larra
31330 Grenade-sur-Garonne
Haute-Garonne
Tel: (0)5 61 82 62 51

From Toulouse, D632 towards Tarbes. After 75km, right on D90 to Péguilhan; auberge is on left before village.

Map No: 15   MM 235-33

Annie & Sabine CASTEX
Ferme-Auberge de Péguilhan
31350 Péguilhan
Haute-Garonne
Tel: (0)5 61 88 75 78

Your host sometimes feels that restoring his former abbey hospital is a life's work, but no matter, he takes great pride in the task. The place oozes atmosphere and history and one feels privileged to walk in its soothing cloister and imagine one is hearing its ancient chants. The guestrooms are in fact the two gîtes in the grounds that have been restored with consummate skill, patience and taste. Christophe is a woodworker and furniture designer who also organises cabinet-making and dance workshops in the summer.

Rooms: 2 double rooms with shared bathroom.

Price: 220 Frs for two, including breakfast.

Meals: 75 Frs, including wine & coffee.

Open: All year.

Gîtes for 13 people

Madame has been praised for her warm and genuine interest in people, manifested with "a mix of the formidable and the lovable, the dignified and the mischievous". In an elegant house full of old pictures, books, comfortable chairs and antiques, her visitors are immersed in the French way of life and sleep in beautiful rooms with views across the green oaks. Step out on a warm morning and enjoy your breakfast — often with homemade cakes — in the large, lush garden. When the temperature soars head for those oaks. Lake and tennis court next door.

Rooms: 2 double, 2 twin, all with bath or shower & wc.

Price: 400 Frs for two, including breakfast.

Meals: Restaurant 4km.

Open: All year.

From Toulouse, N117 to Boussens. There, D365 towards Aurignac. In Le Frechet, follow signpost 'N.D. de Lorette'.

Map No: 15   MM 235-37

Christophe FERRY
Notre-Dame de Lorette
31420 Alan
Haute-Garonne
Tel: (0)5 61 98 98 84/94 58 (Engl)
Fax: (0)5 61 98 98 84

From Toulouse A68 towards Albi exit 3 for Montastruc-la-C. onto D30 towards Lavaur for 4.5km; turn right (before Montpitol) & follow signs.

Map No: 16   MM 235-30

Claudette FIEUX
Stoupignan
31380 Montpitol
Haute-Garonne
Tel: (0)5 61 84 22 02
Fax: (0)5 61 84 22 02

"The house of joy," is how Inge likes to describe her home, a fine old house with stables deep in the woods beside a stream. Forget about work, relax in the arms of Nature, fish, ride, paint — Inge will give you lessons. Passionate about horses, she trains her own and horse-keeping definitely takes priority over house-keeping. She serves good food in the pretty hall (the dining-room only seats four) and offers light, eclectically-decorated, long-bedded rooms with separate bathrooms. Lovely garden to explore.

Rooms: 4 double, each with bath or shower & wc.

Price: 200, 250 or 280 Frs for two, including breakfast.

Meals: 80 Frs, excluding wine.

Open: All year.

Gerard taught philosophy and Chantal taught English, hence the well-stocked library. They love music, too. The hous was recently a working farm: the hay loft, bread-oven and well are still there and a huge inglenook with all the expected oak beams and a nail where Grandma hung her money hidden among the washing. A large terrace overlooks the hills (kites available); a grassy courtyard has a barbecue, table tennis and homemade exercise machines. No antiques, but we loved it for its unpretentious simplicity.

Rooms: 2 triple, 1 twin, 1 double + bunk, each with bath or shower & wc.

Price: 250 Frs for two, including breakfast. Extra person 50 Frs.

Meals: 75 Frs, including wine.

Open: All year.

From Boulogne-sur-Gesse, D635 towards St Gaudens & Ciadoux. After about 7km, fork left towards Ciadoux; after a few metres, left down small private road; house on right.

Map No: 15   MM 234-36

Ingeborg ROEHRIG
Ciadoux
31350 Boulogne-sur-Gesse
Tarn-et-Garonne
Tel: (0)5 61 88 10 88

From A68 exit 3 to Montastruc then onto D30 towards Lavaur for 5km. Left on D30c to Azas; through village for about 2km; signposted towards Garrigue (D22g).

Map No: 16   MM 235-26

Chantal & Gérard ZABÉ
En Tristan
31380 Azas
Haute-Garonne
Tel: (0)5 61 84 94 88
Fax: (0)5 61 84 94 88

Hiding at a remote edge of the world, a restored farmhouse with lots of beams, white walls and a big fireplace, set 1000 feet up on 45 hectares of woodland looking out over the valley. Walk or ride straight into the Pyrenean foothills or go on one of Bob's picnics. The highly entertaining Dutch owners raise horses and Newfoundland dogs. They will regale you, in several languages, with stories of sailing the Atlantic or the Caribbean: don't miss dining with them. Superb value and " the best breakfast in France". Pets by arrangement.

Rooms: 1 double, 1 twin, 2 triple, all with shower & wc.

Price: 220 Frs for two, including breakfast. Book early.

Meals: 70 Frs, including wine.

Open: Mid-March to mid-November.

Gîtes for 10 people

People come just to look for one type of orchid or bird, although Nick lists about 200 different birds sighted and over 50 orchids. He is a fauna and flora guide, so knows his stuff, and Julie is a midwife. They are in a three-house hamlet with breathtaking views up to the mountains and across miles of fields, farms, forests and valleys; it is ineffably lovely. The house has been totally renovated, is simple with smallish rooms, and has a cosy family living-room. They'll pick you up from the airport as part of a week's package.

Rooms: 2 double, 1 twin, each with shower & wc.

Price: 240 Frs for two, including breakfast.

Meals: 85 Frs, including wine.

Open: All year.

From Foix, D17 towards Col de Marrous. After 8km, in La Mouline; signposted up 1.5km unmade track.

Map No: 16   MM 235-42

Bob et Jenny BROGNEAUX
Le Poulsieu
Serres-sur-Arget
09000 Foix
Ariège
Tel: (0)5 61 02 77 72
Fax: (0)5 61 02 77 72

From St Girons D117 E for 7km. Just before fork for Mas d'Azil see Chambres d'Hôtes sign on left. Follow signs up this tiny, metalled track for 2km.

Map No: 15   MM 235-42

Nick & Julie GOLDSWORTHY
La Baquette
Lescure
09420 Rimont
Ariège
Tel: (0)5 61 96 37 67
Fax: (0)5 61 96 37 67

An isolated renovated farmhouse/ hamlet that looks towards the Pyrenees. The artistic among you may care to plan your stay during one of Madame's weekend art courses. You could stop a while, forget the maps and itinerary — you are in a world of ceramics, watercolours, weaving or sculpture. The rooms feel right, light, not over-decorated and adorned with Dutch Jeanne's handiwork. Guests have their own living-room and kitchen facilities but dinner — cooked rather well by Guy — is served *en famille*.

Rooms: 1 double, 2 triple, each with bath or shower & wc.

Price: 230-250 Frs for two, including breakfast.

Meals: 90 Frs, including wine & coffee.

Open: All year.

Gîtes for 9 people

Driving up the majestic avenue to this imposing house, you understand why the Spanish president took up residence here while on official business. The owners and abode are as charming as each other and good-natured laughter comes easily (Madame teaches English). Rooms fit for VIPs — maybe a *chaise-longue*, a canopied bed and a bathroom big enough for a game of *pétanque* — are reached by a wooden spiral staircase. A banquet of a breakfast (drop scones, *crêpes*, homemade bread and jam) is as delectable as dinner.

Rooms: 3 suites with bath & wc.

Price: 350 Frs for two, including breakfast. Extra bed 100 Frs.

Meals: 150 Frs, including aperitif, wine & coffee.

Open: May to October.

From Belpech take road behind public gardens towards Gaudies. After 4km, at crossroads, left following Chambres d'Hôtes signposts.

Map No: 16   MM 235-38

Jeanne & Guy GOSSELIN
Certes
09700 Gaudies
Ariège
Tel: (0)5 61 67 01 56
Fax: (0)5 61 67 42 30

From Foix D919 to Loubens. There turn right at signs for Château.

Map No: 16   MM 235-42

Michel Pierre LELONG
Château de Loubens
09120 Loubens
Ariège
Tel: (0)5 61 05 38 41
Fax: (0)5 61 05 30 61

Your hosts have moved on from their hippy days of communes into sharing in a rather more organised way. Over 25 years of renovation have made this rural idyll what it is today. Dine *en famille* in a huge living/dining room (village dances were organised here!) and share the Loizances' local knowledge — you may even be treated to their charming daughter's range of magic tricks. Walk in summer or cross-country ski in winter. A home with real heart.

Rooms: 3 double, 1 triple, all with own shower & wc.

Price: 220 Frs for two, including breakfast.

Meals: 70 Frs, including wine & coffee.

Open: All year.

You don't have to like horses to enjoy yourself here, but if you do you'll love it! Guests stay in an independent ivy-clad house at this riding centre perched 1750 feet up in the Pyrenees. A spiral wooden staircase leads from a cosy living-room (with fires in winter) to clean, simple rooms with stone walls and pine furniture (plus more basic rooms for groups of up to 19). Spectacular views and plenty of invigorating walks for those who prefer to use Shanks's pony. Children made very welcome by the warm, friendly and relaxed hosts.

Rooms: 2 double, 2 twin, all with bath or shower & wc.

Price: 180-190 Frs for two, including breakfast.

Meals: 60 Frs, including wine & coffee.

Open: All year.

From Foix D17 towards Col-des-Marrous for 15km. 'Hameau de Madranque' signposted on right.

Map No: 16   MM 235-42

Birgit & Jean-Claude LOIZANCE
Madranque
09000 Le Bosc
Ariège
Tel: (0)5 61 02 71 29

From Foix, D617 towards St Martin-de-Caralp. Turn left onto D145 and left again onto D11. Cantegril is on the left.

Map No: 16   MM 235-42

Mlle Élisabeth PAGÈS
Ecole d'Equitation de Cantegril
09000 Saint-Martin-de-Caralp
Ariège
Tel: (0)5 61 65 15 43
Fax: (0)5 61 02 96 86

This old mill in its magical valley was once a *cloutier* (nails were made here) but the beds are made of softer stuff and the water rushing past outside will lull you to sleep. The room isn't large but there's a lovely terrace and you'll want to be out by the stream anyway, catching trout in the right season. Your hosts will gladly harness up their horse and cart to take you for a day trip in the mountains with picnic lunch on board. Magnificent setting. Small pets welcome and there's a little cooking place you can use.

Rooms: 1 twin with shower & wc. Extra bed available. Kitchenette.

Price: 190 Frs for two, including breakfast.

Meals: 70 Frs, including wine & coffee.

Open: All year.

Gîtes for 4 people

A friendly reception is guaranteed from your elderly hosts in their long, low, home. The most memorable features are the greenery, the riot of flowers all around the south-facing terrace and the sound of water in the background. The room for guests has an immaculate new bed, a mass of books, and central heating. The Orient Express loo on the landing will appeal to train buffs. There's good wine — Monsieur will ask you to choose — with the homely dinners (sometimes *en famille*).

Rooms: 1 double room with shower, sharing wc.

Price: 200 Frs for two, including breakfast.

Meals: 80 Frs, including wine & coffee.

Open: Mid-April to mid-October.

From Foix, D21 to Ganac. After 5km take route to Micou 'Les Carcis'. Right just after small bridge.

Map No: 16   MM 235-42

Sylviane PIEDNOËL & Guy DROUET
Les Carcis
09000 Ganac
Ariège
Tel: (0)5 61 02 96 54

From Tarascon, D618 towards Massat. 3km after Saurat turn right. Chambres d'Hôtes signposted.

Map No: 16   MM 235-46

Roger & Monique ROBERT
Layrole
09400 Saurat
Ariège
Tel: (0)5 61 05 73 24

Set in a mountain valley, this sociable older couple's home reminds one of a Swiss chalet. It is as neatly kept as an English boarding house with a garden full of buddleia and hydrangea. He is Dutch and great fun; she is Norman and more serious; both enjoy good conversation. The guestrooms (one with a small sitting area) are traditional in style, with modern bathrooms. In winter, the huge breakfasts set you up for skiing. In summer you can barbecue in the flower garden.

Rooms: 1 double, 1 twin, each with shower or bath, sharing wc.

Price: 230 Frs for two, including breakfast.

Meals: Good choice in Tarascon.

Open: All year.

To buy another antique or dig the turf? Olivier loves his small-holding but the house is witness to his eclectic taste in 'old pieces'. The leitmotif in the main guestroom is *la mer:* there are literally dozens of sea paintings, adding an oceanic touch to the mostly antique furnishings. Don't miss dinner (not always available); Mireille's regional cooking is inspired. A relaxed, simple and happy home — and family (with the inevitable dogs and cats) — and a perfect place to take the children.

Rooms: 1 double + 1 single, sharing bathroom (for a family).

Price: 240 Frs for two, including breakfast (reduction 3 nights).

Meals: 75-90 Frs, including wine & coffee (reservation only).

Open: All year.

Gites for 10 people

From Tarascon-sur-Ariège take D8. Follow signpost to Capoulet Junac and B&B is on left.

Map No: 16   MM 234-35

Pierre & Yvonne VAN HOORN
Capoulet Junac
09400 Tarascon-sur-Ariège
Ariège
Tel: (0)5 61 05 89 88

From Auch N21 towards Tarbes for 2km then left on D929 towards Lannemezan. In Masseube, left towards Simorre for 4 km then left towards Bellegarde. House first turning on left.

Map No: 15   MM 234-36

Mireille & Olivier COUROUBLE
La Garenne
Bellegarde
32140 Masseube
Gers
Tel: (0)5 62 66 03 61
Fax: (0)5 62 66 03 61

Revolutionaries destroyed the local château but some of the stone was put to good use here (superb steps). It is a big, solid old farmhouse owned by genial English folk (ex-Ghurkas) who have made it extremely comfortable: roll-top baths, gold taps, crystal at dinner. Bedrooms ('Dragon' or 'Himalayan') have crisp linen, good beds, some antiques and colonial comfort. Definitely not French but a splendid house in a fine setting and lots of luxury if you want curry with your home-made chutney and a good night's sleep.

Rooms: 1 suite for 4, 1 double, 1 twin, each with bath, shower & wc.

Price: 500-600 Frs for two, including breakfast.

Meals: 180 Frs, including wine & coffee.

Open: All year except 2 weeks Dec-Jan.

From Auch N124 W dir. Vic-Fézenac for 5km; left on D943 through Barran, Montesquiou, Bassoues. After Bassoues follow D943 LEFT dir. Marciac. Scieurac-Flourès signed off this road. In village bend left by church; house first on right.

Map No: 15   MM 234-32

Michael & Christine FURNEY
Setzères
Scieurac-et-Flourès
32230 Marciac
Gers
Tel: (0)5 62 08 21 45
Fax: (0)5 62 08 21 45

This is a real working farm rearing capons and beef cattle and the house has plenty of French *paysan* warmth. Breakfast is at a long table before a huge open hearth and there's a kitchen area where guests can cook if they like. It is all down-to-earth and clean with proper country charm. The bedrooms, which open onto the balcony overlooking the courtyard, have nice old rickety wooden floors and some endearing features like Granny's wedding furniture. Secluded setting amidst grain fields and pastures.

Rooms: 1 double, 1 triple, 1 suite ideal for families, each with own bathroom.

Price: 220 Frs for two, including breakfast.

Meals: Self-catering facilities.

Open: All year.

From Auch, N21 towards Tarbes. 6km after Mirande, house signposted on left.

Map No: 15   MM 234-32

Louis & Marthe SABATHIER
Noailles
32300 Saint-Maur
Gers
Tel: (0)5 62 67 57 98

We hope for feedback about this simple, good-value house. The ground-floor rooms are modern in chalet style, a shade cramped; upstairs there are balconies but still a cramped feeling and sharing a wc. Decor generally heavy floral, with dark modern furniture, polyester sheets. Red vinyl chairs in the dining room. Good regional cooking; they make *foie gras* and *confits* for a living. There is a campsite behind the house and a gite across the yard, but the dining table is for B&B guests only.

Rooms: 2 double, each with shower & wc; 2 triple, each with shower in room + 1 triple with bathroom in corridor, all 3 sharing wc.

Price: 200 Frs for two, including breakfast.

Meals: 100 Frs, including wine & coffee.

Open: All year except November.

Gîtes for 6 people

The best reason for being here is the Gorges de l'Aveyron — a paradise of clear water, cliffs, wildlife, canoeing and wild scenery. Johnny and Véronique, suitably, are sports teachers — all tan and dynamism. They have renovated their house beyond the constraints of its origins — its rooms are simple, modern and functional, with little that is memorable or quintessentially French. But the food is good and generous and so are your friendly hosts. Very busy in summer so don't expect family intimacy then.

Rooms: 2 double & 3 twin, each with bath or shower & wc.

Price: 260-310 Frs for two, including breakfast.

Meals: 100 Frs, including wine & coffee (book ahead).

Open: All year.

From Condom, D7 towards Lectoure. After Caussens, right onto D204; signposted for 2km.

Map No: 15   MM 234-24

Robert VIGNAUX
Bordeneuve
Béraut
32100 Condom
Gers
Tel: (0)5 62 28 08 41

From Cahors, N20 to Caussade then D964 towards Gaillac. At Montricoux, D115 towards Nègrepelisse; after 500m, signposted.

Map No: 16   MM 235-22

Johnny & Véronique ANTONY
Les Brunis
82800 Nègrepelisse
Tarn-et-Garonne
Tel: (0)5 63 67 24 08
Fax: (0)5 63 67 24 08

Once a hunting lodge, it still has its own pigeon tower — the luckless bird often features at meals. Rooms are huge and high-ceilinged, the main bedroom decorated with a seamless panorama of hunting scenes from the famous Zubert paper factory. The *salon* has a massive open fire, always a treat, and the pool is lovely. The house is stuffed with *objets*: copper pots, forge bellows, ivories, African trinkets; a few garish touches, perhaps, but your hosts are interesting, well-travelled conversationalists. Quite an experience.

Rooms: 1 double, 1 twin & 1 suite for 4, each with bath & wc.

Price: 350-500 Frs for two, including breakfast.

Meals: 150 Frs, including aperitif, wine & coffee.

Open: All year.

From A62, Valence d'Agen exit onto D953 through Valence & towards Cahors. After Lalande, left on D46. House is after main square in Castelsagrat; signposted.

Map No: 15   MM 235-17

Georges & Danielle CLÉMENT
Le Castel
82400 Castelsagrat
Tarn-et-Garonne
Tel: (0)5 63 94 20 55
Fax: (0)5 63 94 20 55

An exceptional working farm/B&B where quiet Gilbert will take you egg-hunting or goose-feeding of a morning. Smiling, big-hearted Michèle has won prizes for her recipes, invents sauces, makes her own aperitif. Rooms are comfortable (beware waist-low beams) but food is definitely the priority here. Fishing rods on loan to use in the pond; footpaths out from the gate; proper hiking trails a bit further away; the treasures of Moissac, lovely villages, caves, are within easy reach. Well-behaved children and small pets welcome.

Rooms: 1 double, 1 twin, each with shower & wc. Extra beds available.

Price: 240 Frs for two, including breakfast.

Meals: 90 Frs, including wine & coffee.

Open: All year.

Gites for 4 people

From Moissac, D7 towards Bourg-de-Visa about 14km. Before Brassac and just before a bridge, right towards Fauroux. Farm 2km along; signposted.

Map No: 15   MM 235-17

Gilbert & Michèle DIO
La Marquise
Brassac
82190 Bourg-de-Visa
Tarn-et-Garonne
Tel: (0)5 63 94 25 16

The Hunts are agreeable, relaxed hosts. The distinctive feature of their farmhouse is the *Quercy blanc* stone which so kindly sets off the fresh blue of the shutters. The setting is tranquil, wooded grounds with sweeping views and there's a huge, artificial lake and beach quite close. Comfortably worn-around-the-edges, the rooms vary in size and have smallish shower rooms — the ones over the courtyard were our favourites. Children will enjoy the badminton, ping-pong and pool. This is good value.

Rooms: 1 double, 2 twin, 2 family rooms for 3/4, each with shower & wc.

Price: 180-230 Frs for two, including breakfast.

Meals: 70 Frs, including wine & coffee. Under 2s free.

Open: All year.

Gîtes for 2 people

It's hard to find fault here! The rooms could grace the pages of a magazine — lovely prints, old wardrobes, terracotta tiles. All is fresh, light and a happy marriage of old and new. Varied breakfasts and delicious dinners — regional and exotic dishes and an excellent cheeseboard. Sunflowers, farmland and a dreamy hamlet surround the 19th-century farmhouse which has been lovingly restored by its present owners, a Franco-Dutch family who enjoy sharing their summers here with guests. Not to be missed!

Rooms: 1 suite for 2-4 & 1 double, each with shower & wc.

Price: 250 Frs for two, including breakfast.

Meals: 85 Frs, including wine & coffee.

Open: July & August.

On 'Bis' route half way between Périgueux and Toulouse. Sign 'Chambres d'Hôtes' on D2, 5km south of Montaigu-de-Quercy.

Map No: 15   MM 235-13

Arthur & Deborah HUNT
Les Chênes de Sainte Croix
82150 Montaigu-de-Quercy
Tarn-et-Garonne
Tel: (0)5 63 95 30 78
Fax: (0)5 63 95 30 78

From Agen, A62 east, exit 8 towards Gramont. After Mansonville, follow signs to Lachapelle; house on right on entering village.

Map No: 15   MM 235-21

M & Mme VAN DEN BRINK
Au Village
82120 Lachapelle
Tarn-et-Garonne
Tel: (0)5 63 94 14 10 or
        (0)1 39 49 07 37

You are woken by a (relatively) unobtrusive cockerel... an authentic rural touch. There are others: Grandma squelching around the farm in her wellies, an old pigeon tower, pigs, ducks, rabbits and turkeys, grain silos on view and the glow of a distant nuclear reactor at night. The house is part 14th-century but the rooms are in a modern extension, nothing special but quite adequate. It is altogether a down-to-earth, friendly place... a genuine French small-holding and well worth experiencing.

Rooms: 2 double, 1 triple, 1 quadruple, each with shower & wc.

Price: 230 Frs for two, including breakfast. Extra person 60 Frs.

Meals: 85 Frs, including aperitif, wine & coffee. Under 4s free; 4-10 yrs 55 Frs.

Open: April to October.

Coffee in a bowl — and you feel you've found the 'real' France. This is a working farm with roaming chickens, ducks and pigs. Dinner is uncompromisingly, deliciously 'farmhouse' with portions suitable for a farmer returning from a hard day's work. Madame greeted us from the milking shed, her hands dripping with the evidence; she and her husband, both lively and empathetic, share their home easily, without fuss. The guests' rustic, cluttered dayroom has a dining table and open fire; bedrooms are simply furnished and pleasing.

Rooms: 1 double, 1 suite, both with shower & wc.

Price: 210 Frs for two, including breakfast.

Meals: 80 Frs, including wine & coffee.

Open: All year.

From A62 exit 8 onto D953 S dir. Château de Gramont for 1.5km then fork left on D88, same direction. 3km before Gramont left following La Ferme des Garbès signs.

Map No: 15   MM 235-21

Simone VARGAS & Patrice GAILLARD
Ferme des Garbès
82120 Gramont
Lot-et-Garonne
Tel: (0)5 63 94 07 81

N20 south from Cahors to Caussade. Left on D926 through Septfonds. 3km beyond, left towards Gaussou. Farm is 1km on, signposted.

Map No: 16   MM 235-18

Françoise & Jean-Louis ZAMBONI
Ferme du Gendre
82240 Lavaurette
Tarn-et-Garonne
Tel: (0)5 63 31 97 72

This ancient *ferme-auberge* combines austerity and comfort to suit both backpacker and motorist: rooms like Fra Angelico's cells, views that go on forever with maybe an eagle circling, a swimming hole in the dammed river, owners who also raise animals and are passionate about their mountains. Sunday lunch (Catalan and French) is a riotously convivial affair; everything except the bread is home-made or home-grown and served by the two teenage children before a magnificent stone fireplace. Exceptional!

Rooms: 4 triple, 1 quadruple, 1 double, each with shower & wc.

Price: 290 Frs for two, including breakfast.

Meals: 100 Frs, including aperitif, wine & coffee.

Open: Mid-March to mid-Nov.

On French-Spanish border. From A9 exit 43 onto D115 W through Prats de Mollo and 10km beyond to Col d'Arès. Farm on left.

Map No: 16   MM 235-56

Roussillon – Languedoc – Cévennes

Michelle & Gilbert LANAU
Ferme Auberge La Costa de Dalt
Route du Col d'Arès
66230 Prats de Mollo
Pyrénées-Orientales
Tel: (0)4 68 39 74 40
Fax: (0)4 68 39 74 40

A delightful couple of ex-chamber musicians live in this quiet valley so close to Matisse's beloved Collioure — you can see the Mediterranean from the shady garden. The rooms are light and large, there's a superb electronic music machine in the sitting area and a lovely pool outside. Jane and Ian, "super folk", can arrange visits to local *vignerons*; they also serve local aperitifs and wines with delicious dinners. Many are lured here by the sea but inland treasures — cloisters, Cathar castles, mountain walks, trips to Spain — will seduce you too.

Rooms: 2 double & 1 twin, 1 triple, 1 family, all with shower or bath & wc.

Price: 295 Frs for two, including breakfast.

Meals: 95 Frs, including aperitif, wine & coffee. 150 Frs wine-tasting menu.

Open: All year.

Louis and Chantal are young farmers — they grow organic kiwis — who have gradually converted this old farmhouse to provide six large functional guestrooms. Floors are tiled throughout for coolness; furnishings are simple — almost basic — and practical; showers are small and modern. Dine on Chantal's excellent Catalan cuisine beneath the kiwi trees (there may be 20-odd guests at table), share a joke with your good-natured host, enjoy his spontaneous approach to running his B&B... and see the Pyrenees.

Rooms: 5 double & 1 suite, all with shower & wc.

Price: 210 Frs for two, including breakfast.

Meals: 80 Frs, including aperitif & wine.

Open: All year.

From A9 exit Perpignan Sud towards Thuir. At entrance to Thuir, towards Elne for 2km then right towards Céret for 5.5km to Fourques. There, right onto D2 to Caixas (11km) then follow Mairie/Eglise. In Caixas, house is next to church.

Map No: 16   MM 235-52

Jane RICHARDS & Ian MAYES
Mas Saint Jacques
66300 Caixas
Pyrénées-Orientales
Tel: (0)4 68 38 87 83
Fax: (0)4 68 38 87 83
e-mail: MasStJacq@aol.com

From Perpignan, N114 to Elne. In village take D612 to Bages; signs after 500-600m.

Map No: 16   MM 235-52

Louis & Chantal TUBERT
Mas de la Couloumine
Route de Bages
66200 Elne
Pyrénées-Orientales
Tel: (0)4 68 22 36 07

Strange demonstrative architecture in the middle of the humble Aude vineyards, and the decor is flock-based too... There's plenty to occupy you — billiards, ping-pong and a pool, not to mention the surrounding countryside nursing the secrets of its Cathar past. Homemade food and estate wine for dinner but not *en famille*: don't expect a home-from-home experience despite the gorgeous baby boy. Spotless rooms, new bedding, but towels and hospitality may seem measured, according to one reader — do let us know.

Rooms: 4 double, 1 twin with bathrooms.

Price: 280 Frs for two, including breakfast.

Meals: 140 Frs, including wine & coffee.

Open: 1 April to 30 September.

From Carcassonne, N113 to Trèbes then D610 towards Béziers. On entering Puichéric, left towards Rieux & follow signs.

Map No: 16   MM 235-40

Claude BERGÉ
Château de Saint-Aunay
11700 Puichéric
Aude
Tel: (0)4 68 43 72 20
Fax: (0)4 68 43 76 72

You could never feel cramped in this C19 gentleman farmer's house and there's space to hide in bad weather — the finely-furnished study is a highly civilised refuge while the bedrooms are so vast that the (fairly basic) furniture looks almost lost. Madame, open and welcoming, chats to guests in her attractive kitchen/dining-room and enjoys their travellers' tales. Her freshly-decorated house is full of character (and new mattresses) and the huge, restful park beckons, as do nearby Carcassonne, the Canal du Midi, and the vineyards.

Rooms: 1 double, 1 triple, 1 suite for 4/5, each with shower & wc.

Price: 280-350 Frs for two, including breakfast. Extra person 85 Frs.

Meals: 95 Frs, including wine. Under 10s: 65 Frs.

Open: All year.

Gîtes for 5 people

From Carcassonne D119 E for 6km then left at sign for Alairac onto barely tarmacked track. House is 500m on right.

Map No: 16   MM 235-39

Isabelle CLAYETTE
Domaine des Castelles
11170 Caux-et-Sauzens
Aude
Tel: (0)4 68 72 03 60
Fax: (0)4 68 72 03 60

This beautifully-converted farmhouse rejoices in huge beams, an open fireplace and impeccable taste throughout. There are five pretty rooms to choose from (one for the disabled), utter quiet to relax into and wonderful walks. Your hosts revel in their area, its birdlife, wild flowers, history and wine. They have lovely children and even give language courses in winter. Superb meals made with local produce are served in the enormous dining-room or outside. And all this just 5km from Carcassonne.

Rooms: 3 double, 1 twin, 1 triple, all with bath or shower & wc.

Price: 325-370 Frs for two, including breakfast. 2 nights min. July & August.

Meals: By arrangement 130 Frs, including wine and coffee.

Open: All year.

The rooms are all named after Cathar castles and are ordered rather than cosy. The cool impression of alarm clocks and televisions is dispelled by the warm personal attention to your needs and the huge library of 1,000 books, many on the Cathars. Breakfast is hearty, with up to four types of bread, honey, cheese, homemade cakes and 6 homemade jams. Supper could be grilled salmon with lemon sauce and Madame's *crème caramel*. Nearby is the fortified city of Carcassonne, also Foix and Mirepoix. Wonderful setting.

Rooms: 2 double, 1 twin, each with shower & wc (+ children's room).

Price: 320-340 Frs for two, including breakfast. Extra bed 80 Frs.

Meals: 110 Frs, including aperitif, wine & coffee.

Open: Easter to October.

From Carcassonne, D142 to Cazilhac. Left in front of 'Mairie' on D56 towards Villefloure (bear left at cemetery). La Sauzette signposted to left after 2km.

Map No: 16   MM 235-39

Chris GIBSON & Diana WARREN
Ferme de la Sauzette
Route de Villefloure, Cazilhac
11570 Palaja
Aude
Tel: (0)4 68 79 81 32
Fax: (0)4 68 79 65 99

From Limoux D620 towards Chalabre for 7km then fork right on D626 to Peyrefitte. Signposted from village.

Map No: 16   MM 235-43

Jean-Pierre & Marie-Claire ROPERS
Domaine de Couchet
11230 Peyrefitte-du-Razès
Aude
Tel: (0)4 68 69 55 06
Fax: (0)4 68 69 55 06

Your hosts' families have lived in the village for generations — Jacques used to attend classes in Saint-Jérôme, once his school now his (thoroughly modernised) home, and they are deeply rooted in the agricultural lore and practice of their area. Jacques is big-hearted and enthuses about his food, which has earned a place in the local top ten guide. The decor and smallish bedrooms are fairly banal but the welcome is hugely generous. There is also a small camping site.

Rooms: 1 double, 1 twin, one with shower & wc, one with shower sharing wc.

Price: 225 Frs for two, including breakfast.

Meals: 70 Frs, including wine & coffee.

Open: All year.

A sense of refined luxury, even opulence, pervades this beautifully-restored house where 43 large ebony beams, brought from Madagascar as repatriation luggage when the family moved back..., were used for the job. There is a happy, humorous family atmosphere with many traces of those years on exotic shores, in the cooking as well as the bathrooms. The large, pretty bedrooms are immaculate, the people most unusual, both refined and down-to-earth, country-comfortable and artistic. (If they haven't heard from you by 8pm they may re-let the room.)

Rooms: 1 double, 1 twin, both with bath or shower & wc.

Price: 250 Frs for two, including breakfast.

Meals: 95 Frs, including wine & coffee.

Open: All year.

small

From Gaillac, D964 towards Castelnau-de-Montmirail. There, turn off for Les Barrières and follow sign for Chambres d'Hotes. House next to the church.

Map No: 16   MM 235-22

Jacques & Huguette CAMALET
Saint-Jérôme
81140 Castelnau-de-Montmirail
Tarn
Tel: (0)5 63 33 10 09

From Rabastens, D12 towards Coufouleux. Cross river Tarn then immediately left on D13 towards Loupiac. Just before village right by cemetery; skirt cemetery taking right fork & follow signs for La Bonde 1km.

Map No: 16   MM 235-26

Maurice & Bernadette CRÉTÉ
La Bonde-Loupiac
81800 Rabastens
Tarn
Tel: (0)5 63 33 82 83
Fax: (0)5 63 57 46 54

The sort of home we all dream of — on a hill in a beautiful corner of the Tarn, approached by an avenue of old oaks. Your heart will stir to the beauty of home and setting — and the startlingly-positioned pool. Huge dayrooms, heavy ancient doors, beams and open fires and some Louis XIII furniture. One of the rooms is richly furnished with a bathroom in the tower, the other is brighter, simpler, Mediterranean-inspired — both are worthy of the praise heaped upon them by visitors. And equally elegant, civilised hosts.

Rooms: 2 double, each with bath or shower & wc.

Price: 275 Frs for two, including breakfast. 2 nights min. July/Aug.

Meals: 3 restaurants in village. Mini-kitchen for hire in summer.

Open: All year (bookings only Oct-April).

We've had mixed reports about Le Fourchat, run by a mother-and-daughter team. Our inspectors have waxed quite lyrical about the delicious meals and the welcome they've received when visiting anonymously. Homemade bread and lots of homegrown fruit and vegetables. However, the rooms are all alike, slightly soulless, arranged in a row above a living-room in a converted barn But they are in a lovely, wild, undiscovered area, well off the beaten track and great for kids.

Rooms: 3 double and 2 twin, all with own shower & wc.

Price: 200 Frs for two, including breakfast.

Meals: 70 Frs, including wine (book ahead).

Open: All year.

Gîtes for 4 people

From Gaillac D964 towards Caussade. 4km before Larroque left on D1 for 3km. House signposted on right.

Map No: 16   MM 235-22

Minouche & Christian JOUARD
Meilhouret
81140 Larroque
Tarn
Tel: (0)5 63 33 11 18
Fax: (0)5 63 33 11 18

From Mazamet, D118 towards Carcassonne. Right on D53 to Aiguefonde; signposted.

Map No: 16   MM 235-35

Véronique PECH & Simone LELIÈVRE
Le Fourchat
Aiguefonde
81200 Mazamet
Tarn
Tel: (0)5 63 98 12 62

The huge cool entrance hall and the massive stone staircase winding up through four floors, the trompe-l'œil 'marble' alcoves, the high ceilings and southern colours — deep blue shutters, white walls — make it almost colonially grand. Add the owners' passion for Napoleon III furniture, oil paintings and gilt-framed mirrors and the mood is formal rather than family. Bedrooms are antique-furnished, breakfast is on the terrace overlooking the square — nice to be in a town for once with friendly, utterly French people.

Rooms: 1 suite, 4 double, 1 twin, all with bath or shower & wc.

Price: 240 Frs for two, suite 360 Frs, including breakfast.

Meals: Plenty of places in town.

Open: All year.

Madame is a delight, still spritely enough at 90+ to show her guests round her 13th-century *château fort* — up and down two spiral staircases — and clearly enjoy it. Staying in this rare, rustic and ancient place is an unforgettable experience. Breakfast is served in the big old kitchen dominated by a massive ancient fireplace and you sleep in huge tower bedrooms with high Renaissance coffered ceilings, where the beds are made with spotless old French linen. Primitive bathrooms and an advanced state of decorative decay — we still love it.

Rooms: 2 double, sharing shower & wc.

Price: 250 Frs for two, including breakfast.

Meals: Not available.

Open: May to November.

Gîtes for 9 people

In centre of Gaillac, directly opposite St Michel abbey church as you come in across bridge from A68 Toulouse-Albi road.

Map No: 16   MM 235-27

Lucile PINON
8 place Saint-Michel
81600 Gaillac
Tarn
Tel: (0)5 63 57 61 48
Fax: (0)5 63 41 06 56

In Noailles, coming from Cordes, turn left. The Château is on your right, beside the river.

Map No: 16   MM 235-23

Gabriel & Félicie RAHOUX
Le Château
81170 Noailles
Tarn
Tel: (0)5 63 56 81 26

Mas du Sudre is a warm friendly house, just like its owners. George and Pippa are ideal B&B folk — relaxed, good-natured, at ease with people and enthusiastic about their corner of France. Dinners are delicious and convivial, *dégustations* can be arranged and there's a large shady garden set in rolling vineyards and farmland where you can sleep off any excesses. For the more energetic there's are bikes, a pool, badminton and ping-pong. Children are welcome and guests are encouraged to treat the house as their own.

Rooms: 2 double & 2 twin, all with own shower & wc.

Price: 300 Frs for two, including breakfast.

Meals: 100 Frs, including wine & coffee.

Open: All year.

Gîtes for 10 people

From Gaillac centre take road to Cordes. Cross railway; fork immediately left onto D964 towards Castelnau de Montmirail for 1km then left on D18 towards Montauban. After 400m right onto D4 for 1.5km — 1st left, 1st house on right.

Map No: 16   MM 235-27

Pippa & George RICHMOND-BROWN
Mas de Sudre
81600 Gaillac
Tarn
Tel: (0)5 63 41 01 32
Fax: (0)5 63 41 01 32

Annie and Christian have lavished care on their fine rooms. Most have a fireplace and all are airy, with views of Cordes. We weren't too sure about the satiny bedspreads but that's splitting hairs. Your hosts may be a little reserved at first but their dry humour warms up over dinner — most of which they'll proudly tell you they produced themselves. Children are welcome; there are *boules*, ping pong and a small park where you can picnic if you wish. This estate was once a flourishing tile factory and the manager lived in this house.

Rooms: 1 twin, 2 double, 1 triple, 1 quadruple, all with shower & wc.

Price: 260 Frs for two, including breakfast.

Meals: 95 Frs, including wine & coffee.

Open: All year.

From Albi D600 to Cordes. There follow signs 'Parking 1 & 2'. Then signposted.

Map No: 16   MM 235-23

Annie & Christian RONDEL
Les Tuileries
81170 Cordes-sur-Ciel
Tarn
Tel: (0)5 63 56 05 93
Fax: (0)5 63 56 05 93

Utterly charming and speaking a little English, Monique Sallier takes charge of things in this family-style château, serving breakfast in her farmhouse kitchen so that she can chat more easily to her guests while preparing dinner. The bedrooms have a comfortable, lived-in feel and have kept their original 19th-century charm, including a newly-restored rare wallpaper dated 1850. Altogether a very welcoming country house comfortably worn around the edges, with swimming pool and tennis court.

Rooms: 2 twin, 2 suite, each with shower & wc.

Price: 360-400 Frs for two, including breakfast.

Meals: 120-130 Frs, including wine & coffee.

Open: All year.

Former diplomats, the Thornleys have entertaining in their blood. The stones of their fabulous house are mute witnesses to the passage from rough Middle Ages to calmer farming days and decorative flourishes from their global travels add spice. The big rooms are sensitively furnished with the perfect minimum, each has a private balcony or patio and views worth contemplating. Books, paintings and fabulous walks entice you to stay (let their 7-day deal tempt you). Patricia's infectious laugh and sense of fun will brighten your mornings.

Rooms: 1 suite for 4, 2 double, 1 twin, all with bath or shower & wc.

Price: 260 Frs for two, including breakfast.

Meals: Wide choice in Cordes, or barbecue.

Open: Easter to November.

From Revel, D622 towards Castres. 9km along, left on D12 to Lempaut. At Lempaut, right on D46 towards Lescout. La Bousquétarié is on your left.

Map No: 16   MM 235-31

Monique & Charles SALLIER
La Bousquétarié
81700 Lempaut
Tarn
Tel: (0)5 63 75 51 09

From Albi D600 to Cordes. There take upward 'Cité' road on right of 'Maison de la Presse' for 500m then fork left towards Le Bouysset then left at hairpin bend and right 200m on at 2nd hairpin bend into Aurifat.

Map No: 16   MM 235-23

Denis & Patricia THORNLEY
Aurifat
81170 Cordes-sur-Ciel
Tarn
Tel: (0)5 63 56 07 03

You will be serenaded by birds, bees and sheep in this lovely and largely undiscovered part of France. Your Anglo-French hosts are welcoming and helpful. Their deeply converted 200-year-old farmhouse (they plan to re-expose the old beams soon) is a deliciously secluded place to stay and walk or bike out into the country. They grow their own vegetables and summer dinners are on the terrace overlooking the lovely Tarn valley. Local sheep farmers (who supply Rocquefort with milk) will show you their milking sheds if asked(!).

Rooms: 1 twin, 1 triple, each with shower or bath & wc, 1 twin sharing a bathroom.

Price: 210 Frs for two, including breakfast.

Meals: 90 Frs, including wine & coffee.

Open: All year.

It is easy to see why La Cerisaie seduced this sophisticated Dutch couple into leaving advertising for a simpler life. Its very grand façade is softened by an exotic mix of hydrangea, bamboo, palms and wisteria. A lovely old staircase sweeps up to the bedrooms which are roomy, marble-fireplaced, old-furnished and light. The young artistic owners have a flair for decoration and pride themselves on their fine French food — "those who dine here once dine every evening thereafter". Pets by arrangement.

Rooms: 3 double, 2 twin, each with bath or shower & wc.

Price: From 340 Frs for two, including breakfast.

Meals: 120 Frs, excluding wine.

Open: All year.

Gîtes for 6 people

From Albi, D999 towards Millau. At La Croix Blanche (25km), left down to Cambon du Temple and up to La Barthe on D163. Turn right; house is first on left.

Map No: 16   MM 235-27

Michèle & Michael WISE
La Barthe
81430 Villefranche-d'Albigeois
Tarn
Tel: (0)5 63 55 96 21
Fax: (0)5 63 55 96 21

From A9 Béziers Ouest exit on D64 then N112 towards Castres/Mazamet/St Pons. 1km before St Pons right on D908 towards Riols/Bédarieux. House signposted on left leaving Riols.

Map No: 16   MM 240-25

Monique DEGENAAR & Reinoud WEGGELAAR
La Cerisaie
1 Avenue de Bédarieux
34220 Riols
Hérault
Tel: (0)4 67 97 03 87
Fax: (0)4 67 97 03 88

Salasc, with its ornate fountain, is a typical Languedocian village set in the dramatic red hills that enfold the turquoise Salagou lake (superb swimming). With 20 years of B&B behind them, the Delages run a pretty, warm and welcoming house. The rooms are small, perfect in summer, each with its tiny private terrace, and the *auberge* serves excellent country meals under the leafy pergola. It is quiet, unpretentious and hospitable. Monsieur breeds horses with passion, Madame cooks beautifully and both love having guests.

Rooms: 1 quadruple, 2 double, 2 triple, 1 twin, all with shower & wc.

Price: 250 Frs for two, including breakfast. Half board 420F for two.

Meals: 90 Frs, including wine & coffee.

Open: All year.

From Clermont l'Hérault, D908 W towards Bédarieux. After 4.5km right (D8e) towards Mourèze and Salasc. 1.5km after Salasc, turn left; signposted.

Map No: 16   MM 240-22

Jocelyne & Lionel DELAGE
Auberge Campagnarde La Vallée du Salagou, Route de Mas Canet
34800 Salasc
Hérault
Tel: (0)4 67 96 15 62/
    (0)4 67 88 13 39
Fax: (0)4 67 96 15 62

Sarah, who has just written a cookery book and Dennis, an accomplished photographer, have decorative flair too, clearly visible within these golden rag-painted walls. The fine townhouse has lovely spaces, just enough antiques, careful use of light and fabrics, inviting guestrooms. You can walk, ride, climb rocks; swim, canoe in the river; follow Dennis's wine trail; visit the town's succulent garden — and return drunk with exertion and beauty for a superb, civilised meal on the terrace. Very special.

Rooms: 2 double, 1 twin, 1 suite, all with shower & wc.

Price: 300-395 Frs for two, including breakfast.

Meals: Dinner 125-145 Frs, excluding wine (50 Frs+).

Open: All year.

From Béziers N112 W towards St Pons for 1-2km; then right on D14 through Maraussan, Cazouls-lès-Béziers, Cessenon to Roquebrun. House signposted in village.

Map No: 16   MM 240-26

Dennis & Sarah LA TOUCHE
Les Mimosas
Avenue des Orangers
34460 Roquebrun
Hérault
Tel: (0)4 67 89 61 36
Fax: (0)4 67 89 61 36
e-mail: la-touche.les-mimosas@wanadoo.fr

All is light, sun and simplicity here in superbly wild surroundings (good walks and rock climbing). Madame is gentle, welcoming and most proud of her restored barn which houses the guest quarters, furnished with old country pieces, fitted with pretty curtains and new bedding, rejoicing in fireplace and fully-equipped kitchen. She will even come to the rescue with fresh eggs for your supper. There is a lovely terrace for breakfast which has a different kind of bread every day, or cheese, or walnuts, or honey... Really lovely people.

Rooms: 1 double and 1 twin, each with bath & wc.

Price: 260 Frs for two, including breakfast.

Meals: Self-catering. Restaurants nearby.

Open: April to September.

Not a pelican in sight, nothing out-of-place either on this superb estate with it mulberry-lined drive, woods, hills, vineyards and wonderful family atmosphere (the couple have a small, active child). The large *auberge* dining-room gives onto a covered terrace and rows of vines — just the place to try a glass of estate wine followed by deliciou regional cooking. The fresh-coloured bedrooms are new and mezzanined and the delightful, hard-working owners have decorated their family house with the utmost care.

Rooms: 2 double/quadruple, each with shower & wc.

Price: 300 Frs for two, including breakfast.

Meals: 110 Frs, including wine.

Open: All year.

From Mazamet, N112 towards St Pons-de-Thomières. At Courniou, left to Prouilhe; farm on left.

Map No: 16   MM 240-25

Eliane & Jean-Louis LUNES
La Métairie Basse
Hameau de Prouilhe
34220 Courniou
Hérault
Tel: (0)4 67 97 21 59
Fax: (0)4 67 97 21 59

Leave Gignac centre eastwards towards Montpellier. At the edge of town: Littérault Cuisines on right — turn right (signed) and follow signs for 3km.

Map No: 17   MM 240-22

Isabelle & Baudouin THILLAYE de BOULLAY
Domaine du Pélican
34150 Gignac
Hérault
Tel: (0)4 67 57 68 92

The venerable, plane-lined, eminently cyclable Canal du Midi runs through this charming old village: the warmly friendly Anglo-Australian Viners willingly house cyclists and mounts in their 'terraced château'. They have lovingly restored their C15-to-C18 house with its dark panelling, magnificent *trompe-l'œil* tiled hall and fine painted ceilings (with *scènes du Languedoc*). The big, comfortable rooms include 2m-long beds, power showers and much attention to authentic detail. You are only 5km from the sea.

Rooms: 2 double, 2 twin, all with bath or shower & wc.

Price: 260 Frs for two, including breakfast.

Meals: 85 Frs, including wine.

Open: All year.

From Béziers, N112 towards Agde. Pass under motorway then right on D37 into Villeneuve; house in centre opposite Hôtel de Ville.

Map No: 16   MM 240-30

Andrew & Jennifer-Jane VINER
7 rue de la Fontaine
34420 Villeneuve-lès-Béziers
Hérault
Tel: (0)4 67 39 87 15
Fax: (0)4 67 39 87 15

Monsieur keeps horses so stop on your ride to Compostela (it happens often!) or, more prosaically, on the road to Spain or Montpellier airport (the Domaine is just off the motorway so there is inevitably some road noise). It is a fine old 19th-century wine-grower's house with the remains of a 12th-century chapel. A quiet breakfast can be had in the courtyard in summer or before the kitchen fireplace in winter. Good, clean rooms and Madame is delightful, taking children to feed the rabbits or the old tortoise.

Rooms: 2 double, 2 twin, all with own bathrooms.

Price: 200 Frs for two, including breakfast.

Meals: Wide choice nearby.

Open: All year.

Gites for 4 people

From Montpellier, N113 towards Lunel. House signposted in Baillargues.

Map No: 17   MM 240-23

Michèle & Michel VITOU
Domaine de Saint-Antoine
34670 Baillargues
Hérault
Tel: (0)4 67 70 15 58

This magical 17th-century moated château (parts of it 12th-century) has its very own ghost, *la Dame à la Rose*. Towers overlook the monumental courtyard where Mary Stuart once walked. Madame runs a cultural centre and stages a summer music festival in this beautiful setting. Breakfast is in the courtyard or in the dining-room. The exceptional bedrooms, with round tower bathrooms, have just been renovated with colourful details such as bright new satin canopies. The pool-with-sauna is a seductive addition.

Rooms: 3 double, 2 triple, 1 twin, all with bath & wc.

Price: 500 Frs for two, including breakfast.

Meals: Choice 5-10km.

Open: All year.

If you need a break near Nîmes, you could call in on this 18th-century farmhouse where, once you're enjoying a welcoming drink under the mulberry tree or beside the swimming pool, the slight intrusions of a little traffic on the nearby D135 and a distant view of warehouses will fade behind the vegetation. The interior has been well and truly renovated and is bursting with inherited Provençal furniture. Friendly and talkative, Madame cooks Provençal dinners too and the 'second best golf course in France' is 10km away.

Rooms: 1 suite for 4 with bath & wc.

Price: 350 Frs for two, including breakfast. Extra bed 120 Frs.

Meals: 120 Frs, including wine.

Open: All year.

From Avignon, N580 towards Bagnols-sur-Cèze. At junction in L'Ardoise, left along D9 towards Laudun; signposted.

Map No: 17   MM 240-12

Gisèle & Jean-Louis BASTOUIL
Château de Lascours
30290 Laudun
Gard
Tel: (0)4 66 50 39 61
Fax: (0)4 66 50 30 08

From Nîmes D42 through Caissargues, then D135 towards Vauvert. After sign 'Vauvert 8' (DON'T go to Aubord), turn right.

Map No: 17   MM 240-20

Mireille BOURDIN
Mas Pellet
3 chemin des Canabières
30620 Aubord
Gard
Tel: (0)4 66 71 00 05
Fax: (0)4 66 71 21 18

This ancient abode, with flower-filled terrace, large private orchard and views of the Cévennes mountains, is home to an artist/art historian and a designer. Supremely quiet — the only passer-by is the local winegrower — it offers a choice of styles: an 11th-century vaulted ground-floor room with private courtyard or a first floor remodelled in the 1920s, all ice-cream colours, long, elegant windows and patterned tiled floors with private balcony access. Dinner of regional dishes may be rounded off with organic, home-grown fruit.

Rooms: 2 double with bath or shower & wc.

Price: 280 Frs for two, including breakfast.

Meals: 100 Frs, including wine & coffee.

Open: All year.

From Nîmes D999 towards Le Vigan for 27km then right to Bragassargues. House in village centre.

Map No: 17   MM 240-15

David & Patricia CHAPMAN
La Maison des Rêves
Le Village
30260 Bragassargues
Gard
Tel: (0)4 66 77 13 45
Fax: (0)4 66 77 13 45

A path through the woods leads from the house to the river by the Pont du Gard, a World Heritage site — the setting is truly wonderful. Indoors, the decor is fulsome, almost whacky — a net canopy over one of the beds, hanging hats, splayed fans, silk flowers, etc. The rooms are themed. *La Provençale* has a small adjoining room with bunk beds and soft toys for the younger guest. Monsieur works in Nîmes but gives all his remaining time to welcoming and caring for his guests. A new swimming pool is being built.

Rooms: 1 suite, 2 double, 1 twin with bath or shower & wc.

Price: 370 Frs for two, including breakfast. Extra bed 70 Frs.

Meals: Auberges by Pont du Gard, 800 metres.

Open: March-October.

Gîtes for 4 people

From Remoulins follow signs for Pont du Gard 'rive droite'. Signposted on right 'La Terre des Lauriers'.

Map No: 17   MM 240-16

Gérard CRISTINI
La Terre des Lauriers
Rive Droite — Pont du Gard
30210 Remoulins
Gard
Tel: (0)4 66 37 19 45
Fax: (0)4 66 37 19 45

Where to sit in the château's large drawing-room? There are over a dozen French armchairs for the sedentary to choose from. The ambulant might wander onto the balcony with its panoramic views across river, dramatic viaduct and red-roofed village to the terraced hills beyond. The large elegant bedrooms have a perfect château feeling with their dark-coloured walls. Madame, one of an old French family in the silk industry who have lived here for several generations, is delightful and practical.

Rooms: 2 twin, 1 double, each with bath or shower & wc; 2 double, 1 single, sharing bath & separate wc.

Price: 250-350-450 Frs for two, including breakfast.

Meals: 100 Frs, including wine.

Open: All year.

Gîtes for 7 people

For over 2,000 years the nearby track (with chariot wheel-marks) has borne the *transhumance*. A courtyard provides a summer dining area, a Banksia rose shades the garden table, the olive grove is perfect for a good read. John is an ex-publisher/designer/teacher and they both have a gift for colours and decor. The warm sandstone house has a golden, light atmosphere inside, old beams painted white, natural shapes. You can be independent with your own kitchen. Perfect for a family holiday and the setting is wonderful.

Rooms: 1 double, 1 twin, sharing bath, shower & wc, sitting-room & kitchen.

Price: 250-350 Frs for two, including breakfast.

Meals: 100 Frs, including wine & coffee (on request). Self-catering.

Open: All year.

From Millau S on N9 for 19 km. At La Cavalerie left onto D7 towards Le Vigan for about 50km to Bez. Before bridge, little château signposted on left.

Map No: 16/17   MM 240-14

Françoise du LUC
Château Massal
Bez-et-Esparon
30120 Le Vigan
Gard
Tel: (0)4 67 81 07 60
Fax: (0)4 67 81 04 60

From Alès D50/D129 SW to Anduze then D982 dir. Nîmes for 4km. Right at fork on D35 for Quissac. 400m after Bouzène fork right; 2km to Aspères, turn right, 2nd house on left.

Map No: 17   MM 240-15

Marie-Laure & John MARSH
Mas des Loriots
Aspères
30140 Tornac
Gard
Tel: (0)4 66 61 88 25
Fax: (0)4 66 61 88 25

The pool and the flower-filled garden are reason enough to stay here, so is the shady pergola for reading beneath... and the sense of having got away from it all. Edna has created something utterly English — books, pictures, trinkets, a certain kind of comfort — but it is so well done, the colours and space so carefully thought out, the day/dining-room so big and pleasant, that we think you will like La Fauguière too. Breakfast is as good as the rooms are comfortable and children are as welcome as you are.

Rooms: 1 double, 1 twin, each with bath & wc; 1 double, 1 twin each with shower & handbasin, sharing wc.

Price: 325 Frs or 425 Frs for two, including breakfast.

Meals: Wide choice 10km.

Open: All year.

The roofscape alone is proof of the loving care lavished on this finely-renovated old farmhouse which stands at the foot of an unspoilt listed village, visible from pool and guestrooms. The very comfortable rooms are traditional in style (two done in chintz) and named after flowers. Indeed, flowers abound; Monsieur is green-fingered, while Madame turns her hand to old porcelain. Guests may use a summer kitchen. Try not to arrive too late or bring pets who don't like cats. Attractive river and waterfall nearby.

Rooms: 3 double, 3 triple, all with shower & wc.

Price: 280-320 Frs for two, including breakfast.

Meals: Self-catering.

Open: From Easter to 31 October.

From Alès, N110 south, right on D910 dir. Anduze; after 500m, left on D24 to Canaules. There, right on D149 to St Nazaire-des-G., right at railway bridge, up hill to 'Mairie', turn left. House at bottom of hill on left.

Map No: 17   MM 240-15

Edna & Ted PRICE
Mas de la Fauguière
30610 Saint-Nazaire-des-Gardies
Gard
Tel: (0)4 66 77 38 67
Fax: (0)4 66 77 11 64

From Pont-St-Esprit, N86 towards Bagnols-sur-Cèze. Just before Bagnols right on D980 towards Barjac. After 11km, left on D166 for La Roque-sur-Cèze. House on left in village, opposite telephone kiosk.

Map No: 17   MM 240-12

Pierre & Yolande RIGAUD
La Tonnelle
30200 La-Roque-sur-Cèze
Gard
Tel: (0)4 66 82 79 37

As well as *chambres d'hôtes* the Simonots run a pottery workshop and the atmosphere is busy and creative with lots of interesting people around. The guestrooms are separate from the main house; they are simply furnished and guests have a sitting-room with a fireplace. Breakfast (and dinner on request) is served on the terrace or in the dining-room. Lovely landscape, rolling hills and woods; ideal for hikers as well as potters.

Rooms: 1 twin, 1 double, each with shower & wc.

Price: 240-270 Frs for two, including breakfast.

Meals: 75 Frs, including wine (book ahead).

Open: All year.

Monsieur, a stonemason, restored this former mediæval Templar headquarters himself; it is now a working farm. The C15 house is set among well-tended lawns. After bringing up four children, Madame attended agricultural college and now raises sheep and poultry — children love all the animals. The simple comfortable rooms have fine beds, large cupboards and roomy bathrooms and there is a small *salon*. The pool has sweeping views across the surrounding countryside. A friendly, farming atmosphere.

Rooms: 2 double, 1 twin, 1 suite for 2/4 people, all with shower & wc.

Price: 280 Frs for two, including breakfast.

Meals: Dinner (arrival day, by arrangement). Auberge 5km.

Open: All year.

From Alès, D16 through Salindres to Allègre; left onto D241; signposted.

Map No: 17   MM 240-11

Michel & Françoise SIMONOT
Mas Cassac
30500 Allègre
Gard
Tel: (0)4 66 24 85 65
Fax: (0)4 66 24 80 55

From Alès D6 E dir. Bagnols-sur-Cèze for 6/7km then left on D747/746 to Servas; at church right on D147 dir. Navacelles for 300m then left; after another 700m left again. Signposted.

Map No: 17   MM 240-11

Myriam & Daniel SORDI
Mas des Commandeurs
30340 Servas
Gard
Tel: (0)4 66 85 67 90

No frills in this simple village home where guests have two vaulted ground-floor rooms. Although it's right on the street there's very little traffic but lots of pine and many African souvenirs. Helen, who was a nurse and Jacques, an agriculturist, an interesting and concerned couple, met when working in Africa (10% of their B&B income goes to development projects). The pretty, peaceful, terraced garden is not really suitable for adventurous toddlers. Super folk with whom to share good conversation over cosy suppers.

Rooms: 1 suite for 4 with shower & wc.

Price: 250 Frs for two, including breakfast. Extra bed 50 Frs.

Meals: 70 Frs, including wine.

Open: All year.

This substantial *bastide*, which has been in the same family for 200 years, stands next to the Ardèche River with its own private 'beach'. Monsieur can accompany you on canoe trips — if you're lucky you might see otter. There are simple but functional rooms inside, an enormous stone staircase, a leafy courtyard, a swimming pool, red squirrels in the garden, and plenty to visit in the area. Breakfast is served outside or in the family kitchen. There is also a small campsite on the property, but room for all.

Rooms: 1 quadruple, 1 triple, 1 double, each with shower & wc; 1 double, 1 twin, each with shower, sharing wc.

Price: 300 Frs for two, including breakfast.

Meals: In village.

Open: All year.

Gîtes for 8 people

From Avignon & Villeneuve N580 towards Bagnols-sur-Cèze then right on D377 & D177 to Pujaut. In village follow signs for 'Mairie' — 'Saba'ad' is 300m into the old village from Mairie and church.

Map No: 17   MM 240-16

Helen THOMPSON & Jacques
SERGENT
Saba'ad
Places des Consuls
30131 Pujaut
Gard
Tel: (0)4 90 26 31 68
Fax: (0)4 90 26 31 68

From A7, Bollène exit onto D994 to Pont-St-Esprit. N86 towards Bourg St-Andéol; signposted before bridge across Ardèche river.

Map No: 17   MM 240-12

Mme de VERDUZAN
Pont d'Ardèche
30130 Pont-Saint-Esprit
Gard
Tel: (0)4 66 39 29 80

A mini-hamlet in the calm green Aveyron where there is so much space. Two rooms, in the main house, each with a little terrace, look out over a typical old mediæval château; the third, in an outbuilding, has a mezzanine; all are welcoming, two have cooking facilities. The garden is full of flowers, the view stupendous, your hosts solicitous and keen to help, providing for all your needs. The food is "outstanding and imaginative" — Pierre and Monique used to run a restaurant. Well-behaved children and animals welcome.

Rooms: 2 double, each with bath or shower & wc. In separate house: 2 double beds, bath & wc.

Price: 230-250 Frs for two, including breakfast.

Meals: 85 Frs, including aperitif, wine & coffee.

Open: All year.

Gîtes for 8 people

The Auvergne

From Villefranche, D922 south towards Albi; at entrance to Sanvensa, follow signs on right to 'Monteillet Chambres d'Hôtes'.

Map No: 16   MM 235-15

Monique & Pierre BATESON
Monteillet-Sanvensa
12200 Villefranche-de-Rouergue
Aveyron
Tel: (0)5 65 29 81 01
Fax: (0)5 65 29 81 01

The five Laurens children and their large placid dog greet guests to the tiny family hamlet — with the Cantal hills tumbling down behind the house, the scene is set for an open-armed welcome from these charming dairy farmers. The main house has a characteristic steep shingle roof and three light, fresh rooms. The separate *studio*, equipped for disabled guests, has a kitchenette hidden in an old *armoire*, a washing machine and a private terrace. Madame is delightful and serves delicious, copious, varied breakfasts with her own dandelion jam.

Rooms: 2 double (corner kitchen), 1 twin/quadruple 'studio' (corner kitchen), 1 suite for 5, each with bath or shower & wc.

Price: 260-350 Frs for two, including breakfast. Extra bed 90 Frs.

Meals: Restaurants nearby + self-catering.

Open: January to August

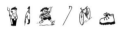

From Entraygues, D904 towards Mur-de-Barrez. 4.5km after Lacroix-Barrez, right to Vilherols; signposted.

Map No: 16   MM 235-8

Catherine & Jean LAURENS
Vilherols
12600 Lacroix-Barrez
Aveyron
Tel: (0)5 65 66 08 24
Fax: (0)5 65 66 19 98

Superb for wildlife and outdoors lovers — orchids and other rare species plus canoeing, rock-climbing, hang-gliding — this is a *Gîte Panda* and Jean knows his region well. The C16 farmhouse has been restored with terracotta floors, old beams and white walls throughout. Jean made much of the pine furniture (one splendid 'mediæval' bed). The dining-room has tapestries on the walls and antique farm furniture with the patina and fragrance of years of polish. Home-produced organic meat and veg are used for excellent regional meals.

Rooms: 1 for 4/5, 5 double, each with bath or shower & wc.

Price: 270 Frs for two, including breakfast.

Meals: 85-100 Frs, excluding wine (50 Frs) (not Mon).

Open: April to mid-Nov.

From Millau N9 N to Aguessac. Just after leaving village right onto D547 to Compeyre; left in village and follow signs for 2km.

Map No: 16   MM 240-10

Jean & Véronique LOMBARD-PRATMARTY
Quiers
12520 Compeyre
Aveyron
Tel: (0)5 65 59 85 10
Fax: (0)5 65 59 80 99

They are the sweetest couple: warm, simple, unpretentious like their house. Their great, great grandparents were born in Ols and their farm is a centre of activity in this small hamlet in wild Aveyron country. The biggest room is very fine with its old books and furniture and village prospect; you can sit in the pleasant garden and admire the ever-changing view. There are delightful footpaths to explore from the house or you can hire a horse or a bike locally. This is genuine farmhouse B&B at its best.

Rooms: 2 twin, 1 double, 1 triple, all with handbasins; shared bathroom.

Price: 200 Frs for two, including breakfast.

Meals: Occasionally, at 75 Frs, including wine. Barbecue possible.

Open: All year.

Your young hosts escaped from heaving Paris to this rural paradise. Their brilliant conversion of an old Cantal farmhouse has preserved the scullery ledge and sink made of vast slabs of stone, the beams, the inglenook fireplace. They now aim to convert their neighbours to better environmental (get the scrap metal off the hillside) and social (more respect for your woman?) attitudes. The rooms are well and simply done, the meals are feasts, the Balleux a most interesting and happy couple.

Rooms: 1 double, 1 twin, 1 suite (D+2S) in main house; 2 suites in cottage; all with bath or shower & wc.

Price: 240-280 Frs for two, including breakfast.

Meals: 80 Frs, including wine & coffee. Half-board 190 Frs p.p.

Open: All year.

From Figeac, N122 towards Villefranche-de-Rouergue. In Villeneuve d'Aveyron, D48 towards Cajarc and Ols. In Ols, right following signpost for 'Chambres d'Hôtes'.

Map No: 16   MM 235-15

Marie-José & Gaston VIGUIÉ
Ols
12260 Villeneuve
Aveyron
Tel: (0)5 65 81 61 47

From Aurillac D920 to Arpajon; left on D990 for 10km (DON'T go to St Etienne de Carlat) then left towards Caizac; signposted.

Map No: 11   MM 239-41

Francine & Jacky BALLEUX
Lou Ferradou
Caizac
15130 Saint-Etienne-de-Carlat
Cantal
Tel: (0)4 71 62 42 37

This may smack of the holiday business (gîtes, small camping site) but the Lacazes were so warm and friendly, enthusing about the happy communal barbecues on hot summer's evenings, that we feel their farm is ideal for walkers and families (there are swings, too). The converted barn you sleep in is superb with vast timbers and space, the result of years of honest hard work. Simple, country furnishings, magnificent landscapes, good breakfasts at the long table in the old dairy. It feels good.

Rooms: 1 quadruple, 2 triple, 2 twin, all with bath or shower & wc.

Price: 210-230 Frs for two, including breakfast.

Meals: In village or self-catering.

Open: Mid-April to mid-November.

Gîtes for 8 people

Like the rest of the attractive old village this house, dated 1777, is built from volcanic stone. Monsieur's shop down below sells *objets* in the same stuff. Superb views of the (extinct) volcano from the rear of the house; try to get one of these rooms. All six rooms are identical inside, quite small but functional. Your hosts, who live in the next house, are young, active, efficient and welcoming; breakfast in their dining-room or on the terrace is a treat with fresh bread and piping hot coffee. And there's a lovely garden.

Rooms: 6 double, all with shower & wc (extra beds for children available).

Price: 230 Frs for two, including breakfast.

Meals: Choice in village.

Open: All year.

From Aurillac N122 towards Cahors, Montauban, Decazeville. At Le Rouget right towards Pers. Go through village (NOT towards Viescamp). Farm signposted on left.

Map No: 11   MM 239-40

Janine & Charles LACAZE
Ferme Accueil de Viescamp
15290 Pers
Cantal
Tel: (0)4 71 62 25 14
Fax: (0)4 71 62 28 66

From Aurillac, D922 towards Mauriac. After 35km, right on D680 to Salers. From Place Tyssandier d'Escour, take first left; signposted 'Chambres d'Hôtes'.

Map No: 11   MM 239-29

Philippe & Claudine PRUDENT
Rue des Nobles
15410 Salers
Cantal
Tel: (0)4 71 40 75 36

The lava of the surrounding volcanoes provided the stone flags for the dining-room floor of this handsome, family house. Élisabeth is bright and enthusiastic, her interior is uncluttered, sober and furnished with antiques and soft textiles. Each room is named after an ancestor; we liked *Guillaume* best — canopied bed, Japanese grass paper, lovely Louis XV *armoire*, cabinet full of old *objets* — but they are all superb, the garden a treat for sunlit breakfasts, the *Godin* stove warming in winter, the outbuildings full of character.

Rooms: 3 double, all with en-suite shower & wc.

Price: 300-350 Frs for two, including breakfast.

Meals: Wide choice 5-8km.

Open: All year (Nov to March by arrangement only).

Acres of parkland, a walled garden, a 12th-century vaulted chapel. The splendid rooms are utterly in keeping, from the vast, panelled, period-furnished drawing and dining-rooms to big, beautiful bedrooms, with here a canopied bed, there an exquisite little dressing-room, everywhere shimmering mirrors, fabulous views of ancient trees or the Puy-de-Dôme. A perfect hostess, Madame makes you feel immediately at ease and helps you plan your day, all over a most delicious breakfast. She can also show you how to make lace (*dentelle du Puy*).

Rooms: 2 double, 2 twin, 2 suites, all with bath and/or shower & wc.

Price: 380-550 Frs for two, including breakfast.

Meals: 150 Frs, including wine (by arrangement); not July or August; 3 restaurants nearby.

Open: April to October.

From A71, Riom exit, N144 towards Combronde & Montluçon. 2.5km after Davayat, right onto D122 to Chaptes.

Map No: 11   MM 239-7

Mme Élisabeth BEAUJEARD
8 route de la Limagne
Chaptes
63460 Beauregard-Vendon
Puy-de-Dôme
Tel: (0)4 73 63 35 62

From Clermont-Ferrand, A75, exit 13 to Parentignat. There D999 towards St Germain-l'Hermite for 6km; signposted on right. (8km from A75 exit.)

Map No: 11   MM 239-20

Henriette MARCHAND
Château de Pasredon
63500 Saint-Rémy-de-Chargnat
Puy-de-Dôme
Tel: (0)4 73 71 00 67
Fax: (0)4 73 71 08 72

Peaceful at the end of a long drive, this is a special place, albeit more formal than some. The Montaignacs are elegant, immaculate and gracious, like their dining-room with its panelling and breakfast silver — the epitome of Old France. Choose the ground-floor, original-parqueted, fireplaced suite or glide up the fine staircase past the ancestors to the double room. Both welcome you with antiques, old engravings, personality. Monsieur knows books-worth of fascinating history; Madame is quietly attentive.

Rooms: 1 suite for 2-4 people, 1 twin, both with bath or shower & wc.

Price: 470-500 Frs for two, including breakfast.

Meals: Choice within 9km.

Open: All year (by arrangement October to May).

A typical and charming 19th-century French manor, square and confident in its 5 acres of parkland (with tennis court) and the hugely famous Troisgros restaurant just 8km down the road. You are guests in a family home, your bedroom has its own character and is furnished with antiques, the bath is a claw-footed marvel (plenty of towels and bathrobes to go with it) and Madame a gentle friendly widow. She loves sharing a welcome cup with new people and guiding them to the hidden delights of this lovely area.

Rooms: 1 double with shower & wc; 1 suite for 3/4 with bath & wc.

Price: 350 Frs for two, 500 Frs suite for three, including breakfast.

Meals: Choice within 3km; Roanne 8km.

Open: Mid-March to mid-Nov; winter by arrangement only.

small

From Montluçon, N145 towards Chamblet; signposted on the right.

Map No: 11   MM 238-44

Yves & Jacqueline de
MONTAIGNAC
Château du Plaix
03170 Chamblet
Allier
Tel: (0)4 70 07 80 56

From Roanne D53 for 8km. Right into village & follow signs.

Map No: 12   MM 239-10

Mme GAUME
Domaine de Champfleury
42155 Lentigny
Loire
Tel: (0)4 77 63 31 43

Once upon a time, kindly Anne-Marie lived in a big town. One day she found her dream house in the Auvergne near deep mysterious woods and babbling brooks so she left the city, lovingly restored her house, installed her old family furniture and opened the door so that visitors could share her dream. So, after a delicious supper, before the roaring fire, Anne-Marie may treat guests to a fairy-tale of her own making. (She also offers breathing and relaxation courses.) Thus they all live happily ever after and never forget this exceptional woman.

Rooms: 2 triple, 2 twin, 1 double, each with shower & wc.

Price: 230-300 Frs for two, including breakfast. Extra person 80 Frs.

Meals: 70 Frs, including wine.

Open: All year.

Once part of the ramparts of this ancient city, the old townhouse has been furnished and decorated by mother and daughter in classically French manner with proper antiques on stylish parquet floors. Dinner both looks and tastes good — true Gallic cuisine enhanced by bone china, family silver and Bohemian crystal. Hear the great organ nearby and the famous music festival (August), walk the excellent hiking paths from the back door, then return to wallow in the gentle, floral, boudoir-like comfort of La Jacquerolle.

Rooms: 2 triple, 2 double, 1 twin, each with bath or shower & wc.

Price: 280-300 Frs for two, including breakfast. Extra bed 80 Frs.

Meals: 100 Frs, including wine.

Open: All year.

From A72 exit 4 onto D53 E to Champoly. Here D24 E to St Marcel-d'Urfé then D20 S towards St Martin-la-Sauveté and follow signs.

Map No: 12   MM 239-22

Anne-Marie HAUCK
Il fut un temps
Les Gouttes
42430 Saint-Marcel-d'Urfé
Loire
Tel: (0)4 77 62 52 19
Fax: (0)4 77 62 52 19

From Brioude D19 to La Chaise-Dieu. Follow signs to 'Centre Ville' and in front of Abbey turn right to Place du Monument. Park here — house is just off the square at bottom right-hand corner.

Map No: 12   MM 239-33

Jacqueline & Carole CHAILLY
La Jacquerolle
Rue Marchédial
43160 La Chaise-Dieu
Haute-Loire
Tel: (0)4 71 00 07 52

Remote, unsung, green wooded hills, secret streams... and such a welcome! The old farmhouse exudes warmth from its rare original panelling (clock case included) to its great stone fireplace. The stables (a 15-metre tree carries the ceiling) have become a magnificent breakfast/sitting room, full of the Champels' lovely treasures. The rooms, formerly the children's, are all full of character, with excellent bathrooms. And your hosts are generous, well-travelled people. A great place to stay and go for long walks.

Rooms: 2 double, 2 twin, all with shower & wc (2 ensuite, 2 separate).

Price: 300 Frs for two, including breakfast.

Meals: Choice 5km. Picnics possible.

Open: All year.

In few places in France can you eat so well for so little — almost everything is produced on the farm. Bread and jam are homemade, their bees produce the honey and you can help with the milking. Bugeac is a tiny hamlet high up in the Massif Central, worth every metre you travel; the walking is wonderful and the house is a pæan to wood; Paul has fashioned it into plank, wardrobe, bed and table. The rooms have wooden floors and ceilings, simple fabrics and pretty iron beds. When the snow blankets the world around it is still lovely.

Rooms: 1 double, 1 twin, 1 triple, 1 family room for 4/5, each with shower & wc.

Price: 200 Frs for two, including breakfast.

Meals: 65 Frs, including wine.

Open: All year.

From Le Puy-en-Velay N102 towards Brioude for 10km then D906 towards La Chaise Dieu for 15km then D1 through Craponne onto D498 towards St Etienne for 3km; following signs, turn left up hill, house is 1st on left.

Map No: 12　　　　　MM 239-46

Éliane & François CHAMPEL
Paulagnac
43500 Craponne-sur-Arzon
Haute-Loire
Tel: (0)4 71 03 26 37
Fax: (0)4 71 03 26 37

From A75 exit 34 dir. St Chély d'Apcher then NE on D989 to Le Malzieu. Just after Le Malzieu right on D48/D33 for Saugues, over 'Pas de l'Ane' pass; signposted on arrival in Bugeac.

Map No: 11　　　　　MM 239-45

Martine & Paul CUBIZOLLE
Bugeac
43170 Grèzes
Haute-Loire
Tel: (0)4 71 74 45 30
Fax: (0)4 71 74 45 30

THE AUVERGNE

Small, simple rooms with basic pine furniture, pretty curtains, functional shower rooms and a solid stone farmhouse to enclose them. Those stones, and wood and tiles, are visible all over the house. There are no frills but you lack for nothing. The family are delightfully natural, gentle and connected to real life; the children help out with breakfast and you feel the peace of the deep countryside. The area is an 'animal refuge' where the landowner has forbidden shooting so — rare in France — there are lots of animals to be seen.

Rooms: 1 quadruple, 1 triple, 2 double, all with shower & wc.

Price: 230 Frs for two, including breakfast (½ board only mid-June/mid-Sept).

Meals: 60 Frs, including wine & coffee.

Open: All year.

Gîtes for 8 people

small

Walkers! Join a circuit here and walk from B&B to B&B in this superbly unspoilt area; or cross-country ski it in winter. Simple, unaffected people will love Rosa, her somewhat dated decor and her fabulous home-grown, home-made food which oozes genuine natural goodness. A real old soldier, she manages the flock of milk-producing sheep, is surrounded by grandchildren and welcomes all-comers with a 'cup of friendship' before her great granite hearth. The house is warm, the hostess unforgettable.

Rooms: 1 double, 1 twin & 1 triple room, all with own shower & wc.

Price: 200 Frs for two, including breakfast. Terms for children & groups.

Meals: 70 Frs, including wine & coffee.

Open: Mid-Jan to mid-Dec.

From Tence towards Ste Agrève. After roundabout (between supermarket and 'Gendarmerie') D185 for 800m then left at 'La Pomme' sign & follow Chambres d'Hôtes.

Map No: 12   MM 239-36

Elyane & Gérard DEYGAS
Les Grillons
La Pomme
43190 Tence
Haute-Loire
Tel: (0)4 71 59 89 33

From Le Puy-en-Velay, D589 to Saugues then D585 towards Langeac, turning left onto D32 to Venteuges.

Map No: 12   MM 239-45

Rosa DUMAS
Le Bourg
43170 Venteuges
Haute-Loire
Tel: (0)4 71 77 80 66

Catherine, Bill and *Valentin* — a rare trio awaits you in this fairy-tale spot where the forest laps up to the edge of the hill-top village and its once-abandoned inn. The Hays left the bright lights of entertaining — he directed, she acted (opposite Peter Sellers, 007,...) — for the old *auberge* whose name was/will be Bill's in another life (they'll tell you all over dinner, in several languages). He, with great painting talent, has waved his magic wand over walls, furniture, bathtubs; she receives magnificently. Their combined sensitivities make it utterly memorable.

Rooms: 1 suite for 4, 3 double, 1 twin, each with bath or shower & wc.

Price: 270-300 Frs for two, including breakfast. Extra bed 50-70 Frs.

Meals: 100 Frs, including wine.

Open: All year.

From Brioude D19 to La Chaise-Dieu then S on D109 towards Le Puy; after 100m left then follow signs 'Bonneval' for 6km.

Map No: 12   MM 239-34

Bill & Catherine HAYS
Chambres d'Hôtes 'Valentin'
Le Bourg
43160 Bonneval
Haute-Loire
Tel: (0)4 71 00 07 47

This austere old house stands on the slope of an extinct volcano, whence stupendous views (and a hair-raising drive). In a recently-converted *bergerie*, the guestrooms are modern-tiled, candlewicked and functional. Meals, served at separate tables and not *en famille*, are made with organic fruit and vegetables (lots from the garden), local meat and cheeses and homemade desserts. Monsieur, therapist and astrologer (he needs quiet times), speaks fluent English. Pool available early morning and evening .

Rooms: 2 double, 1 twin, 1 suite for 3, each with bath or shower & wc.

Price: 250-320 Frs for two, including breakfast.

Meals: 100 Frs, including wine & coffee.

Open: All year except 2 weeks in June, 2 weeks in September.

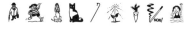

The Rhône Valley

From A7, Loriol exit, N104 to Privas, then towards 'les Ollières'. At Petit Tournon, D260 left to Pourchères and follow signposts.

Map No: 17   MM 245-2

Marcelle & Jean-Nicolas GOETZ
07000 Pourchères
Ardèche
Tel: (0)4 75 66 81 99
Fax: (0)4 75 66 81 99

How to describe paradise in one short paragraph? The setting: high, rural, hidden, silent. The views: long, of mountain peaks, inspiring. The house: lovingly restored, of stone, and wood from the surrounding chestnut forests, light, open, lovely. Bedrooms: just right. Food: organic, home-grown, imaginative... and there's lots of honey. Your hosts are warm and trusting, quickly your friends. Gil is a carpenter in winter and a bee-keeper in summer. Come up the long narrow road to walk, talk, and believe us.

Rooms: 1 suite for 5, 1 triple, 1 double, each with shower & wc.

Price: 250 Frs for two, including breakfast.

Meals: 90 Frs, including aperitif, wine & coffee.

Open: All year except Christmas.

Your host has virtually rebuilt this old mill on its spectacular ravine site where basalt prisms shimmer in the sunlight and the falling stream sings. He knows the country like the back of both hands (use his excellent itineraries), keeps donkeys to clear the land and carry small children (over 5 only), has his own hydroelectric power station, makes lovely wooden toys, chestnut cream, apple juice... Madame cares for five excellent rooms and serves local honey and yoghurt at the long communal breakfast table. Remarkable.

Rooms: 5 twin rooms, all with bath & wc.

Price: 250 Frs for two, including breakfast. Extra bed 85 Frs.

Meals: Occasionally 90-100 Frs, incl. wine & coffee. Restaurants 3-6km.

Open: All year.

Gîtes for 15 people

From Aubenas N102 W towards Le Puy for 8.5km. At Lalevade left to Jaujac. Here, by 'Café des Lorsips', cross river & follow signs 4km along narrow mountain road.

Map No: 12   MM 239-48

Marie & Gil FLORENCE
Les Roudils
07380 Jaujac
Ardèche
Tel: (0)4 75 93 21 11

From Aubenas D104 to Vals-les-Bains then D578 towards Le Cheylard. On leaving Vals, left on D243 to La Bastide-sur-B. There D254 towards Aizac, past tennis courts; 300m after crossing bridge right down sharp bend.

Map No: 17   MM 239-48

Bernadette & Jean-Michel FRANÇOIS
Le Château
07600 La Bastide-sur-Besorgues
Ardèche
Tel: (0)4 75 88 23 67
Fax: (0)4 75 88 23 67

Let the wild Ardèche landscape be your playground or the backdrop for total relaxation. Take walking boots, jodhpurs, bike, canoe, hang-glider, or just yourselves, and you'll be warmly welcomed. Surrounded by almond trees, fields of lavender and mountains, this peaceful, renovated farmhouse is truly *en pleine nature*. Monsieur has elevated 'home brew' onto a new plane, making aperitifs and digestifs to go with Madame's local dishes, eaten *en famille*. Simply-furnished guestrooms and a charming stone-vaulted dayroom.

Rooms: 1 quadruple, 1 triple, 2 double, all with bath or shower & wc.

Price: 250 Frs for two, including breakfast. Extra bed 60-80 Frs.

Meals: 85 Frs, including wine & coffee.

Open: All year.

After ten hairpin bends you have earned the healing sight of this isolated house, a place to stay and unwind. Bright flowers tumble over the terraces, the house has nooks and crannies around a small stone courtyard. No stunning bedroom views (the house turns it back to the wild) but, after a swim in the heated pool and a sauna, take a drink to the terrace overlooking the Vallée de la Beaume. A refined house (despite some curtained-off showers) and hosts. Breakfast includes 10 homemade jams; dinners are made with produce from local farms.

Rooms: 3 double, 1 twin, 2 quadruple, all with shower & wc.

Price: 270-360 Frs for two, including breakfast. Extra bed 130 Frs.

Meals: 100 Frs, including wine & coffee.

Open: April to December (book ahead in winter).

From Bourg-St-Andéol D4 to St Remèze then D362 towards Gras. Signposted on right.

Map No: 17   MM 240-8

Sylvette et Gérard MIALON
La Martinade
07700 Saint-Remèze
Ardèche
Tel: (0)4 75 98 89 42
Fax: (0)4 75 04 36 30

From Joyeuse D203 towards Valgorge. At Pont du Gua cross bridge and take narrow paved road up hillside to La Roche (10 hairpins in 3km!).

Map No: 17   MM 240-3

Henri & Jacote ROUVIÈRE
La Petite Cour Verte
07110 La Roche-Beaumont
Ardèche
Tel: (0)4 75 39 58 88
Fax: (0)4 75 39 43 00
e-mail: henrirouviere@wanadoo.fr

"Good food AND good conversation", we are told: tucked away in beautiful wooded Ardèche country Myriam, Claude and their children surely inhabit a corner of paradise; come commune with nature. Claude will ride horseback with you, there are magnificent walks, river pools for swimming, a very special meal to come back to with home-produced cheese, honey, fruit, vegetables... and a chance to hear Claude's traveller's tales (the vociferous *quacamayo* parrot came back with him from South America).

Rooms: 1 double with own shower & wc; 2 double, 1 twin, each with shower, sharing wc.

Price: 240-280 Frs for two, including breakfast.

Meals: 85 Frs, including wine & coffee.

Open: All year.

Set in vineyards facing Mont Ventoux, this ancient farmhouse provides honest hospitality with efficient service from a mother-and-son team. The bedrooms, small and basic (one shower room curtained off), have individual entrances. Despite the area's vast store of cultural delights (Vaison-la-Romaine, Mont Ventoux, hill-top villages and wine cellars), it is for Madame's Provençal cooking that guests return. Her skills are recognised in the local good food guide and her dinner, with homegrown vegetables, really makes the grade.

Rooms: 3 double, 2 twin and 1 family room, all with shower & wc.

Price: 220 Frs for two, including breakfast.

Meals: 80 Frs, including wine & coffee.

Open: 15 February to 15 November.

From Montélimar, N102 to Aubenas; N104 towards Alès 16km; right onto D5 to Largentière; D24 towards Valgorge 12km then left into Rocles; 300m after church.

Map No: 17   MM 240-3

Myriam & Claude ROUVIÈRE
La Croze
07110 Rocles
Ardèche
Tel: (0)4 75 88 31 43

From Vaison-la-Romaine, D938 towards Malaucène; after 2km, left onto D54 to Entrechaux, then D13 and D5 to Mollans-sur-Ouvèze, then D46 towards Faucon for 2km.

Map No: 17   MM 245-17

Jean-Luc & Rose-Marie BERNARD
Quartier Ayguemarse
26170 Mollans-sur-Ouvèze
Drôme
Tel: (0)4 75 28 73 59

An ancient, three-quarter-timbered rural retreat, doubtless several centuries old, where nobody will think of looking for you. For those who want to escape into the countryside, there are doors on all sides. True nature-lovers will enjoy sharing with the warmly down-to-earth owner-occupiers and contact with the local fauna is likely to be direct, soft and odorous. Beds are natural and organic too. Indeed, this place is almost Hugolian in its closeness to Nature — you couldn't find more authentically rural French.

Rooms: Open-plan central living area becomes sleeping quarters at night. Field facilities en-suite.

Price: 200 Frs-worth of oats for two, including breakfast.

Meals: Unrefined organic cereals and fresh farm milk *à volonté*.

Open: All year except calving time.

Madame is the grandmother we all dream of, a sprightly, delightful woman who cossets her guests, putting candies and fruit in the bedrooms. This old stone farmhouse facing the Vercors mountains is definitely a family home (the family has been here since 1380!), so meals of regional dishes with local wine can be very jolly with family, friends and guests all sharing the long wooden table in the kitchen. The roomy, old-fashioned bedrooms have lovely walnut *armoires* and the bright, new suite has a tiny single attached for children.

Rooms: 2 triple, both with bath & wc.

Price: 190 Frs for two, including breakfast.

Meals: Half board at 190 Frs for one.

Open: All year.

From Bouviers, take small lane NE towards Foing-lès-Écuries; park in village square and walk 500 yards up track marked 'Pré-aux-Vaches'. House on right inside gate.

Map No: 17   MM 244-44

Ferdinand & Jonquille de BOVINE
Grange Nouvelle
26999 Foing-lès-Ecuries
Drôme
Tel: (0)4 12 34 56 78

From A6 exit Valence Sud on D68 to Chabeuil. There, cross river and turn left on D154 towards Combouin for 5km; signposted.

Map No: 12   MM 244-37

Mme Madeleine CABANES
Les Péris
CD 154
26120 Châteaudouble
Drôme
Tel: (0)4 75 59 80 51
Fax: (0)4 75 59 48 78

Madame Dumond's kindliness infuses her home — one that, at first glance, is coy about its age or charms. She will gladly share stories with you of her last trip to London and of her family (and show you the photographs). The slightly fading carpets, small shower rooms and loos down the hall all become incidental after a short while. Enjoy, instead, the peace of the leafy garden and relish breakfast — homemade jams and *gâteau*, eggs, organic honeys, cheese and toast.

Rooms: 2 twin, 1 single/twin, all with own shower & wc.

Price: 220-270 Frs for two, including breakfast.

Meals: Restaurant 2km away.

Open: All year.

The hard-working Cornillons bought this ruined 1769 farmhouse in the 1960s and have laboured diligently to create their beautiful property and the surrounding vineyards. The bedrooms have dark beams, lovely old doors forming cupboards and views out across lavender fields or the chestnut-shaded courtyard. The dining/sitting room, with an open fire for winter warmth after a truffle expedition, is very snug and everyone eats together at the long wooden table. There is a cleverly-hidden swimming pool, too.

Rooms: 3 double, 1 twin, 1 triple, all with bath & wc.

Price: From 360 Frs for two, including breakfast.

Meals: 140 Frs, excluding wine (60 Frs)(not Sun).

Open: All year.

Gîtes for 3 people

From A7 Valence Sud exit onto A49 towards Grenoble. At roundabout No33 right onto D538a towards Beaumont. After 2.2km signposted on right.

Map No: 12   MM 244-36

Mme Lina de CHIVRÉ-DUMOND
Germon
26760 Beaumont-lès-Valence
Drôme
Tel: (0)4 75 59 71 70
Fax: (0)4 75 59 75 24
e-mail: linadechivredumond@minitel.net

From Montélimar, N7 for Orange. At Bollène, D994 to Suze-la-Rousse. There, D59 for St Paul-Trois-Châteaux; right on D117 to La Baume-de-Transit; signposted.

Map No: 17   MM 240-8

Ludovic & Eliane CORNILLON
Domaine de Saint-Luc
26130 La Baume-de-Transit
Drôme
Tel: (0)4 75 98 11 51
Fax: (0)4 75 98 19 22

Perched 2,000 feet up in *Drôme Provençale*, you have glorious views of the foothills of the Alps. The ochres and pastels of the blue-shuttered building reinforce the happy marriage of the sophisticated and the homespun. The Fortunatos (Italian/Spanish) have a daughter and love having small guests: there's a playground (visible from the bedrooms), walks, woods and fields to run in — will they want to leave? Dinner includes homegrown veg, own chicken, bread made with their own wheat and cooked in their old bread oven.

Rooms: 3 double, 2 triple, all with shower & wc.

Price: 280-300 Frs for two, including breakfast. Extra bed 70 Frs.

Meals: 105 Frs, excluding wine.

Open: All year.

From the north: A7 exit Valence Sud then D111 to Crest. There, D538 through Bordeaux & towards Dieulefit for 5km. Right on D192 towards Truinas. House on right.

Map No: 17   MM 245-4

Pilar & Carlo FORTUNATO
Les Volets Bleus
26460 Truinas
Drôme
Tel: (0)4 75 53 38 48
Fax: (0)4 75 53 49 02

This artistic, caring couple are deeply concerned with social and ecological issues. They have renovated their farmhouse with sensitivity and an eye for detail, using nothing but authentic materials. Art-lovers will enjoy the summer exhibitions and courses as well as Madame's beautifully-made china dolls. Guest quarters, in a separate building, have good rooms and handsome carpentry by Mado's son. Organic meals with home-grown vegetables and fruit in season are served in the vaulted guest dining-room or on the terrace.

Rooms: 3 double, 1 suite for 4, all with bath or shower & wc.

Price: 250-380 Frs for two, including breakfast.

Meals: 85 Frs, including wine & coffee.

Open: All year.

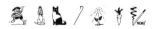

From Chabeuil, D538 towards Crest for 5km (ignore signs for Montvendre). Left at sign 'Les Dourcines'; house 700m on right next to 'Auberge-Restaurant' sign.

Map No: 12   MM 244-37

Mado GOLDSTEIN & Bernard DUPONT
Les Dourcines
26120 Montvendre
Drôme
Tel: (0)4 75 59 24 27

Sample the simple country life at this friendly, hard-working poultry and frog farm which has been in the family for a century. Despite 5000 eggs to collect before breakfast, Madame always finds time to spend with guests. The bedrooms are in a separate wing of the farm with unfussy modern interiors, nice antique beds and pretty floral linen. Meals of regional food are served family-style and include home-produced vegetables, fruit and eggs. The setting, at the foot of Mont Vercors, is very peaceful.

Rooms: 2 double, 1 triple, each with shower or bath & wc.

Price: 255 Frs for two, including breakfast. Extra bed 64 Frs.

Meals: 70 Frs, including wine & coffee. 45 Frs under 10s.

Open: All year.

There's a 70s feel to this villa high above the valley outside Valence. Your hostess is deliciously enthusiastic and her welcome is huge, a gift inherited from Armenian parents. Breakfast, with hot croissants and homemade organic jam, on the terrace whence the magnificent chalk escarpments of the Vercors range are visible. The rooms are big with flowery wallpaper. A little traffic noise can be heard in the daytime but this is an excellent stopover. There's a B&B on each side of the road but, following our instructions, this one is on the LEFT.

Rooms: 1 twin with shower & wc, 1 double with bath & wc.

Price: 270-300 Frs for two, including breakfast.

Meals: Vast choice in Valence.

Open: All year.

From Romans D538 to Alixan. On entering Alixan, turn left following 'Chambres d'Hôtes' signs for St Didier. House down short track on right 3km from Alixan.

Map No: 12   MM 244-37

Christiane & Jean-Pierre IMBERT
Le Marais
26300 Saint-Didier-de-Charpey
Drôme
Tel: (0)4 75 47 03 50

From A7 Valence Nord exit through Bourg-lès-Valence centre then left on N532 towards Romans/Grenoble. Exit to St Marcel. At 'Place de la Mairie' follow signs. House on LEFT.

Map No: 12   MM 244-36

Marie-Jeanne KATCHIKIAN
La Pineraie
383 Chemin Bel Air
26320 Saint-Marcel-lès-Valence
Drôme
Tel: (0)4 75 58 72 25
e-mail: marie.katchikian@club.francetelecom.fr

Enjoy walks in the enchanting garden or a swim in the nearby river. This busy, lively château, set in wild, beautiful countryside, is also open to groups studying meditation, music and massage in the summer. The views to the Vercors hills are stunning. All the food is organic and there are vegetarian dishes. The large bedrooms with their hardwood floors have some fine antiques. The bathrooms, across the corridor, are a little basic. Madame has a dormitory upstairs which can sleep 60 for groups during courses!

Rooms: 3 twin, one with shower & wc, one with shower, sharing wc, one sharing shower & wc.

Price: 260-310 Frs for two, including breakfast.

Meals: Occasionally 90 Frs, excluding wine.

Open: All year (bookings only).

The stone cross-vaulting in the dining-room is wonderful and Francis has renovated the rest of the house with love too. He has poured his energy into giving new life to old beams and tiles. He was once an engineer. Jackie is an artist... "And it shows", says a reader. There is a huge organic vegetable garden, producing the basics, plus fruit and eggs, for some superb meals. The rooms are perfectly simple, not a frill too many. Lively and charming people living in lovely countryside.

Rooms: 2 triple, 1 double, 1 twin, each with shower & wc.

Price: 285-315 Frs for two, including breakfast.

Meals: 115 Frs, including wine & coffee.

Open: All year.

From Crest, D93 to Mirabel et Blacons. Château on left as you leave village with sign 'Galerie Arbre de Vie' on wall.

Map No: 17   MM 245-4

Evelyne LATUNE
Château de Blacons
26400 Mirabel et Blacons, Crest
Drôme
Tel: (0)4 75 40 01 00
Fax: (0)4 75 40 04 97

From Montélimar D540 E to La Batie Rolland (10km). In village left onto D134 towards St Gervais; signposted on left.

Map No: 17   MM 240-4

Francis & Jackie MONEL
La Joie
26160 La Batie Rolland
Drôme
Tel: (0)4 75 53 81 51
Fax: (0)4 75 53 81 51

If you enjoy real people doing real hands-on work on the land, if you don't mind somewhat basic sleeping quarters, if all things goaty (sight/smell/cheese/milk) appeal in their total authenticity, then do go and stay with the generous, well-educated, happy and relaxed Pagis family who run a thriving goat farm in this forgotten corner of the Drôme. Breakfast and dinner include homemade jams, own veg, eggs and — *quelle surprise!* — goat cheese. And moreover, Jean-Jacques plays trumpet in the local salsa band.

Rooms: 1 double, 1 quadruple, sharing a bath & wc.

Price: 190 Frs for two, including breakfast.

Meals: 75 Frs, including wine.

Open: March to November.

From Vaison-la-Romaine D938 towards Malaucène for 4km. Left on D13 for 8km. Right on D40 to Montbrun-les-Bains then right towards Sault. House 1km along on left.

Map No: 17   MM 245-18

Jean-Jacques & Agnès PAGIS
Le Chavoul
Reilhanette
26570 Montbrun-les-Bains
Drôme
Tel: (0)4 75 28 80 80

The ever-delightful and energetic Prothons are now renovating a C17 coaching inn. The great high hay barn has been put to superb use: each guestroom has a mezzanine and views through one normal and one roof window to the magnificent countryside. Lots of nice old furniture, and two rooms will have antique loos! Meals, in the family dining-room, are made with fresh products from the younger Prothons' farm; there is a welcoming fireplace; and truffle weekends in winter. A hard-working and wonderfully friendly place.

Rooms: 2 triple/quadruple, each with shower & wc (2 more rooms in 1999).

Price: 280-300 Frs for two, including breakfast.

Meals: 80-100 Frs, including wine.

Open: All year except 15 Dec to 15 Jan.

Gites for 5 people

1999

From A7 exit 18 onto N7 S towards Avignon for 2km then left on D133 towards Grignan for 5km. Just before Valaurie, right towards St Paul 3 Châteaux (D133) for 2 km — house on right.

Map No: 17   MM 240-8

Marie-Claire (Mick) & François PROTHON
Val Léron
26230 Valaurie
Drôme
Tel: (0)4 75 98 52 52
Fax: (0)4 75 98 52 52

Satin cushions, swags and curly legs: your fun-loving hosts brought their standards from their previous home on the Riviera, which means you will want for nothing. Such care, attention and unbridled luxury, including superb beds and great bathrooms, may not make for a 'homely' atmosphere but the meals... Madame is not only charming, she's a stupendous cook (*bouillabaisse* a speciality). Breakfast is a banquet of homemade jams, *brioche*, cake, and more. The half-acre garden provides rest and... flowers for indoors.

Rooms: 3 double, 1 twin, 2 suites, all with own bath and wc.

Price: 370-470 Frs for two, including breakfast.

Meals: 185 Frs, including (abundant) wine & coffee.

Open: All year.

From Lyon, A43 Chimilin/Les Abrets exit towards Les Abrets & follow signs.

Map No: 12   MM 244-28

Christian & Claude CHAVALLE REVENU
La Bruyère
38490 Les Abrets
Isère
Tel: (0)4 76 32 01 66
Fax: (0)4 76 32 06 66

Come here to experience the charming, authentically aristocratic lives of your hosts: no pretence or prissiness (2 screened-off bathrooms), just unselfconscious style. The richly-decorated *salon* has a piano, books and open fireplace. The garden has a pool, a summer-house, a large terrace, 150 species of trees, an organic vegetable garden and a statue of Grandad. Madame is too busy cooking to eat with guests but welcomes company as she's preparing dinner. Children love it — there's a room packed with toys, and the hosts' two children to play with.

Rooms: 2 double with bath or shower & wc; 1 twin with shower & wc.

Price: 350 Frs for two, including breakfast. Extra bed 50 Frs.

Meals: 120 Frs, excluding wine.

Open: All year.

From A6 exit Macon Sud/Belleville then N6 to Romaneche and Lancié. In village take road towards Fleurie into Square Les Pasquiers.

Map No: 12   MM 244-2

Jacques & Laurence GANDILHON
Les Pasquiers
69220 Lancié/Belleville
Rhône
Tel: (0)4 74 69 86 33
Fax: (0)4 74 69 86 57

Climb the old wooden stairs to your room and note the complete works of Shakespeare in French and English. Madame is delightfully theatrical and loves to make ceremonies out of daily habits. She pours tea from silver into porcelain and artfully moves the breakfast table butter as the sun rises. At night she'll light your bedside lamp and even leave a book open at a carefully chosen page for you to read after a game of (French) Scrabble. The rooms? Beautiful Persian carpets, trompe-l'œil, antiques, fresh flowers. Superb.

Rooms: 1 double with bathroom & wc; 1 double and 1 twin sharing shower & wc.

Price: 500 Frs for two, including breakfast. Children under 10 free.

Meals: Good restaurant 3km.

Open: All year.

From Bourg-en-Bresse, N83 towards Lyon. At Servas right on D64 towards Condeissiat for 5km, then left at sign 'Le Marmont' into tree-lined avenue.

Map No: 12   MM 244-4

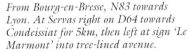

Geneviève & Henri GUIDO-ALHÉRITIÈRE
Manoir de Marmont
01960 Saint-André-sur-Vieux-Jonc
Ain
Tel: (0)4 74 52 79 74

This house flourishes with the loving care its owners lavish upon it. "Luxury without ostentation" is their aim and their passion for antiques, interior decorating, gourmet cuisine and entertaining ensures just that. A vast brunch for all and 4/5 course dinners on request: French-Canadian Denyse was a food journalist. The rooms are all different: the blue Albanaise, the raspberry Aixoise, the oak-beamed Écossaise. You choose. Beautiful Annecy with its gleaming lake, Chamonix-Mont Blanc, the towering Alps, swinging Geneva, are all nearby.

Rooms: 2 double, 1 twin, each with bath or shower & wc.

Price: 575 Frs for two, including breakfast.

Meals: 175 Frs, including wine & coffee.

Open: All year.

Gîtes for 3 people

From A41 junction Alby/Rumilly, N201 towards Chambéry. In Saint-Félix, in front of church onto D53, pass cemetery, go 300m then left (sign towards Mercy) to statue, turn right and immediately left, pass farm and go through gate.

Map No: 13   MM 244-18

Denyse & Bernard BETTS
Les Bruyères
Mercy
74540 Saint-Félix
Haute-Savoie
Tel: (0)4 50 60 96 53
Fax: (0)4 50 60 94 65

The Alps

Wood, wood and more wood, outside and in, plus lovely fabrics and furniture, make this brand new traditional-style chalet warm and reassuring. It has panoramic views south across the valley to rising green Alpine pastures and mountains. The roomy guestroom has doors to the garden and that fabulous view. Your hosts are great fun, energetic and enthusiastic about their new house, the 135km of marked mountain trails, and their two lovely labradors who enjoy the walking too. Delightful Annecy is just two dozen kilometres and a few bends away.

Rooms: 1 double with shower & wc.

Price: 300 Frs for two, including breakfast.

Meals: 85 Frs, including wine.

Open: All year.

Hospitality is a family tradition; Anne-Marie speaks fluent English, keeps horses and organises rides or walks to the Alpine pastures above the valley. The walking is indeed exceptional and you may see chamois and marmots if you go far enough. The chalet has a 'museum' depicting life on an Alpine farm in the old days. Dinner (served late to allow guests time to settle) is eaten at the long wooden table, with grandmama's recipes cooked on a wood-fired stove: "simple ingredients well prepared; delicious cheeses". Readers love it.

Rooms: 1 triple with shower & wc, 5 double sharing 3 showers & 3 wc's.

Price: 180 Frs for EACH GUEST: half-board only.

Meals: Dinner (incl. wine & coffee) included in price.

Open: All year.

From Annecy, D909 to Thones then D12 towards Serraval & Manigod; very shortly after, take D16 to Manigod. Through village then follow signs to 'Les Murailles'. House is 4th on right.

Map No: 13   MM 244-19

Colin & Alyson BROWNE
Les Murailles
74230 Manigod
Haute-Savoie
Tel: (0)4 50 44 95 87
Fax: (0)4 50 44 95 87

From Thonon-les-Bains, D26 towards Bellevaux; house is 2km before Bellevaux on the left — signposted.

Map No: 13   MM 244-9

Anne-Marie FELISAZ-DENIS
Le Chalet
La Cressonnière
74470 Bellevaux
Haute-Savoie
Tel: (0)4 50 73 70 13
Fax: (0)4 50 73 70 13

Halfway between France and Switzerland, in green hilly country, this chalet was built by Monsieur himself. You will warm to his earthy, jovial manner and appreciate Madame's enthusiastic welcome. The guestrooms are functional, the furniture is well-worn, the first-floor room is next to the kitchen and its bathroom opposite. Dinner dishes are Savoyard with ingredients from the large kitchen garden and poultry farm (now run by younger members of the family). A chorus of readers say, "good folk, excellent value".

Rooms: 1 double with shower & own wc, 1 double with bath & wc on landing.

Price: 200 Frs for two, including breakfast.

Meals: 80 Frs, including wine.

Open: April to October.

Stone and wood, white paint, dried flowers and good furniture combine to give this 200-year-old Savoyard farmhouse a light, harmonious air that matches Madame's smartly energetic presence. She keeps a kitchen garden which provides fresh vegetables for her good and varied dinners and will do anything for you. Monsieur shares his extensive wine knowledge and interest in mushroom-collecting. There is a sitting-room for guests with an unusual half-moon window at floor level.

Rooms: 1 double, 2 twin, each with shower & wc (one behind curtain).

Price: 280 Frs for two, including breakfast.

Meals: 85 Frs, including wine (not Sundays).

Open: March to mid-November.

From Annecy, N201 towards Geneva. Soon after Cruseilles, left onto D27 to Copponex. Through village then left at cemetery; sign for Chambres d'Hôtes Châtillon — 1.5km. House on right.

Map No: 13   MM 244-7

Maryse & Aimé GAL
Châtillon
74350 Copponex
Haute-Savoie
Tel: (0)4 50 44 22 70

From Annecy, N201 towards Geneva. 1km after Cruseilles, D27 left to Copponex. Through village, left at cemetery; signs to Chambres d'Hôtes Châtillon. House on left.

Map No: 13   MM 244-7

Suzanne & André GAL
La Bécassière
Châtillon
74350 Copponex
Haute-Savoie
Tel: (0)4 50 44 08 94

There are many reasons to head for this Savoyard chalet — not least of which are relaxed hosts, a daughter willing to babysit and a kind micro-climate: the nearby mountains apparently attract the clouds, leaving the sun to beat a clear path to your door. Breakfast only is provided but the hosts, both locals, recommend restaurants and provide kitchen facilities. The rooms, in a little chalet that shares the garden (with swings and ropes), are basic but the garden is a pleasant surprise. Only 10km from Annecy.

Rooms: 2 double (+ convertible sofa) in cottage, each with shower & wc. 1 double in house with shower & wc.

Price: 240 Frs for two, including breakfast.

Meals: Self-catering possible.

Open: All year.

Gîtes for 6 people

In mind-boggling Alpine beauty, this C19 chalet embodies the tradition of French B&B. From the moment you arrive you are one of the family, welcome to join in Madame's activity — for smilingly, tirelessly active she will be! Do let her know it matters little they don't speak English. Dinners are solid Savoyard affairs where you may sit with guests staying a week or two. Rooms are fairly ordinary. The setting, at the end of a valley, is truly lovely; footpaths lead up the valley to a small lake, and up, and up, and up...for the more adventurous.

Rooms: 4 double & 1 twin, all with bath & wc.

Price: 235 Frs for two, including breakfast.

Meals: 80 Frs, including wine.

Open: All year.

From Annecy (sud) D16 towards Rumilly. Enter Marcellaz-Albanias and go immediately left on D38 towards Chapeiry for 1km. Right towards Chaunu; house 100m up on right.

Map No: 13   MM 244-18

Claudie & Jean-Louis MARTIN
Chemin de Chaunu
74150 Marcellaz-Albanais
Haute-Savoie
Tel: (0)4 50 69 73 04

From Thonon-les-Bains, D26 to Bellevaux. There, left to La Clusaz then towards La Chèvrerie — house on right (6km from Bellvaux & soon after entering La Clusaz).

Map No: 13   MM 244-9

Francis & Geneviève PASQUIER
La Clusaz — Vallon
74470 Bellevaux
Haute-Savoie
Tel: (0)4 50 73 71 92

A farm with a difference; in the family for five generations, it produces trees and organic fertilisers. They also run an art gallery just up the road (where the pool and Monsieur's B&B rooms are...). Madame's unaffected warmth melts any shyness you may feel and her love of art is reflected in the decoration and *objets*. She may play the piano, Monsieur the accordion; there is classical music almost all the time and good simple food in the evening; very comfortable rooms and good 'presence'.

Rooms: 3 double, 2 twin, 1 triple: 5 with shower & wc, 1 with shower sharing wc.

Price: 288 Frs for two, including breakfast.

Meals: 85 Frs, including wine.

Open: All year.

Gîtes for 4 people

 30 Frs

This is a year-round Alpine dream. In summer it's all flowers, bees, birds and rushing streams. In winter, you can easily reach the vast ski areas of Les Arcs and Val d'Isère, ski cross-country or snow-walk nearer to home. The cuisine is as good and honest as the young hosts, cooked in the outside wood oven in summer. Children are catered for with early suppers, son Boris is a willing playmate and Claude will babysit in the evening. Guests have their own comfortable dayroom with a refrigerator. Readers love both people and food.

Rooms: 1 suite for 4/5, 1 double for 2/3, each with shower & wc.

Price: 240 Frs for two, including breakfast (reduction children & long stays).

Meals: 85 Frs, including wine & coffee. Children's prices.

Open: All year.

From Aix-les-Bains, D913 to Trévignin ('direction Le Revard') then follow signs.

Map No: 13   MM 244-18

Josseline & Daniel CHAPPAZ
La Jument Verte
Place de l'Eglise
73100 Trévignin
Savoie
Tel: (0)4 79 61 47 52

From Albertville N90 to Moutiers then D85 towards Bourg-St-Maurice. Right on D87 (later D225) to Peisey-Nancroix. Signposted in village.

Map No: 13   MM 244-32

Claude COUTIN & Franck CHENAL
Maison Coutin, T12 Peisey
73210 Peisey-Nancroix
Savoie
Tel: (0)4 79 07 93 05/
        (0)6 14 11 54 65
Fax: (0)4 79 07 93 05

Another Savoyard farm, another stupendous set of views across the surrounding massif (beyond a pretty messy farmyard, it must be said). Masses of home-grown vegetables and meat for dinner *en famille*, round a table big enough to seat a rugby team, with regional specialities centre stage. Proper meals are considered essential for those planning to explore the area, be it on skis or on foot. Bedrooms (due for redecoration) may seem like country cousins with their old beds and shared loo, but they are excellent value.

Rooms: 2 double + bunk beds, each with shower, sharing wc.

Price: 225 Frs for two, including breakfast.

Meals: Dinner 75 Frs.

Open: All year.

Gîtes for 4 people

Blazing fires, natural wood — all pure Savoyard ; big rooms and luxury bathrooms — such a treat. The televisions and the cardphone in the hall give a slight 'hotelly' feel, but what matter? Perched on the edge of a mountain, you have a superb view of peaks above and villages below, be you in your room, in the jacuzzi, or rolling in the snow after your sauna. After a hearty breakfast your Franco-American hostess will gladly help you map out your itinerary — mountain-lake fishing in summer, skiing in winter, superb walking all year.

Rooms: 2 suites for 4, 3 double (queen or king-size beds), all with bath or shower & wc.

Price: 550-750 Frs for two, including breakfast.

Meals: 185 Frs, including wine & coffee (twice a week); good restaurants within walking distance.

Open: Dec to April & June to Sept.

Gîtes for 9 people

From Albertville, N212 towards Megève. After 22km, left to Saint Nicolas-la-Chapelle; follow signs.

Map No: 13   MM 244-20

André & Michelle JOLY
Le Passieux
Ferme du Mont Charvin
73590 Saint-Nicolas-la-Chapelle
Savoie
Tel: (0)4 79 31 62 89 /69 37
Fax: (0)4 79 31 62 89

From Bourg-St-Maurice D902 towards Val d'Isère through Ste Foy-Tarentaise. After La Thuile left towards Ste Foy Station and follow wooden signposts.

Map No: 13   MM 244-21

Nancy TABARDEL
Yellowstone Chalet
Bonconseil Station
73640 Sainte-Foy-Tarentaise
Savoie
Tel: (0)4 79 06 96 06
Fax: (0)4 79 06 96 05

THE ALPS

The heart fills upon arrival at this house on the edge of the Vanoise National Park, 4000 feet up near the Italian border. Bernard is a qualified summer and winter guide for walkers and the Trigons do know about walking, in boots or snow-shoes; delicious packed lunches are easily made and dinner in the stone-vaulted dining-room is a convivial feast. Rooms are large, sober, just right. Authenticity abounds: hamlet, house, hills and mountains, food, activities and atmosphere. It is a friendly family house and you will want to stay. Accompanied treks for guests.

Rooms: 3 twin, 1 triple, all with bath & wc.

Price: 260 Frs for two, including breakfast.

Meals: 70 Frs, excluding wine.

Open: All year.

Each high moment in the history of France has left its mark on this listed, partly 12th-century château which is surrounded by village houses. Mitterand, for example, was with the Resistance here. It is definitely a fine setting for the summer evening spectaculars that the owners stage. Despite its illustrious past it must be said the rooms themselves offer less than the grandness you might be led to expect. They are a little small and dim but the splendour of the whole place — and its ghostly mysteries — will surely overcome that.

Rooms: 3 suites, each with antechamber, shower & wc.

Price: 450 Frs for two, including breakfast.

Meals: Choice 1.5-6km.

Open: All year.

From Chambéry, N6 towards Turin. 4km before Modane, left to St André/L'Orgère. Through village then signs on left to Le Villard.

Map No: 13   MM 244-31

Bernard & Michèle TRIGON
Le Villard
73500 Saint-André
Savoie
Tel: (0)4 79 05 27 17

From Gap, D994 towards Veynes. 4km before Veynes, take D320 towards Dévoluy; Montmaur is 2km on, visible from the road. Drive along château wall then towards church.

Map No: 18   MM 245-6

Raymond & Élise LAURENS
Château de Montmaur
05400 Veynes
Hautes-Alpes
Tel: (0)4 92 58 11 42
Fax: (0)4 92 58 11 42

There is a fine acacia over the terrace, the garden rambles in and out of shade; inside, there are fireplaces and decorative platters of fruit. One bedroom: lavender colour-washed walls, stripped wooden floors and good country furniture, with a rolled-edge cast-iron bath and period basin. Now to breakfast: served under mature trees with vineyards and distant mountains... try the Scottish pancakes and homemade jam. Dinner is delicious too; Michael is an imaginative chef and his sense of hospitality has been praised to the skies.

Rooms: 1 suite for 4, 2 double, each with bath or shower & wc.

Price: 270-350 Frs for two, including breakfast.

Meals: 125 Frs, including aperitif, wine & coffee.

Open: All year.

Gites for 2/3 people

From Vaison-la-Romaine D938 N towards Nyons for 5km then right on D46 dir. Buis-les-Baronnies for 4km. On entering Faucon, house on right at crossroads with D205 (blue gate & shutters).

Map No: 17   MM 245-17

Provence – Riviera

Michael BERRY
Les Airs du Temps
Quartier les Aires
84110 Faucon
Vaucluse
Tel: (0)4 90 46 44 57
Fax: (0)4 90 46 44 57

Simplicity is the theme in this recently-restored farmhouse. Its clean and basic rooms include good beds with Provençal covers and views over the fields. According to one of our readers, "Madame is a star with a lovely sense of humour"; fortunately she is up and shining during the daytime as well... and she and her family create a good atmosphere round the table. The fare is traditional, with home-grown vegetables.

Rooms: 5 double, all with bath or shower & wc.

Price: 280 Frs for two, including breakfast (420 Frs for two, half board).

Meals: 80 Frs, including wine & coffee.

Open: All year.

Set in a large walled garden, this 18th-century *mas de vigneron* (the vats are still intact) has been well renovated by the current owners, a Swiss couple who were formerly in the book trade. The rooms are immaculate, each named after a Provençal author and stocked with his or her books! Your hosts' attention to detail is superb: desks with headed paper, lavender bouquets, childrens' toys and, downstairs, a summer kitchen, table-tennis and a drinks fridge. And fabulous walking of course.

Rooms: 3 double, 1 triple, 1 for four people, all with shower & wc.

Price: 240-330 Frs for two, including breakfast.

Meals: Barbecue possible in summer.

Open: April to October.

From Apt, N100 towards Avignon. At Lumières, D106 towards Lacoste, then D218 to Ménerbes; second farm on the left.

Map No: 17   MM 245-31

Maryline & Claude CHABAUD
Mas Marican
84220 Goult
Vaucluse
Tel: (0)4 90 72 28 09

From A7, Bollène exit onto D994 and D8 towards Carpentras. At La Bégude-de-Mazenc, D977 to Violès; signposted in the village.

Map No: 17   MM 245-16

Augustine & Jean-Claude CORNAZ
La Farigoule
Le Plan de Dieu
84150 Violès
Vaucluse
Tel: (0)4 90 70 91 78

A C18 château of great character — its chapel includes part of the Roman town wall. Monsieur has done much of the restoration himself, recently adding a swimming pool. The wonderful entrance hall has its own grand piano. The very large guestrooms feature antiques, old tiles and fireplaces and two of the bathrooms, with their old-fashioned claw-footed baths, are built into the restored tower. Meals, which include home-grown fruit, are served on the terrace or in the dining-room. Big house: let the telephone ring at length.

Rooms: 3 triple, each with bath & wc.

Price: 500-550 Frs for two, including breakfast. Extra bed 50 Frs.

Meals: 130 Frs, including coffee, excluding wine (50 Frs). Cold supper 85 Frs.

Open: All year.

We need pages to do justice to this gem. The hosts own the locals' favourite shop, 'Epicerie Fine', and Madame is a renowned cook. For breakfast she may serve her special *galette de pomme* and her evening meals are outstanding. The beauty of the interior — sunshine yellows, fresh flowers, natural stone, charming furniture — is partnered by the stunning exterior, a well-planted garden offering shade, a field of sunflowers (in July) and views of the Luberon. Simply arrive, absorb and wonder what on earth you did to deserve it all.

Rooms: 1 suite, 2 quadruple, 2 double, all with shower & wc.

Price: 400-700 Frs for two, including breakfast. Extra bed 100 Frs.

Meals: 150 Frs, including aperitif, wine & coffee.

Open: All year.

From Roman theatre in Vaison follow signs for Malaucène/Mt Ventoux. Left onto 'Chemin des Planchettes'. Signposted.

Map No: 17   MM 245-17

Rémy & Cécile DAILLET
Château de Taulignan
Saint-Marcellin-lès-Vaison
84110 Vaison-la-Romaine
Vaucluse
Tel: (0)4 90 28 71 16
Fax: (0)4 90 28 77 42

From Avignon, N7 then D22 towards Apt. After 'Le Petit Palais', signposted on right.

Map No: 17   MM 245-30

Isabelle & Rolland GOUIN
La Ferme des 3 Figuiers
Le Petit Jonquier
84800 Lagnes
Vaucluse
Tel: (0)4 90 20 23 54
Fax: (0)4 90 20 25 47

Set among vineyards below the Montmirail hills, this simple, Provençal farmhouse has a courtyard shaded by a lovely linden tree. The views across the surrounding country and unspoilt villages are wonderful. Madame grows organic vegetables and fruit and considers dinners with her guests, in dining-room or courtyard, as the most interesting part of doing B&B. Meals are also showcases for local specialities. The interior decoration is in a bright, traditional French country style with old family furniture.

Rooms: 2 suites, 1 double, 1 twin, each with shower & wc.

Price: 220 Frs for two, including breakfast.

Meals: 75 Frs, including wine.

Open: March to mid-November.

Built in the 18th century, renovated with an excellent mix of old Provence (stones, floors, ceilings) and modern comforts (bathrooms and bedding), surrounded by orchards (visitors may help themselves in season), this is a well ordered house for discerning guests. Madame has years of experience and likes to do things by the book. Each bedroom is different, modern and spotless with attractive fabrics and good bedding, and your widely-travelled host serve delicious dinners after which they join their guests.

Rooms: 6 twin, all with shower & wc.

Price: 480 Frs for two, including breakfast.

Meals: 150 Frs, including wine & coffee.

Open: All year.

From Carpentras D7 N through Aubignan & Vacqueyras; fork right, still on D7, towards Sablet; 500m after 'Cave des Vignerons de Gigondas' turn right; signposted.

Map No: 17   MM 245-17

Sylvette GRAS
La Ravigote
84190 Gigondas
Vaucluse
Tel: (0)4 90 65 87 55
Fax: (0)4 90 65 36 11

From A7, Avignon-Sud exit, D22 towards Apt; house is 2km after the signpost 'Petit Palais', near junction with N100.

Map No: 17   MM 245-30

Monique & François GRECK
Le Mas du Grand Jonquier
84800 Lagnes
Vaucluse
Tel: (0)4 90 20 90 13
Fax: (0)4 90 20 91 18

The friendly, energetic Kozlowskis have turned the garden round their C18 stone farmhouse into a luxuriant mass of roses, lavender and olives and the entrance to the pretty guestrooms is shaded by a pergola. The rooms, furnished with a growing collection of country antiques, are in a converted *bergerie* which leads directly onto the garden. Breakfast is eaten in the handsome vaulted dining-room with its long trestle table. The views to Mont Ventoux across a panorama of pure Provence are spectacular.

Rooms: 1 double and 3 twin, all with bath or shower & wc.

Price: 450-550 Frs for two, including breakfast (3 nights min).

Meals: In village or within 5km.

Open: March to October.

A warm welcome and a real guestroom in a real home where the friendly Lawrences thoroughly enjoy their role as hosts. The room has its own dressing-room and a newly-tiled shower. The new house is built of old stone in traditional local style and surrounded by hills, woods, fields and vineyards with lovely views across the valley towards Bonnieux and the Luberon. The Lawrences worked overseas for 40 years, he in public works, she in the diplomatic, and the house is full of attractive *objets* from their travels.

Rooms: 1 triple with shower & wc.

Price: 260 Frs for two, including breakfast. Extra bed 80 Frs.

Meals: Good choice 5km.

Open: All year.

Gîtes for 4 people

From Avignon, N100 towards Apt. 10km after Lumières, right towards Bonnieux, Pont Julien. Cross Roman bridge & take D149 towards Bonnieux for 2km; signposted on right.

Map No: 17   MM 245-31

Shirley & Jan KOZLOWSKI
Jas des Eydins
Route du Pont Julien
84480 Bonnieux
Vaucluse
Tel: (0)4 90 75 84 99
Fax: (0)4 90 75 96 71

From Avignon N100 for Apt. At Coustellet, D2 for Gordes. After Les Imberts right on D207 & D148 to St Pantaléon. Pass church, stay on D104 for 50m, left onto small uphill road; THIRD drive on the right.

Map No: 17   MM 245-80

Pierrette & Charles LAWRENCE
Villa La Lèbre
Saint-Pantaléon
84220 Gordes
Vaucluse
Tel: (0)4 90 72 20 74
Fax: (0)4 90 72 20 74

In pretty Lourmarin, this is still one of our favourites. The former 17th-century staging post is decorated with great refinement and filled with antiques and exquisite fabrics by the cultivated and interesting owners. Monsieur is an interior decorator and has his shop on the ground floor. There are bikes for guests' use — Madame, a keen cyclist, is ready to advise on routes and leads such an active life that she may just not be there to greet you or dust your room! For the less athletic or the saddle-sore there's a cool, shaded garden.

Rooms: 2 double and 3 twin, all with bath or shower & wc.

Price: 300-400 Frs for two, including breakfast.

Meals: Choice locally.

Open: All year.

Set in great walking country among spectacular fields of lavender with vast views, this fine C19 farmhouse is built around a courtyard shaded by a spreading linden tree. The family living/dining-room is homely and warm with a large table and a fireplace for cooler weather. The comfortable, light-filled rooms are carefully decorated in an unpretentious mix of new and old. Monsieur is a keen cook and prepares Provençal dishes using local produce and herbs while the charming, enthusiastic Madame makes the desserts.

Rooms: 1 suite for 4, 1 suite for 3, 3 triple, all with bath or shower & wc.

Price: 390-450 Frs for two, including breakfast.

Meals: 135 Frs, including wine & coffee.

Open: All year except Jan & Feb.

From Aix-en-Provence, N96 and D556 to Pertuis. There, D973 to Cadenet and then D943 towards Bonnieux until you reach Lourmarin.

Map No: 17   MM 245-31

M & Mme LASSALLETTE
Villa Saint-Louis
35 rue Henri de Savornin
84160 Lourmarin
Vaucluse
Tel: (0)4 90 68 39 18
Fax: (0)4 90 68 10 07

From Carpentras, D941/D1 to Sault (41km) then D942 towards Aurel. Just before Aurel, left at signpost.

Map No: 17   MM 245-18

Christian & Visnja MICHELLE
Richarnau
84390 Aurel
Vaucluse
Tel: (0)4 90 64 03 62
Fax: (0)4 90 64 03 62

They are a delightful older couple who thoroughly enjoy caring for guests at their farmhouse just outside the very pretty village of Le Thor. The house is surrounded by refreshingly cool, green gardens and a countryside of fields, vineyards and hills. The rooms are quiet and comfortable with lots of books and paintings. Madame prepares breakfast in the separate kitchen in the guest wing and they will sometimes take guests for walks or visits to nearby attractions.

Rooms: 3 double, all with bath or shower & wc.

Price: 360 Frs for two, including breakfast. Min. 2 nights.

Meals: 90 Frs, including wine (arrival day only); choice 3km.

Open: April to September.

Don't pick up that broken saucer — it's part of an artist's installation. A fascinating contemporary arts centre run by a Franco-Polish couple who offer artists a spell of creative peace and sympathetic B&B guests a chance to share the privilege of an art-centred atmosphere. Pierre will even take you sketching. The old Provençal house has an authentic patina and lovely worn tiles; the sparse furniture is designer-perfect; the artwork everywhere; the garden reached by a bridge across the street; the whole feel incomparably special.

Rooms: 2 double, 1 twin, each with bath or shower & wc.

Price: 300 Frs for two, including breakfast.

Meals: 120 Frs, including wine.

Open: All year except January.

From A7 exit Avignon-Sud, towards Cavaillon for 1km then left to Caumont. After village, D1 to Le Thor and once there, telephone (this is essential!).

Map No: 17   MM 245-17

André & Bénita MOURGES
La Palasse
2345 route de Saint-Saturnin D98
84250 Le Thor
Vaucluse
Tel: (0)4 90 33 92 38
Fax: (0)4 90 33 76 05

Saignon is 3km SE of Apt. In Saignon, park near PTT Post Office. On main street, house is on right, 30m after PTT.

Map No: 17   MM 245-31

Kamila REGENT & Pierre JACCAUD
Chambre de Séjour avec Vue...
84400 Saignon-en-Luberon
Vaucluse
Tel: (0)4 90 04 85 01
Fax: (0)4 90 04 85 01

The solid old aristocratic *bastide* was built on the foundations of a 12th-century water-mill and the thick stone walls keep the house cool. There is a very big pool in the large, landscaped, tree-filled garden surrounding it (though the busy road tends to make its presence felt). Breakfast is wonderful out on the terrace or in the family dining-room, dinners include Madame's Provençal specialities. The house is full of interesting mementoes of the owners' time in various North African countries.

Rooms: 2 double, 1 twin, all with bath or shower & wc.

Price: 330 Frs for two, including breakfast.

Meals: 100 Frs, excluding wine (except weekends).

Open: All year.

The Secchis' mansion possesses a cool charm: granite floors, simple rooms, the odd antique. The welcome, though, warms things up considerably. The Italian owner, the chic, suited Monsieur Secchi, and his French wife, will draw you into engaging conversation from the moment you arrive. There are homemade jams for breakfast and the evening meal may be taken with your hosts and include regional dishes and organic wine made from their own grapes. Apple orchards, vineyards and woods surround this impressive house.

Rooms: 5 double with shower & wc, 1 twin with bath & wc.

Price: 350-450 Frs for two, including breakfast. Extra bed 100 Frs.

Meals: 130 Frs, including wine.

Open: All year.

From Carpentras, D974 towards Bédoin/Mont Ventoux; stay on this road, do NOT enter Crillon village. The mill is on the left below signpost.

Map No: 17   MM 245-17

Bernard & Marie-Luce RICQUART
Moulin d'Antelon
84410 Crillon-le-Brave
Vaucluse
Tel: (0)4 90 62 44 89
Fax: (0)4 90 62 44 90

From L'Isle sur la Sorgue D938 towards Carpentras. After 2nd roundabout look for sign 'Pépiniériste Le Chêne Vert' — road on right here.

Map No: 17   MM 245-17

Josette SECCHI
Château des Costières
1634 route de Carpentras
84800 L'Isle-sur-la-Sorgue
Vaucluse
Tel: (0)4 90 38 39 19
Fax: (0)4 90 38 39 19

Narrow, cobbled streets lead to this fascinating, impeccably-furnished house that was once part of the C17 Bishop's Palace. The Verdiers are charming, cultivated people — he an architect/builder, she a teacher — with a keen interest in antiques and in protecting mediæval Vaison from 'progress'. The guestrooms and cosy *salon* have a warm, Provençal feel. Well-presented breakfasts on the terrace come complete with French and English newspapers and, best of all, the magnificent view to the Roman bridge.

Rooms: 2 double, 2 twin, each with bath or shower & wc.

Price: 380-420 Frs for two, including breakfast.

Meals: Choice in Vaison.

Open: All year except 2 weeks in November.

This modern, Provençal-style house sits high above the surrounding vineyards and orchards as if in a Cézanne: the view of the Montagne Sainte Victoire is breathtaking. A good base for a family holiday where guests have a large room with mezzanine and kitchenette in a separate little house (illustrated); there is a fine pool, table tennis, *boules* for all, the sea 45 minutes away and lovely old Aix within easy reach. The Babeys, with four sons, are relaxed and easy. One reader wrote: "A favourite, such caring and phlegmatic hosts".

Rooms: Cottage for 4 : double/twin on ground floor, double on mezzanine, bathroom and kitchenette.

Price: 360 Frs for two, including breakfast. Extra bed 120 Frs.

Meals: Self-catering. Restaurants in village 2km.

Open: All year.

From Orange, D975 to Vaison. In town, follow 'Ville Médiévale' signs.

Map No: 17   MM 245-17

Aude & Jean-Loup VERDIER
L'Évêché, Rue de l'Évêché
84110 Vaison-la-Romaine
Vaucluse
Tel: (0)4 90 36 13 46
Fax: (0)4 90 36 32 43

From Aix, N7 towards Nice for 20km. Left after Château de La Bégude; Chemin des Prés is on right. House at end.

Map No: 18   MM 245-32

Jean-Pierre & Sophie BABEY
Les Bréguières
Chemin des Prés
13790 Rousset
Bouches-du-Rhône
Tel: (0)4 42 29 01 16
Fax: (0)4 42 29 01 16

Guests have been very happy with their room (superbly Provençal in style, boasting a view of the mountains and an excellent bathroom), the lush shrubby garden which protects from the encroaching urbanisation, and the well-furnished reception rooms. You can be as independent as you like but Madame, an intelligent mother of four students who welcomes children, enjoys spending time with her guests and pointing them to the best local treasures. Breakfast is on the terrace or in the dining-room.

Rooms: 1 twin with bath & wc.

Price: 300 Frs for two, including breakfast.

Meals: Full choice in Aix.

Open: All year except August.

A fine old house, once a magistrate's summer residence, is what remains of a huge estate that has been sold off by the city for business premises so the Bouvants' 18th-century manor and formal French garden and park (great old trees) are now an island surrounded by buildings. Once inside, all is fine furniture and timeless elegance with the original chapel (now a wine cellar), charming rooms, an attic sitting-room full of old radios and records to be played. Also a genuinely warm welcome from your Franco-Dutch hosts.

Rooms: 1 double, 2 twin/double, all with shower or bath & wc.

Price: 260 or 300 Frs (shower) or 340 Frs (bath) for two, including breakfast.

Meals: 100 Frs, including wine & coffee.

Open: All year.

To get there: In Aix, from Place de la Rotonde take Blvd de la République onto Ave de Lattre de Tassigny; right at 4th traffic light; 50m after Pharmacie is a red-brick building: Bastide Brunet is behind this.

Map No: 17   MM 245-31

Mme de BELLECOMBE
Bastide Brunet
Verte Colline
13090 Aix-en-Provence
Bouches-du-Rhône
Tel: (0)4 42 96 42 83
Fax: (0)4 42 96 41 93

From Aix A51 towards Marseille, 3rd exit Bouc Belair; right on D59 to Pôle d'Activités Aix-en-Provence. After roundabout, continue 3.4km. House on right after tennis court.

Map No: 17   MM 245-31

Hervé & Miriam BOUVANT
Domaine du Frère
495 rue Ampère (D59)
ZA des Milles
13852 Aix-en-Provence
Bouches-du-Rhône
Tel: (0)4 42 24 24 62
Fax: (0)4 42 24 37 89

On the beautiful, residential side of Aix and only 10 minutes walk from the centre, you'll find tranquillity in the vast garden of this 1960s house designed by Monsieur himself. The decoration, especially in two of the larger rooms, is more 60s-contemporary than Provence-rural but it is all in good taste. There's a pool and the garden has olive trees from which the helpful, cheery hosts make their own oil (though the 1997 frost was painful). Children are welcomed. Extra rooms may be available.

Rooms: 2 double and 1 twin, all with bath or shower & wc.

Price: 250-400 Frs for two, including breakfast (2 nights preferred).

Meals: Wide choice in Aix.

Open: All year.

In Aix, from Place de la Rotonde, past Tourist Information, turn into Boulevard Victor Hugo. At 9th traffic light only, turn into Route du Tholonet; l'Enclos is at second roundabout — two tall gateposts on right.

Map No: 17	MM 245-31

Mauricette & René IUNG
L'Enclos, Route du Tholonet
2 av du Général Préaud
13100 Aix-en-Provence
Bouches-du-Rhône
Tel: (0)4 42 96 40 52

Set in its charming, rose-filled garden, this 18th-century *bastide* is in the very heart of the pretty village of Peynier. It once belonged to the painter Vincent Roux and memories of Cézanne are here for all eyes to see. The house has been beautifully restored in appropriate Provençal style and the atmosphere and welcome have been much praised. The guestroom has antique furniture and a pleasing, traditionally-tiled bathroom down the corridor. Guests return year after year. Older children welcome.

Rooms: 1 double, with own bathroom; extra bed available.

Price: 350 Frs for two, including breakfast.

Meals: In village.

Open: All year, except first three weeks in August.

From Aix-en-Provence, A8 towards Nice. Canet exit on D6 towards Trets. 4km before Trets, right on D57 to Peynier.

Map No: 18	MM 245-45

Mme LAMBERT
Mas Sainte Anne
3 rue d'Auriol
13790 Peynier
Bouches-du-Rhône
Tel: (0)4 42 53 05 32
Fax: (0)4 42 53 04 28

A *maison de maître* with really ancient origins, right in the heart of old Tarascon, in a quiet cobbled street, it has been beautifully renovated without losing any of the patina of stone walls and old tiles. It is built round an ochre-hued courtyard where breakfast is served. The rooms have fine old furniture, beams, stone flags. Christiane is an artist who spent years in the States; Henry is an Australian painter and he, too, has his studio in the house. They are quiet, interesting people who are there when needed.

Rooms: 2 double, 1 twin, each with bath or shower & wc.

Price: 300-390 Frs for two, including breakfast.

Meals: Choice in town.

Open: All year (book ahead).

Cats sit like kings on cushions in the cosiest corners of this restored *mas*, which has lots of interesting bits and pieces, such as an old water pump and some carved stones on the façade. The quiet, amiable owners have amassed a collection of books about the region. *Objets* and pretty fabrics complement antiques in the simple rooms. Copious breakfasts are served under plane trees or in the dining-room in an old barn. Unpretentious Provence at its best.

Rooms: 3 double : 1 with shower & wc, 2 with shower & washbasin, sharing wc.

Price: 280 Frs for two, including breakfast.

Meals: Restaurant in village.

Open: April to 10 September.

In Tarascon centre take Rue du Château opposite the château (well signposted) — No 24 is along on right.

Map No: 17   MM 245-28

From Avignon, D571 to Châteaurenard and D571 towards Eyragues. After 3.5km take a small road left; signposted.

Map No: 17   MM 245-29

Christiane & Henry LEWIS
24 rue du Château
13150 Tarascon
Bouches-du-Rhône
Tel: (0)4 90 91 09 99
Fax: (0)4 90 91 09 99

Christiane & Robert POLI
Le Mas des Chats qui Dorment
Chemin des Prés
13630 Eyragues
Bouches-du-Rhône
Tel: (0)4 90 94 19 71

Valérie and Rémy have done a lot of work on their 17th-century *mas* over the last few years. The new suites are sybaritically luxurious with big bathrooms and lovely antiques. The original bedrooms are slightly small but charming and the garden, terrace and pool (with bar) make them well worth the price. Valérie serves refined meals in the dining-room or on the terrace. It is a beautiful setting, nestled in the *Alpilles* among pine forests and beside a lake. Horse-lovers will appreciate the stables.

Rooms: 2 double, 3 suites (1 for 4), 1 cottage, all with shower, bath & wc.

Price: Double 500 Frs, suite 900 Frs, cottage 1400 Frs, for two, including breakfast.

Meals: 260 Frs, including wine & coffee. Self-catering in cottage.

Open: All year.

Madame, who owns an antique shop, has used her knowledge and imagination to furnish this townhouse in one of Fontvieille's busy main streets with great taste. Everything here is refined and in impeccable order. Both bedrooms have beautiful antiques as well as thick woollen carpets, fine linens and large bathrooms; both overlook the small garden. There is a large, very handsome guest *salon*. Breakfast is served on old silver, a typically elegant touch. Your enthusiastic hosts enjoy sharing their love of music and Provence.

Rooms: 1 double, 1 triple, each with bath, shower & wc.

Price: 500 Frs for two, including breakfast.

Meals: Choice within walking distance.

Open: Easter to 30 October.

From A7, Cavaillon exit onto D99 to St Rémy. There, D5 towards Maussane; right towards 'Le Lac de St Rémy'; pass the lake — it is the last house.

Map No: 17   MM 245-29

Rémy REBOUL & Valérie SCHNEIDER
Mas de Gros, Route du Lac
13210 Saint-Rémy-de-Provence
Bouches-du-Rhône
Tel: (0)4 90 92 46 85
Fax: (0)4 90 92 47 78
e-mail: reboul-schneider@wanadoo.fr

From Arles, D17 to Fontvieille; follow signs to 'Regalido' Hotel. House is 50m beyond on left.

Map No: 17   MM 245-29

Jean-Marie & Édith-Claire RICARD DAMIDOT
Le Mas Ricard
107 avenue Frédéric Mistral
13990 Fontvieille
Bouches-du-Rhône
Tel: (0)4 90 54 72 67
Fax: (0)4 90 54 64 43

A lesson in how to make a modern house feel like a charming old home, but then Jean-Pierre does run an association to promote Provençal traditions. Both he and Véronique are warmly, southernly friendly. The 3 ground-floor rooms with tiled floors, old beams, antiques and Provençal fabrics, look out to a garden surrounded by oak woods. One is named after *grandmère* Camille whose photograph hangs on the wall. The *salon* with its fireplace and antiques leads to a large roofed terrace for summer breakfasts.

Rooms: 1 double/quadruple, 1 double, 1 triple, each with bath or shower & wc.

Price: 280-320 Frs for two, including breakfast.

Meals: Choice 1.5-5km.

Open: All year except 5 Jan to end Feb.

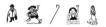

The interior of this manicured farmhouse is as cool as the welcome is warm from its French/Irish owners; they just wish you'd linger after your croissants. Natural stone, oak beams, terracotta floors and cool colours give a wonderfully light and spacious feel. Outside, centuries-old plane trees, a vine tunnel, three hectares of cypresses and horses (why not head for the *Alpilles* mountains?) add to the magic. An oft-tinkled piano is there for you to play.

Rooms: 3 double, 3 twin, all with shower & wc.

Price: 400 Frs for two, including breakfast. Extra bed 75 Frs.

Meals: Choice in Saint Rémy.

Open: All year.

From Salon-de-Pr. D16 S to Grans (6km) then left on D19 dir. Lançon-de-Pr. for 1.5km; left on Chemin des Bergers — signposted. Follow to end of road then left on Chemin de la Transhumance; house at end.

Map No: 17   MM 245-30

Jean-Pierre & Véronique RICHARD
Domaine du Bois Vert
Quartier Montauban
13450 Grans
Bouches-du-Rhône
Tel: (0)4 90 55 82 98
Fax: (0)4 90 55 82 98

From St Rémy D571 towards Avignon. After 2 roundabouts, left at 2nd bus stop (Lagoy) onto Chemin de Velleron & Prud'homme. House is 5th on right.

Map No: 17   MM 245-29

Christiane & John WALSH
Mas Shamrock
Chemin de Velleron & du Prud'homme
13210 Saint-Rémy-de-Provence
Bouches-du-Rhône
Tel: (0)4 90 92 55 79
Fax: (0)4 90 92 55 80

A mother-and-son team run this simple house, with mother in the kitchen and son 'front of house'. Although B&B is the main focus, the farm also produces aromatic plants and saffron, so what you may lose in 'homeliness' you gain in aromatic interest. If there's a full house, dinner (Provençal dishes a speciality) could be shared with 17 others — a potential party! — and if Maman's cake is anything to go by, it will be wonderful. Décor is whitewashed walls with splashes of deliciously rich colour. Jean-Pierre has bikes and makes a friendly cycling companion.

Rooms: 1 suite, 3 triple, 2 double, all with own shower & wc.

Price: 285-310 Frs for two, including breakfast.

Meals: 95 Frs, including wine & coffee.

Open: April to October.

Gîtes for 15 people

On sunny summer days, breakfast is eaten and life is lived on the peaceful terrace beside the pool of this modern villa. Monsieur, a very able watercolourist, personally designed the house in the Provençal style, adding extensions over the years. The spotlessly clean, if somewhat impersonal, guestrooms are named *Papillon* and *Provence*. They are light and airy and have direct access to the flower-filled garden and the swimming pool. An excellent base and there are many good local beaches.

Rooms: 1 double, 1 twin, each with shower & wc.

Price: 350 Frs for two, including breakfast.

Meals: 70-80 Frs, including wine.

Open: May to September.

In St Maximin take D28 towards Bras for 3km to signpost on right. From here follow narrow road 3km further.

Map No: 18   MM 245-33

Jean-Louis & Pierrette BAUDE
Domaine de Garrade
Route de Bars
83470 Saint-Maximin-la-Sainte-Baume
Var
Tel: (0)4 94 59 84 32
Fax: (0)4 94 59 83 47
e-mail: garrade@aol.com

In Fréjus N7 dir. Cannes; pass memorial to 'Morts en Indochine' on right. After 1km enter 'Les Jardins de César' development on left; 1st left = Pline l'Ancien; No 7 on left.

Map No: 18   MM 245-36

Yvette BERTIN
Les Jardins de César
7 allée Pline l'Ancien
83600 Fréjus
Var
Tel: (0)4 94 53 17 85

This delicious old manor house was built in 1760 as a silkworm farm — mulberry trees still shade the wonderful terrace that gives onto a mature garden, a meadow area with children's games, a summer pool and a stupendous view to the distant hills. Inside it is just as authentic: old tiles with good rugs, beams, white walls and simple, comfortable antique furniture. Unlike our other owners, Nicola is here four months of the year only; her Norwegian friends receive you, in perfect English, at other times. They are all delightful.

Rooms: 1 double, 1 twin, each with shower & wc; 1 double, 1 twin, sharing shower & wc.

Price: 350-400 Frs for two, including breakfast.

Meals: Wide choice within walking distance.

Open: All year.

From A8 exit 13 onto N7 E to Vidauban then left on D48 to Lorgues. In main street, post office on right: right and right again (behind post office). At T-junction left into Place Arariso. Leave square on left into Rue de la Canal; house along on left.

Map No: 18   MM 245-35

Nicola & Mario D'ANNUNZIO
La Canal
177 rue de La Canal
Quartier le Grand Jardin
83510 Lorgues
Var
Tel: (0)4 94 67 68 32
Fax: (0)4 94 67 68 69

Hospitable? The Dyens spontaneously de-iced our car without our asking! Their C18 château stands alone, surrounded by the vineyards where Monsieur, who is fluent in English, toils. It has a thoroughly lived-in appearance and atmosphere. Wine tastings and local produce are always available and there's usually a glass of Monsieur's own, notably the Blanc de blanc, at dinner. The rooms are big and furnished just as you'd expect. It is wonderfully civilised and relaxed and guests can swim or play tennis at the owners' little club 500m away.

Rooms: 1 double, 1 suite for 4, each with bath & wc.

Price: 300 Frs for two, including breakfast. Extra bed 50 Frs.

Meals: 150 Frs, including estate wine.

Open: All year.

From A8 exit Le Cannet des Maures onto N558 towards La Garde Freinet for 2km. At crossroads turn left — house 200m along.

Map No: 18   MM 245-48

Lucette & Paul DYENS
Château de Roux
Le Cannet des Maures
83340 Le Luc-en-Provence
Var
Tel: (0)4 94 60 73 10
Fax: (0)4 94 60 89 79

Your hosts were born in this unspoilt part of the Var where beautiful views of the Alps across vineyards and hills — and genuine human warmth — await you at their modernised farmhouse (19th-century foundations). The smallish bedrooms feature typical Provençal fabrics and antiques, the bathrooms are new and spotless. Breakfast is brought to you on the private terrace or in the dining-room. Monsieur, a tenant farmer, loves to talk about his *métier* and village. Madame is a kindly hostess. Readers have amply confirmed this.

Rooms: 1 triple, 1 double, 1 twin, all with shower & wc.

Price: 280 Frs for two, including breakfast. Extra bed 100 Frs.

Meals: In village (1km) or 3km away. Barbecue available.

Open: All year.

Arable fields envelop this 17th-century farmhouse that has guestrooms in a new wing, with its own entrance and a small wicker-furnished terrace. The *domaine* is a working cereal farm and has an organic vegetable garden. Rooms are modest but comfortable in simple, country style and Madame is so helpful and warm and glad to share her knowledge of the area. She also serves a wholesome farm supper on a long welcoming table in the new dining-room, where guests eat with the family and friends.

Rooms: 4 double, 1 twin, all with bath & wc.

Price: 295 Frs for two, including breakfast. Extra bed 80 Frs.

Meals: 110 Frs, including wine & coffee.

Open: All year.

Gîtes for 5 people

From Aups, D9 and D30 to Montmeyan. There, D13 towards Quinson. House is on left of road, 1km along; signposted.

Map No: 18   MM 245-34

Dany & Vincent GONFOND
Mas Saint Maurinet
Route de Quinson
83670 Montmeyan
Var
Tel: (0)4 94 80 78 03
Fax: (0)4 94 80 78 03

From Rians, D23 towards Ginasservis; right on D30 towards La Verdière. After 3km, you will see grain silos; house is 300m along.

Map No: 18   MM 245-33

Paule & Charley GRECH
Domaine Espagne
83560 Ginasservis
Var
Tel: (0)4 94 80 11 03

The Hennys came to this bright pink 1868 farmhouse from their native Holland 25 years ago and now run it as a working farm. The position is delightful, with good views of the Var hills, vineyards and orchards to be savoured from the attractive sun terrace. More energetic guests can play outdoor games or help with the harvest. Each room is named after a colour and bathrooms are decorated with beautiful Provençal tiles. Breakfast and delicious meals using home produce are served on the terrace or in the dining-room.

Rooms: 2 suites for 4 with kitchenette, 1 double, each with bath or shower & wc.

Price: From 350 Frs for two, including breakfast. 3 nights min.

Meals: 100 Frs, including wine & coffee. Self-catering.

Open: 20 March to 20 October.

Gîtes for 25 people

"SUCH delightful, cultivated people". Here is a chance to stay with a warm, lively family (four teenage children) on a working farm/vineyard with a timeless feel to it. The first-class bedrooms, impeccably decorated in authentic Provençal style, and the guests' dayroom (with mini-kitchen) are in a separate wing; breakfast on the terrace, weather permitting. Monsieur, an historian, is happy to share his encyclopædic knowledge of the monuments and sights of the area and readers simply write: "Armelle is wonderful".

Rooms: 2 twin/double & 1 suite for 4, all with bath or shower & wc.

Price: 280-320 Frs for two, including breakfast.

Meals: Self-catering. Restaurant nearby.

Open: All year.

From Salernes centre go 200m towards Entrecasteaux, right over bridge then left; right at fork. House is 2.5km further on down a track.

Map No: 18   MM 254-34

Karel & Caroline HENNY
La Bastide Rose
Quartier Haut-Gaudran
83690 Salernes
Var
Tel: (0)4 94 70 63 30
Fax: (0)4 94 70 77 34

From A8, Saint Maximin/La Sainte Baume exit onto D560 through Barjols. There, continue D560 towards Draguignan; entrance opposite D60 turning for Pontevès.

Map No: 18   MM 245-33

Guillaume & Armelle de JERPHANION
Domaine de Saint Ferréol
83670 Pontevès
Var
Tel: (0)4 94 77 10 42
Fax: (0)4 94 77 19 04

The setting is incomparable, way up in the hills with deep views from the flowered, terraced garden; miles from anywhere (take care on the road up) the 20-year-old house comes as a surprise. But inside all is definitely old France where a certain formality about place and people commands respect. The guest quarters are on the mezzanine (single bed) and in the double room off it with a modern shower room. Your hosts, much-travelled ex-Parisians, are eager to guide you to the unknown delights of the area. Children over 7 welcome.

Rooms: 1 double, 1 single with shower & wc.

Price: 320 Frs for two, including breakfast. 3rd person 130 Frs.

Meals: 95 Frs, including aperitif, wine & coffee.

Open: Easter to September.

You'll share this busy farm with myriad livestock from humble chicken to friendly dog, majestic peacock to Arab thoroughbred. The hosts manage both menagerie and human guests beautifully. In the oldest building, the rooms, with soft lighting and smart bedcovers, offer clean, crisp simplicity. It's a short walk to the main living/dining-room to eat (home-grown fruit and veg), *en famille* whenever possible, then you may settle to enjoy the books and fire. Botanic walks, horse rides and visits to local wine cellars can be arranged.

Rooms: 3 suites for 3, 1 triple, 1 twin, all with bath or shower & wc.

Price: 300 Frs for two, including breakfast. Extra bed 80 Frs.

Meals: 100 Frs, including wine.

Open: All year.

From A38 exit 36 onto N555/D955 N through Draguignan to Montferrat (15km). Just before Montferrat left after service station and up narrow road; at top signposted Le Chifflet on right.

Map No: 18   MM 245-35

Danièle & Bernard de LA BROSSE
Le Chifflet
83131 Montferrat
Var
Tel: (0)4 94 70 92 77
Fax: (0)4 94 70 92 77

From Ginasservis D23 towards Rians for 1.5km then left on D22 towards Esparron for 1km. Signposted 'Aubanel' on left.

Map No: 18   MM 245-33

Fatia & Michel LAZÈS
Aubanel
83560 Ginasservis
Var
Tel: (0)4 94 80 11 07
Fax: (0)4 94 80 11 04

A gorgeous *domaine viticole*, an 18th-century manor that the shy but friendly Roubauds have carefully restored and where they produce 'organic' wines, with a cellar and tasting (much favoured by German wine buffs too). The house overlooks vine-covered hillsides and is within easy reach of several charming Var villages. Rooms are decorated and furnished in traditional Provençal style and have independent kitchen facilities.

Rooms: 3 double and 1 twin, all with bathrooms.

Price: 320 Frs for two, including breakfast. (Min. 3 nights July & August.)

Meals: 110 Frs, including wine. & coffee. Self-catering.

Open: March to October.

Close to the mediæval village of Castellet, a pleasing, modern house, designed by its architect-owner and thoughtfully integrated into its surroundings. There is a large, shaded and beautifully-kept terraced garden, with a swimming pool. Rooms are decorated in Provençal style with lovely Salerne bathroom tiles and are very comfortable; one has its own garden with table and chairs. Monsieur's slight shyness is concealed by Madame's smiling efficiency.

Rooms: 2 double, 1 twin, 1 suite for 4, all with bath or shower & wc.

Price: 350 Frs for two, 500 Frs suite, including breakfast.

Meals: In village.

Open: All year.

Gîtes for 4 people

From A8, Brignoles exit north onto D554 through Le Val; then D22 through Montfort-sur-Argens, towards Cotignac. 5km along, turn left; signposted.

Map No: 18   MM 245-34

Nathalie & Jean-François ROUBAUD
Domaine de Nestuby
83570 Cotignac
Var
Tel: (0)4 94 04 60 02
Fax: (0)4 94 04 79 22

From A50 exit to Le Beausset & follow signs for 'Circuit du Castellet'. After 2nd roundabout turn right opposite 'Casino' supermarket for 1.5km. 100m after a right bend, left up track; signposted.

Map No: 18   MM 245-46

Charlotte & Marceau ZERBIB
Les Cancades
Chemin de la Fontaine
83330 Le Beausset
Var
Tel: (0)4 94 98 76 93
Fax: (0)4 94 90 24 63

For walkers who want to get off the beaten track and into the Mediterranean mountains, this is an ideal base. The house takes its name from a nearby waterfall and sits in peaceful isolation in this rugged landscape. You can quickly pick up walking trails which lead straight into the surrounding hills, or you can take in the scenery from the ground-floor guestrooms, all of which have mountain views. Madame cooks using the farm's own organic produce and dinner is usually eaten *en famille.* Masses of country activities available in the village.

Rooms: 2 double, 1 twin & 3 quadruple, all with bath & wc.

Price: 270-290 Frs for two, including breakfast.

Meals: From 80 Frs, excluding wine & coffee.

Open: All year except November & 1 week in February.

Near the top of one of those stunning hilltop villages, the house itself is nothing spectacular but it has a sheer rock face rising above it (where mountaineers practise) and incredible views down to the sea 10km below. The terraced garden is alive with sub-tropical vegetation, the old Provençal house has later additions and is decorated with old furniture and good taste. Your host is a retired colonel who enjoys having guests, Madame is a management consultant of charm and intelligence and they love children.

Rooms: 2 double, 1 twin, each with bath, shower & wc.

Price: 350-450 Frs for two, including breakfast. Children under 10 free.

Meals: In village.

Open: All year.

From Grasse, D2085 to Châteauneuf and D3 to Bramafan. There, right to Courmes. Follow signs from village centre for 0.6km.

Map No: 18   MM 245-37

From A8 St Laurent-du-Var exit on D118 then D18/D2210 to St Jeannet. Into village along narrow (2-way) street; fork right into Rue St Claude: No 136 is 300m along. Or park in P at entrance and walk (10 mins).

Map No: 18   MM 245-37

Patrice BARACCO & Isabelle DUPIN
La Cascade
06620 Courmes
Alpes-Maritimes
Tel: (0)4 93 09 65 85

Guy & Michelle BENOIT SÈRE
L'Olivier Peintre
136 rue Saint-Claude
06640 Saint-Jeannet
Alpes-Maritimes
Tel: (0)4 93 24 78 91

In this enviable position on the Cap itself, no traffic hums, any summer breeze is felt and there is sun all year round. Walk 10 minutes to swim, sail or dive in the sea. Your charming hosts fled hyper-agitated Paris and are happy to guide you in your exploration of the Riviera, but not on bikes (too dangerous!). Bernard, an architect, and Clarisse have made the most of every inch of the small, pretty, Provençal-style rooms and she takes pride in her breakfasts in the lovely garden. Children over 5 welcome. Pets by arrangement. (Book early!)

Rooms: 1 double with bath & wc; 1 double/twin + 2 singles with bath & wc.

Price: 420-480 Frs for two, including breakfast. Reservations only.

Meals: Good choice in town.

Open: All year.

He is an Italian builder, so every column of his new house is turned to a T and every gnome on the entrance bridge painted to perfection. He and his English wife (she came from Yorkshire years ago and stayed...) have taken advantage of every square inch of the steep site and the views are stupendous, so what matter the insalubrious quarter of Menton you go through to get there, the rather basic bathrooms and a bit of satin overkill? It is simple, clean, welcoming and deliciously breezy by the pool in summer.

Rooms: 4 double, each with bath & wc.

Price: 320 Frs for two, including breakfast.

Meals: 120 Frs, including wine (by arrangement).

Open: All year except December & January.

From Antibes centre towards Cap d'Antibes. At palm-tree roundabout towards Cap d'Antibes 'Direct'. At next junction, towards Cap d'Antibes. 1st right into Chemin du Crouton; 1st left. At end of cul-de-sac left on drive. At No17, Panko is 2nd house on right.

Map No: 18   MM 245-37

Clarisse & Bernard BOURGADE
Villa 'Panko'
17 chemin du Parc Saramartel
06160
Cap d'Antibes
Alpes-Maritimes
Tel: (0)4 93 67 92 49
Fax: (0)4 93 61 29 32

From Menton D24 towards Castellar (NOT Ciappes de Castellar). Follow numbers (odds on left) and park above house.

Map No: 18   MM 245-39

M & Mme Paul GAZZANO
151 route de Castellar
06500 Menton
Alpes-Maritimes
Tel: (0)4 93 57 39 73

Annick is a well-travelled former riding instructress, good with horses (though she rides less now) and good with people. The garden has awesomely ancient olive trees, like old men with a few whisps of hair, dotted about on the terraces. Over this looks the garden suite, a treat for those who want to self-cater with its most delightful kitchen — light-filled, quarry-tiled and attractive. The blue room is charming, smaller, with its own entrance, a vast antique wardrobe and old wooden bed.

Rooms: 2 double, each with bath or shower & wc.

Price: 300-400 Frs for two, including breakfast.

Meals: In village. Self-catering in suite.

Open: All year except January & February.

Le Rouret is on D2085 between Grasse & Cagnes. South of village, left on D7 — La Colle-sur-Loup/Roquefort-Notre Dame road. On leaving village, right down lane signed 'Chambres d'Hôtes'.

Map No: 18   MM 245-37

Mme Annick LE GUAY
Les Coquelicots
30 route de Roquefort
06650 Le Rouret
Alpes-Maritimes
Tel: (0)4 93 77 40 04
Fax: (0)4 93 77 40 04

Madame, in her lively 70s and a talented painter, inherited this house from an uncle, loves it to bits and wants to share it with others. It is like a dolls house; indeed, the small single room is full of antique dolls. The main bedroom, which looks across the lushly Mediterranean, statue-decorated, terraced garden to the Alps, has delightful French antiques, a well-equipped kitchenette and a modern shower room. Amazing peace so near the centre of Nice and good walking and biking nearby.

Rooms: 1 double & 1 single sharing shower & wc.

Price: 390 Frs for two, including breakfast. 190 Frs single.

Meals: In village.

Open: All year.

From A8 exit 54 Nice Nord on D14 to Gairaud. After village follow towards Aspremont. Pass Auberge du Mas Fleuri on left. Ave Panéra is 1km along on left; house a few yards down hill.

Map No: 18   MM 245-38

Mme Pia MALET KANITZ
Villa Pan 'É' Râ
8 avenue Panéra — Gairaut Supérieur
06100 Nice
Alpes-Maritimes
Tel: (0)4 92 09 93 20
Fax: (0)4 92 09 93 20

Cascades of bougainvillea and blushes of pelargonium beloved by colour-loving Riviera gardeners tumble over this modern townhouse. Antibes' sea front is an easy 15-minute walk and Juan-les-Pins just a few minutes more. Madame, who fills the rooms with fresh flowers, took a crash course in English before opening her rooms and takes great care of her guests: she took the trouble to walk to the Place de Gaulle to meet us to guard against any wayward wanderings. The house, garden and terrace are remarkably quiet for the area.

Rooms: 1 double with salon, shower & wc.

Price: 350-280 Frs for two, including breakfast.

Meals: Wide choice in Antibes.

Open: All year.

After careful renovation using the appropriate materials, simple, sensitive good taste has been employed in the decoration and furnishing of this stately home. The bedrooms with original frescoes look over five hectares of old parkland with fountain and monastery — and Madame's father's sculptures. Far from traffic and tourists, you may feel a little smug at making such a discovery. The 19th-century maisonette in the garden is perfect for a family of four. Very fine walking, riding, bird-watching country.

Rooms: 1 triple, 2 double, each with shower & wc; 1 twin, 1 double, each with shower, sharing wc.

Price: 280-400 Frs for two, including breakfast (2 nights minimum).

Meals: In Sospel 3km.

Open: All year.

In Antibes centre, from Place de Gaulle take Rue Aristide Briand; left at roundabout and follow railway 600m; right into impasse with barrier, marked 'Privé'; house at end on right.

Map No: 18   MM 245-37

Martine & Pierre MARTIN-CATOIRE
Villa Maghoss
8 impasse Lorini
06600 Antibes
Alpes-Maritimes
Tel: (0)4 93 67 02 97
Fax: (0)4 93 67 02 97

From Menton, D2566 to Sospel; at 'Mairie' (town hall), left towards Col de Turini for 1.9km then left towards 'La Vasta' & 'Campings'. Domaine is 1.3km along on right after ranch & sharp bend.

Map No: 18   MM 245-26

Mme Marie MAYER
Domaine du Paraïs
Chemin du Paraïs
La Vasta
06380 Sospel
Alpes-Maritimes
Tel: (0)4 93 04 15 78

You can ride into the centre of Nice on the local bus that stops just outside this late 19th-century Italianate house on the residential hills outside Nice. The garden is both terraced and colourful. Madame is an ex-hotelier and runs her B&B with crisp but thoughtful efficiency. Guestrooms are irreproachable and have views over the garden and hills. In the sparkling bathrooms are lots of toiletries and a chocolate appears on your pillow at night. Breakfasts are generous, with cheese, ham, *compotes*, cakes and yoghurts.

Rooms: 3 double rooms with bath, shower & wc.

Price: 500 Frs for two, including breakfast. Extra bed 170 Frs.

Meals: Vast choice in town.

Open: All year.

The happy marriage of modern technique and traditional design has inspired this very appealing Provençal-type villa. The setting is entrancing — umbrella pines, palms, the southern skies — and the house lies between lovely old Valbonne and hi-tech Sophia Antipolis, France's silicon valley. Your charming and enthusiastic hosts have created old out of new, paved their generous terrace with lovely old squares, and furnished the rooms with an appropriate mix of the antique and the contemporary.

Rooms: 2 double/twin, 1 double, all with bath & wc.

Price: 320-420 Frs for two, including breakfast. Children under 2 free.

Meals: In village. Self-catering on request.

Open: All year (book ahead).

In Nice, from Place St Philippe take Ave Estienne d'Orves. Over level crossing. After sharp bend, turn into small private road left of the hill (rough track); second house.

Map No: 18   MM 245-38

Mme Jacqueline OLIVIER
Le Castel Enchanté
61 route de Saint-Pierre-de-Féric
06000 Nice
Alpes-Maritimes
Tel: (0)4 93 97 02 08
Fax: (0)4 92 15 07 87

From A8 Antibes exit on D103 dir. Antibes. Across Les Bouillides roundabout dir. Valbonne village for 3km. 100m after 'Bois Doré' restaurant left by yellow bus stop into private lane (iron gate); No 205 is at beginning of lane.

Map No: 18   MM 245-37

Alain & Christine RINGENBACH
Le Cheneau
205 route d'Antibes
06560 Valbonne
Alpes-Maritimes
Tel: (0)4 93 12 13 94
Fax: (0)4 93 12 91 85
e-mail: ringbach@club-internet.fr

Geographically not far from the tourist shops, potteries and madding crowds of Vallauris but a world away in atmosphere. Your hosts restored this old building on a terraced vineyard when they retired from the hectic life of running a brasserie in Paris 15 years ago, so they understand the value of peace. The house is light, cheery, well furnished and eclectically decorated with collections of antique glass and mugs. The fabulous garden with its swimming pool is a place to pamper yourself and relax to the sound of chirruping cicadas.

Rooms: 1 double with shower & wc, 1 twin with bath & wc.

Price: 380-400 Frs for two, including breakfast.

Meals: Choice in town.

Open: All year.

Another new Provençal-style house on a flat, carefully planted-and-pooled piece of land. In a separate guest wing, each ground-floor room has its own patio area and shares the indoor sitting space with kettle etc. Madame's careful taste has furnished the rooms in simple floral style with plain pale walls and rugs on tiled floors. She is genuinely interested to see that you enjoy yourself, offers a welcome rosé and chocolates on turned-down beds. She also runs a family of teenagers... Children over 7 welcome.

Rooms: 2 double, 1 twin, each with bath or shower & wc.

Price: 300-380 Frs for two, including breakfast. Children 50 Frs.

Meals: Choice in village or St Paul-de-Vence (2km).

Open: All year (book ahead).

From A8 Antibes exit towards Vallauris. There follow signs 'Route de Grasse' from centre; go through 2 roundabouts then hairpin bend; at next crossroads left into forest (signed Mas du Mûrier) — 50m up track.

Map No: 18   MM 245-37

M & Mme G. RONCÉ
Mas du Mûrier
1407 route de Grasse
06220 Vallauris
Alpes-Maritimes
Tel: (0)4 93 64 52 32
Fax: (0)4 93 64 23 77

From A8 exit 48 dir. St Paul-de-Vence for 3km. Fork right on D536/D7 to La Colle. Right at flashing light, cont. straight down hill; 100m after telephone box on right rutn right into Chemin de la Rouguière; first house on left.

Map No: 18   MM 245-37

Béatrice RONIN PILLET
Le Clos de Saint Paul
71 chemin de la Rouguière
06480 La Colle-sur-Loup
Alpes-Maritimes
Tel: (0)4 93 32 56 81
Fax: (0)4 93 32 56 81

FRENCH WORDS & EXPRESSIONS used in this book

Mairie and *Hôtel de Ville* mean town and city hall respectively. They are useful landmarks, easy to find in town centres, flying the tricolour and adorned with noticeboards.

Gîte Panda identifies houses inside national or regional parks where the owners provide detailed information about plants and animals in the park, walking itineraries, sometimes guided walks, will lend you binoculars and even rucksacks and where there is B&B or self-catering.

Château refers to a mansion or stately home built for aristocrats between the 16th and 19th centuries. A 'castle', with defences and fortifications, is a *château fort*.

Maison bourgeoise and *maison de maître* are both big, comfortable houses standing in quite large grounds and built for well-to-do members of the liberal professions, captains of industry, trade, etc.

Bastide has two meanings : it can be a stronghold, a small fortified village or, in Provence, it can simply be another word for *mas*.

Mas is a Provençal country house, usually long and low and beautifully typical in its old stone walls, pan-tiled roof and painted shutters.

Malouinière Malouin means 'of Saint Malo'. A *malouinière* is a local style of large house built for Corsairs or wealthy fishing families.

And *Les Malouines* is the French name for the Falkland Islands - first discovered by sailors from Saint Malo - which in turn is the source of the Argentinian name for them: *Las Malvinas*. Remember?

Maison vigneronne is, obviously, a house in a wine-growing area, and can be anything from a tiny vine-worker's cottage (usually part of a row of cottages) to a comfortable house owned by the estate manager or proprietor.

Marais means marsh or marshland. There are one or two well-known marshlands in France - the most spectacular is perhaps the *Marais Poitevin* with its miles of little waterways to be explored by boat - and the 4th *arrondissement* of Paris, once a miserable, unhealthy, low-lying slum, is known as *Le Marais* and is now in the process of gentrification.

Armoire is a wardrobe, a very French wardrobe with more or less elaborate regional-style carving (Norman, Breton, Burgundian,...) and often a mirrored front.

Lit clos is the type of bed that poor peasants slept in, some until very recently. It was basically a wooden box with a canopy over the top, a fairly small double bed inside and doors to shut once you'd climbed in. Thus, you could share your one room with your animals and keep out the rats. Some of them, Marriage Beds, were also very richly carved. They are much sought after nowadays for conversion to hi-fi cabinets or computer corners or telly tubs...

Potager has two meanings, the commonest being kitchen garden, whence the French word for everyday vegetable soup: *potage*. The other is the ancestor of the hotplate. It is a waist-high stone structure with a number of dish-shaped holes in the top - the number depended on the size of the household and probably its wealth - and a space beneath the holes to put burning embers brought over from the kitchen range.

Déguster means to taste, sample or savour and *une dégustation* is a tasting - of wine, oysters, any speciality. Note that it is NOT necessarily free.

A volonté means 'as much as you want'.

Viennoiserie - literally 'things from Vienna' - covers all those relatively plain flaky-pastry concoctions served for breakfast or tea : *croissants, pains au chocolat,* etc.

TIPS FOR TRAVELLERS IN FRANCE

- Buy a phonecard *(télécarte)* on arrival; they are on sale at post offices and tobacconists' *(tabac)*. Keep some small change for the (very few) non-card phone boxes; phone boxes are generously distributed throughout France.
- Be aware of public holidays; many national museums and galleries close on Tuesdays, others close on Mondays (e.g. Monet's garden in Giverny) as do many country restaurants, and opening times may be different on the following days:

New Year's Day (1 January)	Bastille Day (14 July)
Easter Sunday & Monday	Assumption of BVM (15 August)
May Day (1 May)	All Saints (1 November)
Liberation 1945 (8 May)	Armistice 1918 (11 November)
Ascension Thursday	Christmas Day
Whit Sunday & Monday	(Pentecost)

- Beware also of mass exodus over public holiday weekends, both the first day – outward journey - and the last - return journey.

Medical and Emergency procedures
- If you are an EC citizen, have an E111 form with you for filling in after any medical treatment. You will subsequently receive a refund for only part of your payment, so it is advisable to take out private insurance.
- French emergency services are:
  – the public service called *SAMU* or the Casualty Department - *Services des Urgences* - of a hospital;
  – the private service called *SOS MÉDECINS*.

Roads and driving
- Current speed limits are: Motorways 130 kph (80 mph), RN National trunk roads 110 kph (68 mph), other open roads 90 kph (56 mph), in towns 50 kph (30 mph). The road police are very active and can demand on-the-spot payment of fines.
- One soon gets used to driving on the right but complacency leads to trouble; take special care coming out of car parks, private drives, narrow one-lane roads and coming onto roundabouts.

French Motorways *(Autoroutes)* are mostly toll-paying	*Autoroutes á Péage*
Blue road signs = motorways	*Autoroutes*
Green road signs = alternative routes or routes leading to motorways	*Itinéraires bis*

Many roads coming from the right still have priority - and drivers take it, come what may, so expect it **always!**
The mysterious command 'Use your engine braking' is a literal translation of *'Utilisez votre frein moteur'*, a sign often seen at the top of long steep motorway slopes. In English we would expect 'Keep in low gear'.

- Directions in towns
  The French drive towards a destination and use road numbers far less than we do. Thus, to find your way *á la française,* know the general direction you want to go, i.e. the towns your route goes through, and when you see *Autres Directions* or *Toutes Directions* in a town, forget road numbers (they probably aren't marked anyway), just follow towards the place name you're heading for or through - and have faith!

AVOIDING CULTURAL CONFUSIONS & SHOCKS

GREETINGS & FORMS OF ADDRESS

We drop far more easily into first-name terms than the French. This reluctance on their part is not a sign of coldness, it's simply an Old National Habit, to be respected, we feel, like any other tribal ritual. So it's advisable to wait for the signal from <u>them</u> as to when you have achieved more intimate status.

The French do not say "Bonjour Monsieur <u>Dupont</u>" or "Bonjour Madame <u>Jones</u>" - this is considered rather familiar. They just say "Bonjour Monsieur" or "Bonjour Madame" - which makes it easy to be lazy about remembering people's names.

À TABLE
(Don't be alarmed by all the etiquette below; making mistakes can be as much fun as getting it right!)

Breakfast
There may be only a bowl/large cup* and a teaspoon per person on the table. If so, you are expected to butter your bread *on your hand* or on the tablecloth (often the kitchen oilcloth) using the knife in the butter dish, then spread the jam with the jam spoon. This method has recently been described to us as The Only Proper Way to Eat Breakfast by an extremely aristocratic French country gentleman (tip of tongue in cheek? we're not absolutely sure).

A well-bred English lady would never dream of 'dunking' her croissant, toast or teacake in her cup - it is perfectly acceptable behaviour in French society.

Lunch/Dinner

1. EQUIPMENT
Glasses are centred at the top of the plate, not to the right, and you are expected to put your glass/glasses down in the same place each time and not allow them to wander back and forth, left to right, as the whim takes you.

Cutlery is laid <u>concave</u> face upwards in 'Anglo-Saxon' countries; in France it is proper to lay forks and spoons <u>convex</u> face upwards (crests are engraved accordingly). Do try and hold back your instinctive need to turn them over!

To the right of your plate, at the tip of the knife, you may find a **knife-rest**. This serves two purposes : to lay your knife on when you are not using it, rather than leaving it in your plate; to lay your knife AND fork on (points downwards) if you are asked to '*garder vos couverts*' (keep your knife and fork) while the plates are changed - e.g. between starter and main dish.

2. FOOD
Cheese comes BEFORE pudding in France - that's the way they do it! The proper order is -
Entrée - starter (rather than main dish à la Mrs Beeton)
Plat - main dish of meat and vegetable(s)
Salade - usually just green leaves
Fromage - can be just one perfect Camembert or a vast tray with a dozen cheeses to choose from; in very smart places, there will be a second board for goat cheese; the middle-of-the-road place has all cheeses are on one board with one knife for cow and ewe and another for goat.
Dessert - ranging from plain fresh fruit to superbly complicated creamy structures.

It is becoming more and more acceptable to serve/ask for the cheese to be served at the same time as the salad.

In the past it was absolute dogma that **salads**, and especially lettuce, should not be approached with a knife (a hangover from the days of non-stainless knives which gave a metallic taste to delicate foods), but folded neatly onto the fork with a piece of bread as 'pusher' - your hostess having prepared small enough pieces (by tearing the lettuce in the kitchen, not cutting it) for this to be feasible. The bread pusher, however, has now fallen into disgrace among modern figure-conscious eaters.

Cutting cheese
Cut a round cheese as you would cut a round cake - in triangular segments. When a ready-cut segment such as a piece of Brie is presented, the rule is to 'preserve the point', i.e. do not cut it straight across but take an angle which removes the existing point but makes another one.

Seasoning
It is considered rather insulting to the cook to add salt and pepper to a dish before tasting it. Thus, many restaurants do not automatically put seasonings on the table : you have to ask for them.

REGIONAL FOOD LABELS - À la manière de.../In the manner of...

À l'Alsacienne	*With sauerkraut and sausage.*
À l'Américaine	*A corruption of À l'Armoricaine, Armor being the Celtic name for Brittany: with tomato sauce and shallots.*
À l'Anglaise	*Plain boiled.*
À l'Ardennaise	*With juniper berries.*
À l'Auvergnate	*With cabbage and bits of bacon.*
À la Basquaise	*With onions, sweet peppers, rice and possibly Bayonne cured ham.*
À la Bordelaise	*Bordeaux style, with red wine, shallots and bone marrow.*
À la Bourguignonne	*Burgundy style, with red wine, onions, mushrooms and bacon.*
À la Bretonne	*With leeks, celery and beans (cf. Américaine above for another Bretonne).*
À la Dauphinoise	*With cream, garlic and sometimes cheese.*
À la Dijonnaise	*With mustard sauce.*
À la Flamande	*Flemish style: cooked in beer or vinegar.*
À la Lyonnaise	*With onions, wine, vinegar, and often sausage.*
À la Niçoise	*With anchovies and olives.*
À la Normande	*With cream.*
À la Périgourdine	*With goose liver and truffles.*
À la Provençale	*With tomatoes, garlic, olive oil.*
À la Savoyarde	*With cream and cheese.*

A FEW FALSE FRIENDS

En-suite can lead to terrible confusions in France. One booking for two 'en-suites', made with B&B owners who speak good English, became a disaster when the owners reserved their only *suite* for these guests: the two adult couples were less than gruntled at having to fit into a double room leading to a 'children's' twin room leading to a shared bathroom.

Biologique & Organic
Vegetables called 'organic' in English are known as *de culture biologique* in French, *bio* for short. If you talk about *organique* people will imagine you have trouble with your organs.

Biscuit & Gâteau
Biscuit literally means 'twice cooked' and properly applies to dehydrated army rations or the base for some sticky puddings. The usual words for sweet or savoury biscuits are *gâteaux secs* or *petits gâteaux*, also *gâteaux d'apéritif*.
So if you are offered a 'little gateau', it does not come dangerously rich and slathered in cream, it comes looking like first cousin to a Rich Tea or a Smith's Crisp. If you are given *gâteau maison* at breakfast, it will probably be a simple sponge-cake with jam or a French-style fruit cake (also called *du cake*, just to make things easier).

Tourte - Tarte - Tartine - Pie - Pis
Tourte is the closest the French have to 'pie', i.e. with pastry above and below.
Tarte is an open tart or flan.
Tartine is a half baguette (usually) sliced in half and buttered, i.e. breakfast food.
Une pie is a magpie. *Un pis* (same pronunciation as *une pie*) is a cow's udder.
Scotch means adhesive tape or whisky - the context should help.
Soda is a non-alcoholic, probably sweet, fizzy drink of some kind. If you want soda water you should ask for *eau gazeuse*.
Trouble You can send a bottle of wine back for this - it means cloudy, murky.
Mousse is : froth, foam, lather (beer, sea, soap) or foam rubber or... moss.
Pomme de pin is fircone. Pineapple is *ananas*. *Pamplemousse* is grapefruit.
Raisin Is a fresh grape or grapes. Steinbeck's book is called *Les Raisins de la Colère*. Dried fruit is : *Raisins de Corinthe* (currants - see the derivation?); *Raisins de Smyrne* (sultanas); *Raisins secs* (raisins!).
Grappe is a bunch of grapes - *une grappe de raisins*.
Prune is a fresh plum. A prune is *pruneau*.
Myrtille is bilberry - they grow wild and delicious on the hills of southern France and make for a wonderful tart. Myrtle is *myrte*.
Verger An orchard : many a greengrocer's shop is called *Aux Fruits du Verger*.
Marmelade means stewed fruit. Marmalade is called *confiture d'oranges amères*.

Cheminée is French for fireplace, flue or chimney stack (the flue is also called *le conduit de cheminée*). *Un feu <u>dans la</u> cheminée* does not mean you need to call the fire brigade but *un feu <u>de cheminée</u>* does.
Une Commode is a chest of drawers. A commode is *une chaise percée*.
Grange simply means barn, not a big country house.

Actuel - Actuellement
A great pitfall this one - it means current, present - currently, presently, NOW and not As a Matter of Fact.

Éventuel - Éventuellement
Possible - should the occasion arise.

Un Christmas is a Christmas <u>card.</u> The French used only to send each other visiting cards with hand-written New Year greetings. The English and American custom of sending decorative cards for Christmas only caught on fairly recently and the object was naturally given the (truncated) English name.

Correspondance applies to travel connections between flights, trains and metro lines.

ACTIVITIES

Courses, workshops, lessons, events and facilities you may find at the listed B&Bs.

Historical and Cultural Visits
10 • 16 • 35 • 49 • 50 • 51 • 52 • 54 • 80 • 84 • 91 • 112 • 115 • 134 • 140 • 158 • 180 • 206 • 225 • 239 • 241 • 262 • 269 • 277 • 295 • 297 • 299 • 302 • 316 • 327 • 337 • 374 • 382 • 383 • 392 • 395 • 396 • 406 • 409 • 412 • 445 • 450 • 468 • 501 • 503 • 532 • 535 • 553 • 556 • 564 • 584 • 587 • 596 • 598 • 603 • 604 • 616 • 624 • 647 • 660

Theatrical Events
97 • 156 • 313 • 616

Music lessons or practice
97 • 291 • 306 • 346 • 363 • 387 • 417 • 421 • 432

Musical events
49 • 84 • 97 • 116 • 156 • 166 • 217 • 295 • 306 • 313 • 363 • 373 • 417 • 503 • 552 • 597 • 611 • 616

Painting
31 • 73 • 80 • 84 • 97 • 104 • 132 • 134 • 151 • 233 • 256 • 296 • 311 • 316 • 332 • 343 • 368 • 373 • 386 • 395 • 405 • 430 • 436 • 459 • 497 • 505 • 554 • 594 • 597 • 598 • 611 • 620 • 629 • 636

Pottery – Sculpture
16 • 233 • 266 • 296 • 459 • 509 • 560

Needlework: lace, patchwork, embroidery, weaving, tapestry
42 • 84 • 227 • 233 • 236 • 262 • 332 • 344 • 364 • 436 • 451 • 511 • 572 • 594

Help with your French - lessons or conversation
42 • 49 • 50 • 53 • 112 • 113 • 150 • 239 • 244 • 281 • 284 • 299 • 306 • 317 • 341 • 344 • 363 • 373 • 395 • 397 • 406 • 408 • 440 • 450 • 467 • 516 • 524 • 532 • 542 • 552 • 553 • 584 • 603 • 660

Cookery: from jams to regional specialities
16 • 42 • 54 • 72 • 73 • 80 • 104 • 113 • 115 • 119 • 150 • 153 • 158 • 163 • 180 • 229 • 284 • 295 • 297 • 317 • 332 • 341 • 344 • 368 • 395 • 397 • 410 • 411 • 412 • 428 • 438 • 440 • 444 • 445 • 450 • 461 • 477 • 479 • 524 • 526 • 544 • 547 • 549 • 553 • 564 • 572 • 582 • 586 • 587 • 598 • 600 • 614 • 621 • 623 • 644 • 649 • 650

Wine-growing - Wine-tasting
2 • 37 • 42 • 49 • 53 • 56 • 72 • 78 • 79 • 91 • 94 • 97 • 98 •
117 • 118 • 140 • 270 • 284 • 293 • 295 • 317 • 344 • 354 • 379
• 406 • 440 • 462 • 464 • 471 • 472 • 473 • 475 • 476 • 477 •
479 • 480 • 528 • 553 • 564 • 592 • 596 • 602 • 621 • 631 •
647 • 650

Mushroom collecting - Truffle hunting
118 • 154 • 257 • 564 • 592 • 600 • 608

Local flora and fauna
8 • 72 • 79 • 109 • 112 • 180 • 190 • 237 • 262 • 269 • 272 •
293 • 332 • 396 • 441 • 450 • 501 • 508 • 606 • 644 • 647 • 660

Horse-riding
37 • 63 • 106 • 113 • 115 • 172 • 175 • 192 • 200 • 220 • 229 •
234 • 272 • 322 • 432 • 452 • 489 • 505 • 507 • 512 • 587 • 604
• 606 • 643

Horse-drawn rides – Carriage-driving lessons
38 • 57 • 63 • 115 • 166 • 185 • 233 • 272 • 305 • 452 • 507 •
513

Stables or pasture available
3 • 8 • 30 • 37 • 38 • 42 • 49 • 64 • 106 • 112 • 113 • 127 • 162
• 166 • 182 • 217 • 237 • 261 • 272 • 297 • 315 • 388 • 420 •
432 • 452 • 467 • 470 • 477 • 512 • 513 • 611 • 640

Boating
35 • 89 • 112 • 125 • 234 • 236 • 256 • 277 • 286 • 302 • 310 •
327 • 368 • 378 • 396 • 398 • 399 • 403 • 428 • 436 • 441 • 604

Fishing
30 • 35 • 48 • 49 • 51 • 65 • 89 • 91 • 101 • 109 • 112 • 113 •
156 • 175 • 189 • 192 • 221 • 228 • 229 • 230 • 237 • 239 • 246
• 256 • 264 • 269 • 286 • 293 • 297 • 302 • 310 • 315 • 343 •
368 • 378 • 393 • 396 • 398 • 402 • 403 • 409 • 428 • 432 • 441
• 445 • 450 • 452 • 463 • 469 • 500 • 505 • 513 • 515 • 522 •
527 • 552

Aromatherapy - Yoga - Relaxation
80 • 121 • 147 • 163 • 204 • 215 • 296 • 297 • 474 • 482 • 489 •
497 • 575 • 627

Tennis
44 • 49 • 51 • 109 • 113 • 115 • 175 • 217 • 234 • 313 • 334 •
335 • 373 • 395 • 399 • 400 • 407 • 420 • 443 • 451 • 461 • 471
• 486 • 540 • 542 • 574 • 604 • 647

Some of the wonderful places in
Special Places to Stay in Spain and Portugal

Discover undiscovered Spain, explore unexplored Portugal - and stay in our hand-picked hilltop castles, cosy cottages, country estates, historic townhouses.

North Spain
La Casona de Villanueva

This grand old 18th-century village house has been lovingly restored and decorated in warm pastel colours, every corner a careful balance of antiques, paintings, fabrics and plants. Attentive hosts, a lovely garden, flowers complete the picture.

Tel: 985412590

Catalonia
Can Fabrica

On top of a hill with heart-stopping views, the friendly young farmers have created a blissful corner of peace and country quiet.
The simple, perfect rooms are smallish, the breakfasts deliciously Catalan, the area full of treasures.

Tel: 972594629

Andalusia
Monte de la Torre

An Edwardian country house on the southern edge of Spain and an English name established here for generations. Here are elegance, heirlooms and period bathrooms, long views, lovely palm-strewn gardens and gracious hosts: a superb place to stay.

Tel: 956660000

Portugal
Convento do Santo António

A Portuguese feast of hand-crafted terracotta and tiles, rich alcobaça fabrics and hand-knotted rugs, this former monastery has cloister and character, antiques and atmosphere, Gregorian chant at breakfast. The 'Special' rooms are, indeed, very special

Tel: (0)81-325632

Alastair Sawday's Special Places to Stay in Spain and Portugal

SPECIAL PLACES TO STAY

Spain & Portugal

Over 280 of the most delightful places to stay in Spain & Portugal - chosen for their character, comfort and value.

Edited by
Guy Hunter-Watts

The guide that takes you to the places that your friends would (privately) recommend.

No other guide gives you this wonderful selection of remarkable places to stay in both Spain and Portugal. To the magic that we worked for Spain in our first edition, with its 200 Special Places, we now add the magic of Portugal. Its houses and hotels are quite delightful, with an atmosphere all of their own. We have found about 80 of them, great country houses and little beach-side hotels, old religious buildings etc... all of them selected because they, and their owners, are special in some way.
So, you can now find authenticity, character and charm in every corner of Spain and Portugal, and wonderful value for all budgets.
Order your copies from us, or harry your local book-shop.
Price £10.95.

Some of the wonderful places in
Special Places to Stay in Britain

From castle to cottage, from elegant to simple - a very personal selection of places to stay for your special holiday in Britain.

Somerset
The Manor House
The lintel is carved 1630, the dovecote is 14th-century, the Reformation left a priesthole - this house oozes history. The fine old furniture breathes elegance and peace and the smell of your hostess's baking wafts deliciously to welcome you.

Tel: (0)1225-832027

Devon
Tor Cottage
There is luxury here in fluffy robes, huge bedrooms, a heated outdoor pool and a fountain in the breakfast room. More soothing water runs in the stream and your easy-going hostess can provide inspired vegetarian cooking too.

Tel: (0)1822-860248

Scotland
Chipperkyle
Sensitively restored, Chipperkyle stands proudly Georgian in a superb setting in one of the unexplored corners of Scotland. It is a warm, relaxed family home with children, chickens and donkeys, ideal for walkers and outdoor enthusiasts.

Tel: (0)1556-650223

Wales
Penyclawdd Court
A Tudor manor of staggeringly ancient beauty where every bedroom has dramatic views of the Welsh mountains, the grounds have knot garden and yew maze, the Welsh bedroom is lit by candles. Patina, a sense of history and good company.

Tel: (0)1873-890719

Special Places to Stay in BRITAIN

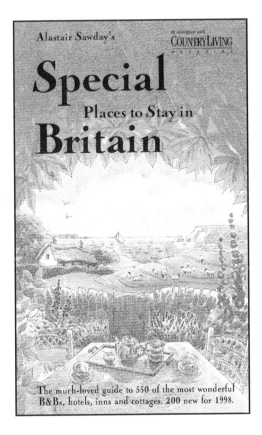

If you, too, wince at the sight of another lovely old 17th-century room vandalised to make way for a bathroom... then this book (ALL our books) is for you.

Britain is over-run by chain hotels, bad taste and commercial 'establishments'. Even private homes that do B&B are squeezed mercilessly to fit into the mould. So we have searched the country for what WE consider to be the nicest, the most friendly, and genuinely attractive houses, hotels and inns. (Most are very comfortable too.)

Our standards are high: places HAVE to be special. Then we accept them, and let them do their own thing. With over 500 special places to stay throughout the British Isles this book is a MUST for the sensitive traveller.
Price £10.95.

Some of the wonderful places in
Special Places to Stay in Ireland

Here are 180 varied and fascinating places you can trust. They have character, authenticity, eccentricity... and high standards. Genuinely nice people too.

Galway
Delphi Lodge
Miles of dramatic scenery: mountain, bog, rock and water. Fabulous fishing, wonderful walking, and a supremely congenial country house party atmosphere where dinners are gastronomic and conversational high spots and rooms are utterly civilised.

Tel: 095-42211

Galway
Man of Aran Cottage
In a perfect Aran Island hideaway right by the sea, this house was built in the 1930s as an 'old cottage' for a film. Perfect hosts, with a passion for organic vegetables and the natural way, the Wolfes create a thoroughly relaxed atmosphere.

Tel: 099-61301

Monaghan
Castle Leslie
A castle with four lakes in the grounds yet a genuine family home, it has a cathedral room, a haunted room, a bamboo room, all full of family memorabilia (a throne for the Pope...), decorated with flair and humour and amazing bathrooms.

Tel: 047-88109

Monaghan
Hilton Park
One of Ireland's most imposing country houses, it has stunning grounds, a fine panelled dining room, huge high four-posters, great bath tubs, and delightfully easy, helpful owners. Breakfast is taken in floods of morning light.

Tel: 047-56007

Alastair Sawday's Special Places to Stay in Ireland

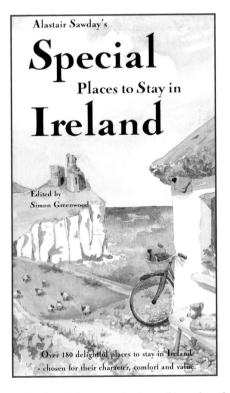

All the magic of Ireland in our choice of lovely places to stay.

Ireland - one of the last havens in Western Europe still unspoilt by mass tourism - is the perfect setting for the fifth Sawday guide. Our inspectors have collected a series of gems that nestle in this wide and wild land where taking in weary travellers is part of the Celtic tradition. The Irish of today are definitely worthy descendents of their ancestors on this score.

Each of the 200-odd B&Bs, farmhouses, mansions and family-run hotels boasts something that makes it truly special - usually a welcome stemming not from the contents of your wallet but from your hosts' genuine enjoyment in meeting people.

We have weeded out any hint of over-commercialism, pretension or half-heartedness in the owners' approach and brought you the loveliest, gentlest, most seductive places to stay in this green and misty country.
Full colour photography, masses of detail, reliable practical information. Available for £10.95.

Alastair Sawday's Guide to Special Paris Hotels

Alastair Sawday's

GUIDE TO

Special Paris Hotels

Some of the best hotels in Paris, selected for their authenticity, character, charm.....and superb value.

A night in Paris is far too precious to be spent in the wrong hotel.

You are off to Paris, full of hope, but there is a nagging doubt: where to stay? So you ask friends who went last year, or before... and cross your fingers. The risk of ending up in a touristy monster, or recently-spoiled favourite, is ever-present.

This book is like an up-to-date and ultra-reliable friend who knows *all* the Paris hotels and makes choices for you... whether you are rich or poor, artistic or not.

Written with wit and style by an Englishwoman living in Paris, this highly personal selection of 70 of Paris's nicest, most attractive and welcoming hotels is all you need to make your visit a complete success. You can easily save the cost in just one night's sleep in the right hotel.

Colour photographs and lots of detail. A delightful book and the only one of its kind. Price: £8.95

ORDER FORM for the UK. See over for USA.

All these books are available in the major bookshops but we can send them to you quickly and without effort on your part. Post and packaging is FREE if you order 3 or more books.

	No. of copies	Price each	Total value
French Bed & Breakfast – 4th Edition		£12.95	
Special Paris Hotels		£8.95	
Special Places to Stay in Spain & Portugal		£10.95	
Special Places to Stay in Britain – 2nd Edition		£10.95	
Special Places to Stay in Ireland		£10.95	
Add Post & Packaging: £1 for Paris book, £2 for any other, **FREE** if ordering 3 or more books.			
TOTAL ORDER VALUE *Please make cheques payable to Alastair Sawday Publishing*			

We are moving towards a system of annual publishing, whereby we get new books out before Christmas and publish the next edition automatically one year later.

All orders to: Alastair Sawday Publishing, 44 Ambra Vale East, Bristol BS8 4RE Tel: 0117 9299921. (Sorry, no credit card payments).

Name

Address

Postcode

Tel   Fax

If you do not wish to receive mail from other companies, please tick the box ☐   FBB4

ORDER FORM for USA.

These books are available at your local bookstore, or you may order direct. Allow two to three weeks for delivery.

	No. of copies	Price each	Total value
French Bed & Breakfast – 4th Edition		$19.95	
Special Paris Hotels		$14.95	
Special Places to Stay in Spain & Portugal		$19.95	
Special Places to Stay in Britain		$19.95	
Special Places to Stay in Ireland		$19.95	
Add Post & Packaging: $4 for Paris book, $4.50 for any other.			
TOTAL ORDER VALUE *Please make cheques payable to Publishers Book & Audio*			

All orders to: Publishers Book & Audio, P.O. Box 070059, 5446 Arthur Kill Road, Staten Island, NY 10307, phone (800) 288-2131. For information on bulk orders, address Special Markets, St. Martin's Press, 175 Fifth Avenue, Suite 500, New York, NY 10010, phone (212) 674-5151, ext. 724, 693, or 628.

Name

Address

Zip code

Tel   Fax

FBB4

REPORT FORM

Comments on existing entries and new discoveries.

If you have any comments on existing entries, please let us have them.

If you have a favourite house or a new discovery in France, please let us know.

Please send reports to: Alastair Sawday Publishing, 44 Ambra Vale East, Bristol BS8 4RE, UK.

Report on:

Entry no. _____   New Recommendation ☐ Date _____

Names of owners _____

Name of house _____

Address _____

_____

_____ Tel. No: _____

My reasons are _____

_____

_____

_____

_____

_____

_____

_____

_____

_____

_____

_____

_____

_____

_____

_____

_____

_____

_____

_____

_____

_____

_____

_____

_____

My name and address:

Name _____

Address _____

_____

Tel. No.: (only if you don't mind) _____

I am not connected in any way with the owners of this property

Signed _____

Please send the completed form to:
Alastair Sawday Publishing, 44 Ambra Vale East,
Bristol BS8 4RE, UK.

THANK YOU SO MUCH FOR YOUR HELP!

BULLETIN DE RÉSERVATION
Booking Form

À l'attention de :
To : ....

....

Date: ....

Madame, Monsieur,

Veuillez faire la réservation suivante au nom de :
Please make the following booking for (name):

....

Pour .... nuit(s).   Arrivant le: jour .... mois .... année ....
For   night(s)   *Arriving: day   month   year*

                             Partant le: jour .... mois .... année ....
                             Leaving: day   month   year

Si possible, nous aimerions .... chambres, disposées comme suit:
We would like   rooms, arranged as follows:

À grand lit	....
Double bed	
À lits jumeaux	....
Twin beds	
Pour trois	....
Triple	
À un lit simple	....
Single	
Suite	....

Nous aimerions également réserver le dîner pour .... personnes.
We would also like to book dinner for   people

Veuillez nous envoyer la confirmation à l'adresse ci-dessous:
Please send confirmation to the following address:

Nom: ....
Name:
Adresse: ....
Address:

Fax No: ....

Special Walks

If you enjoy this book, and also enjoy a good country walk, then you may be interested to hear that our travel company, Alastair Sawday's Tours, is about to launch a new walking programme.

We have been around since 1984. Among other things we run a programme of guided walks all over Europe, mainly for the US market. We have built an international reputation for using the most interesting and experienced guides and staying in the most wonderful places... many of them now from our Special Places books.

The publishing venture grew out of the travel company, when we realised that private homes and small family-run hotels etc were such wonderful value, and such FUN.

WHAT IS SO SPECIAL ABOUT OUR WALKS? We use a magical combination of imagination, deep knowledge of the areas, special places to stay, and delightful local guides who LIVE in their areas. Our walks last a week, can be put together back-to-back, cover about 8-16 easy miles a day, consume glorious picnics, use interesting hotels and private homes, and cost about £790. There are usually 6-12 people.

Further afield, we also do tours to South India and Sri Lanka, both of which involve some good walking.

If you would like to be among the first British people to experience our new walks, with a special 5% discount as a recent reader of Special Places (send us your receipt or proof of use), then fill in the form below and send it to AST, 44 Ambra Vale East, Bristol BS8 4RE.

....

Name: .... **Age:** ....

Address:

....

....

County: .... **Post Code:** ....

Tel no: .... **Fax No:** .... **E-mail:** ....

Which areas are you interested in? (please circle): Andalucia; Spanish Pyrenees; The Lot; Provence; Burgundy; Dordogne; Tuscany; Umbria; Italian Lakes; Romania; Austria; Norway; South India; Sri Lanka

Others:..

Dates I prefer:

....

Friends who may also be interested: ....

....

The Barge Company

INDEPENDENT BARGE BOOKERS

Luxury European Barge Cruises

The Barge Company offers you cruises on luxury 'hotel' and charter barges operating on the canals and rivers of France, England, Scotland, Ireland, Holland and Belgium.

The barges are run by experienced, friendly and English-speaking crews providing a high standard of cuisine, comfort and service.

For further details contact: The Barge Cruise Company Ltd
12 Orchard Close, Felton, Bristol, UK BS40 9YS
Tel: 01275 474034 Toll free from US: 1-800-688-0245
Fax: 01275 474673 E-mail: barge.co@btinternet.com

Relax, unwind and let the world float by......

INDEX of PLACES

OWNERS Entry

Abbaye (Ferme de l'), *Ecrammeville* . . . . .FAUVEL 177
Aguzan, *La Sauzaie* . . . . .LANGER 413
Airs du Temps (Les), *Faucon* . . . . .BERRY 617
Alcyone (L'), *Carnac-Plage* . . . . .BALSAN 263
Allée du Château, *Villefargeau* . . . . .SEPTIER 124
Allées Maroselli, *Luxeuil-les-Bains* . . . . .JOHNSON 82
Alteville (Château d'), *Dieuze* . . . . .BARTHÉLÉMY 70
Ancienne Chaumière (L'), *Fonds-Brulé* . . . . .PIROMAN 96
Arclais, *Pont d'Ouilly* . . . . .LEBATARD 185
Arfentière (Domaine de l'), *Uchizy* . . . . .SALLET 98
Ariston Fils, *Brouillet* . . . . .ARISTON 56
Arnac (Château d'), *Nonards* . . . . .WEBB 443
Aubanel, *Ginasservis* . . . . .LAZÈS 653
Aufragère (L'), *Fourmetot* . . . . .DUSSARTRE 153
Aurifat, *Cordes* . . . . .THORNLEY 543
Ayguemarse (Quartier), *Mollans-sur-Ouvèze* . . . . .BERNARD 588
Bailleau le Pin, *Chauffours* . . . . .HASQUENOPH 326
Balous (Château), *Damazan* . . . . .SAVY-TAQUET 469
Bangin (Le), *Beauchamps-sur-Huillard* . . . . .DHUIT 334
Bannay (Ferme de), *Montmort Lucy* .CURFS 59
Bannay, *St-Germain-des-Bois* . . . . .CHAMBRIN 338
Baquette (La), *Lescure* .GOLDSWORTHY 508
Barabie (La), *Lamonzie-Montastruc* . . . . .ARCHER 444
Barthe (La), *Villefranche-d'Albigeois* . . . . .WISE 544
Bas du Gast (Le), *Laval* . . . . .WILLIOT 308
Basse-Cour de St-Martin, *Ste-Marie* . . . . .JANDET 110
Bastide Brunet, *Aix-en-Provence* . . . . .BELLECOMBE 634
Bastide Rose (La), *Salernes* . . . . .HENNY 650
Bavelincourt, *Villers Bocage* . . . . .VALENGIN 40
Bazoches (Ferme Auberge de) . . . . .PERRIER 114
Beaulieu (Château de), *Saumur* .MICHAUT 292
Beauséjour (Domaine de), *Panzoult* . . . . .CHAUVEAU 356
Bécassière (La), *Châtillon* . . . . .GAL Suzanne & André 608
Bergerie (La), *Villers-sur-Authie* . . . . .SINGER de WAZIÈRES 39
Berthiers (La Ferme les), *Sepmes* . . . . .VERGNAUD 375
Besnardière (La), *Fougeré* . . . . .RIMELL 296
Bezassade (La), *Laurière* . . . . .CHANUDET 426
Bihourderie (La), *Azay-sur-Indre* . . . . .BOUIN 353
Birdy Land, *Le Touquet* . . . . .VERSMÉE 22
Biza (La), *Missy-sur-Aisne* . . . . .DUFFIÉ 48
Blacons (Château de), *Mirabel et Blacons* . . . . .LATUNE 597
Bois Bonance (Le), *Port-le-Grand* . . . . .MAILLARD 32
Bois de Tilly (Ferme du), *Vendeuvre* . . . . .VANHOUTTE 197
Bois Dousset (Logis du Château du), *Lavoux* VILLOUTREYS de Brignac 395
Bois Goulu (Le), *Pouant* . . . . .PICARD 389

INDEX

Bois Vert (Domaine du), *Grans* ....RICHARD   642
Boissière (Manoir de la), *La Croix-St-Leufroy* ....SÉNÉCAL   159
Bonabry (Château de), *Hillion* ....FOU de KERDANIEL   237
Bonavis, *(Ferme de)*, Banteux ....DELCAMBRE   24
Bonde-Loupiac (La), *Rabastens* ....CRÉTÉ   535
Bonnets Rouges (Les), *Bourges* ....BROUSTE   337
Borde (La), *St-Bonnet-l'Enfantier* ....BUGE   438
Bordeneuve, *Béraut* ....VIGNAUX   519
Borderie (La), *St-Pierre-Bellevue* ....DESCHAMPS   435
Bordes (Les), *Crucheray* ....TONDEREAU   324
Bouchaud (Le), *Vendoire* ....DURIEUX   450
Bouère Salée (La), *St-Lambert-des-Levées* ....BASTID   278
Boufray, *Maulay* ....MONTAL   388
Boulancourt (Domaine de), *Montier-en-Der* ....VIEL-CAZAL   65
Boulinière (La), *Journet* ....EARLS   380
Bourg-Ville (Domaine de), *Monts-sur-Guesnes* ....FOUQUENET   382
Bournand (Château de), *Bournand* ....LAURENS   301
Boursaie (La), *Tortisambert* ....DAVIES   175
Bousquétarié (La), *Lempaut* ....SALLIER   542
Bouteuille, *Alluy* ....LEJAULT   111
Bréguières (Les), *Rousset* ....BABEY   633
Breucq (Le), *Belle-et-Houllefort* ....MONTIGNY   16
Brunis (Les), *Nègrepelisse* ....ANTONY   520
Bruyère (La), *Les Abrets* ....CHAVALLE REVENU   601
Bruyères (Les), *St-Félix* ....BETTS   604
Bugeac, *Grèzes* ....CUBIZOLLE   578
Buissonets (Les), *Bruges* ....BOURGHELLE   484
Butte de l'Épine (La), *Continvoir* ....BODET   352
Cabalus, *Vézelay* ....CABALUS   116
Campseissillou (Ferme), *St-Pé-de-Bigorre* ....ARRAMONDE   493
Canal (La), *Lorgues* ....D'ANNUNZIO   646
Cancades (Les), *Le Beausset* ....ZERBIB   655
Cantegril (Ecole d'Equitation), *St-Martin-de-Caralp* ....PAGÈS   512
Cantemerle, *Vertheuil-Médoc* ....TARDAT   480
Cantepie (Manoir de), *Cambremer* ....GHERRAK   178
Cantet (Château de), *Samazan* ....LA RAITRIE   467
Capcazal de Pachioü (Maison), *Mimbaste* ...DUFOURCET-ALBERCA   481
Capitainerie (La), *Verneuil-sur-Indre* ....MASSELOT   366
Capoulet Junac, *Tarascon-sur-Ariège* ....VAN HOORN   515
Carcis (Les), *Ganac* ....PIEDNOËL & DROUET   513
Carcotage Beauceron (Le), *Pré-St-Martin* ....VIOLETTE   332
Carrefour des Fosses, *Brémoy* ....LALLEMAN   183
Cascade (La), *Courmes* ....BARACCO & DUPIN   656
Cassac (Mas), *Allègre* ....SIMONOT   560
Castel Enchanté (Le), *Nice* ....OLIVIER   664
Castel (Le), *Castelsagrat* ....CLÉMENT   521
Castelles (Domaine des), *Caux-et-Sauzens* ....CLAYETTE   531
Caussolière (La), *St-Sornin* ....PINEL-PESCHARDIÈRE   416
Cèdre Bleu (Le), *Marcigny* ....CHEVALLIER   89
Cerisaie (La), *Riols* ....DEGENAAR & WEGGELAAR   545
Certes, *Gaudiès* ....GOSSELIN   509
Chabonne, *Vouneuil-sur-Vienne* ....PENOT   390
Chalet (Le), *Bellevaux* ....FELISAZ-DENIS   606
Chalopinière (La), *Le Vieil-Baugé* ....KITCHEN   290
Chambon (Le Château du), *Bersac-sur-Rivalier* ..PERRIN des MARAIS   434
Chambre de Séjour avec Vue..., *Saignon* ......REGENT & JACCAUD   629
Champfleury (Domaine de), *Lentigny* ....GAUME   574
Champvent (Manoir de), *Chardonnay* ....RULLIÈRE   97

Chanteclair, *Cancon* . . . . .LARRIBEAU 468
Chantelouve, *Sains-lès-Fressin* . . . . .RIEBEN 18
Chapelle (La), *Château-Chervix* .LESPAGNOL 431
Charmaie (Domaine de la), *St-Sève* . . . . .CHAVEROU 476
Charrières (Les), *Trambly* . . . . .GAUTHIER 93
Chasse (La), *Tendu* . . . . .MITCHELL 348
Châtaigneraie (La), *Dissay-sous-Courcillon* . . .LETANNEUX & GUYON 313
Château (Ferme du), *Levéville* . . . . .VASSEUR 331
Château (Le), *La Bastide-sur-Besorgues* . . . . .FRANÇOIS 584
Château (Le), *Le Rozel* . . . . .GRANDCHAMP 211
Château (Le), *Marcey-les-Grèves* . . . . .TURGOT 223
Château (Le), *Noailles* . . . . .RAHOUX 539
Chatelard (Le), *Passirac* . . . . .CASTELBAJAC 421
Châtillon, *Copponex* . . . . .GAL Maryse & Aimé 607
Chats qui Dorment (Le Mas des), *Eyragues* . . . . .POLI 639
Chaume (La), *Rians* . . . . .PROFFIT 344
Chavoul (Le), *Reilhanette* . . . . .PAGIS 599
Chemin d'Aisey, *Châtillon-sur-Seine* . . . . .DARTOIS 102
Chemin de Bois Soleil, *Rochecorbon* . . . . .GAY 362
Chemin de Chaunu, *Marecellaz-Albanais* . . . . .MARTIN 609
Chemin du Golf, *Dieppe* . . . . .NOËL 147
Cheneau (Le), *Valbonne* . . . . .RINGENBACH 665
Chênes de Ste Croix (Les), *Montaigu-de-Quercy* . . . . .HUNT 523
Chesnaie (La), *Bois-en-Ardres* . . . . .LÉTURGIE 14
Cheviré, *Savigny-en-Véron* . . . . .CHAUVELIN 357
Chez Elvire, *Chauffour* . . . . .DUCHET 108
Chez Quimand, *Ecoyeux* . . . . .FORGET 411
Chézeaux (Les), *Le Blanc* . . . . .JUBARD 347
Chifflet (Le), *Montferrat* . . . . .LA BROSSE 652
Chiron (Le), *Salles-d'Angles* . . . . .CHAINIER 422
Ciadoux, *Boulogne-sur-Gesse* . . . . .ROEHRIG 505
Clair Matin, *Reuilly* . . . . .TREVISANI 160
Clé des Champs (La), *Aumagne* . . . . .DESCHAMPS 407
Clé des Champs (La), *Tricqueville* . . . . .LE PLEUX 155
Clos de l'Ormeau (Le), *Huismes* .BUREAU 354
Clos de Saint Paul (Le), *La Colle-sur-Loup* . . . . .RONIN PILLET 667
Clos du Pausa (Le), *Thillombois* .TANCHON 68
Clos Grincourt (Le), *Duisans* . . . . .SENLIS 21
Clos (Le), *Chérêt* . . . . .SIMONNOT 54
Clos Vincents (Le), *Fléré-la-Rivière* . . . . .RENOULT 350
Closerie du Guilhat (La), *Salies-de-Béarn* . . . . .POTIRON 492
Clusaz - Vallon (La), *Bellevaux* . . . . .PASQUIER 610
Coët Caret (Château de), *Herbignac* . . . . .MONNERAYE 272
Colombié, *Dévillac* . . . . .PANNETIER 470
Colombier des Rivières (Le), *Prailles* . . . . .DUVALLON 397
Commanderie (La), *Brizay* . . . . .VAURIE 374
Commandeurs (Mas des), *Servas* . . . . .SORDI 561
Coquelicots (Les), *Le Rouret* . . . . .LE GUAY 660
Corbinais (La), *St-Michel-de-Plélan* . . . . .BEAUPÈRE 234
Costa de Dalt (Ferme Auberge), *Prats de Mollo* . . . . .LANAU 527
Costières (Château des), *L'Isle-sur-la-Sorgue* . . . . .SECCHI 631
Cottage de la Voisinière (Le), *Percy* . . . . .DUCHEMIN 204
Couchet (Domaine de), *Peyrefitte-du-Razès* . . . . .ROPERS 533
Couloumine (Mas de la), *Elne* . . . . .TUBERT 529
Cour Beaudeval (La), *Faverolles* .LOTHON 327
Courtepointe (La), *Boussac* . . . . .GROS & COLSENET 436
Coustet, *Buzet-sur-Baïse* . . . . .GELIX 466
Coutin (Maison), *Peisey* . . . . .COUTIN & CHENAL 612

INDEX

Crennes (Château de), *Urou-et-Crennes* . . . . .LE BOUTEILLER   165
Croix d'Etain (La), *Grez-Neuville* . . . . .BAHUAUD   276
Croix (Ferme la), *Villy-lez-Falaise* . . . . .THOMAS   194
Croze (La), *Rocles* . . . . .ROUVIÈRE   587
Cruchet (Le), *Mézangers* . . . . .NAY   306
Cure (La), *Foissy* . . . . .RENY   105
Demeure de Latillé (La), *Latillé* . . . . .FLAMBEAU   381
Dés (Les), *Mansle* . . . . .JOLLEY   424
Désiré (Ferme de), *Le Gault-Soigny* .BOUTOUR   57
Deux Aiguilles (Les), *Laz* .THOMPSON   262
Domaine du Teilleul (Le), *St-Sauveur-de-Flée* . . . . .VITTON   299
Dourcines (Les), *Montvendre* . . . . .GOLDSTEIN & DUPONT   594
Drucas (Château de), *Auxi-le-Château* . . . . .AUGUSTIN   1
Eaux Vives (Les), *Vallée de l'O* . . . . .TREMPE-LINEAU   425
Écots (Les), *Availles-Limousine* . . . . .SALVAUDON   393
Écuries du Château (Les), *Tostat* . . . . .RIVIÈRE D'ARC   499
En Tristan, *Azas* . . . . .ZABÉ   506
Enclos (L'), *Aix-en-Provence* . . . . .IUNG   636
Enclos (L'), *Lavergne* . . . . .RUBBENS   457
Escale (L'), *Richelieu* . . . . .LAWRENCE   363
Espagne (Domaine), *Ginasservis* . . . . .GRECH   649
Étang (Domaine de l'), *Neuvy-sur-Loire* . . . . .PASQUET   112
Évêché (L'), *Vaison-la-Romaine* . . . . .VERDIER   632
Farigoule (La), *Violès* . . . . .CORNAZ   619
Fauguière (Mas de la), *St-Nazaire-des-Gardies* . . . . .PRICE   558
Ferme de l'Ecluse (La), *Frise* . . . . .RANDJIA   35
Ferme de l'Eglise (La), *St-Nicolas-de-Pierrepont* . . . . .CLAY   202
Ferme de l'Etang (La), *Vergoncey* .GAVARD   208
Ferme de Wolphus (La), *Zouafques* . . . . .BEHAGHEL   2
Ferme des Forges (La), *Legé* . . . . .PEAUDEAU   273
Ferme des Tourelles (La), *La Musse* . . . . .MARÉCHAL   328
Ferme du Colombier (La), *Savignies* . . . . .LETURQUE   46
Ferme (La), *Bissy-sous-Uxelles* . . . . .LA BUSSIÈRE   95
Ferme (La), *Heudreville-sur-Eure* . . . . .BOURGEOIS   150
Fèvrerie (La), *Ste-Geneviève* . . . . .CAILLET   201
Fière (La), *Ste-Mère-l'Église* . . . . .BLANCHET   199
Flaynac, *Pradines* . . . . .FAYDI   460
Fleury La Tour, *Tintury* . . . . .GUÉNY   109
Foncher (Manoir de), *Villandry* . . . . .SALLES   372
Font Bétou (La), *Orignolles* . . . . .TARROU & FLUDE   418
Forêt d'Othe (Relais de la), *Sussy-en-Othe* . . . . .DUFAYET   121
Foucaucourt (Château de), *Foucaucourt* . . . . .ROCQUIGNY   37
Fougeolles, *Eymoutiers* . . . . .MONTANT   432
Fourchat, *Aiguefonde* . . . . .PECH & LELIÈVRE   537
Franquette (La), *Montsalvy* . . . . .HAUCHECORNE   461
Fredelin, *Coutures* . . . . .ARNAULT   275
Frère (Domaine du), *Aix-en-Provence* . . . . .BOUVANT   635
Gacogne (La), *Azincourt* . . . . .FENET   10
Gage (La), *Roullours* . . . . .MARIE   188
Gains (Les), *Survie* . . . . .WORDSWORTH   168
Garbès (Ferme des), *Gramont* . . . . .VARGAS & GAILLARD   525
Garencière, *Champfleur* . . . . .LANGLAIS   311
Garenne (La), *Bellegarde* . . . . .COUROUBLE   516
Garenne (La), *Thevet-St-Julien* . . . . .FRENKEL   346
Garrade (Domaine de), *St-Maximin-la-Ste-Baume* . . . . .BAUDE   644
Garz ar Bik, *Brasparts* . . . . .CHAUSSY   249
Gautrais (La), *St-James* . . . . .TIFFAINE   221
Gaxottière (La), *Jaux-Varanval* . . . . .GAXOTTE   43

Gendre (Ferme du), *Lavaurette* . . . . .ZAMBONI 526
Germon, *Beaumont-lès-Valence* . . . . .CHIVRÉ-DUMOND 591
Giloutière (La), *Châtillon-sur-Loire* . . . . .LEFRANC 336
Godiers (Les), *Lavoux* . . . . .RABANY 391
Goupillon (Château du), *Neuillé* . . . . .CALOT 280
Gourdet (Château de), *St-Mariens* . . . . .CHARTIER 475
Grand Boucaud, *Rimons* . . . . .LÉVY 479
Grand Bus (Château du), *Thiberville* . . . . .PRÉAUMONT 157
Grand Cèdre (Le), *St-Pé-de-Bigorre* . . . . .PETERS 498
Grand Jonquier (Le Mas du), *Lagnes* . . . . .GRECK 623
Grand' Maison (La), *Haute Escalles* . . . . .BOUTROY 4
Grand-Rullecourt (Château de), *Avesnes-le-Comte* . . . . .SAULIEU 20
Grande Ferme (La), *Sainte-Eugénie* . . . . .MAURICE 167
Grande Mouline (La), *Bourgneuf* . . . . .MALOT & CHARLON 341
Grande Noë (La), *Moulicent* . . . . .LONGCAMP 166
Grange de Coatélan (La), *Plougonven* . . . . .TERNAY 261
Grange Nouvelle, *Foing-de-Paillès* . . . . .BOVINE 589
Grange Rouge (La), *Géruge* . . . . .VERJUS 85
Grange Rouge (Relais de la), *Milly-la-Forêt* . . . . .DESFORGES 130
Grave (Château de la), *Bourg-sur-Gironde* . . . . .BASSEREAU 472
Grenier (Le), *Yffiniac* . . . . .LOQUIN 242
Grenouille (La), *St-Adjutory* . . . . .CASPER 420
Grenouillère (La), *Dangé-St-Romain* . . . . .BRAGUIER 378
Grillons (Les), *Tence* . . . . .DEYGAS 579
Gros (Mas de), *St-Rémy-de-Provence* . . . . . . .REBOUL & SCHNEIDER 640
Guérandière (La), *Cerisy-la-Salle* . . . . .TROUT 222
Guillonnière (Château de la), *Dienné* . . . . .REBILLARD 392
Haizean (Maison), *Urrugne* . . . . .NARDOU 490
Hameau ès-Adams, *Sottevast* .LEBARILLIER 214
Hamelinais (La), *Cherruiex* . . . . .GLÉMOT 226
Haut Billy (Le), *Yvetot-Bocage* . . . . .DUBOST 205
Haut Joreau (Le), *Gennes* . . . . .BOISSET 279
Haute Bigne (La), *Clécy* . . . . .REGNIER 193
Haute-Rive (Ferme de), *Cuvry* .MORHAIN 73
Hauts Champs (Les), *Nicorps* . . . . .POSLOUX 220
Hauts (Les), *St-Jean-le-Thomas* . . . . .LEROY 217
Hazaie (Manoir de la), *Planguenoual* . . . . .MARIVIN 243
Hazeville (Château d'), *Wy-dit-Joli-Village* . . . . .DENECK 134
Herbe de Grâce (L'), *Buyon* . . . . .PILLON 34
Hermos (Manoir d'), *St-Eloi-de-Fourques* . . . . .NOËL-WINDSOR 156
Huntagneres (Maison), *Guiche* .LAPLACE 487
Il fut un temps, *St-Marcel-d'Urfé* .HAUCK 575
Ithurburia (Ferme), *St-Michel* . . . . .OURTIAGUE 491
Jacquerolle (La), *La Chaise-Dieu* . . . . .CHAILLY 576
Jacquot (Château), *Ste-Magnance* . . . . .COSTAILLE 119
Jaquetterie (La), *Plassay* . . . . .LOURADOUR 414
Jardins de César (Les), *Fréjus* . . . . .BERTIN 645
Jarnages (Château de), *Jarnages* . . . . .LOMBARDI 437
Jas des Eydins, *Bonnieux* . . . . .KOZLOWSKI 624
Jean-Pierre (Domaine de), *Pinas* . . . . .COLOMBIER 496
Jeanne (Domaine des), *Vic-sur-Aisne* . . . . .MARTNER 51
Joie (La), *La Batie-Rolland* . . . . .MONEL 598
Jonvilliers (Château de), *Jonvilliers-Ecrosnes* . . . . .THOMPSON 330
Jument Verte (La), *Trévignin* . . . . .CHAPPAZ 611
Kerambris, *Port Manech* . . . . .GOURLAOUEN 251
Kerantum, *Mahalon* . . . . .OLIER 258
Kerdavid-Duchentil, *Pluvigner* . . . . .COLLET 264
Kerfaro, *Querrien* . . . . .LE GALLIC 256

INDEX

Kergrec'h (Manoir de), *Plougrescant* . . . . ROQUEFEUIL 246
Kerguéréon (Manoir de), *Lannion* . . . . BELLEFON 235
Kerimel, *Ploemel-Carnac* . . . . MALHERBE 267
Kerlarec (Château de), *Arzano* . . . . BELLIN 248
Kerloaï, *Scaër* . . . . PENN 259
Kermezen (Château de), *Pommerit-Jaudy* . . . . KERMEL 239
Kernévez, *Cléder* . . . . GRALL 252
Kervent (Manoir de), *Pouldavid* . . . . LEFLOCH 254
Kervren, *St-Yvi* . . . . LE GALL 255
Kreisker, *Botmeur* . . . . SOLLIEC 260
La Lèbre (Villa), *St-Pantaléon* . . . . LAWRENCE 625
Labarom (Château de), *Chéneché* . . . . LE GALLAIS 386
Lachapelle . . . . VAN DEN BRINK 524
Lamolère, *Campet-Lamolère* . . . . MONREDON 483
Lancournet, *Glanges* . . . . DESMAISON 427
Lande (Château de la), *Cerqueux* . . . . MASLIAH 191
Landreville (Château de), *Bayonville* . . . . MEIXMORON 55
Lanévry, *Kerlaz* . . . . GONIDEC 250
Lann Kermane, *St-Philibert* . . . . CUZON du REST 265
Lanot (Le), *Sames* . . . . MICKELSON 488
Lapeyère, *Ste-Sabine* . . . . BERTHOLOM 446
Larra (Château de), *Grenade-sur-Garonne* . . . . CARRIÈRE 501
Lascours (Château de), *Laudun* . . . . BASTOUIL 552
Lay-Lamidou . . . . DESBONNET 485
Layrole, *Saurat* . . . . ROBERT 514
Le Mazis . . . . ONDER DE LINDEN 33
Léchelle (Ferme), *Berzy-le-Sec* . . . . MAURICE 52
Les Charmontois . . . . PATIZEL 61
Lezerhy, *Bieuzy-les-Eaux* . . . . MAIGNAN & BOIVIN 266
Licorne (La), *Valojoulx* . . . . MILLIEZ & VAN EECKHOUDT 454
Liffernet Grange, *Lunan* . . . . NIELSON de LAMOTHE 462
Locherie (La), *Mamers* . . . . LORIEUX 314
Loge (La), *Chaunac* . . . . PICQ 415
Logis d'Arnières (Le), *St-Cyr-sous-Dourdan* . . . . DABASSE 129
Logis de l'Epine (Le), *Plassay* . . . . CHARRIER 405
Logis de la Filanderie (Le), *Bécherel* . . . . CANET 225
Logis Du Ray (Le), *St-Denis-d'Anjou* . . . . LEFEBVRE 305
Logis du Sacriste (Le), *Cormery* . . . . McGRATH 367
Logis (Le), *Le Gué-de-Velluire* . . . . RIBERT 403
Logis (Le), *St-Romans-lès-Melle* . . . . RABANY 399
Londe (La), *Tilly-sur-Seule* . . . . AMEY 170
Loriots (Mas des), *Tornac* . . . . MARSH 557
Lou Ferradou, *St-Etienne-de-Carlat* . . . . BALLEUX 568
Loubarré (Le), *Gauchin Verloingt* . . . . VION 23
Loubens (Château de), *Loubens* . . . . LELONG 510
Louisière (La), *Beaumont-la-Ronce* . . . . CAMPION 355
Louisière (La), *Les Barballières* . . . . HERVÉ 384
Loutarès (Ferme), *Haut-de-Bosdarros* . . . . MONTEVERDE 489
Macquelines (Ferme de), *Betz* . . . . HAMELIN 44
Madranque, *Le Bosc* . . . . LOIZANCE 511
Maghoss (Villa), *Antibes* . . . . MARTIN-CATOIRE 662
Magny-les-Villiers . . . . GIORGI 103
Maison des Bois (La), *Paunat* . . . . SIMAND 458
Maison des Rêves (La), *Bragassargues* . . . . CHAPMAN 554
Maison des Violettes (La), *Fressin* . . . . JAMES 12
Maison du Charron (La), *Pfettisheim* . . . . GASS 76
Maison du Vert (La), *Ticheville* . . . . KIRK 163
Maison Fleurie, *Dieffenbach-au-Val* . . . . ENGEL-GEIGER 75

Maison JLN, *Chartres* ....CUISINIEZ 325
Maison Marchand, *La Bastide-Clairence* ....FOIX 486
Maison Royale (La), *Pesmes* ....HOYET 81
Malik, *Plélan-le-Petit* ....VIANNAY 247
Mallouet, *Granville* ....LAISNÉ 213
Malposte (La), *Reviers* ....BLANLOT 171
Malvoisine, *Écuillé* ....LA BASTILLE 291
Manoir de la Duchée, *St-Briac-sur-Mer* ....STENOU 233
Manoir Francis, *Marles-sur-Canche* ....LEROY 13
Manoir (Le), *Bonningues-lès-Ardres* ....DUPONT 9
Manoir (Le), *Montfarville* ....GABROY 207
Marais (Le), *St-Didier-de-Charpey* ....IMBERT 595
Marcelet (Ferme de), *Tournières* ....ISIDOR 182
Marchoux (Le), *Nonards* ....GREENWOOD 439
Mardelle (La), *Noyers-sur-Cher* ....CHOQUET 318
Marette (La), *Melleville* ....GARÇONNET 145
Marican (Mas), *Goult* ....CHABAUD 618
Marmont (Manoir de), *St-André-de-Vieux-Jonc* GUIDO-ALHÉRITIÈRE 603
Marnis (Le), *Courtomer* ....GOFF 162
Marquise (La), *Brassac* ....DIO 522
Marquise (La), *St-Gratien-Savigny* ....PERREAU 113
Martinade (La), *St-Remèze* ....MIALON 585
Massal (Château), *Le Vigan* ....LUC 556
Massigny, *Velluire* ....NEAU 402
Maunit-Chemellier ....EDON 285
Mazeyrolles ...................................MARESCASSIER 452
Meilhouret, *Larroque* ....JOUARD 536
Mercerais (La), *Blain* ....PINEAU 274
Mésangeau (Le), *Drain* ....MIGON 293
Mesnil de Benneville (Le), *Cahagnes* ....GUILBERT 180
Mesnil (Le), *Occagnes* ....LAIGNEL 164
Messey (Château de), *Ozenay* ....FACHON 91
Métairie Basse (La), *Corniou* ....LUNES 548
Metairie Haute (La), *Sarlat* ....PINARD-LEGRY 456
Millaud-Montlabert (Château), *St-Émilion* ....BRIEUX 473
Mimosas (Les), *Roquebrun* ....LA TOUCHE 547
Mirambeau, *St-Vivien-de-Médoc* ....LANNEAU 478
Mirvault (Château de), *Château-Gontier* ....AMBRIÈRES 302
Monbet (Château du), *St-Lon-les-Mines* ....LATAILLADE 482
Mondounet, *Fargues* ....SCOTT 464
Monhoudou (Château de), *Monhoudou* ....MONHOUDOU 315
Mont Epinguet (Château), *Brix* ....BERRIDGE 198
Mont Eventé (Le), *Menneville* ....DESALASE 8
Montanjus (Le), *Ettuefont* ....ELBERT 80
Montaupin (Château de), *Oizé* ....DAVID & DUBOIS 309
Monteillet-Sanvensa, *Villefranche-de-Rouergue* ....BATESON 564
Montet (Le), *Pouligny-St-Martin* ....PESSEL 349
Montgouverne (Château de), *Rochecorbon* ....DESVIGNES 360
Montmaur (Château de), *Veynes* ....LAURENS 616
Montour (Manoir de), *Beaumont-en-Véron* ....ARBON 351
Montpierreux (Domaine de), *Venoy* ....CHONÉ 118
Montreuil (Château de), *Montreuil-sur-Loir* ....BAILLIOU 277
Morillons (Domaine des), *Mt-St-Sulpice* ....BRUNOT 115
Motte aux Chauff (La), *St-Coulomb* ....POMMARE 231
Motte (Château de la), *Baracé* ....FRANÇOIS 286
Motte Obin (La), *Muncq-Nieurlet* ....BRETON 5
Mouclade (Villa La), *Le Crotoy* ....WEYL 41
Mouettes (Les), *St-Suliac* ....ROUVRAIS 232

INDEX

Moulin d'Antelon, *Crillon-le-Brave* . . . . .RICQUART 630
Moulin de Fresquet, *Gramat* . . . . .RAMELOT 463
Moulin de la Crouzille (Le), *Tourtoirac* . . . . .ARMITAGE 445
Moulin de la Quine (Le), ...ELMES 408
Moulin de Marsaguet, *Coussac-Bonneval* . . . . .GIZARDIN 428
Moulin de Montrésor (Le), *Montrésor* . . . . .WILLEMS 376
Moulin du Bignon (Le), *Lassy* . . . . .KRUST 229
Moulin (Le), *Fléré-la-Rivière* . . . . .AUMERCIER 345
Moulin (Le), *Samouillan* . . . . .CALLEN & MISSELBROOK 500
Moulin (Le), *St-Hymer* . . . . .VALLE 196
Moulin (Le), *St-Jean-St-Germain* . . . . .PAGE & HUTTON 368
Moulin Neuf (Le), *Paunat* . . . . .CHAPPELL & SHIPPEY 448
Moulinot (Le), *Vermenton* . . . . .WOOTTON & ROBERTSON 125
Moulins (Les), *Antezant* . . . . .FALLELOUR 409
Mouterre-Silly . . . . .BRÉMAUD 379
Mozardière (La), *Legé* . . . . .DESBROSSES 271
Murailles (Les), *Manigod* . . . . .BROWNE 605
Mûrier (Mas du), *Vallauris* . . . . .RONCÉ 666
Musardière (La), *Lidrezing* . . . . .MATHIS 72
Musseaux (Les), *Cruzy-le-Châtel* . . . . .CHERVAUX 117
Namaste, *Galan* . . . . .FONTAINE 497
Nestuby (Domaine de), *Cotignac* . . . . .ROUBAUD 654
Noailles, *St-Maur* . . . . .SABATHIER 518
Nobles (Château de), *La Chapelle-sous-Brancion* . . . . .CHERISEY 88
Notre-Dame de Lorette, *Alan* . . . . .FERRY 503
Olivier Peintre (L'), *St-Jeannet* . . . . .BENOIT SÈRE 657
Ols, *Villeneuve* . . . . .VIGUIÉ 567
Ombelles (Les), *Dangu* . . . . .SAINT PÈRE 158
Orgerie (L'), *St-Vigor-des-Monts* .GOUDE 210
Ormeaux (Les), *Chambon* . . . . .RAFFIN 417
Ormeraie (L'), *Corberon* . . . . .BALMELLE 100
Ormoie (L'), *St Laurent-des-Eaux* . . . . .LIBEAUT 322
Ozeville (Le Manoir d'), *Appeville* . . . . .LEJOUR & WOOSTER 215
Palasse (La), *Le Thor* . . . . .MOURGES 628
Pan 'É' Râ (Villa), *Nice* . . . . .MALET KANITZ 661
'Panko' (Villa), *Cap d'Antibes* . . . . .BOURGADE 658
Paraïs (Domaine du), *Sospel* . . . . .MAYER 663
Paris, *Châtelet district* . . . . .SAUNIER 142
Paris, *Châtelet district* . . . . .PIERROT 141
Paris, *Montmartre district* 138
Paris, *Montparnasse district*. . . . . .MONBRISON 140
Paris, *Mouffetard district* . . . . .COHEN-SCALI 137
Paris, *National Assembly/Invalides district* . . . . .MARCHAL 139
Paris, *Notre Dame/Saint Michel district* . . . . .CHATIGNOUX 136
Pasquiers (Les), *Lancié/Belleville* . . . . .GANDILHON 602
Pasredon (Château de), *St-Rémy-de-Chargnat* . . . . .MARCHAND 572
Passieux, *St-Nicolas-la-Chapelle* . . . . .JOLY 613
Pastourelle (La), *Plancoët* . . . . .LEDÉ 240
Patis du Vergas (Le), *Lavenay* . . . . .DÉAGE 310
Patrus (Domaine des), *l'Épine-aux-Bois* . . . . .ROYOL 53
Paulagnac, *Craponne-sur-Arzon* . . . . .CHAMPEL 577
Pauliac, *Ribérac* . . . . .EDWARDS 451
Péguilhan (Ferme-Auberge de), *Péguilhan* . . . . .CASTEX 502
Pélican (Domaine du), *Gignac* . . . . .THILLAYE de BOULLAY 549
Pellet (Mas), *Aubord* . . . . .BOURDIN 553
Pen-Kear, *Plouescat* . . . . .LE DUFF 253
Pennerest, *Noyal Pontivy* . . . . .ROBERTS 268
Péris (Les), *Châteaudouble* . . . . .CABANES 590

Petit Brassac, *Labouquerie* . . . . .MARESCASSIER 453
Petit Carqueron (Le), *Le Lion d'Angers* . . . . .CARCAILLET 281
Petit Manoir (Le), *Servon* . . . . .GÉDOUIN 209
Petit Moulin du Rouvre (Le), *St-Pierre-de-Plesguen*MICHEL-QUÉBRIAC 230
Petit Pey (Le), *Monmarves* . . . . .BOSREDON 447
Petit Verdus (Château le), *Sadirac* . . . . .AURIOL 471
Petite Cour Verte (La), *La Roche Beaumont* . . . . .ROUVIÈRE 586
Petits Augustins (Demeure des), *Montreuil-Bellay* . . . . . . .GUÉZÉNEC 288
Pichonnière (La), *Charcé* . . . . .COLIBET 283
Pigeonnerie (La), *St-Martin-du-Bois* . . . . .DIGARD & PAJAK 284
Pince-Guerre, *Montpezat d'Agenais* . . . . .GASQUY 465
Pineraie (La), *St-Marcel-lès-Valence* . . . . .KATCHIKIAN 596
Pit (Le), *Confolens* . . . . .EVERITT 423
Place de l'Eglise, *Vauchelles-lès-Quesnoy* . . . . .CRÉPELLE 29
Place de l'Eglise, *Venouse* . . . . .GARNIER 122
Place de la Liberté, *Senan* . . . . .DEFRANCE 120
Place des Templiers, *Forest-l'Abbaye* . . . . .BECQUET-CHATEL 28
Place Jean Graffin, *Pontvallain* . . . . .VIEILLET 316
Place Saint-Michel, *Gaillac* . . . . .PINON 538
Plaix (Château du), *Chamblet* . . . . .MONTAIGNAC 573
Plateau (Le), *Montreuil-Juigné* . . . . .HUEZ 289
Plessis (Château du), *Pont-St-Martin* . . . . .BELORDE 269
Plessis Vegetarian Guesthouse (Le), *Plumaudan* . . . . .JUDGES 238
Plessis-Brezot (Château), *Monnières* . . . . .CALONNE 270
Point du Jour (Le), *Jarzé* . . . . .PAPIAU 294
Pointe (La), *Liancourt-St-Pierre* . . . . .GALLOT 42
Pont Chauvet (Ferme-Auberge), *La Celle-Condé* . . . . .MANSSENS 342
Pont d'Ardèche, *Pont-St-Esprit* . . . . .VERDUZAN 563
Pont Ricoul (Le), *St-Pierre-de-Plesguen* . . . . .GROSSET 228
Pont Rouge (Manoir au), *St-Loup-Hors* . . . . .CHILCOTT 174
Portail Bleu (Le), *Châtres* . . . . .LAURENT 126
Pouch, *Rignac* . . . . .BELL 459
Poulsieu (Le), *Serres-sur-Arget* . . . . .BROGNEAUX 507
Pourchères . . . . .GOETZ 582
Poux (Domaine de), *Sorges* . . . . .DELAIRE 449
Pré Ménot (Le), *Grévilly* . . . . .DEPREAY 90
Presbytère (Le), *La Motte Ternant* . . . . .AYLETT 99
Presbytère Tregrom (Le), *Plouaret* . . . . .MORCHOVEN 244
Pressignoise (La), *Le Petit Pressigny* . . . . .LIMOUZIN 365
Pressoir (Le), *Berville* . . . . .DUHAMEL 176
Prevasy (Manoir de), *Carhaix* . . . . .NOVAK 257
Prézat (Le), *Albussac* . . . . .LARDNER 442
Prieuré de l'Epinay, *St-Georges-sur-Loire* . . . . .GAULTIER 287
Prieuré de la Chaise, *St-Georges-sur-Cher* . . . . . .DURET-THERIZOLS 320
Prieuré de Vendanger (Le), *Le Guédeniau* . . . . .TOUTAIN 297
Prieuré des Granges, *Savonnières* . . . . .SALMON 373
Prieuré (Le), *Azay-sur-Indre* . . . . .PAPOT 369
Prieuré (Le), *Fouchères* . . . . .BERTHELIN 62
Prieuré (Le), *St-Quentin-de-Baron* . . . . .CASTILHO 474
Provostière (La), *Aucey-la-Plaine* . . . . .FEUVRIER 206
Puy d'Arçay (Château du), *Arçay* . . . . .LEROUX de LENS 387
Puymartin (Château de), *Sarlat-la-Canéda* . . . . .MONTBRON 455
Quiers, *Compeyre* .LOMBARD-PRATMARTY 566
Randonnées du Précheny (Les), *Velles* . . . . .ROUSSELOT 63
Ravigote (La), *Gigondas* . . . . .GRAS 622
Reculée (La), *Montigny* . . . . .GRESSIN 340
Relais de la Vignette (Le), *Tour-en-Bessin* . . . . .GIRARD 179
Relais (Le), *Caumont l'Éventé* . . . . .BOULLOT 172

INDEX

Religieuses (Les), *Richelieu* . . . . .LE PLATRE   364
Renardais (La), *Plouer-sur-Rance* . . . . .ROBINSON   245
Rennebourg (Domaine de), *St-Denis-du-Pin* . . . . .FRAPPIER   412
Réserve (La), *Giverny* . . . . .BRUNET   151
Réserve (La), *St-Léonard-de-Noblat* . . . . . . .JANSEN de VOMÉCOURT   429
Ressons (Ferme de), *Mt-St-Martin* . . . . .FERRY   49
Rhétorerie (La), *St-Ebremond-de-Bonfossé* . . . . .OSMOND   219
Ricard (Le Mas), *Fontvieille* . . . . .RICARD DAMIDOT   641
Richarnau, *Aurel* . . . . .MICHELLE   627
Riffets (Château des), *Bretteville-sur-Laize* . . . . .CANTEL   173
Rivière (Ferme de la), *Géfosse-Fontenay* . . . . .LEHARIVEL   186
Rivière (Ferme de la), *Sept Vents* . . . . .ACHARD   169
Rivière (Ferme de la), *St-Germain-du-Pert* . . . . .MARIE   190
Rivièrette (La), *Caours* . . . . .LAMARLIÈRE   30
Roche (La), *Eymoutiers* . . . . .JAUBERT   430
Roche Martel (Château de la), *Roiffé* . . . . .CASTELBAJAC   300
Roches (Les), *Le Sap* . . . . .BOURGAULT   161
Roches (Les), *Mozé-sur-Louet* . . . . .CATROUILLET   282
Roque de Bas (La), *Canville-la-Roque* . . . . .VASSELIN   224
'Rose Arts', *Vernantois* . . . . .RYON   84
Roseraie (La), *La Guiche* . . . . .BINNS   86
Rosier Sauvage (Le), *Nieul-sur-Autize* . . . . .CHASTAIN-POUPIN   401
Rouaudière (La), *Mégaudais* . . . . .TRIHAN   307
Roudils (Les), *Jaujac* . . . . .FLORENCE   583
Route de Castellar, *Menton* . . . . .GAZZANO   659
Route de Conty, *Lœuilly* . . . . .RICHOUX   36
Route de la Limagne, *Chaptes* . . . . .BEAUJEARD   571
Roux (Château de), *Le Cannet-des-Maures* . . . . .DYENS   647
Rue Anatole France, *Le Vésinet* . . . . .ALBAUT   131
Rue aux Ours, *Rouen* . . . . .AUNAY-STANGUENNEC   143
Rue Carnot, *Maizières* . . . . .COTEL   74
Rue Chanzy, *Loigny-la-Bataille* . . . . .NIVET   329
Rue de Coëtquen, *Dinan* . . . . .LOCKWOOD   241
Rue de Coole, *Maisons-en-Champagne* . . . . .COLLOT   58
Rue de l'Abbaye, *Maillezais* . . . . .BONNET   400
Rue de l'Église, *Echingen* .BOUSSEMAERE   3
Rue de l'Église, *Fosseux* . . . . .GUILLUY-DELACOURT   11
Rue de l'Église, *Poigny-la-Forêt* . . . . .LE BRET   133
Rue de l'Église, *St-Georges-des-Coteaux* . . . . .TROUVÉ   419
Rue de l'Hôtel de Ville, *Château-du-Loir* . . . . .LE GOFF   312
Rue de la Fontaine, *Villeneuve-lès-Béziers* . . . . .VINER   550
Rue de la Gare, *Saulty* . . . . .DALLE   6
Rue de la Mare, *Buicourt* . . . . .VERHOEVEN   47
Rue de la Motte, *Droyes* . . . . .STEIN   64
Rue de la Petite Corniche, *Perros-Guirec* . . . . .BIARNES   236
Rue de la République, *Caudebec-en-Caux* . . . . .VILLAMAUX   149
Rue de Meuves, *Onzain* . . . . .LANGLAIS   321
Rue des Hannetons, *Lille* . . . . .HULIN   25
Rue des Lilas, *La Ménardière* .FERCHAUD   410
Rue des Martyrs de la Résistance, *Bourbourg* . . . . .VANDEWALLE   27
Rue des Nobles, *Salers* . . . . .PRUDENT   570
Rue des Trois Épis, *Katzenthal* . . . . .KLUR-GRAFF   79
Rue du Breuil, *Samer* . . . . .MAUCOTEL   15
Rue du Camp Romain, *Banville* .LESAGE   187
Rue du Château, *Tarascon* . . . . .LEWIS   638
Rue du Chef de Ville, *Armentières-en-Brie* . . . . .WOEHRLÉ   128
Rue du Général de Gaulle, *Marlenheim* . . . . .GOETZ   77
Rue du Paradis, *St-Thierry* . . . . .HARLAUT   60

Rue du Vieux Moulin, *Rahling* . . . . .BACH   69
Rue Dutems, *Mer* . . . . .MORMICHE   323
Rue Élise Lucas, *Coulon* . . . . .CHOLLET   396
Rue Faidherbe, *Wattignies* . . . . .LE BOT   26
Rue Flahaut, *Boulogne-sur-Mer* . . . . .DELABIE   7
Rue Georges Lourdel, *Ennery* . . . . .DUBOSCQ   135
Rue Grande, *Orbec* . . . . .VAILLÈRE   195
Rue Grimaux, *Dury* . . . . .SAGUEZ   38
Rue Gustave Courbet, *Plaisir* . . . . .CASTELNAU   132
Rue Hénault, *Mt-St-Aignan* . . . . .GOGNY   144
Rue Jacquard, *Mirebeau* . . . . .JEANNIN   385
Rue Lorraine, *Burtoncourt* . . . . .CAHEN   71
Rue Maréchal Foch, *Dambach-la-Ville* . . . . .RUHLMANN   78
Rue Paul Dubois, *Le Coudray-St-Germer* . .Le MARCHAND de St Priest   45
Rue Paul Verlaine, *Fampoux* . . . . .PEUGNIEZ   17
Rue Pilate, *Neuvy-le-Roi* . . . . .COUESNONGLE   359
Rue Principale, *Aix-en-Issart* . . . . .SANTUNE   19
Rue Principale, *Creuse* . . . . .LEMAÎTRE   31
Rue Saint-Rémy, *Braine* . . . . .MARTIN   50
Rue Verte (La Ferme de la), *Flamanville* . . . . .QUEVILLY BARET   148
Ruppaley (Le), *Bernesq* . . . . .MARIE   189
Saba'ad, *Pujaut* .THOMPSON & SERGENT   562
Saint Ferréol (Domaine de), *Pontevès* . . . . .JERPHANION   651
Saint Jacques (Mas), *Caixas* . . . . .RICHARDS & MAYES   528
Saint Jean (Manoir), *Tourlaville* . . . . .GUÉRARD   212
Saint Maurinet (Mas), *Montmeyan* .GONFOND   648
Saint-Antoine (Domaine de), *Baillargues* . . . . .VITOU   551
Saint-Aunay (Château de), *Puichéric* . . . . .BERGÉ   530
Saint-Jérôme, *Castelnau-de-Montmirail* . . . . .CAMALET   534
Saint-Léger, *Quibou* . . . . .LEPOITTEVIN   216
Saint-Louis (Villa), *Lourmarin* . . . . .LASSALLETTE   626
Saint-Luc (Domaine de), *La Baume-de-Transit* . . . . .CORNILLON   592
Sainte Anne (Mas), *Peynier* . . . . .LAMBERT   637
Sainte-Hélène (Domaine de), *Vannes-sur-Cosson* CELERIER NOULHIANE   333
Salans (Château de), *Salans* . . . . .OPPELT   83
Salles (Château des), *St-Fort-sur-Gironde* . . . . .COUILLAUD   406
Saulières, *Monceaux-sur-Dordogne* . . . . .LAFOND   441
Sauzette (Ferme de la), *Cazilhac* . . . . .GIBSON & WARREN   532
Semelin, *Châtillon-en-Bazois* . . . . .DELTOUR   107
Sercy . . . . .BIWAND   87
Serre (La), *Charenton-Laugère* . . . . .MOREAU   343
Servon . . . . .LESÉNÉCHAL   218
Setzères, *Marciac* . . . . .FURNEY   517
Shamrock (Mas), *St-Rémy-de-Provence* . . . . .WALSH   643
Siouvre, *St-Savin* . . . . .BARBARIN   377
Sombrun (Château de), *Sombrun* . . . . .BRUNET   495
Souvigne (La), *Forgès* . . . . .HOARE   440
Stoupignan, *Montpitol* . . . . .FIEUX   504
Sudre (Mas de), *Gaillac* . . . . .RICHMOND-BROWN   540
Suhardière (La), *Livry* . . . . .PETITON   192
Suppey (Le), *Villiers-Fossard* . . . . .BUISSON   200
Tail (Château du), *Castelnau-Rivière-Basse* . . . . .BOLAC   494
Tarperon (Manoir de), *Aignay-le-Duc* . . . . .CHAMPSAVIN   101
Taulignan (Château de), *St-Marcellin-lès-Vaison* . . . . .DAILLET   620
Tennessus (Château de), *Amailloux* . . . . .FREELAND   398
Terre des Lauriers (La), *Pont du Gard* . . . . .CRISTINI   555
Thébaïde (La), *Pouillac* . . . . .BILLAT   404
Thiau (Domaine de la), *Briare* .FRANÇOIS   335

INDEX

Thoveyrat, *Bellac* ....MORICE 433
Thuillère (La), *Marcigny* ....GALLAND 92
Tilleuls (Les), *Saché* ....PILLER 370
Tinailler d'Aléane (Le), *La Roche Vineuse* ....HEINEN 94
Tonnelle (La), *La Roque-sur-Cèze* ....RIGAUD 559
Tour Gaillon (La), *Vézelay* ....GINISTY 123
Tourpes (Manoir des), *Bures-sur-Dives* ....LANDON & CASSADY 184
Travaillères (Les), *Le Lion d'Angers* ....VIVIER 298
Tremblais (La), *La Couyère* ....GOMIS 227
Trois Figuiers (La Ferme des), *Lagnes* ....GOUIN 621
Tuilerie (La), *Noaillac* ....LABORDE 477
Tuileries (Les), *Cordes* ....RONDEL 541
Val de la Mer, *Senneville-sur-Fécamp* ....LETHUILLIER 146
Val (Le), *Vengeons* ....DESDOITS 203
Val Léron, *Valaurie* ....PROTHON 600
'Valentin' (Chambres d'Hôtes), *Bonneval* ....HAYS 581
Vallée des Grottes (La), *St-Germain-sur-Vienne* ....DUBARRY 361
Vallée du Salagou (Auberge La), *Salasc* ....DELAGE 546
Vau (Château du), *Ballan-Miré* ....CLÉMENT 358
Vaudredon (Manoir de), *Sancerre* ....CIROTTE 339
Vaujours, *Château-la-Vallière* ....RIBERT 371
Vaumoret (Château de), *Poitiers* ....VAUCAMP 394
Veaudepierre (La), *Chauvigny* ....GIAFFERRI 383
Venteuges ....DUMAS 580
Verger de la Bouquetterie, *St-Mathurin-sur-Loire* ....PINIER 295
Vert Saint-Père (Ferme), *Crisenoy* ....MAUBAN 127
Viescamp (Ferme Accueil de), *Pers* ....LACAZE 569
Vieux Château (Le), *Bémécourt* ....LALLEMAND-LEGRAS 154
Vieux Cognet (Le), *Blois* ....COSSON 319
Vieux Presbytère (Le), *Montreuil-Poulay* ....LEGRAS-WOOD 304
Vilherols, *Lacroix-Barrez* ....LAURENS 565
Villa des Prés (La), *St-Révérien* ....BÜRGI & BEER 106
Villa des Roses, *Clermont-en Argonne* ....CHRISTIAENS 66
Villa Le Clos, *Darcey* ....GOUNAND 104
Villa Médicis (La), *Macé* ....CABIN-SAINT-MARCEL 317
Villard (Le), *St-André* ....TRIGON 615
Villeprouvé, *Ruille-Froid-Fonds* ....DAVENEL 303
Volets Bleus (Les), *Truinas* ....FORTUNATO 593
Vouilly (Château de), *Vouilly* ....HAMEL 181
Vouthon-Bas ....ROBERT 67
Yellowstone Chalet, *Ste-Foy-Tarentaise* ....TABARDEL 614